A Longman Cultural Edition

THE HISTORY OF THE ADVENTURES OF JOSEPH ANDREWS

by Henry Fielding

Edited by

Adam Potkay

New York   San Francisco   Boston
London   Toronto   Sydney   Tokyo   Singapore   Madrid
Mexico City   Munich   Paris   Cape Town   Hong Kong   Montreal

Editor-in-Chief: Joseph P. Terry
Executive Marketing Manager: Megan Galvin-Fak
Production Manager: Ellen MacElree
Project Coordination and Electronic Page Makeup: Stratford/TexTech Inc.
Cover Design Manager: Wendy Ann Fredericks
Cover Art: Plate from Fielding's *Joseph Andrews*, 1805,
    Princeton University Library
Manufacturing Manager: Mary Fischer
Printer and Binder: R.R. Donnelley/Harrisonburg
Cover Printer: Coral Graphics

Library of Congress Cataloging-in-Publication Data

Fielding, Henry, 1707–1754.
    The history of the adventures of Joseph Andrews / by Henry Fielding;
edited by Adam Potkay.
        p. cm. — (A Longman cultural edition)
    Includes bibliographical references (p.) and index.
    ISBN-13: 978-0-321-20937-5 (alk. paper)
    ISBN-10:   0-321-20937-0 (alk. paper)
    1. Young men—Fiction. 2. Domestics—Fiction. 3. Male friendship—
Fiction. 4. Social classes—Fiction. 5. England—Fiction. 6.Clergy—Fiction.
I. Potkay, Adam, 1961– II. Title.
    PR3454.J65 2008
    823'.5—dc22

2007016560

Please visit us at http://www.ablongman.com

ISBN 13: 978-0-321-20937-5

ISBN 10:   0-321-20937-0

1 2 3 4 5 6 7 8 9 10—DOH—10 09 08 07

Contents

List of Illustrations

About Longman Cultural Editions

Reading always vibrates with the transformations of the day—now, yesterday, and centuries ago when presses first put printed language into circulation. So too, literary culture is always open to change, with new pulses of imagination confronting older practices, texts transforming under new ways of reading and new perspectives of understanding, canons shifting and expanding, traditions reviewed and renewed, recast and reformed. Inspired by the innovative *Longman Anthology of British Literature,* Longman Cultural Editions present key texts in contexts that illuminate the lively intersections of literature, tradition, and culture. In each volume, a principal work gains new dimensions from materials that relate it to its past, present, and future: to informing traditions and debates, to the conversations and controversies of its own historical moment, to later eras of reading and reaction.

The series is designed for several kinds of readers and several situations of reading: the cultural editions offer appealing complements to the *Anthology,* as well as attractive resources for a variety of coursework, or for independent encounters. First-time readers will find productive paths to investigate, while more-seasoned readers will enjoy the fresh perspectives and provocative juxtapositions. The contexts for adventure vary from volume to volume, but the constants (in addition to handsome production and affordable pricing) are an important literary work, expertly edited and helpfully annotated; an inviting introduction; a table of dates to track its composition, publication, and reception in relation to biographical, cultural and historical events; and a guide for further study. To these common measures and uncommon enhancements, we invite your attention and curiosity.

Susan J. Wolfson, General Editor
Professor of English, Princeton University

About This Edition

This edition of *Joseph Andrews* places Fielding's landmark novel in several enriching contexts—literary, philosophical, and theological. In response to recent interest in the global, trans-historical story of the novel, my Introduction analyzes Fielding's innovative relation to a romance tradition stretching from the Greek-speaking world of the early Christian era to seventeenth-century continental Europe. A contextual section on "The Romance Tradition" illuminates aspects of Fielding's novel with passages drawn from Heliodorus, Cervantes, and Scarron. Fielding also engages in philosophical and religious controversies of his day, and the section on "Ethics and Theology" brings these to light through selections from two Christian clergymen and one secular philosopher who figure by name in the novel. The questions Fielding raises through these thinkers are still of interest: for example, can sympathy and benevolence supply a sufficient basis for morality? Do moral rules require divine sanction and the threat of eternal punishment for noncompliance? Another question raised by the novel—one very important to its contemporary readers—concerns what it means to laugh at someone or something. Do we laugh only at persons or things that we consider somehow inferior to us? This question is taken up in the section on "The Psychology of Laughter" and also in "What Contemporaries Said." In a passage quoted there, Sarah Fielding (Henry's sister and herself a novelist) argues that Parson Adams—the central comic character of *Joseph Andrews*—is not a proper object of derisive laughter.

The novel's history begins in February 1742 with its anonymous publication, in two duodecimo volumes,[1] as *The History of the*

---

[1] An economic form of printing, a duodecimo volume was made from printing 12 pages on each side of a sheet of paper, to yield a 24-page bundle which was then stitched together with other such bundles.

Adventures of Joseph Andrews, and of his Friend Mr. Abraham Adams. Written in Imitation of the Manner of Cervantes, Author of Don Quixote. A second edition, substantially revised and expanded, appeared in June. (In this and subsequent editions the novel's title lost one "of," becoming *The History of the Adventures of Joseph Andrews, and his Friend Mr. Abraham Adams.*) The third edition, published in March 1743, was again revised, though much less extensively, and is the first to feature Fielding's name on the title page. It has twelve copper-plate illustrations by James Hulett, one of which is reprinted in this volume. A fourth edition followed in October 1748 (misdated 1749) but this is, as Fredson Bowers notes, "the most untrustworthy of all the revised editions," introducing far more printer's errors than authoritative changes.[2] The fifth and last edition to appear in Fielding's lifetime, published in December 1751, was not revised by Fielding and thus its variants lack authority.

The text of *Joseph Andrews* presented here is the third edition of March 1743, the most reliable and authoritative edition to appear in Fielding's lifetime, to which I have done only minor typographical updating (substantive revisions in the fourth edition are footnoted). I have retained all of Fielding's capitalizations of nouns (a conventional feature of earlier eighteenth-century texts); I retain capitalization but not italics for proper names. Italics are retained for words Fielding stresses, most foreign or dialect words, and for short character utterances that Fielding italicizes rather than encasing in quotation marks. I have regularized Fielding's use of quotation marks according to modern standards, deleting the quotation marks that in the original head every line of a long speech. While silently correcting a number of apparent typesetting errors (e.g., a period coming mid-sentence where a comma or colon should be), I have retained the inconsistencies and peculiarities of style that reveal printed language in vibrant flux: for example, Fielding uses "heroick" with a final k but "public" without it; sometimes a speech is "cried" and sometimes "cry'd"; "though" alternates with "tho'," and "God" with "G—." Fielding's art of punctuating his sentences is explained in a note to my Introduction.

My annotations draw wherever possible upon eighteenth-century reference works. For definitions of obscure or outdated words, I principally quote from Samuel Johnson's *Dictionary of the*

---

[2] Bowers, "Textual Introduction" to Martin Battestin's important Wesleyan edition of the novel (Wesleyan University Press, 1967), p. xli.

English Language (1755) and Captain Francis Grose's *A Classical Dictionary of the Vulgar Tongue* (3rd ed., 1796). I turn to the standard *Oxford English Dictionary* when a word is to be found neither in Johnson nor in Grose, or when on occasion the two conflict. Some familiar-looking words meant entirely different things to Fielding from what they mean today: "manners," which now we think of as polite behavior, is defined by Johnson as either "character of the mind" or "general way of life"; "nervous" meant "strong, vigorous"; "pathetic" meant "passionate" or "moving." For references to classical mythology I use John Lemprière's *Classical Dictionary* (1788). Fielding's allusions to Homer and Virgil, and his Latin quotations of the latter, are illumined by the standard verse translations of his day, Dryden's Virgil and Pope's Homer. All other translations from Greek and Latin, as well as from French and (garbled) Italian, are my own.

My Table of Dates for Fielding's life is based on Martin and Ruthe Battestin, *Henry Fielding: A Life* (London: Routledge, 1989).

I am throughout this edition much indebted to all the Fielding scholars whose work appears in the section on Further Reading and particularly to the work of Ronald Paulson, John Richetti, Jill Campbell, Simon Dickie, and James Lynch. I have also benefitted from the extensively annotated editions of *Joseph Andrews* by Martin Battestin (Wesleyan University Press, 1967) and Homer Goldberg (W. W. Norton, 1987). My work on this edition has been aided and abetted by a number of scholars and friends, including Bill Walker and Monica Brzezinski Potkay. My special thanks go out to my Longman series editor, Susan Wolfson; to my colleague Robert Maccubbin, for his editing as well as his insights into eighteenth-century life; and to my two William and Mary research assistants, Jessica Clawson and Elizabeth Derby, for helping me to record the changes Fielding made between his first, second, third and fourth editions of the novel.

Introduction

The History of the Adventures of Joseph Andrews, and His Friend Abraham Adams (1742) is among the earliest novels in English, the first comic novel in English, and still one of the greatest novels in English. In his Preface, Fielding defines "the Comic" as a realistic representation of human life and manners with an eye to what is "ridiculous," particularly vanity (people pretending to be something they're not) and hypocrisy (people trying to conceal what they are). The comic mode of *Joseph Andrews* exposes liars and cheats, especially those who violate the Christian principles of charity or general good-neighborliness. The feeling of sympathy and the charitable actions that result from it are the novel's normative values, against which a host of characters—country squires, lawyers, judges, innkeepers, and a variety of clergymen—are judged and found wanting. Another key value is the companionate and sexually warm marriage—the Wilsons in Book III and Joseph and his beloved Fanny Goodwill at the novel's end—set against a panorama of lechery, adultery, lewdness, and attempted rape. Pierre Desfontaines, a contemporary reviewer of the novel, sung the praises of Fielding's moral vision. *Joseph Andrews,* he wrote, is "a judicious and moral novel, full of salt" (by which he meant wit, merriment); it "makes us love virtue and is infinitely interesting. . . . The style is everywhere comic, except for the passages which interest us in a tender and lawful love."

Yet not all the novel's comedy or laughter is governed by a "judicious and moral" design. *Joseph Andrews* is full of farcical humor, the comedy of antics and pratfalls. Parson Adams, a feisty, strong-fisted, but generally hapless clergyman, is at the center of the physical comedy. He prances about wildly when overjoyed; falls and rolls down a hill when scared by "ghosts"; walks waist-deep through a mud puddle for lack of sense to look for a route around it. In several skirmishes he is drenched in hog's blood, blackened with a mop of dirty water, and jostled by a pack of hunting dogs (see Illustration 6). A practical joke lands him in a tub of cold water (see cover illustration), and he has a starring role in the extended bedroom farce at the novel's comic climax (IV.14); for good measure, he falls off his horse in the final chapter (16). Laughter at the good Parson's expense derives more from popular traditions of anti-clerical humor than from any moral purpose. We may even find ourselves given to the malicious (or at least superior) laughter that Fielding rejects in his Preface. Sarah Fielding, Henry's sister and herself a novelist from 1744, argued that Adams is not a proper object of ridicule (see under Contexts in this volume); yet her very need to argue the point concedes the provocation.

No wonder Fielding took such pains, in his Preface and in the introductory chapters to the first three of the novel's four "Books," to explain what he's trying to do in *Joseph Andrews*. Some of this has to do with Fielding's self-conscious sense that he was inventing a new (novel) English form. Today, the novel is our pre-eminent literary genre, and we have certain expectations about what novels do: they depict more or less realistic characters going about the business of life in more or less plausible ways, even if their lives are more colorful and dramatic than our own. For Fielding such conventions were not yet in place. The term "novel" referred, as Samuel Johnson defined it in his great *Dictionary* (1755), to "a small tale, generally of love."

Fielding had other ideas. But working in a new genre was a source of anxiety as well as pride. In Fielding's day, innovation was not viewed as an unqualified good. The Greek and Roman classics were still the basis of elite education and the standard of literary excellence. In Parson Adams, Fielding gives us a strong proponent of the value of classical learning, and displays through the Parson's learned disquisitions (particularly in III.2) that he himself is no mean classicist. Thus Fielding validates his new mode of writing by giving it a respectable literary and cultural heritage. Invoking the Homeric epic—epic was the "highest" literary genre—he calls *Joseph Andrews* "a comic Epic-poem in Prose," and in the reflections on genre that begin the first three Books he associates his literary form with biography and history, other genres with classical roots.

Fielding has contemporary influences as well as classical ones. Fielding's Preface invokes William Hogarth (1697–1764), dubbed by Fielding a "Comic History-Painter." Paintings from scriptural, classical-mythological, and Greco-Roman political history had the highest status, but Fielding admired Hogarth's "histories" of his own times. One celebrated history was the eight-print series *The Rake's Progress* (1733–35). Hogarth takes satiric aim at a wealthy middle-class young man who comes to ruin and to madness through affecting the fashionable vices of the aristocracy, including dueling, drinking, whoring, and gambling. *The Rake's Progress* provides much of the frame-by-frame narrative for Mr. Wilson's "History of his Life" in *Joseph Andrews* III.3. Like Hogarth's rake, Wilson whittles away his patrimony on fashionable attire and leisure pursuits, debauches a young woman, picks up a series of venereal diseases, drinks all night with loose companions, loses all at gambling, tries his luck as a playwright, and is imprisoned for debt. Unlike Hogarth's rake, however, Mr. Wilson is saved by the good graces of Miss Harriet Hearty, whom he happily marries. Fielding, finally more comic than Hogarth, was generally unwilling to trace a downward spiral to the point of no return.

This edition reproduces two Hogarth prints, one of which may lie behind and one of which stems from Fielding's theory of comedy. Fielding claims: "The only Source of the true Ridiculous (as it appears to me) is Affectation," and in his subsequent illustration of "a poor House," where we find the "Affectation of Riches and Finery," we appear to enter Hogarth's print "The Distrest Poet," a scene of squalor littered with signs of the poetaster's ambitions—a shirt and lace cuffs before the fire, a great coat and gentleman's sword on the floor, a map of Peruvian riches on the wall. Fielding also distinguishes the comic, an exact "copying of Nature," from "*caricatura,*" which aims "to exhibit Monsters, not Men." Hogarth illustrated Fielding's distinction in "Characters Caricaturas." On the left bottom of the print we see one idealized and two comic profiles copied from Raphael cartoons; on the right are several caricatures. Amidst the more than one hundred comic heads that float above the bottom panel are, in the print's lower center, caricatures of Fielding, famous for his long nose, and the pug-faced Hogarth, facing one another and smiling.

Yet for all his affinities to Hogarth, Fielding calls his literary creation not just a "comic history" but also "a comic Romance." He allies *Joseph Andrews* with the traditional form of the "romance," derived from *roman,* the old French term used to designate narratives of quest, adventure, and erotic love, written in Western European vernacular languages from the Middle Ages onwards. English critical tradition usually distinguishes the prose "romance" (improbable and conventional) from the "novel" (plausible and original); but it's important to note that this distinction is not so vivid in other literary cultures. French, along with other Continental languages, has no separate words for "novel" and "romance" (both are called *roman*). Thus, a French work that influenced Fielding—Paul Scarron's *Le Roman Comique* (1651–57), about the adventures of two young lovers in an acting troupe—may be translated either as *The Comic Novel* or as *The Comic Romance*. Both designations could apply to *Joseph Andrews*.

Yet, unlike Scarron's *Roman*, *Joseph Andrews* is full of social detail, from the workings of church and judicature, to the relations between the classes, to basic matters of money, such as how much things cost and how much people make. With an interest in social realism, Fielding censures the absurd extravagances of the romance tradition and uses the word "romance" in a pejorative sense when referring to Madeleine de Scudéry's *Artamène ou le Grand Cyrus* (1649–53) and other seventeenth-century French "heroic romances," all of which are massive, multi-volume sagas of aristocratic love and honor set in exotic, fanciful locales. Fielding's "comic romance" is rendered in the mode of social probability and fidelity to common life. Distinguishing *Joseph Andrews* from the English "modern Novel" as well (III.1), Fielding pegs that genre, with a slight, to tales of sexual intrigue featured in the novellas of Eliza Haywood (1693–1756) and the scandal chronicles of Mary de la Rivière Manley (1663–1724). All these distinctions, from heroic romance and the English novel, argue for the respectability and moral usefulness of *Joseph Andrews*. As Desfontaines noted, *Joseph Andrews* is "without the least touch of libertinage."

Fielding's chief rival for novelistic fame in the 1740s, Samuel Richardson (1689–1761), wrote in an avowedly, even doggedly, moral vein—but with traces of the libertine novel he eschewed. Book I of *Joseph Andrews* begins as a burlesque of Richardson's extraordinarily popular novel, *Pamela, or Virtue Rewarded* (November 1740). Servant girl Pamela Andrews, having successfully resisted the sexual advances of her master, "Squire B——" (as though he were a real person whose reputation needs to be protected), is finally asked for her hand in marriage and becomes an exemplary upper-class matron. Fielding thought this a bad novel stylistically—it is composed of fictive letters, most of them by the unsophisticated, prosy Pamela—and morally, both for its titillating scenes of attempted seduction and (as he saw it) its ultimately mercenary lesson that the virtue of chastity is rewarded by status and wealth. Fielding first attacked *Pamela* in his novella *An Apology for the Life of Mrs. Shamela Andrews* (April 1741): Richardson's Pamela is travestied in the carnal and conniving Shamela, who reels in "Squire Booby" while carrying on an affair with the antinomian Parson Williams. In *Joseph Andrews*, Pamela Andrews returns under her Richardsonian name but as a sanctimonious prig (IV.7), while "Squire Booby" returns under his travesty name but as an intelligent and generous character. It is the squire's aunt, Lady Booby, who assumes the libertine role "Squire B—" had played in *Pamela*. She lusts for Pamela's (presumed) brother, the servant Joseph, who (in a parody of the Biblical story of Joseph's resistance to Potiphar's lustful wife [Genesis 39]) resists her.

When Joseph responds to Lady Booby's advances with ludicrously solemn talk about his innocence and virtue, it costs him his employment in London at the close of the first part of the novel (I.1–10). The second part (I.11 to the end of Book 3) is set on the road: Joseph sets out for his country home and his beloved Fanny, even while Fanny sets out for London to find Joseph; and their country parson, Abraham Adams, journeys towards London in the naïve hope of publishing his sermons. The burlesque of *Pamela* is left behind for a new focus on charity, and Joseph changes from a ridiculous figure into the novel's ardent, courageous, impetuous—but also reasonable—hero.

As a hero, moreover, he is the foil to the new fool: the quixotic and fallible Parson Adams. Fielding wrote on his title page that his work was *Written in Imitation of the Manner of Cervantes, Author of* Don Quixote, and Adams is his Quixote. Cervantes' *Don Quixote de la Mancha* (1605–15), an English translation of which was overseen by Peter Motteux in 1700–1703, concerns the adventures of a poor Spanish gentleman besotted with chivalric romances. Setting himself up as a knight upon a bare-ribbed nag Rosinante, he goes in quest of noble adventures, oblivious to mundane life. He tilts at windmills as though they were giants and enters a cheap inn filled with prostitutes as though it were a castle of virtuous maidens. Yet Quixote is no despicable fool. He is "God's fool," embodying an ideal of service and moral simplicity against which the actual world may be judged. Similarly, Fielding's Parson Adams is devoted to an ideal of charity sorely lacking in the English countryside. But in a further irony, the Parson not only preaches charity but is in continual need of it because of his imprudence, his inability to look ahead and provide for himself.

Don Quixote helped Fielding to create the character of Adams—by Fielding's account, "the most glaring in the whole"— but it did not afford him a plot. In both the second part of *Joseph Andrews* and its third and last part—Book IV, set in the Somersetshire countryside around Booby Hall, and concerning Joseph and Fanny's discovery of their proper social place—Fielding bases his narrative on a Greek romance plot as old as Heliodorus's *Ethiopian Story* (4th century CE?), about the trials, sufferings, and eventual success of two lovers. Heliodorus's work was imitated by many romance writers of the Renaissance and seventeenth century, including Cervantes and Scarron, and was in Fielding's lifetime translated into English as *The Adventures of Theacles and Chariclia, A Romance. Being the Rise, Progress, Tryals, and happy Success of the Heroic Loves of those Two Illustrious Persons* (Charles Gildon, 1717). Heliodorus's lovers, repeatedly separated (often through abduction) and reunited, their love recurrently tested by erotic rivals and by attacks on their chastity and mutual fidelity, finally find the haven in which their true identities may be revealed and their marital happiness secured. Fielding's Joseph and Fanny, buffeted by fortune, reach their destination (the countryside around Booby Hall), where, after they are united in full self-knowledge, the curtain falls on "the Happiness of this Couple," and Joseph declares he will imitate his fond parents in a life of rural retirement.

But Fielding's last line, "nor will [Joseph] be prevailed on by any Booksellers, or their Authors, to make his Appearance in *High-Life*," twists back to the novel's beginnings in burlesque with one last jab at Richardson's literary heroine: Fielding alludes to an unauthorized sequel to *Pamela* by another author (John Kelly), *Pamela's Conduct in High Life* (May 1741). Instead of closing on a romance note, Fielding ends with a self-reflexive notice of the novel's literary precursors and of its precarious place in a roiling literary marketplace. It is this deft balance of sentiment and satire, high life and low, and romance conventions and the practicalities of writing and publishing in the 1740s that, more than any other feature of *Joseph Andrews,* marks Fielding's distinctive contribution to the development of the novel.

A Note on Money in Fielding's Novel

A *pound* (£) consisted of 20 *shillings*. Each shilling (s) was worth 12 *pence* (p) or "pennies." As sure as "a Shilling was worth twelve pence," Adams declares, his manuscript sermons are "well worth a hundred Pound" (he's sadly mistaken about this).

The penny was divided into *half-pennies* and then *farthings*, or quarter-pennies, the smallest coin. ("I value thee not a farthing," Fielding says to "Vanity" at the end of I.15.) In II.14, Adams and company incur a debt of 7 shillings and have only 6 and a half pence between them. Adams is delighted to receive a loan of 6 shillings, 6 pence from a poor peddler, a sum that allows him to pay his bill with one half-penny left over.

Six shillings was the original cost of the two bound, pocket-size volumes of *Joseph Andrews* that appeared in February 1742. This would have been 3.75 percent of Joseph's £8 annual salary as a servant, or 7.5 percent of his annual disposable income, as he sends half his wages home to his aged mother and father. Fielding's novel might seem more within the reach of Parson Adams—if he read novels—but he too may have been hard-strapped to spare six shillings on a book of dubious value. He supports a wife and six children on his curate's salary of £23 a year, or £1, 18s a month. Lady Booby is scornful of the Adams's genteel poverty: "there was not such another ragged Family in the Parish," she tells a visiting gentleman (IV.9). She is an aristocrat with a likely annual income of thousands of pounds (the historical Duke of Newcastle had an annual income of £40,000).

Two other units of money we encounter in *Joseph Andrews* (initially in II.16) are the *Half-Crown*, worth 2s 6p, and the *Guinea*, a gold coin worth £1 1s (or 21 shillings). The coin's name derived from the Guinea coast of West Africa, which supplied much of the gold used in its minting.

A Note on Fielding's Punctuation and Style

Today, we punctuate sentences in order to clarify grammatical relations: a *colon* may introduce a definition or explanation of something; *commas*, when used properly, separate the several clauses of a sentence; *semi-colons* separate two or more independent but closely related sentences. These conventions were not codified in the eighteenth century. Fielding uses punctuation, as we do, to separate the portions of a sentence into manageable units. But he also uses it rhetorically to guide the reader, whom he imagines reading aloud, through the proper pacing of his sentences. To grammarians of the late seventeenth century and early eighteenth century, the comma, semi-colon, and colon indicate *pauses* of increasing duration: a comma presents a stop for the length of time it takes to say "one," a semi-colon to say "one-two," and a colon, "one-two-three-four." Keeping this in mind will help you more fully comprehend and enjoy Fielding's prose style. Take, for example, the very first sentence of Fielding's Preface (p. 3). Six clauses are separated by three commas and two semi-colons, the latter used rhetorically to indicate a longer pause. This sentence is also a *period* or "periodic sentence," one in which grammatical completion is pleasurably delayed, here until the word "Writing," 58 words into a sentence of 71 words. Fielding's sentences are complex but propulsive, energetic but leisurely. In 1874, novelist George Eliot (the pen name of Mary Ann Evans) paid Fielding this tribute: "he seems to bring his arm chair to the proscenium and chat with us in all the lusty ease of his fine English. But Fielding lived when the days were longer (for time, like money, is measured by our needs), when summer afternoons were spacious, and the clock ticked slowly in the winter evenings" (*Middlemarch* Bk. 2, Chap. 15). In the twenty-first century, the clock ticks faster than ever. Yet, in reading Fielding at his proper pace we may recapture the delight of measuring time not by machines but by the rhythm and flow of the human voice.

Table of Dates

Henry Fielding (1707–54)

1700–1703   Peter Motteux arranges a new English translation of Cervantes' *Don Quixote.*

1707   **22 April, Henry Fielding** (HF, hereafter) born, the first son of a distinguished family in Dorsetshire. Father, Edmund Fielding, a senior army officer and younger son of a younger son of the aristocracy; Mother, Sarah Gould, is the daughter of Sir Henry Gould, one of England's most senior law officers. Six siblings follow, five daughters surviving.

1710   8 November, **Sarah Fielding** born, the future novelist (active 1744–68) and HF's favorite sister.

1711   Anthony Ashley Cooper, the third earl of Shaftesbury, publishes *Characteristicks of Men, Manners, Opinions, Times* (1711), a two-volume collection of his treatises and dialogues that will have a significant influence on moral philosophy and aesthetics in Britain and on the continent.

1712   English translation of Paul Scarron's *Roman Comique, or Comical Romance.*

1717   Charles Gildon's English translation of Heliodorus's ancient Greek novel, *The Ethiopian Story*, as *The Adventures of Theacles and Chariclia, A Romance.*

1718   April, death of HF's mother, Sarah Gould.

1718–19   Edmund Fielding (EF, hereafter), in London, marries a Roman Catholic widow. A long and acrimonious court case ensues over custody of the Fielding children between EF and Sarah Gould's mother, Lady Gould, who removes the children to her own house in Salisbury. The suit is eventually decided in favor of Lady Gould. EF remarries twice more before his death in 1741 and has more children, including the son who would later become Sir John Fielding, HF's fellow London magistrate in 1751 and successor after 1754.

1719–1723/24   **HF at Eton College,** one of England's great "public schools," where he is educated in ancient Greek and Latin.

1721–42   **Sir Robert Walpole** serves as first lord of the Treasury and chancellor of the Exchequer and becomes England's first effective "prime minister" (the title was not yet an official one). He solidifies his position in the House of Commons through doling out and retracting court patronage (or "corruption," as his detractors called it). **"Court Whigs"** are ascendant in Parliament (over **Tories** and **"Opposition"** or **"Patriot" Whigs**).

1725   Late Spring/Summer, HF in London; sees the hanging of Jonathan Wild, notorious crime-lord and fence for stolen goods, the original for Peachum in John Gay's ballad opera, *Beggar's Opera.*

1728   January, Gay's *Beggar's Opera* begins a run of 63 consecutive nights. February, Opening of HF's first play, *Love in Several Masques.* It runs for a respectable 4 nights.

1728–29   HF studies at University of Leyden (Holland).

1729–37   **HF a successful comic playwright in London;** comes to manage the "Little Theatre," Haymarket. He writes over 25 plays.

1730   Staging of HF's burlesque of heroic drama, *Tom Thumb. A Tragedy.*

1731   Publication of *The Tragedy of Tragedies, or the Life and Death of Tom Thumb the Great,* with an editorial apparatus by "H. Scriblerus Secundus" that borrows from the mock-pedantic works of Swift and Pope.

1734   HF marries Charlotte Craddock (d. 1744), with whom he has three children. Only one, Harriet, lives to adulthood.

1735   William Hogarth publishes his 8-print comic series, *A Rake's Progress,* having arranged in February for **An Engraver's Copyright Bill** to be drafted and introduced to the House of Commons. On 25 June 1735, the Act, which became known as Hogarth's Bill, received royal assent and passed into law.

1736–37   Fielding stages two political satires, *Pasquin* (1736) and *The Historical Register for 1736* (1737), which attacked the Walpole government and were partly the instigation for Walpole's retaliatory measure, the **Licensing Act of z1737,** which effectively ended HF's career as a playwright. The Licensing Act, passed June 21, was a landmark of censorship, requiring all new plays to be submitted for the approval of the Lord Chamberlain before staging, and limiting serious drama to two royal patent theatres, Covent Garden and Drury Lane.

1739–41   HF writes the periodical *The Champion,* essays on moral, social, and political topics. 1739: George Whitfield, Calvinist Methodist, publishes his sermons.

1740   April, HF receives patronage from George Bubb Doddington, a "patriot" Whig in opposition to Walpole. HF writes *Mr. Jonathan Wild the Great* (pub. 1743), with Wild a Walpole figure.

1740   June, HF admitted to the bar as a barrister (defense attorney). November, Samuel Richardson publishes the epistolary novel *Pamela, or Virtue Rewarded.*

1741   April, anonymous publication of *Shamela,* a parody of *Pamela,* a work almost certainly by Fielding but which he never acknowledges. Summer/Autumn: HF meets his future benefactor Ralph Allen, probably visiting his estate Prior Park, near the city of Bath.

1742   February, HF publishes, anonymously, *Joseph Andrews.* It goes through five editions by 1751; the 3rd edition of March 1743 is the first with HF's name on the title page.

1744   Sarah Fielding publishes *Adventures of David Simple* with a preface by HF.

1745	July to April 1746: (Second) Jacobite Rebellion. Bonnie Prince Charlie's Scottish army takes Scotland and marches into England as far south as Derby; is routed at the Battle of Culloden. HF publishes anti-Jacobite pamphlets and the journal *The True Patriot.*
1747	November, HF marries his servant Mary Daniel in the 6th month of her pregnancy. With Mary, HF has three children; the sons William and Allen live into the 19th century.
1747–48	HF writes the pro-ministerial periodical *The Jacobite's Journal* (in the ironic guise of "John Trott-Plaid," a bigoted Jacobite).
1748	October, HF writes Richardson a letter of admiration for his new novel, *Clarissa*. Richardson, in turn, remains HF's bitter enemy, deploring his "continued lowness."
1748	November, HF begins a 5-year stint as a London magistrate, Justice of the Peace for Westminster and (in January 1749) for Middlesex County. He holds court on Bow Street.
1749	January–February, HF publishes **Tom Jones.** Goes through four editions (4th is revised) by December.
1751	January, HF publishes *An Enquiry into the Causes of the Late Increases of Robbers*. July, HF's half-brother John Fielding is appointed to the magistracy of Westminster, becoming HF's assistant with Bow Street business. December, HF publishes his third novel, **Amelia.**
1752	HF's last periodical, *The Covent Garden Journal* (satires on moral and social ills).
1753	January, *Proposal for Making an Effectual Provision for the Poor* (advocates county workhouses for the poor and separate workhouses for criminals, with morning and evening chapel compulsory). HF establishes nucleus of a professional metropolitan police force, known as the "Bow-Street Runners." HF suffers from gout and cirrhosis of the liver.

1754   Summer, HF retires with his family to Lisbon, Portugal (later reduced to rubble in the earthquake of 1755). **Dies October 8, age 47.**

1755   Posthumous publication of HF's *Journal of a Voyage to Lisbon.*

1762   HF's publisher, Andrew Millar, puts out HF's collected *Works.*

1768   Death of Sarah Fielding.

THE

HISTORY

OF THE

ADVENTURES

OF

JOSEPH ANDREWS,

And his FRIEND

Mr. *ABRAHAM ADAMS.*

Written in Imitation of

The *Manner* of CERVANTES,
Author of *Don Quixote.*

By HENRY FIELDING, Esquire

The THIRD EDITION, illustrated with CUTS.

IN TWO VOLUMES.

VOL. I.

LONDON:
Printed for A. MILLAR, opposite to *Katharine
Street*, in the *Strand.* M. DCC.XLIII

Preface

As it is possible the mere English Reader may have a different Idea of Romance with the Author of these little Volumes; and may consequently expect a kind of Entertainment not to be found, nor which was even intended, in the following Pages; it may not be improper to premise a few Words concerning this kind of Writing, which I do not remember to have seen hitherto attempted in our Language.

The EPIC, as well as the DRAMA, is divided into Tragedy and Comedy. Homer, who was the Father of this Species of Poetry, gave us a Pattern of both these, tho' that of the latter kind is entirely lost; which Aristotle tells us, bore the same Relation to Comedy which his *Iliad* bears to Tragedy.[1] And perhaps, that we have no more Instances of it among the Writers of Antiquity, is owing to the Loss of this great Pattern, which, had it survived, would have found its Imitators equally with the other Poems of this great Original.

And farther, as this Poetry may be Tragic or Comic, I will not scruple to say it may be likewise either in Verse or Prose: for tho' it wants one Particular, which the Critic enumerates in the constituent Parts of an Epic Poem, namely Metre; yet, when any Kind of Writing contains all its other Parts, such as Fable, Action, Characters, Sentiments, and Diction, and is deficient in Metre only; it seems, I think, reasonable to refer it to the Epic; at least, as no Critic hath thought proper to range it under any other Head, nor to assign it a particular Name to itself.

Thus the *Telemachus* of the Archbishop of Cambray[2] appears to me of the Epic Kind, as well as the *Odyssey* of Homer; indeed, it

---

[1] In *Poetics* 4, Aristotle attributes to Homer a lost burlesque epic, *Margites*.

[2] Françoise de Salignac de la Mothe Fénelon (1651–1715), Archbishop of Cambrai from 1696, published in 1699 a prose epic on the moral education of Telemachus, the son of Odysseus.

is much fairer and more reasonable to give it a Name common with that Species from which it differs only in a single Instance, than to confound it with those which it resembles in no other. Such are those voluminous Works commonly called *Romances,* namely, *Clelia, Cleopatra, Astraea, Cassandra,* the *Grand Cyrus,* and innumerable others, which contain, as I apprehend, very little Instruction or Entertainment.[3]

Now a comic Romance is a comic Epic-Poem in Prose; differing from Comedy, as the serious Epic from Tragedy: its Action being more extended and comprehensive; containing a much larger Circle of Incidents, and introducing a greater Variety of Characters. It differs from the serious Romance in its Fable and Action, in this; that as in the one these are grave and solemn, so in the other they are light and ridiculous: It differs in its Characters, by introducing Persons of inferior Rank, and consequently of inferior Manners, whereas the grave Romance sets the highest before us; lastly, in its Sentiments and Diction; by preserving the Ludicrous instead of the Sublime. In the Diction, I think, Burlesque itself may be sometimes admitted; of which many Instances will occur in this Work, as in the Descriptions of the Battles, and some other Places, not necessary to be pointed out to the Classical Reader; for whose Entertainment those Parodies or Burlesque Imitations are chiefly calculated.

But tho' we have sometimes admitted this in our Diction, we have carefully excluded it from our Sentiments and Characters: for there it is never properly introduced, unless in Writings of the Burlesque Kind, which this is not intended to be. Indeed, no two Species of Writing can differ more widely than the Comic and the Burlesque: for as the latter is ever the Exhibition of what is monstrous and unnatural, and where our Delight, if we examine it, arises from the surprizing Absurdity, as in appropriating the Manners of the highest to the lowest, or *è converso;*[4] so in the former, we should ever confine ourselves strictly to Nature, from the just Imitation of which, will flow all the Pleasure we can this way convey to a sensible Reader. And perhaps there is one Reason why a Comic Writer should of all others be the least excused for deviating from Nature, since it may not be always so easy for a serious Poet to meet

---

[3] French heroic romances by Madeleine de Scudéry (*Clélie,* 1654–60, *Artamène ou le Grand Cyrus,* 1649–53); Gauthier de Costes de la Calprenède (*Cléopâtre,* 1647–56, *Cassandre,* 1644–50); and Honoré d'Urfé (*Astrée,* 1607–28).

[4] "Vice Versa."

with the Great and the Admirable; but Life every where furnishes an accurate Observer with the Ridiculous.

I have hinted this little concerning Burlesque; because, I have often heard that Name given to Performances which have been truly of the Comic Kind, from the Author's having sometimes admitted it in his Diction only; which, as it is the Dress of Poetry, doth, like the Dress of Men, establish Characters, (the one of the whole Poem, and the other of the whole Man) in vulgar Opinion, beyond any of their greater Excellencies: But surely, a certain Drollery in Style, where the Characters and Sentiments are perfectly natural, no more constitutes the Burlesque, than an empty Pomp and Dignity of Words, where every thing else is mean and low, can entitle any Performance to the Appellation of the true Sublime.

And I apprehend, my Lord Shaftesbury's Opinion of mere Burlesque agrees with mine, when he asserts, "There is no such Thing to be found in the Writings of the Antients."[5] But perhaps, I have less Abhorrence than he professes for it: and that not because I have had some little Success on the Stage this way;[6] but rather, as it contributes more to exquisite Mirth and Laughter than any other; and these are probably more wholesome Physic for the Mind, and conduce better to purge away Spleen, Melancholy and ill Affections than is generally imagined. Nay, I will appeal to common Observation, whether the same Companies are not found more full of Good-Humour and Benevolence, after they have been sweetened for two or three Hours with Entertainments of this Kind, than when soured by a Tragedy or a grave Lecture.

But to illustrate all this by another Science, in which, perhaps, we shall see the Distinction more clearly and plainly: Let us examine the Works of a Comic History-Painter,[7] with those Performances which the Italians call *Caricatura;* where we shall find the true Excellence of the former to consist in the exactest copying of Nature; insomuch, that a judicious Eye instantly rejects any thing *outré;* any Liberty which the Painter hath taken with the Features of

---

[5] Anthony Ashely Cooper, third earl of Shaftesbury (1671–1713), makes a remark to this effect in *Sensus Communis: An Essay on the Freedom of Wit and Humour* (1709) I.5.

[6] Fielding's most popular theatrical burlesques were *Tom Thumb* (1730) and its expanded version, *The Tragedy of Tragedies* (1731), which parody scenes and speeches from many seventeenth- and eighteenth-century tragedies and heroic dramas.

[7] That is, William Hogarth (see Introduction pp. xiv–xv).

that Alma Mater.—Whereas in the *Caricatura* we allow all Licence. Its Aim is to exhibit Monsters not Men; and all Distortions and Exaggerations whatever are within its proper Province.

Now what *Caricatura* is in Painting, Burlesque is in Writing; and in the same manner the Comic Writer and Painter correlate to each other. And here I shall observe, that, as in the former the Painter seems to have the Advantage; so it is in the latter infinitely on the side of the Writer: for the *Monstrous* is much easier to paint than describe, and the *Ridiculous* to describe than paint.

And tho' perhaps this latter Species doth not in either Science so strongly affect and agitate the Muscles as the other; yet it will be

Characters Caricaturas, William Hogarth, 1743. (Special Collections, University of Virginia Library.)

owned, I believe, that a more rational and useful Pleasure arises to us from it. He who should call the Ingenious Hogarth a Burlesque Painter, would, in my Opinion, do him very little Honour: for sure it is much easier, much less the Subject of Admiration, to paint a Man with a Nose, or any other Feature of a preposterous Size, or to expose him in some absurd or monstrous Attitude, than to express the Affections of Men on Canvas. It hath been thought a vast Commendation of a Painter, to say his Figures *seem to breathe;* but surely, it is a much greater and nobler Applause, that they *appear to think.*

But to return—The Ridiculous only, as I have before said, falls within my Province in the present Work.—Nor will some Explanation of this Word be thought impertinent by the Reader, if he considers how wonderfully it hath been mistaken, even by Writers who have profess'd it: for to what but such a Mistake, can we attribute the many Attempts to ridicule the blackest Villanies; and what is yet worse, the most dreadful Calamities? What could exceed the Absurdity of an Author, who should write the *Comedy of Nero, with the merry Incident of ripping up his Mother's Belly;*[8] or what would give a greater Shock to Humanity, than an Attempt to expose the Miseries of Poverty and Distress to Ridicule? And yet, the Reader will not want much Learning to suggest such Instances to himself.

Besides, it may seem remarkable, that Aristotle, who is so fond and free of Definitions, hath not thought proper to define the Ridiculous. Indeed, where he tells us it is proper to Comedy, he hath remarked that Villany is not its Object: but he hath not, as I remember, positively asserted what is. Nor doth the Abbé Bellegarde, who hath writ a Treatise on this Subject, tho' he shews us many Species of it, once trace it to its Fountain.[9]

The only Source of the true Ridiculous (as it appears to me) is Affectation. But tho' it arises from one Spring only; when we consider the infinite Streams into which this one branches, we shall presently cease to admire at the copious Field it affords to an Observer. Now Affectation proceeds from one of these two Causes; Vanity or Hypocrisy: For as Vanity puts us on affecting false Characters, in order to purchase Applause; so Hypocrisy sets us on an Endeavour to avoid Censure, by concealing our Vices under an

---

[8] The Roman emperor Nero ordered his mother's murder in 59 CE, commanding that she be stabbed in the womb (Tacitus, *Annals* 14.8).

[9] Jean Baptiste Morvan de Bellegarde (1648–1743), *Reflexions sur le ridicule* (1696).

Appearance of their opposite Virtues. And tho' these two Causes are often confounded, (for there is some Difficulty in distinguishing them) yet, as they proceed from very different Motives; so they are as clearly distinct in their Operations: For indeed, the Affectation which arises from Vanity is nearer to Truth than the other; as it hath not that violent Repugnancy of Nature to struggle with, which that of the Hypocrite hath. It may be likewise noted, that Affectation doth not imply an absolute Negation of those Qualities which are affected: and therefore, tho' when it proceeds from Hypocrisy, it be nearly allied to Deceit; yet when it comes from Vanity only, it partakes of the Nature of Ostentation: for instance, the Affectation of Liberality in a vain Man differs visibly from the same Affectation in the Avaricious; for tho' the vain Man is not what he would appear, or hath not the Virtue he affects, to the degree he would be thought to have it; yet it sits less aukwardly on him than on the avaricious Man, who is the very Reverse of what he would *seem* to be.

From the Discovery of this Affectation arises the Ridiculous— which always strikes the Reader with Surprize and Pleasure; and that in a higher and stronger Degree when the Affectation arises from Hypocrisy, than when from Vanity: for to discover any one to be the exact Reverse of what he affects, is more surprizing, and consequently more ridiculous, than to find him a little deficient in the Quality he desires the Reputation of. I might observe, that our Ben Johnson, who of all Men understood the *Ridiculous* the best, hath chiefly used the hypocritical Affectation.[10]

Now from Affectation only, the Misfortunes and Calamities of Life, or the Imperfections of Nature, may become the Objects of Ridicule. Surely he hath a very ill-framed Mind, who can look on Ugliness, Infirmity, or Poverty, as ridiculous in themselves: nor do I believe any Man living who meets a dirty Fellow riding through the Streets in a Cart, is struck with an Idea of the Ridiculous from it; but if he should see the same Figure descend from his Coach and Six, or bolt from his Chair[11] with his Hat under his Arm, he would then begin to laugh, and with Justice. In the same manner, were we to enter a poor House, and behold a wretched Family shivering with Cold and languishing with Hunger, it would not incline us to

[10] Ben Jonson (1572–1637) satirized hypocrisy in plays including *Volpone* (1606) and *The Alchemist* (1610).

[11] "Chair": "a vehicle borne by men; a sedan" (Johnson). Tom Rakewell is carried by two men in a sedan chair in Hogarth's *A Rake's Progress*, plate 4 (Longman Anthology of British Literature 1C).

Laughter, (at least we must have very diabolical Natures, if it would:) but should we discover there a Grate, instead of Coals, adorned with Flowers, empty Plate or China Dishes on the Sideboard, or any other Affectation of Riches and Finery either on their Persons or in their Furniture; we might then indeed be excused for ridiculing so fantastical an Appearance. Much less are natural Imperfections the Objects of Derision: but when Ugliness aims at the Applause of Beauty, or Lameness endeavours to display Agility; it is then that these unfortunate Circumstances, which at first moved our Compassion, tend only to raise our Mirth.

The Poet carries this very far;

> None are for being what they are in Fault,
> But for not being what they would be thought.[12]

Where if the Metre would suffer the Word *Ridiculous* to close the first Line, the Thought would be rather more proper. Great Vices are the proper Objects of our Detestation, smaller Faults of our Pity: but Affectation appears to me the only true Source of the Ridiculous.

But perhaps it may be objected to me, that I have against my own Rules introduced Vices, and of a very black Kind into this Work. To which I shall answer: First, that it is very difficult to pursue a Series of human Actions and keep clear from them. Secondly, That the Vices to be found here, are rather the accidental Consequences of some human Frailty or Foible, than Causes habitually existing in the Mind. Thirdly, That they are never set forth as the Objects of Ridicule but Detestation. Fourthly, That they are never the principal Figure at that Time on the Scene; and lastly, they never produce the intended Evil.

Having thus distinguished *Joseph Andrews* from the Productions of Romance Writers on the one Hand, and Burlesque Writers on the other, and given some few very short Hints (for I intended no more) of this Species of Writing, which I have affirmed to be hitherto unattempted in our Language; I shall leave to my good natur'd Reader to apply my Piece to my Observations, and will detain him no longer than with a Word concerning the Characters in this Work.

And here I solemnly protest, I have no Intention to vilify or asperse any one: for tho' every thing is copied from the Book of Nature, and scarce a Character or Action produced which I have not

---

[12] William Congreve (1670–1729), "Of Pleasing," ll. 63–64.

The Distrest Poet, William Hogarth, 1740. (The Colonial Williamsburg Foundation.)

taken from my own Observations and Experience; yet I have used the utmost Care to obscure the Persons by such different Circumstances, Degrees, and Colours, that it will be impossible to guess at them with any Degree of Certainty; and if it ever happens otherwise, it is only where the Failure characterized is so minute, that it is a Foible only which the Party himself may laugh at as well as any other.

As to the Character of Adams, as it is the most glaring in the whole, so I conceive it is not to be found in any Book now extant. It is designed a Character of perfect Simplicity; and as the Goodness of his Heart will recommend him to the Good-natur'd; so I hope it will excuse me to the Gentlemen of his Cloth;[13] for whom, while they are worthy of their sacred Order, no Man can possibly have a greater Respect. They will therefore excuse me, notwithstanding the low Adventures in which he is engaged, that I have made him a Clergyman; since no other Office could have given him so many Opportunities of displaying his worthy Inclinations.

---

[13] That is, the clergy.

THE
CONTENTS
OF
VOLUME I.

CHAP. V.

CHAP. VI.

CHAP. VII.

CHAP. VIII.

CHAP. IX.

CHAP. X.

CHAP. XI.

CHAP. XII.

CHAP. XIII.

CHAP. XIV.

CHAP. XV.

CHAP. XVI.

CHAP. XVII.

CHAP. XVIII.

BOOK II.

CHAP. I.

CHAP. II.

CHAP. III.

CHAP. IV.

CHAP. V.

CHAP. VI.

CHAP. VII.

CHAP. VIII.

A notable Dissertation by Mr. Abraham Adams; *wherein that Gentleman appears in a political Light.*

CHAP. IX.

In which the Gentleman descants on Bravery and heroic Virtue, 'till an unlucky Accident puts an end to the Discourse.

CHAP. X.

Giving an Account of the strange Catastrophe of the preceding Adventure, which drew poor Adams *into fresh Calamities; and who the Woman was who owed the Preservation of her Chastity to his victorious Arm.*

CHAP. XI.

What happened to them while before the Justice. A Chapter very full of Learning.

CHAP. XII.

A very delightful Adventure, as well to the Persons concerned as to the good-natur'd Reader.

CHAP. XIII.

A Dissertation concerning high People and low People, with Mrs. Slipslop's *Departure in no very good Temper of Mind, and the evil Plight in which she left* Adams *and his Company.*

CHAP. XIV.

An interview between Parson Adams *and Parson* Trulliber.

THE
CONTENTS
OF
VOLUME II.

BOOK IV.

CHAP. I.

CHAP. IX.

CHAP. X.

CHAP. XI.

CHAP. XII.

CHAP. XIII.

CHAP. XIV.

CHAP. XV.

CHAP. XVI.

THE
HISTORY
OF THE
ADVENTURES
OF
Joseph Andrews, and his Friend
Mr. *Abraham Adams.*

BOOK I.

CHAP. I.

Of writing Lives in general, and particularly of Pamela; *with a Word by the bye of* Colley Cibber *and others.*

IT is a trite but true Observation, that Examples work more forcibly on the Mind than Precepts:[1] And if this be just in what is odious and blameable, it is more strongly so in what is amiable and praise-worthy. Here Emulation most effectually operates upon us, and inspires our Imitation in an irresistible manner. A good Man therefore is a standing

---

[1] Fielding writes in *The Champion* for June 10, 1740: "the Force of Example is infinitely stronger, as well as quicker, than Precept: for which Horace [*Ars Poetica,* ll. 180–82] assigns this Reason, *That our Eyes convey the Idea more briskly to the Understanding than our Ears.*" "On this account," Fielding continues, "I esteem the ingenious Mr. Hogarth as one of the most useful Satyrists any Age hath produced." On Hogarth, see Introduction, pp. xiv–xv. Cf. John Tillotson on Jesus as "living example" in Contexts, pp. 341–42.

Lesson to all his Acquaintance, and of far greater use in that narrow Circle than a good Book.

But as it often happens that the best Men are but little known, and consequently cannot extend the Usefulness of their Examples a great way; the Writer may be called in aid to spread their History farther, and to present the amiable Pictures to those who have not the Happiness of knowing the Originals; and so, by communicating such valuable Patterns to the World, he may perhaps do a more extensive Service to Mankind than the Person whose Life originally afforded the Pattern.

In this Light I have always regarded those Biographers who have recorded the Actions of great and worthy Persons of both Sexes. Not to mention those antient Writers which of late days are little read, being written in obsolete, and, as they are generally thought, unintelligible Languages; such as Plutarch, Nepos, and others which I heard of in my Youth;[2] our own Language affords many of excellent Use and Instruction, finely calculated to sow the Seeds of Virtue in Youth, and very easy to be comprehended by Persons of moderate Capacity. Such are the History of John the Great, who, by his brave and heroic Actions against Men of large and athletic Bodies, obtained the glorious Appellation of the Giant-killer; that of an Earl of Warwick, whose Christian Name was Guy; the Lives of Argalus and Parthenia, and above all, the History of those seven worthy Personages, the Champions of Christendom.[3] In all these, Delight is mixed with Instruction, and the Reader is almost as much improved as entertained.

But I pass by these and many others, to mention two Books lately published, which represent an admirable Pattern of the Amiable in either Sex. The former of these which deals in Male-virtue, was written by the great Person himself, who lived the Life he hath recorded, and is by many thought to have lived such a Life only in order to write it. The other is communicated to us by an Historian

---

[2] The famous biographers Plutarch (c. 46–120 CE) and Cornelius Nepo (c. 100–25 BCE) wrote, respectively, in Greek and Latin. In Fielding's days, these and other classical authors were still read in their original languages in public schools and universities but not all students at these elite institutions could read them well, and readers without a gentleman's education could as a rule not read them at all.

[3] *Jack and the Giants, Guy, Earl of Warwick, Argalus and Parthenia*, and *The Seven Champions of Christendom* were inexpensive, illustrated chapbooks, widely available in the eighteenth century. Fielding had used the chapbook protagonist Tom Thumb in his send-ups of heroic drama, *Tom Thumb* and *The Tragedy of Tragedies* (1730–1731).

who borrows his Lights, as the common Method is, from authentic Papers and Records. The Reader, I believe, already conjectures, I mean the Lives of Mr. *Colley Cibber,* and of Mrs. *Pamela Andrews.*[4] How artfully doth the former, by insinuating that he *escaped* being promoted to the highest Stations in Church and State, teach us a Contempt of worldly Grandeur! how strongly doth he inculcate an absolute Submission to our Superiors! Lastly, how completely doth he arm us against so uneasy, so wretched a Passion as the Fear of Shame! how clearly doth he expose the Emptiness and Vanity of that Fantom, Reputation!

What the Female Readers are taught by the Memoirs of Mrs. Andrews, is so well set forth in the excellent Essays or Letters prefixed to the second and subsequent Editions of that Work, that it would be here a needless Repetition. The authentic History with which I now present the Public, is an Instance of the great Good that Book is likely to do, and of the Prevalence of Example which I have just observed: Since it will appear that it was by keeping the excellent Pattern of his Sister's Virtues before his Eyes, that Mr. Joseph Andrews was chiefly enabled to preserve his Purity in the midst of such great Temptations. I shall only add, that this Character of Male-Chastity, tho' doubtless as desirable and becoming in one Part of the human Species, as in the other, is almost the only Virtue which the great Apologist hath not given himself for the sake of giving the Example to his Readers.

CHAP. II.

Of Mr. Joseph Andrews *his Birth, Parentage, Education, and great Endowment; with a Word or two concerning Ancestors.*

MR. Joseph Andrews, the Hero of our ensuing History, was esteemed to be the only Son of Gaffar and Gammer[1] Andrews, and Brother to the illustrious Pamela, whose Virtue is at present so famous. As to his Ancestors, we have searched with great Diligence,

---

[4] On Richardson's *Pamela, or Virtue Rewarded* (1740), see Introduction, pp. xvi–xvii. "Mrs." or "mistress"—a title suggesting a position of authority—could be used of unmarried as well as married women. Colley Cibber (1671–1757) was an actor, playwright, and theater manager with whom Fielding at first collaborated and later competed during his theatrical career (1728–37). In 1740 Cibber published his autobiography, *An Apology for the Life of Mr. Colley Cibber, Comedian.*

[1] Titles of respect applied to older country people of low social rank.

but little Success; being unable to trace them farther than his Great Grandfather, who, as an elderly Person in the Parish remembers to have heard his Father say, was an excellent Cudgel-player.[2] Whether he had any Ancestors before this, we must leave to the Opinion of our curious Reader, finding nothing of sufficient Certainty to rely on. However, we cannot omit inserting an Epitaph which an ingenious Friend of ours hath communicated:

> Stay Traveller, for underneath this Pew
> Lies fast asleep that merry Man Andrew;
> When the last Day's great Sun shall gild the Skies,
> Then he shall from his Tomb get up and rise.
> Be merry while thou can'st: For surely thou
> Shall shortly be as sad as he is now.

The Words are almost out of the Stone with Antiquity. But it is needless to observe, that Andrew here is writ without an s, and is besides a Christian Name. My Friend moreover conjectures this to have been the Founder of that Sect of laughing Philosophers, since called *Merry Andrews*.[3]

To wave therefore a Circumstance, which, tho' mentioned in conformity to the exact Rules of Biography, is not greatly material; I proceed to things of more consequence. Indeed it is sufficiently certain, that he had as many Ancestors, as the best Man living; and perhaps, if we look five or six hundred Years backwards, might be related to some Persons of very great Figure at present, whose Ancestors within half the last Century are buried in as great Obscurity. But suppose for Argument's sake we should admit that he had no Ancestors at all, but had sprung up, according to the modern Phrase, out of a Dunghil, as the Athenians pretended they themselves did from the Earth, would not this *Autokopros** have been justly entitled to all the Praise arising from his own Virtues? Would it not be hard, that a Man who hath no Ancestors, should therefore be rendered incapable of acquiring Honour, when we see so many who have no Virtues, enjoying the Honour of their Forefathers? At ten Years old (by which Time his Education was advanced to

---

[2] A cudgel is a short, thick stick or club. "Cudgel-play" between two opponents was popular at country fairs; the winner was the first to draw blood from his adversary's head. Joseph himself is later described as an expert cudgel-player (I.12).

[3] Grose defines a "merry Andrews" as a "jester" or "zany . . . dressed in a party-coloured coat."

* *Fielding's note*: In English, sprung from a Dunghil.

Writing and Reading) he was bound an Apprentice, according to the Statute, to Sir Thomas Booby, an Uncle of Mr. Booby's by the Father's side. Sir Thomas having then an Estate in his own Hands, the young Andrews was at first employed in what in the Country they call *keeping Birds*.[4] His Office was to perform the Part the Antients assigned to the God Priapus, which Deity the Moderns call by the Name of Jack-o'-Lent: but his Voice being so extremely musical, that it rather allured the Birds than terrified them, he was soon transplanted from the Fields into the Dog-kennel, where he was placed under the Huntsman, and made what Sportsmen term a *Whipper-in*.[5] For this Place likewise the Sweetness of his Voice disqualified him; the Dogs preferring the Melody of his chiding to all the alluring Notes of the Huntsman, who soon became so incensed at it, that he desired Sir Thomas to provide otherwise for him; and constantly laid every Fault the Dogs were at, to the Account of the poor Boy, who was now transplanted to the Stable. Here he soon gave Proofs of Strength and Agility, beyond his Years, and constantly rode the most spirited and vicious Horses to water with an Intrepidity which surprized every one. While he was in this Station, he rode several Races for Sir Thomas, and this with such Expertness and Success, that the neighbouring Gentlemen frequently solicited the Knight, to permit little Joey (for so he was called) to ride their Matches. The best Gamesters, before they laid their Money, always enquired which Horse little Joey was to ride; and the Betts were rather proportioned by the Rider than by the Horse himself; especially after he had scornfully refused a considerable Bribe to play booty[6] on such an Occasion. This extremely raised his Character, and so pleased the Lady Booby, that she desired to have him (being now seventeen Years of Age) for her own Foot-boy.

Joey was now preferred from the Stable to attend on his Lady, to go on her Errands, stand behind her Chair, wait at her Tea-table, and carry her Prayer-Book to Church; at which Place, his Voice gave him an Opportunity of distinguishing himself by singing

---

[4] That is, keeping them away from crops. In ancient Rome, statues of the fertility god Priapus were used as scarecrows in gardens and orchards. "Jack-o'-Lent" is "a figure of a man, set up to be pelted in a game played during Lent" (*OED*); here, however, the term apparently refers to a scare-crow.

[5] "A huntsman's assistant who keeps the hounds from straying by driving them back with the whip into the main body of the pack" (*OED*).

[6] "Cheating play, where the player purposely avoids winning" (Grose).

Psalms: he behaved likewise in every other respect so well at divine Service, that it recommended him to the Notice of Mr. Abraham Adams the Curate,[7] who took an Opportunity one Day, as he was drinking a Cup of Ale in Sir Thomas's Kitchin, to ask the young Man several Questions concerning Religion; with his Answers to which he was wonderfully pleased.

CHAP. III.

Of Mr. Abraham Adams *the Curate, Mrs.* Slipslop *the Chambermaid, and others.*

MR. Abraham Adams was an excellent Scholar. He was a perfect Master of the Greek and Latin Languages; to which he added a great Share of Knowledge in the Oriental Tongues,[1] and could read and translate French, Italian and Spanish. He had applied many Years to the most severe Study, and had treasured up a Fund of Learning rarely to be met with in a University. He was besides a Man of good Sense, good Parts, and good Nature;[2] but was at the same time as entirely ignorant of the Ways of this World, as an Infant just entered into it could possibly be. As he had never any Intention to deceive, so he never suspected such a Design in others. He was generous, friendly and brave to an Excess; but Simplicity was his Characteristic: he did, no more than Mr. Colley Cibber, apprehend any such Passions as Malice and Envy to exist in Mankind,[3] which was indeed less remarkable in a Country Parson than in a Gentleman who hath past his Life behind the Scenes, a Place which hath been seldom thought the School of Innocence; and where a very little Observation would

---

[7] A *curate* refers in this period to "a clergyman hired to perform the duties of another" (Johnson). Thus Adams is employed at a cut rate by "the Parson of the Parish" (Chap. 3), an absentee *rector* who is entitled to the "tithes" of the parish (a tax of roughly ten percent on the parish's produce) even though he has nothing to do with its spiritual care (including Sunday services, sacraments, marriages, and the running of a small elementary school), which is entirely in Adams's hands. A rector is appointed to his living or "benefice" by a patron, here being Sir Thomas Booby as lay proprietor.

[1] That is, western Asian languages, chiefly Hebrew and Arabic.

[2] Johnson defines "parts" as "qualities, powers, faculties, or accomplishments." For Fielding's expansive definitions of "good nature," see below, "Contexts" pp. 349–50.

[3] "My Ignorance, and want of Jealousy [suspicion] of Mankind has been so strong, that it with Reluctance I even yet believe any Person . . . can be capable of Envy, Malice, or Ingratitude . . ." (Cibber's *Apology* 9).

have convinced the great Apologist, that those Passions have a real Existence in the human Mind.

His Virtue and his other Qualifications, as they rendered him equal to his Office; so they made him an agreeable and valuable Companion, and had so much endeared and well recommended him to a Bishop; that at the Age of Fifty, he was provided with a handsome Income of twenty-three Pounds a Year; which however, he could not make any great Figure with: because he lived in a dear Country, and was a little incumbered with a Wife and six Children.[4]

It was this Gentleman, who having, as I have said, observed the singular Devotion of young Andrews, had found means to question him concerning several Particulars; as how many Books there were in the New Testament? which were they? how many Chapters they contained? and such like; to all which Mr. Adams said he answer'd much better than Sir Thomas, or two other neighbouring Justices of the Peace could probably have done.[5]

Mr. Adams was wonderfully sollicitous to know at what Time, and by what Opportunity the Youth became acquainted with these Matters: Joey told him, that he had very early learnt to read and write by the Goodness of his Father, who, though he had not Interest enough to get him into a Charity School,[6] because a Cousin of his Father's Landlord did not vote on the right side for a Church-warden in a Borough-Town, yet had been himself at the Expence of Sixpence a Week for his Learning. He told him likewise, that ever since he was in Sir Thomas's Family, he had employed all his Hours of Leisure in reading good Books; that he had read the Bible, the *Whole Duty of Man,* and Thomas à Kempis; and that as often as he could, without being perceived, he had studied a great good Book which lay open in the Hall Window, where he had read, *as how the Devil carried away half a Church in Sermon-time, without hurting one of the Congregation;* and *as how a Field of Corn ran away down a Hill with all the Trees upon it, and covered another Man's*

[4] "A handsome income" is ironic: see Introduction, "Note on Money," p. xix. A "dear Country" means a parish or county with a high cost of living. Booby Hall is, we later discover (IV.5), in Somersetshire, a southwestern English county in and around which Fielding spent his boyhood.

[5] In the fourth edition Fielding changed "Mr. Adams said" to "Mr. Adams privately said," making Adams cautious not to insult his superiors in public.

[6] Charity schools, organized by the Society for the Promotion of Christian Knowledge, taught reading, writing, and arithmetic, with a strong emphasis on religious and moral instruction.

Meadow. This sufficiently assured Mr. Adams, that the good Book meant could be no other than *Baker's Chronicle*.[7]

The Curate, surprized to find such Instances of Industry and Application in a young Man, who had never met with the least Encouragement, asked him, if he did not extremely regret the want of a liberal Education, and the not having been born of Parents, who might have indulged his Talents and Desire of Knowledge? To which he answered, 'He hoped he had profited somewhat better from the Books he had read, than to lament his Condition in this World. That for his part, he was perfectly content with the State to which he was called, that he should endeavour to improve his Talent, which was all required of him, but not repine at his own Lot, nor envy those of his Betters.' 'Well said, my Lad,' reply'd the Curate, 'and I wish some who have read many more good Books, nay, and some who have written good Books themselves, had profited so much by them.'

Adams had no nearer Access to Sir Thomas, or my Lady, than through the Waiting-Gentlewoman: For Sir Thomas was too apt to estimate Men merely by their Dress, or Fortune; and my Lady was a Woman of Gaiety, who had been bless'd with a Town-Education, and never spoke of any of her Country Neighbours by any other Appellation than that of *The Brutes*. They both regarded the Curate as a kind of Domestic only, belonging to the Parson of the Parish, who was at this time at variance with the Knight; for the Parson had for many Years lived in a constant State of Civil War, or, which is perhaps as bad, of Civil Law, with Sir Thomas himself and the Tenants of the Manor. The Foundation of this Quarrel was a Modus,[8] by setting which aside, an advantage of several shillings *per Annum* would have accrued to the Rector: but he had not yet been able to accomplish his Purpose; and had reaped hitherto nothing better from the Suits than the Pleasure (which he used indeed frequently to say was no small one) of reflecting that he had utterly undone many of the poor Tenants, tho' he had at the same time greatly impoverish'd himself.

---

[7] *The Whole Duty of Man* (1658), probably by Richard Allestree (1619–81), a popular devotional work; Thomas à Kempis (c. 1380–1471), *De Imitatio Christi*, translated as *The Imitation of Christ*; Richard Baker, *Chronicles of the Kings of England* (1643), some of the more sensational passages of which are here recalled by Joseph.

[8] "Something paid as a compensation for tithes on the supposition of being a moderate equivalent" (Johnson). It seems here that the modus or sum of money regularly paid to the rector in lieu of his tithes is now somewhat less than his tithes would be, and so he works to have his tithes restored.

Mrs. Slipslop the Waiting-Gentlewoman, being herself the Daughter of a Curate, preserved some Respect for Adams; she professed great Regard for his Learning, and would frequently dispute with him on Points of Theology; but always insisted on a Deference to be paid to her Understanding, as she had been frequently at London, and knew more of the World than a Country Parson could pretend to.

She had in these Disputes a particular Advantage over Adams: for she was a mighty Affecter of hard Words, which she used in such a manner, that the Parson, who durst not offend her by calling her Words in question, was frequently at some Loss to guess her Meaning, and would have been much less puzzled by an Arabian Manuscript.[9]

Adams therefore took an Opportunity one Day, after a pretty long discourse with her on the Essence, (or, as she pleased to term it, the *Incense*) of Matter, to mention the Case of young Andrews; desiring her to recommend him to her Lady as a Youth very susceptible of Learning, and one whose Instruction in Latin he would himself undertake; by which means he might be qualified for a higher Station than that of a Footman: and added, she knew it was in his Master's power easily to provide for him in a better manner. He therefore desired, that the Boy might be left behind under his Care.

'La Mr. Adams,' said Mrs. Slipslop, 'do you think my Lady will suffer any *Preambles* about any such Matter? She he is going to London very *concisely*, and I am *confidous* would not leave Joey behind her on any account; for he is one of the genteelest young Fellows you may see in a Summer's Day, and I am *confidous* she would as soon think of parting with a Pair of her Grey-Mares; for she values herself as much on one as the other.' Adams would have interrupted, but she proceeded: 'And why is Latin more *necessitous* for a Footman than a Gentleman? It is very proper that you Clargymen must learn it, because you can't preach without it: but I have heard Gentlemen say in London, that it is fit for no body else. I am *confidous* my Lady would be angry with me for mentioning it; and I shall draw myself into no such *Delemy*.' At which words her Lady's Bell rung, and Mr. Adams was forced to retire; nor could he gain a second Opportunity with her before their London Journey, which happened a few Days afterwards. However, Andrews behaved very thankfully and gratefully to him for his intended Kindness, which he told him he never

---

[9] Mrs. Slipslop anticipates Mrs. Malaprop in Richard Brinsley Sheridan's play *The Rivals* (1775); the latter's solecisms gave the word "malapropism" to the language.

would forget, and at the same time received from the good Man many Admonitions concerning the Regulation of his future Conduct, and his Perseverance in Innocence and Industry.

CHAP. IV.

What happened after their Journey to London.

No sooner was young Andrews arrived at London, than he began to scrape an Acquaintance with his party-colour'd Brethren,[1] who endeavour'd to make him despise his former Course of Life. His Hair was cut after the newest Fashion, and became his chief Care: He went abroad with it all the Morning in Papers, and drest it out in the Afternoon. They could not however teach him to game, swear, drink, nor any other genteel Vice the Town abounded with. He applied most of his leisure Hours to Music, in which he greatly improved himself; and became so perfect a Connoisseur in that Art, that he led the Opinion of all the other Footmen at an Opera, and they never condemned or applauded a single Song contrary to his Approbation, or Dislike. He was a little too forward in Riots[2] at the Play-Houses and Assemblies; and when he attended his Lady at Church (which was but seldom) he behaved with less seeming Devotion than formerly: however, if he was outwardly a pretty Fellow, his Morals remained entirely uncorrupted, tho' he was at the same time smarter and genteeler, than any of the Beaus in Town, either in or out of Livery.

His Lady, who had often said of him that Joey was the handsomest and genteelest Footman in the Kingdom, but that it was pity he wanted Spirit, began now to find that Fault no longer; on the contrary, she was frequently heard to cry out, *Aye, there is some Life in this Fellow.* She plainly saw the Effects which Town-Air hath on the soberest Constitutions. She would now walk out with him into Hyde-Park in a Morning, and when tired, which happened almost every Minute, would lean on his Arm, and converse with him in great Familiarity. Whenever she stept out of her Coach, she would take him by the Hand, and sometimes, for fear of stumbling, press it very hard; she admitted him to deliver Messages at her Bed-side

---

[1] Footmen wore outfits or "liveries" that combined various colors ("party-colored").

[2] "Wild and loose festivity" (Johnson).

in a Morning, leer'd at him at Table, and indulged him in all those innocent Freedoms which Women of Figure may permit without the least Sully of their Virtue.

But tho' their Virtue remains unsullied; yet now and then some small Arrows will glance at the Shadow of it, their Reputation; and so it fell out to Lady Booby, who happened to be walking Arm-in-Arm with Joey one Morning in Hyde-Park, when Lady Tittle and Lady Tattle came accidentally by in their Coach, *Bless me,* says Lady Tittle, *can I believe my Eyes? Is that Lady Booby? Surely,* says Tattle. *But what makes you surprized? Why, is not that her Footman,* reply'd Tittle? At which Tattle laughed and cryed, *An old Business, I assure you, is it possible you should not have heard it? The whole Town hath known it this half Year.* The Consequence of this Interview was a Whisper through a hundred Visits, which were separately performed by the two Ladies* the same Afternoon, and might have had a mischievous Effect, had it not been stopt by two fresh Reputations which were published[3] the Day afterwards, and engrossed the whole Talk of the Town.

But whatever Opinion or Suspicion the scandalous Inclination of Defamers might entertain of Lady Booby's innocent Freedoms, it is certain they made no Impression on young Andrews, who never offered to encroach beyond the Liberties which his Lady allowed him. A Behaviour which she imputed to the violent Respect he preserved for her, and which served only to heighten a something she began to conceive, and which the next Chapter will open a little farther.

CHAP. V.

The Death of Sir Thomas Booby, *with the affectionate and mournful Behaviour of his Widow, and the great Purity of* Joseph Andrews.

At this Time, an Accident happened which put a stop to these agreeable Walks, which probably would have soon puffed up the Cheeks of Fame,[1] and caused her to blow her brazen Trumpet through the Town; and this was no other than the Death of Sir Thomas Booby,

---

* *Fielding's note:* It may seem an Absurdity that Tattle should visit, as she actually did, to spread a known Scandal: but the Reader may reconcile this, by supposing with me, that, notwithstanding what she says, this was her first Acquaintance with it.

[3] "To make generally and openly known" (Johnson); here, to gossip about.

[1] "Report, rumour" (Johnson), here personified.

who, departing this Life, left his disconsolate Lady confined to her House, as closely as if she herself had been attacked by some violent Disease. During the first six Days the poor Lady admitted none but Mrs. Slipslop, and three Female Friends, who made a Party at Cards: but on the seventh she ordered Joey, whom for a good Reason we shall hereafter call JOSEPH,[2] to bring up her Tea-kettle. The Lady being in Bed, called Joseph to her, bade him sit down, and having accidentally laid her Hand on his, she asked him, *if he had never been in Love?* Joseph answered, with some Confusion, 'it was time enough for one so young as himself to think on such things.' 'As young as you are,' reply'd the Lady, 'I am convinced you are no Stranger to that Passion; Come Joey,' says she, 'tell me truly, who is the happy Girl whose Eyes have made a Conquest of you?' Joseph returned, that all Women he had ever seen, were equally indifferent to him. 'O then,' said the Lady, 'you are a general Lover. Indeed you handsome Fellows, like handsome Women, are very long and difficult in fixing: but yet you shall never persuade me that your Heart is so insusceptible of Affection; I rather impute what you say to your Secrecy, a very commendable Quality, and what I am far from being angry with you for. Nothing can be more unworthy in a young Man than to betray any Intimacies with the Ladies.' *Ladies! Madam,* said Joseph, *I am sure I never had the Impudence to think of any that deserve that Name.* 'Don't pretend to too much Modesty,' said she; 'for that sometimes may be impertinent: but pray, answer me this Question. Suppose a Lady should happen to like you; suppose she should prefer you to all your Sex, and admit you to the same Familiarities as you might have hoped for, if you had been born her Equal, are you certain that no Vanity could tempt you to discover her? Answer me honestly, Joseph; Have you so much more Sense and so much more Virtue than you handsome young Fellows generally have, who make no scruple of sacrificing our dear Reputation to your Pride, without considering the great Obligation we lay on you, by our Condescension and Confidence? Can you keep a Secret, my Joey?' 'Madam,' says he, 'I hope your Ladyship can't tax me with ever betraying the Secrets of the Family; and I hope, if you was to turn me away, I might have that Character of you.' 'I don't intend to turn you away, Joey,' said she, and sighed, 'I am afraid it is not in my Power.' She then raised herself a little in her Bed, and discovered one

---

[2] According to Grose's dictionary of slang, a "Joseph" is "a sheepish, bashful young fellow: an allusion to Joseph who fled from Potiphar's wife" (see Genesis 39:7–20).

of the whitest Necks that ever was seen;[3] at which Joseph blushed, 'La!' says she, in an affected Surprize, 'what am I doing? I have trusted myself with a Man alone, naked in Bed; suppose you should have any wicked Intentions upon my Honour, how should I defend myself?' Joseph protested that he never had the least evil Design against her. 'No,' says she, 'perhaps you may not call your Designs wicked; and perhaps they are not so.'—He swore they were not. 'You misunderstand me,' says she; 'I mean if they were against my Honour, they may not be wicked; but the World calls them so. But then, say you, the World will never know any thing of the Matter; yet would not that be trusting to your Secrecy? Must not my Reputation be then in your power? Would you not then be my Master?' Joseph begged her Ladyship to be comforted; for that he would never imagine the least wicked thing against her, and that he had rather die a thousand Deaths than give her any reason to suspect him. 'Yes,' said she, 'I must have Reason to suspect you. Are you not a Man? and without Vanity I may pretend to some Charms. But perhaps you may fear I should prosecute you; indeed I hope you do; and yet Heaven knows I should never have the Confidence to appear before a Court of Justice; and you know, Joey, I am of a forgiving Temper. Tell me Joey, don't you think I should forgive you?' 'Indeed, Madam,' says Joseph, 'I will never do any thing to disoblige your Ladyship.' 'How,' says she, 'do you think it would not disoblige me then? Do you think I would willingly suffer you?' 'I don't understand you, Madam,' says Joseph. 'Don't you?' said she, 'then you are either a Fool, or pretend to be so; I find I was mistaken in you. So get you down Stairs, and never let me see your Face again: your pretended Innocence cannot impose on me.' 'Madam,' said Joseph, 'I would not have your Ladyship think any Evil of me. I have always endeavoured to be a dutiful Servant both to you and my Master.' 'O thou Villain!' answered my Lady, 'Why did'st thou mention the Name of that dear Man, unless to torment me, to bring his precious Memory to my Mind,' (and then she burst into a Fit of Tears.) 'Get thee from my Sight, I shall never endure thee more.' At which Words she turned away from him; and Joseph retreated from the Room in a most disconsolate Condition, and writ that Letter which the Reader will find in the next Chapter.

---

[3] "Neck" here includes cleavage, as it often does in eighteenth-century usage. In Hullett's 1743 illustration of the subsequent seduction scene in I.8, Lady Booby's bosom is almost entirely bare.

CHAP. VI.

How Joseph Andrews *writ a Letter to his Sister* Pamela.

To Mrs. Pamela Andrews, living with Squire Booby.

'Dear Sister,
Since I received your Letter of your good Lady's Death, we have had a Misfortune of the same kind in our Family. My worthy Master Sir Thomas died about four Days ago; and what is worse, my poor Lady is certainly gone distracted. None of the Servants expected her to take it so to heart, because they quarrelled almost every day of their Lives: but no more of that, because, you know, Pamela, I never loved to tell the Secrets of my Master's Family; but to be sure you must have known they never loved one another; and I have heard her Ladyship wish his Honour dead above a thousand times: but no body knows what it is to lose a Friend 'till they have lost him.

Don't tell any body what I write, because I should not care to have Folks say I discover what passes in our Family: but if it had not been so great a Lady, I should have thought she had had a mind to me. Dear Pamela, don't tell any body: but she ordered me to sit down by her Bed-side, when she was in naked Bed; and she held my Hand, and talked exactly as a Lady does to her Sweetheart in a Stage-Play, which I have seen in Covent-Garden, while she wanted him to be no better than he should be.[1]

If Madam be mad, I shall not care for staying long in the Family; so I heartily wish you could get me a Place either at the Squire's, or some other neighbouring Gentleman's, unless it be true that you are going to be married to Parson Williams, as Folks talk,[2] and then I should be very willing to be his Clerk: for which you know I am qualified, being able to read, and to set a Psalm.[3]

I fancy, I shall be discharged very soon; and the Moment I am, unless I hear from you, I shall return to my old Master's Country Seat, if it be only to see Parson Adams, who is the best Man in the World. London is a bad Place, and there is so little good

---

[1] A euphemism, usually applied to a sexually promiscuous woman ("no better than she should be"), which dates back to Motteux's 1700–1703 translation of *Don Quixote* and Fielding's 1730 play, *The Temple Beau* (IV.iii); it remains a common locution in the UK but not the US.

[2] In Richardson's novel Mr. B—, to cloak his designs on Pamela, deceives her parents into thinking she is to marry his chaplain Parson Williams.

[3] To sing a line or two of a psalm in order that the congregation might respond or join in.

Fellowship, that next-door Neighbours don't know one another.
Pray give my Service to all Friends that enquire for me; so I rest

Your Loving Brother,
Joseph Andrews.

As soon as Joseph had sealed and directed this Letter, he walked down
Stairs, where he met Mrs. Slipslop, with whom we shall take this
Opportunity to bring the Reader a little better acquainted. She was a
Maiden Gentlewoman of about Forty-five Years of Age, who having
made a small Slip in her Youth had continued a good Maid ever since.
She was not at this time remarkably handsome; being very short, and
rather too corpulent in Body, and somewhat red, with the Addition of
Pimples in the Face. Her Nose was likewise rather too large, and her
Eyes too little; nor did she resemble a Cow so much in her Breath, as
in two brown Globes which she carried before her; one of her Legs
was also a little shorter than the other, which occasioned her to limp
as she walked. This fair Creature had long cast the Eyes of Affection
on Joseph, in which she had not met with quite so good Success as she
probably wished, tho' besides the Allurements of her native Charms,
she had given him Tea, Sweetmeats, Wine, and many other Delicacies,
of which, by keeping the Keys, she had the absolute Command.
Joseph however, had not returned the least Gratitude to all these
Favours, not even so much as a Kiss; tho' I would not insinuate she
was so easily to be satisfied: for surely then he would have been highly
blameable. The truth is, she was arrived at an Age when she thought
she might indulge herself in any Liberties with a Man, without the
Danger of bringing a third Person into the World to betray them. She
imagined, that by so long a Self-denial, she had not only made amends
for the small Slip of her Youth above hinted at: but had likewise laid
up a Quantity of Merit to excuse any future Failings. In a word, she
resolved to give a loose to her amorous Inclinations, and pay off the
Debt of Pleasure which she found she owed herself, as fast as possible.

With these Charms of Person, and in this Disposition of Mind,
she encountered poor Joseph at the Bottom of the Stairs, and asked
him if he would drink a Glass of something good this Morning.
Joseph, whose Spirits were not a little cast down, very readily and
thankfully accepted the Offer; and together they went into a Closet,
where having delivered him a full Glass of Ratifia, and desired him
to sit down, Mrs. Slipslop thus began:

'Sure nothing can be a more simple *Contract* in a Woman, than
to place her Affections on a Boy. If I had ever thought it would have

been my Fate, I should have wished to die a thousand Deaths rather than live to see that Day. If we like a Man, the lightest Hint *sophisticates*. Whereas a Boy *proposes* upon us to break through all the *Regulations* of Modesty, before we can make any *Oppression* upon him.' Joseph, who did not understand a Word she said, answered, 'yes Madam;—' 'Yes Madam!' reply'd Mrs. Slipslop with some Warmth, 'Do you intend to *result* my Passion? Is it not enough, ungrateful as you are, to make no Return to all the Favours I have done you: but you must treat me with *Ironing?* Barbarous Monster! how have I deserved that my Passion should be *resulted* and treated with *Ironing?*' 'Madam,' answered Joseph, 'I don't understand your hard Words: but I am certain, you have no Occasion to call me ungrateful: for so far from intending you any Wrong, I have always loved you as well as if you had been my own Mother.' 'How, Sirrah!' says Mrs. Slipslop in a Rage: 'Your own Mother! Do you *assinuate* that I am old enough to be your Mother? I don't know what a Stripling may think: but I believe a Man would *refer* me to any Green-Sickness silly Girl *whatsomdever:* but I ought to despise you rather than be angry with you, for *referring* the Conversation of Girls to that of a Woman of Sense.' 'Madam,' says Joseph, 'I am sure I have always valued the Honour you did me by your Conversation; for I know you are a Woman of Learning.' 'Yes but, Joseph,' said she, a little softened by the Compliment to her Learning, 'If you had a Value for me, you certainly would have found some Method of shewing it me; for I am *convicted* you must see the Value I have for you. Yes, Joseph, my Eyes, whether I would or no, must have declared a Passion I cannot conquer.—Oh! Joseph!—'

As when a hungry Tygress, who long had traversed the Woods in fruitless Search, sees within the Reach of her Claws a Lamb, she prepares to leap on her Prey; or as a voracious Pike, of immense Size, surveys through the liquid Element a Roach or Gudgeon, which cannot escape her Jaws, opens them wide to swallow the little Fish; so did Mrs. Slipslop prepare to lay her violent amorous Hands on the poor Joseph, when luckily her Mistress's Bell rung, and delivered the intended Martyr from her Clutches. She was obliged to break off abruptly, and defer the Execution of her Purpose to some other Time. We shall therefore return to the Lady Booby, and give our Reader some Account of her Behaviour, after she was left by Joseph in a Temper of Mind not greatly different from that of the inflamed Slipslop.

CHAP. VII.

*Sayings of wise Men. A Dialogue between the Lady and her Maid;
and a Panegyric, or rather Satire on the Passion of Love, in the
sublime Style.*

IT is the Observation of some ancient Sage, whose Name I have forgot, that Passions operate differently on the human Mind, as Diseases on the Body, in proportion to the Strength or Weakness,
Soundness or Rottenness of the one and the other.

We hope therefore a judicious Reader will give himself some
Pains to observe, what we have so greatly laboured to describe, the
different Operations of this Passion of Love, in the gentle and culti-
vated Mind of the Lady Booby, from those which it effected in the
less polished and coarser Disposition of Mrs. Slipslop.

Another Philosopher, whose Name also at present escapes my
Memory, hath somewhere said, that Resolutions taken in the
Absence of the beloved Object are very apt to vanish in its Presence;
on both which wise Sayings the following Chapter may serve as a
Comment.

No sooner had Joseph left the Room in the Manner we have
before related, than the Lady, enraged at her Disappointment, began
to reflect with Severity on her Conduct. Her Love was now changed
to Disdain, which Pride assisted to torment her. She despised herself
for the Meanness of her Passion, and Joseph for its ill Success. However, she had now got the better of it in her own Opinion, and determined immediately to dismiss the Object. After much tossing and
turning in her Bed, and many Soliloquies, which, if we had no better
Matter for our Reader, we would give him; she at last rung the Bell
as above-mentioned, and was presently attended by Mrs. Slipslop,
who was not much better pleased with Joseph than the Lady herself.

Slipslop, said Lady Booby, *when did you see Joseph?* The poor
Woman was so surprized at the unexpected Sound of his Name, at
so critical a time, that she had the greatest Difficulty to conceal the
Confusion she was under, from her Mistress; whom she answered,
nevertheless, with pretty good Confidence, though not entirely void
of Fear of Suspicion, that she had not seen him that Morning. 'I am
afraid,' said Lady Booby, 'he is a wild young Fellow.' 'That he is,'
said Slipslop, 'and a wicked one too. To my knowledge he games,
drinks, swears and fights eternally: besides he is horribly *indicted*

to Wenching.' 'Ay!' said the Lady! 'I never heard that of him.'
'O Madam,' answered the other, 'he is so lewd a Rascal that if your
Ladyship keeps him much longer, you will not have one Virgin in
your House except myself. And yet I can't conceive what the
Wenches see in him, so be so foolishly fond as they are: in my Eyes
he is as ugly a Scarecrow as I ever *upheld.*' 'Nay,' said the Lady, 'the
Boy is well enough.'—'La Ma'am,' cries Slipslop, 'I think him the
ragmaticallest Fellow in the Family.' 'Sure, Slipslop,' says she, 'you
are mistaken: but which of the Women do you most suspect?'
'Madam,' says Slipslop, 'there is Betty the Chamber-Maid, I am
almost *convicted,* is with Child by him.' 'Ay!' says the Lady, 'then
pray pay her her Wages instantly. I will keep no such Sluts in my
Family. And as for Joseph, you may discard him too.' 'Would your
Ladyship have him paid off immediately?' cries Slipslop, 'for perhaps, when Betty is gone, he may mend; and really the Boy is a good
Servant, and a strong healthy *luscious* Boy enough.' 'This Morning,' answered the Lady with some Vehemence. 'I wish Madam,'
cries Slipslop, 'your Ladyship would be so good as to try him a little
longer.' 'I will not have my Commands disputed,' said the Lady,
'sure you are not fond of him yourself.' 'I Madam?' cries Slipslop,
reddening, if not blushing, 'I should be sorry to think your Ladyship had any reason to *respect* me of Fondness for a Fellow; and if it
be your Pleasure, I shall fulfill it with as much reluctance as possible.' 'As little, I suppose you mean,' said the Lady; 'and so about it
instantly.' Mrs. Slipslop went out, and the Lady had scarce taken
two turns, before she fell to knocking and ringing with great Violence. Slipslop, who did not travel post-haste, soon returned, and
was countermanded as to Joseph, but ordered to send Betty about
her Business without Delay. She went out a second time with much
greater alacrity than before; when the Lady began immediately to
accuse herself of Want of Resolution, and to apprehend the Return
of her Affection with its pernicious Consequences: she therefore
applied herself again to the Bell, and resummoned Mrs. Slipslop
into her Presence; who again returned, and was told by her Mistress, that she had consider'd better of the Matter, and was absolutely
resolved to turn away Joseph; which she ordered her to do immediately. Slipslop, who knew the Violence of her Lady's Temper, and
would not venture her Place for any Adonis or Hercules in the Universe, left her a third time; which she had no sooner done, than the
little God Cupid, fearing he had not yet done the Lady's Business,

took a fresh Arrow with the sharpest Point out of his Quiver, and shot it directly into her Heart: in other and plainer Language, the Lady's Passion got the better of her Reason. She called back Slip-slop once more, and told her, she had resolved to see the Boy, and examine him herself; therefore bid her send him up. This wavering in her Mistress's Temper probably put something into the Waiting-Gentlewoman's Head, not necessary to mention to the sagacious Reader.

Lady Booby was going to call her back again, but could not prevail with herself. The next Consideration therefore was, how she should behave to Joseph when he came in. She resolved to preserve all the Dignity of the Woman of Fashion to her Servant, and to indulge herself in this last View of Joseph (for that she was most certainly resolved it should be) at his own Expence, by first insulting, and then discarding him.

O Love, what monstrous Tricks dost thou play with thy Votaries of both Sexes! How dost thou deceive them, and make them deceive themselves! Their Follies are thy Delight. Their Sighs make thee laugh, and their Pangs are thy Merriment!

Not the Great Rich, who turns Men into Monkeys, Wheelbarrows, and whatever else best humours his Fancy, hath so strangely metamorphosed the human Shape;[1] nor the Great Cibber, who confounds all Number, Gender, and breaks through every Rule of Grammar at his Will, hath so distorted the English Language, as thou dost metamorphose and distort the human Senses.

Thou puttest out our Eyes, stoppest up our Ears, and takest away the power of our Nostrils; so that we can neither see the largest Object, hear the loudest Noise, nor smell the most poignant Perfume. Again, when thou pleasest, thou can'st make a Mole-hill appear as a Mountain; a Jew's-Harp sound like a Trumpet; and a Dazy smell like a Violet. Thou can'st make Cowardice brave, Avarice generous, Pride humble, and Cruelty tender-hearted. It short, thou turnest the Heart of Man inside out, as a Juggler doth a Petticoat, and bringest whatsoever pleaseth thee out from it. If there be any one who doubts all this, let him read the next Chapter.

---

[1] The theater manager John Rich (1682–1761) was earlier satirized by Pope for introducing farcical pantomimes and conjuring shows onto the London stage.

CHAP. VIII.

In which, after some very fine Writing, the History goes on, and relates the Interview between the Lady and Joseph; *where the latter hath set an Example, which we despair of seeing followed by his Sex, in this vicious Age.*

Now the Rake Hesperus had called for his Breeches, and having well rubbed his drowsy Eyes, prepared to dress himself for all Night; by whose Example his Brother Rakes on Earth likewise leave those Beds, in which they had slept away the Day. Now Thetis the good Housewife began to put on the Pot in order to regale the good Man Phoebus, after his daily Labours were over. In vulgar Language, it was in the Evening when Joseph attended his Lady's Orders.[1]

But as it becomes us to preserve the Character of this Lady, who is the Heroine of our Tale; and as we have naturally a wonderful Tenderness for that beautiful Part of the human Species, called the Fair Sex; before we discover too much of her Frailty to our Reader, it will be proper to give him a lively Idea of that vast Temptation, which overcame all the Efforts of a modest and virtuous Mind; and then we humbly hope his Good-nature will rather pity than condemn the Imperfection of human Virtue.

Nay, the Ladies themselves will, we hope, be induced, by considering the uncommon Variety of Charms, which united in this young Man's Person, to bridle their rampant Passion for Chastity, and be at least as mild as their violent Modesty and Virtue will permit them, in censuring the Conduct of a Woman, who, perhaps, was in her own Disposition as chaste as those pure and sanctified Virgins, who, after a Life innocently spent in the Gaieties of the Town, begin about Fifty to attend twice *per diem* at the polite Churches and Chapels, to return Thanks for the Grace which preserved them formerly amongst Beaus, from Temptations perhaps less powerful than what now attacked the Lady Booby.

Mr. Joseph Andrews was now in the one and twentieth Year of his Age. He was of the highest Degree of middle Stature. His Limbs

---

[1] In this extended mock-romance description of evening, Hesperus is the evening star and Thetis a divinity of the sea into which the sun-god Phoebus Apollo sets. Don Quixote employed rhetorically heightened nature-description (see Contexts, p. 330), but Fielding follows Scarron's *Comical Romance* I.1 in puncturing its pretensions: "Right Phoebus had already perform'd above half his Career. . . . To speak more like a Man, and in plainer terms; it was betwixt five and six of the Clock . . ." (1).

were put together with great Elegance and no less Strength. His Legs and Thighs were formed in the exactest Proportion. His Shoulders were broad and brawny; but yet his Arms hung so easily, that he had all the Symptoms of Strength without the least Clumsiness. His Hair was of a nut-brown Colour, and was displayed in wanton Ringlets down his Back. His Forehead was high, his Eyes dark, and as full of Sweetness as of Fire. His Nose a little inclined to the Roman. His Teeth white and even. His Lips full, red, and soft. His Beard was only rough on his Chin and upper Lip; but his Cheeks, in which his Blood glowed, were overspread with a thick Down. His Countenance had a Tenderness joined with a Sensibility inexpressible. Add to this the most perfect Neatness in his Dress, and an Air, which to those who have not seen many Noblemen, would give an Idea of Nobility.

Such was the Person who now appeared before the Lady. She viewed him some time in Silence, and twice or thrice before she spake, changed her Mind as to the manner in which she should begin. At length, she said to him, 'Joseph, I am sorry to hear such Complaints against you; I am told you behave so rudely to the Maids, that they cannot do their Business in quiet; I mean those who are not wicked enough to hearken to your Solicitations. As to others, they may perhaps not call you rude: for there are wicked Sluts who make one ashamed of one's own Sex; and are as ready to admit any nauseous Familiarity as Fellows to offer it; nay, there are such in my Family; but they shall not stay in it; that impudent Trollop, who is with Child by you, is discharged by this time.'

As a Person who is struck through the Heart with a Thunder-bolt, looks extremely surprised, nay, and perhaps, is so too—Thus the poor Joseph received the false Accusation of his Mistress; he blushed and looked confounded, which she misinterpreted to be Symptoms of his Guilt, and thus went on:

'Come hither, Joseph: another Mistress might discard you for these Offences; But I have a Compassion for your Youth, if I could be certain you would be no more guilty—Consider, Child, (laying her Hand carelessly upon his) you are a handsome young Fellow, and might do better; you might make your Fortune—.' 'Madam,' said Joseph, 'I do assure your Ladyship, I don't know whether any Maid in the House is Man or Woman—.' 'Oh fie! Joseph,' answer'd the Lady, 'don't commit another Crime in denying the Truth. I could pardon the first; but I hate a Lyar.' 'Madam,' cries Joseph, 'I hope your Ladyship will not be offended at my asserting my Innocence: and by all that is Sacred, I have never offered more than

Kissing.' 'Kissing!' said the Lady, with great Discomposure of Countenance, and more redness in her Cheeks, than Anger in her Eyes,
'do you call that no Crime? Kissing, Joseph, is but a Prologue to a
Play. Can I believe a young Fellow of your Age and Complexion will
be content with Kissing? No, Joseph, there is no Woman who grants
that but will grant more; and I am deceived greatly in you, if you
would not put her closely to it. What would you think, Joseph, if I
admitted you to kiss me?' Joseph reply'd, 'He would sooner die than
have any such Thought.' 'And yet, Joseph,' returned she, 'Ladies
have admitted their Footmen to such Familiarities; and Footmen,
I confess to you, much less deserving them; Fellows without half
your Charms: for such might almost excuse the Crime. Tell me,
therefore, Joseph, if I should admit you to such Freedom, what
would you think of me?—tell me freely.' 'Madam,' said Joseph, 'I
should think your Ladyship condescended a great deal below yourself.' 'Pugh!' said she, 'that I am to answer to myself: but would not
you insist on more? Would you be contented with a Kiss? Would not
your Inclinations be all on fire rather by such a Favour?' 'Madam,'
said Joseph, 'if they were, I hope I should be able to control them,
without suffering them to get the better of my Virtue.'—You have
heard, Reader, Poets talk of the *Statue of Surprize;* you have heard
likewise, or else you have heard very little, how Surprize made one
of the Sons of Croesus speak tho' he was dumb.[2] You have seen the
Faces, in the Eighteen-penny Gallery, when through the Trap-Door,
to soft or no Musick, Mr. Bridgewater, Mr. William Mills, or some
other of ghostly Appearance, hath ascended with a Face all pale
with Powder, and a Shirt all bloody with Ribbons;[3] but from none
of these, nor from Phidias, or Praxiteles, if they should return to
Life—no, not from the inimitable Pencil of my Friend Hogarth,
could you receive such an Idea of Surprize, as would have entered in
at your Eyes, had they beheld the Lady Booby, when those last
Words issued out from the Lips of Joseph.—'Your Virtue!' (said the
Lady recovering after a Silence of two Minutes). 'I shall never survive
it. Your Virtue! Intolerable Confidence! Have you the Assurance to

---

[2] The mute son of King Croesus was shocked into speech when seeing an enemy
solider approach his father (Herodotus 1.85). Tom Keymer has traced "the *Statue of
Surprize*" to Benjamin Martyn's *Timoleon: A Tragedy* (1730), V.iii, a play parodied
in Fielding's *The Tragedy of Tragedies* (*Notes & Queries* 45 [1998]: 460–61).

[3] Roger Bridgewater (d. 1754) frequently played the ghost in productions of *Hamlet;*
William Mills (d. 1750) played Banquo (and thus Banquo's ghost) in *Macbeth,* and
also the ghost of Tom Thumb's father in *The Tragedy of Tragedies.*

pretend, that when a Lady demeans herself to throw aside the Rules of Decency, in order to honour you with the highest Favour in her Power, your Virtue should resist her Inclination? That when she had conquer'd her own Virtue, she should find an Obstruction in yours?' 'Madam,' said Joseph, 'I can't see why her having no Virtue should be a Reason against my having any: Or why, because I am a Man, or because I am poor, my Virtue must be subservient to her Pleasures.' 'I am out of Patience,' cries the Lady: 'Did ever Mortal hear of a Man's Virtue! Did ever the greatest, or the gravest Men pretend to any of this Kind! Will Magistrates who punish Lewdness, or Parsons, who preach against it, make any scruple of committing it? And can a Boy, a Stripling, have the Confidence to talk of his Virtue?' 'Madam,' says Joseph, 'that Boy is the Brother of Pamela, and would be ashamed, that the Chastity of his Family, which is preserved in her, should be stained in him. If there are such Men as your Ladyship mentions, I am sorry for it; and I wish they had an Opportunity of reading over those Letters, which my Father hath sent me of my Sister Pamela's; nor do I doubt but such an Example would amend them.' 'You impudent Villain,' cries the Lady in a Rage, 'Do you insult me with the Follies of my Relation, who hath exposed himself all over the Country upon your Sister's account? a little Vixen, whom I have always wondered my late Lady John Booby ever kept in her House. Sirrah! get out of my sight, and pre-pare to set out this Night; for I will order you your Wages immedi-ately, and you shall be stripped and turned away.—' 'Madam,' says Joseph, 'I am sorry I have offended your Ladyship, I am sure I never intended it.' 'Yes, Sirrah,' cries she, 'you have had the Vanity to mis-construe the little innocent Freedom I took in order to try, whether what I had heard was true. O my Conscience, you have had the Assurance to imagine, I was fond of you myself.' Joseph answered, he had only spoke out of Tenderness for his Virtue; at which words she flew into a violent Passion, and, refusing to hear more, ordered him instantly to leave the Room.

He was no sooner gone, than she burst forth into the following Exclamation: 'Whither doth this violent Passion hurry us? What Meannesses do we submit to from its Impulse? Wisely we resist its first and least Approaches; for it is then only we can assure our-selves the Victory. No Woman could ever safely say, *so far only will I go*. Have I not exposed myself to the Refusal of my Footman? I cannot bear the Reflection.' Upon which she applied herself to the Bell, and rung it with infinite more Violence than was necessary; the faithful Slipslop attending near at hand: To say the truth, she had conceived a Suspicion at her last Interview with her Mistress; and had waited ever since in the Antichamber, having carefully applied her Ears to the Key-Hole during the whole time, that the preceeding Conversation passed between Joseph and the Lady.

CHAP. IX.

What passed between the Lady and Mrs. Slipslop, *in which we prophesy there are some Strokes which every one will not truly comprehend at the first Reading.*

'SLIPSLOP,' said the Lady, 'I find too much Reason to believe all thou hast told me of this wicked Joseph; I have determined to part with him instantly; so go you to the Steward, and bid him pay him his Wages.' Slipslop, who had preserved hitherto a Distance to her Lady, rather out of Necessity than Inclination, and who thought the Knowledge of this Secret had thrown down all Distinction between them, answered her Mistress very pertly, 'She wished she knew her own Mind; and that she was certain she would call her back again, before she was got half way down stairs.' The Lady replied, 'she had taken a Resolution, and was resolved to keep it.' 'I am sorry for it,' cries Slipslop; 'and if I had known you would have punished the poor Lad so severely, you should never have heard a *Particle* of the Matter. Here's a Fuss indeed, about nothing.' 'Nothing!' returned my Lady; 'Do you think I will countenance Lewdness in my House?' 'If you will turn away every Footman,' said Slipslop, 'that is a lover of the Sport, you must soon open the Coach-Door yourself, or get a Sett of *Mophrodites* to wait upon you; and I am sure I hated the Sight of them even singing in an Opera.'[1] 'Do as I bid you,' says my Lady, 'and don't shock my Ears with your beastly Language.' 'Marry-come-up,' cries Slipslop, 'People's Ears are sometimes the nicest Part about them.'

The Lady, who began to admire the new Style in which her Waiting-Gentlewoman delivered herself, and by the Conclusion of her Speech, suspected somewhat of the Truth, called her back, and desired to know what she meant by that extraordinary degree of Freedom in

---

[1] Slipslop uses her version of *hermaphrodites* to refer to the *castrati* who sang in the Italian-language operas then popular in London. The most famous castrato was Farinelli (1705–82), the subject of a 1994 film by Gérard Corbiau.

which she thought proper to indulge to her Tongue. 'Freedom!' says Slipslop, 'I don't know what you call Freedom, Madam; Servants have Tongues as well as their Mistresses.' 'Yes, and saucy ones too,' answered the Lady: 'but I assure you I shall bear no such Impertinence.' 'Impertinence! I don't know that I am impertinent,' says Slipslop. 'Yes indeed you are,' cries my Lady; 'and unless you mend your Manners, this House is no Place for you.' 'Manners!' cries Slipslop, 'I never was thought to want Manners *nor Modesty neither;* and for Places, there are more Places than one; and I know what I know.' 'What do you know, Mistress?' answered the Lady. 'I am not obliged to tell that to every Body,' says Slipslop, 'any more than I am obliged to keep it a Secret.' 'I desire you would provide yourself,' answered the Lady. 'With all my Heart,' replied the Waiting-Gentlewoman; and so departed in a Passion, and slapped the Door after her.

The Lady too plainly perceived that her Waiting-Gentlewoman knew more than she would willingly have had her acquainted with; and this she imputed to Joseph's having discovered to her what past at the first Interview. This therefore blew up her Rage against him, and confirmed her in a Resolution of parting with him.

But the dismissing Mrs. Slipslop was a Point not so easily to be resolved upon: she had the utmost Tenderness for her Reputation, as she knew on that depended many of the most valuable Blessings of Life; particularly Cards, making Court'sies in public Places, and above all, the Pleasure of demolishing the Reputations of others, in which innocent Amusement she had an extraordinary Delight. She therefore determined to submit to any Insult from a Servant, rather than run a Risque of losing the Title to so many great Privileges.

She therefore sent for her Steward, Mr. Peter Pounce; and ordered him to pay Joseph his Wages, to strip off his Livery, and turn him out of the House that Evening.

She then called Slipslop up, and after refreshing her Spirits with a small Cordial which she kept in her Closet, she began in the following manner:

'Slipslop, why will you, who know my passionate Temper, attempt to provoke me by your Answers? I am convinced you are an honest Servant, and should be very unwilling to part with you. I believe likewise you have found me an indulgent Mistress on many Occasions, and have as little Reason on your side to desire a Change. I can't help being surprized therefore, that you will take the surest Method to offend me. I mean repeating my Words, which you know I have always detested.'

The prudent Waiting-Gentlewoman had duly weighed the whole Matter, and found on mature Deliberation, that a good Place in Possession was better than one in Expectation. As she found her Mistress therefore inclined to relent, she thought proper also to put on some small Condescension; which was as readily accepted: and so the Affair was reconciled, all Offences forgiven, and a Present of a Gown and Petticoat made her as an Instance of her Lady's future Favour.

She offered once or twice to speak in favour of Joseph: but found her Lady's Heart so obdurate, that she prudently dropt all such Efforts. She considered there were more Footmen in the House, and some as stout Fellows, tho' not quite so handsome as Joseph: besides the Reader hath already seen her tender Advances had not met with the Encouragement she might have reasonably expected. She thought she had thrown away a great deal of Sack and Sweet-meats on an ungrateful Rascal; and being a little inclined to the Opinion of that female Sect, who hold one lusty young Fellow to be near as good as another lusty young Fellow, she at last gave up Joseph and his Cause, and with a Triumph over her Passion highly commendable, walked off with her Present, and with great Tranquility paid a visit to a Stone-Bottle, which is of sovereign Use to a Philosophical Temper.

She left not her Mistress so easy. The poor Lady could not reflect, without Agony, that her dear Reputation was in the power of her Servants. All her Comfort, as to Joseph, was, that she hoped he did not understand her Meaning; at least, she could say for herself, she had not plainly express'd any thing to him; and as to Mrs. Slipslop, she imagined she could bribe her to Secrecy.

But what hurt her most was, that in reality she had not so entirely conquered her Passion; the little God lay lurking in her Heart, tho' Anger and Disdain so hoodwinked her, that she could not see him. She was a thousand times on the very Brink of revoking the Sentence she had passed against the poor Youth. Love became his Advocate, and whispered many things in his Favour. Honour likewise endeavoured to vindicate his Crime, and Pity to mitigate his Punishment; on the other side, Pride and Revenge spoke as loudly against him; and thus the poor Lady was tortured with Perplexity, opposite Passions distracting and tearing her Mind different ways.

So have I seen, in the Hall of Westminster, where Serjeant Bramble hath been retained on the right Side, and Serjeant Puzzle on the left;[2] the Balance of Opinion (so equal were their Fees) alternately incline to either Scale. Now Bramble throws in an Argument; and Puzzle's Scale strikes the Beam; again, Bramble shares the like Fate, overpowered by the Weight of Puzzle. Here Bramble hits, there Puzzle strikes; here one has you, there t'other has you; 'till at last all becomes one Scene of Confusion in the tortured Minds of the Hearers; equal Wagers are laid on the Success, and neither Judge nor Jury can possibly make any thing of the Matter; all Things are so enveloped by the careful Serjeants in Doubt and Obscurity.

Or as it happens in the Conscience, where Honour and Honesty pull one way, and a Bribe and Necessity another.—If it was only our present Business to make Similies, we could produce many more to this Purpose: but a Similie (as well as a Word) to the Wise. We shall therefore see a little after our Hero, for whom the Reader is doubtless in some pain.

CHAP. X.

Joseph *writes another Letter: His Transactions with Mr.* Peter Pounce, *&c. with his Departure from Lady* Booby.

THE disconsolate Joseph would not have had an Understanding sufficient for the principal Subject of such a Book as this, if he had any longer misunderstood the Drift of his Mistress; and indeed that he did not discern it sooner, the Reader will be pleased to apply to an Unwillingness in him to discover what he must condemn in her as a Fault. Having therefore quitted her Presence, he retired into his own Garret, and entered himself into an Ejaculation on the numberless Calamities which attended Beauty, and the Misfortunes it was to be handsomer than one's Neighbours.

He then sat down and addressed himself to his Sister Pamela, in the following Words:

Dear Sister Pamela,
Hoping you are well, what News have I to tell you! O Pamela, my Mistress is fallen in love with me—That is, what great Folks call falling in love, she has a mind to ruin me; but I hope, I shall

---

[2] Serjeants were high-ranking lawyers (barristers) who argued cases at Westminster Hall, England's principal court of law until 1825. Fielding, as a law student, 1737–38, attended trials at Westminster.

have more Resolution and more Grace than to part with my Virtue to any Lady upon Earth.

Mr. Adams has often told me, that Chastity is as great a Virtue in a Man as in a Woman. He says he never knew any more than his Wife, and I shall endeavour to follow his Example. Indeed, it is owing entirely to his excellent Sermons and Advice, together with your Letters, that I have been able to resist a Temptation, which he says no Man complies with, but he repents in this World, or is damned for it in the next; and why should I trust to Repentance on my Death-bed, since I may die in my Sleep? What fine things are good Advice and good Examples![1] But I am glad she turned me out of the Chamber as she did: for I had once almost forgotten every word Parson Adams had ever said to me.

I don't doubt, dear Sister, but you will have Grace to preserve your Virtue against all Trials; and I beg you earnestly to pray, I may be enabled to preserve mine: for truly it is very severely attacked by more than one: but, I hope I shall copy your Example, and that of Joseph, my Name's-sake; and maintain my Virtue against all Temptations.

Joseph had not finished his Letter, when he was summoned down stairs by Mr. Peter Pounce, to receive his Wages: for, besides that out of eight Pounds a Year, he allowed his Father and Mother four, he had been obliged, in order to furnish himself with musical Instruments, to apply to the Generosity of the aforesaid Peter, who, on urgent Occasions, used to advance the Servants their Wages: not before they were due, but before they were payable; that is, perhaps, half a Year after they were due, and this at the moderate *Praemium* of fifty *per Cent.* or a little more; by which charitable Methods, together with lending Money to other People, and even to his own Master and Mistress, the honest Man had, from nothing, in a few Years amassed a small Sum of twenty thousand Pounds or thereabouts.

Joseph having received his little Remainder of Wages, and having stript off his Livery, was forced to borrow a Frock and Breeches of one of the Servants:[2] (for he was so beloved in the Family, that they would all have lent him any thing) and being told by Peter, that he must nor stay a Moment longer in the House than was necessary

---

[1] Joseph here echoes the moral sentiments found in Pamela's correspondence with her parents: for example, "O how amiable a Thing is doing good!" (letter 6); "What blessed Things are Trials and Temptations to us, when they be overcome!" (letter 17).

[2] In an apparent inconsistency, Joseph is described as still being dressed in his livery from I.14 through the end of Book III.

to pack up his Linnen, which he easily did in a very narrow Compass; he took a melancholy Leave of his Fellow-Servants, and set out at seven in the Evening.

He had proceeded the Length of two or three Streets, before he absolutely determined with himself, whether he should leave the Town this Night, or procuring a Lodging, wait till the Morning. At last, the Moon, shining very bright, helped him to come to a Resolution of beginning his Journey immediately, to which likewise he had some other Inducements; which the Reader, without being a Conjurer, cannot possibly guess, till we have given him those hints, which it may be now proper to open.

CHAP. XI.

Of several new Matters not expected.

IT is an Observation sometimes made, that to indicate our Idea of a simple Fellow, we say, *he is easily to be seen through:* Nor do I believe it a more improper Denotation of a simple Book. Instead of applying this to any particular Performance, we chuse rather to remark the contrary in this History, where the Scene opens itself by small degrees; and he is a sagacious Reader who can see two Chapters before him.

For this reason, we have not hitherto hinted a Matter which now seems necessary to be explained; since it may be wondered at, first, that Joseph made such extraordinary haste out of Town, which hath been already shewn; and secondly, which will be now shewn, that instead of proceeding to the Habitation of his Father and Mother, or to his beloved Sister Pamela, he chose rather to set out full speed to the Lady Booby's Country Seat, which he had left on his Journey to London.

Be it known then, that in the same Parish where this Seat stood, there lived a young Girl whom Joseph (tho' the best of Sons and Brothers) longed more impatiently to see than his Parents or his Sister. She was a poor Girl, who had been formerly bred up in Sir John's Family; whence, a little before the Journey to London, she had been discarded by Mrs. Slipslop on account of her extraordinary Beauty: for I never could find any other reason.[1]

---

[1] As Slipslop has power of dismissal, Fanny must have been in the household of Sir Thomas Booby; "Sir John" appears to be a mistake.

This young Creature (who now lived with a Farmer in the Parish) had been always beloved by Joseph, and returned his Affection. She was two Years only younger than our Hero. They had been acquainted from their Infancy, and had conceived a very early liking for each other, which had grown to such a degree of Affection, that Mr. Adams had with much ado prevented them from marrying; and persuaded them to wait, till a few Years Service and Thrift had a little improved their Experience, and enabled them to live comfortably together.

They followed this good Man's Advice; as indeed his Word was little less than a Law in his Parish: for as he had shewn his Parishioners by a uniform Behaviour of thirty-five Years duration, that he had their Good entirely at heart; so they consulted him on every Occasion, and very seldom acted contrary to his Opinion.

Nothing can be imagined more tender than was the parting between these two Lovers. A thousand Sighs heaved the Bosom of Joseph; a thousand Tears distilled from the lovely Eyes of Fanny, (for that was her Name) tho' her Modesty would only suffer her to admit his eager Kisses, her violent Love made her more than passive in his Embraces; and she often pulled him to her Breast with a soft Pressure, which, tho' perhaps it would not have squeezed an Insect to death, caused more Emotion in the Heart of Joseph, than the closest Cornish Hug could have done.[2]

The Reader may perhaps wonder, that so fond a Pair should during a Twelve-month's Absence never converse with one another; indeed there was but one Reason which did, or could have prevented them; and that was, that poor Fanny could neither write nor read, nor could she be prevailed upon to transmit the Delicacies of her tender and chaste Passion, by the Hands of an Amanuensis.

They contented themselves therefore with frequent Enquiries after each other's Health, with a mutual Confidence in each other's Fidelity, and the Prospect of their future Happiness.

Having explained these Matters to our Reader, and, as far as possible, satisfied all his Doubts, we return to honest Joseph, whom we left just set out on his Travels by the Light of the Moon.

Those who have read any Romance or Poetry antient or modern, must have been informed, that Love hath Wings; by which they are not to understand, as some young Ladies by Mistake have

---

[2] A stranglehold used by wrestlers from Cornwall.

done, that a Lover can fly; the Writers, by this ingenious Allegory, intending to insinuate no more, than that Lovers do not march like Horse-Guards;[3] in short, that they put the best Leg foremost, which our lusty Youth, who could walk with any Man, did so heartily on this Occasion, that within four Hours, he reached a famous House of Hospitality well known to the Western Traveller. It presents you a Lion on the Sign-Post: and the Master, who was christened Timotheus, is commonly called plain Tim.[4] Some have conceived that he hath particularly chosen the Lion for his Sign, as he doth in Countenance greatly resemble that magnanimous Beast, tho' his Disposition favours more of the Sweetness of the Lamb. He is a Person well received among all sorts of Men, being qualified to render himself agreeable to any; as he is well versed in History and Politics, hath a smattering in Law and Divinity, cracks a good Jest, and plays wonderfully well on the French Horn.

A violent Storm of Hail forced Joseph to take Shelter in this Inn, where he remembered Sir Thomas had dined in his way to Town. Joseph had no sooner seated himself by the Kitchin-Fire, than Timotheus, observing his Livery began to condole the loss of his late Master; who was, he said, his very particular and intimate Acquaintance, with whom he had cracked many a merry Bottle, aye many a dozen in his Time. He then remarked, that all those Things were over now, all past, and just as if they had never been; and concluded with an excellent Observation on the Certainty of Death, which his Wife said was indeed very true. A Fellow now arrived at the same Inn with two Horses, one of which he was leading farther down into the Country to meet his Master; these he put into the Stable, and came and took his Place by Joseph's Side, who immediately knew him to be the Servant of a neighbouring Gentleman, who used to visit at their House.

This Fellow was likewise forced in by the Storm; for he had Orders to go twenty Miles farther that Evening, and luckily on the same Road which Joseph himself intended to take. He therefore embraced this Opportunity of complimenting his Friend with his Master's Horses, (notwithstanding he had received express Commands to the contrary) which was readily accepted; and so after they had drank a loving Pot, and the Storm was over, they set out together.

[3] That is, in the slow, stately pace of troops guarding the royal palace.
[4] Timothy Harris, keeper of the Red Lion Inn at Egham, Surrey.

CHAP. XII.

Containing many surprizing Adventures, which Joseph Andrews *met with on the Road, scarce credible by those who have never travelled in a Stage-Coach.*

NOTHING remarkable happened on the Road, till their arrival at the Inn, whither the Horses were ordered; where they came about two in the Morning. The Moon then shone very bright; and Joseph making his Friend a present of a Pint of Wine, and thanking him for the favour of his Horse, notwithstanding all Entreaties to the contrary, proceeded on his Journey on foot.

He had not gone above two Miles, charmed with the Hopes of shortly seeing his beloved Fanny, when he was met by two Fellows in a narrow Lane, and ordered to stand and deliver.[1] He readily gave them all the Money he had, which was somewhat less than two Pounds; and told them he hoped they would be so generous as to return him a few Shillings, to defray his Charges on his way home.

One of the Ruffians answered with an Oath, *Yes, we'll give you something presently: but first strip and be d—n'd to you.—Strip,* cry'd the other, *or I'll blow your Brains to the Devil.* Joseph, remembring that he had borrowed his Coat and Breeches of a Friend; and that he should be ashamed of making any Excuse for not returning them, reply'd, he hoped they would not insist on his Clothes, which were not worth much, but consider the Coldness of the Night. *You are cold, are you, you Rascal!* says one of the Robbers, *I'll warm you with a Vengeance;* and, damning his Eyes, snapt a Pistol at his Head: which he had no sooner done, than the other levelled a Blow at him with his Stick, which Joseph, who was expert at Cudgel-playing, caught with his, and returned the Favour so successfully on his Adversary, that he laid him sprawling at his Feet, and at the same Instant received a Blow from behind, with the Buttend of a Pistol from the other Villain, which felled him to the Ground, and totally deprived him of his Senses.

The Thief, who had been knocked down, had now recovered himself; and both together fell to belabouring poor Joseph with their Sticks, till they were convinced they had put an end to his miserable Being: They then stript him entirely naked, threw him into a Ditch, and departed with their Booty.

---

[1] That is, "stop and give me your valuables," the highwayman's traditional command.

The poor Wretch, who lay motionless a long time, just began to recover his Senses as a Stage-Coach came by. The Postillion hearing a Man's Groans, stopt his Horses, and told the Coachman, He was certain there was a dead Man lying in the Ditch; for he heard him groan. 'Go on, Sirrah,' says the Coachman, 'we are confounded late, and have no time to look after dead Men.' A Lady, who heard what the Postillion said, and likewise heard the Groan, called eagerly to the Coachman, To stop and see what was the matter. Upon which he bid the Postillion alight, and look into the Ditch. He did so, and returned, 'That there was a Man sitting upright as naked as ever he was born.'—'O J—sus,' cry'd the Lady, 'A naked Man! Dear Coachman, drive on and leave him.' Upon this the Gentlemen got out of the Coach; and Joseph begged them to have Mercy upon him: For that he had been robbed, and almost beaten to Death. 'Robbed,' cries an old Gentleman; 'Let us make all the haste imaginable, or we shall be robbed too.' A young Man, who belonged to the Law answered, He wished they had past by without taking any Notice: But that now they might be proved to have been last in his Company; if he should die, they might be called to some account for his Murder. He therefore thought it adviseable to save the poor Creature's Life, for their own sakes, if possible; at least, if he died, to prevent the Jury's finding *that they fled for it.* He was therefore *of Opinion,* to take the Man into the Coach, and carry him to the next Inn. The Lady insisted, 'That he should not come into the Coach. That if they lifted him in, she would herself alight: for she had rather stay in that Place to all Eternity, than ride with a naked Man.' The Coachman objected, 'That he could not suffer him to be taken in, unless some body would pay a Shilling for his Carriage the four Miles.' Which the two Gentlemen refused to do. But the Lawyer, who was afraid of some Mischief happening to himself if the Wretch was left behind in that Condition, saying, No Man could be too cautious in these Matters, and that he remembered very extraordinary Cases in the Books, threatened the Coachman, and bid him deny taking him up at his Peril; for that if he died, he should be indicted for his Murder, and if he lived, and brought an Action against him, he would willingly take a Brief in it. These Words had a sensible Effect on the Coachman, who was well acquainted with the Person who spoke them; and the old Gentleman abovementioned, thinking the naked Man would afford him frequent Opportunities of shewing his Wit to the Lady, offered to join with the Company in giving a Mug of Beer for his Fare; till partly alarmed by the Threats of the one, and partly by the Promises of the other, and being perhaps a *little* moved with Compassion at the poor Creature's Condition, who stood bleeding and shivering with the Cold, he at length agreed; and Joseph was now advancing to the Coach, where seeing the Lady, who held the Sticks of her Fan before her Eyes, he absolutely refused, miserable as he was, to enter, unless he was furnished with sufficient Covering, to prevent giving the least Offence to Decency. So perfectly modest was this young Man; such mighty Effects had the spotless Example of the amiable Pamela, and the excellent Sermons of Mr. Adams wrought upon him.

Though there were several great Coats about the Coach, it was not easy to get over this Difficulty which Joseph had started. The two Gentlemen complained they were cold, and could not spare a Rag; the Man of Wit saying, with a Laugh, *that Charity began at home;* and the Coachman, who had two great Coats spread under him, refused to lend either, lest they should be made bloody; the Lady's Footman desired to be excused for the same Reason, which the Lady herself, notwithstanding her Abhorence of a naked Man, approved: and it is more than probable, poor Joseph, who obstinately adhered to his modest Resolution, must have perished, unless the Postillion, (a Lad who hath been since transported[2] for robbing a Hen-roost) had voluntarily stript off a great Coat, his only Garment, at the same time swearing a great Oath, (for which he was rebuked by the Passengers) 'That he would rather ride in his Shirt all his Life, than suffer a Fellow-Creature to lie in so miserable a Condition.'

Joseph, having put on the great Coat, was lifted into the Coach, which now proceeded on its Journey. He declared himself almost dead with the Cold, which gave the Man of Wit an occasion to ask the Lady, if she could not accommodate him with a Dram. She answered with some Resentment, 'She wondered at his asking her such a Question; but assured him, She never tasted any such thing.'

The Lawyer was enquiring into the Circumstances of the Robbery, when the Coach stopt, and one of the Ruffians, putting a Pistol in, demanded their Money of the Passengers; who readily gave it them; and the Lady, in her Fright, delivered up a little silver Bottle, of about a half-pint Size, which, the Rogue clapping it to his Mouth, and drinking her Health, declared held some of the best Nantes he had ever tasted: this the Lady afterwards assured the

---

[2] Banished, as a felon, to the American colonies.

Company was the Mistake of her Maid; for that she had ordered her to fill the Bottle with Hungary Water.[3]

As soon as the Fellows were departed, the Lawyer, who had, it seems, a Case of Pistols in the Seat of the Coach, informed the Company, that if it had been Day-light, and he could have come at his Pistols, he would not have submitted to the Robbery; he likewise set forth, that he had often met Highwaymen when he travelled on Horseback, but none ever durst attack him; concluding, that if he had not been more afraid for the Lady than for himself, he should not have now parted with his Money so easily.

As Wit is generally observed to love to reside in empty Pockets; so the Gentleman, whose Ingenuity we have above remark'd, as soon as he had parted with his Money, began to grow wonderfully facetious. He made frequent Allusions to Adam and Eve, and said many excellent things on Figs and Fig-Leaves; which perhaps gave more Offence to Joseph than to any other in the Company.

The Lawyer likewise made several very pretty Jests, without departing from his Profession. He said, 'If Joseph and the Lady were alone, he would be the more capable of making a *Conveyance* to her, as his *Affairs* were not *fettered* with any *Incumbrance*; he'd warrant, he soon suffered a *Recovery* by a Writ of *Entry*, which was the proper way to create *Heirs in Tail*; that for his own part, he would engage to make so *firm* a *Settlement* in a Coach, that there should be no Danger of an *Ejectment*;'[4] with an Inundation of the like Gibbrish, which he continued to vent till the Coach arrived at an Inn, where one Servant-Maid only was up in readiness to attend the Coachman, and furnish him with cold Meat and a Dram. Joseph desired to alight, and that he might have a Bed prepared for him, which the Maid readily promised to perform; and being a good-natur'd Wench, and not so squeamish as the Lady had been, she clapt a large Faggot on the Fire, and furnishing Joseph with a great Coat belonging to one of the Hostlers, desired him to sit down and warm himself, whilst she made his Bed. The Coachman, in the mean time, took an Opportunity to call up a Surgeon, who lived within a few Doors: after which, he reminded his Passengers how late they were, and after they had taken Leave of Joseph, hurried them off as fast as he could.

[3] "Hungary water" was a medicinal drink, while "Nantes" was a strong French brandy.

[4] Double-entendres drawn from the language of property law.

The Wench soon got Joseph to bed, and promised to use her Interest to borrow him a Shirt; but imagined, as she afterwards said, by his being so bloody, that he must be a dead Man: she ran with all speed to hasten the Surgeon, who was more than half drest, apprehending that the Coach had been overturned and some Gentleman or Lady hurt. As soon as the Wench had informed him at his Window, that it was a poor foot Passenger who had been stripped of all he had, and almost murdered; he chid her for disturbing him so early, slipped off his Clothes again, and very quietly returned to bed and to sleep.

Aurora now began to shew her blooming Cheeks over the Hills, whilst ten Millions of feathered Songsters, in jocund Chorus, repeated Odes a thousand times sweeter than those of our Laureate, and sung both *the Day and the Song;*[5] when the Master of the Inn, Mr. Tow-wouse, arose, and learning from his Maid an Account of the Robbery, and the Situation of his poor naked Guest, he shook his Head, and cried, *Good-lack-a-day!* and then ordered the Girl to carry him one of his own Shirts.

Mrs. Tow-wouse was just awake, and had stretched out her Arms in vain to fold her departed Husband, when the Maid entered the Room. 'Who's there, Betty?" 'Yes Madam.' 'Where's your Master?' 'He's without, Madam; he hath sent me for a Shirt to lend to a poor naked Man, who hath been robbed and murdered.' 'Touch one, if you dare, you Slut,' said Mrs. Tow-wouse, 'your Master is a pretty sort of a Man to take in naked Vagabonds, and clothe them with his own Clothes. I shall have no such Doings.—If you offer to touch any thing, I will throw the Chamber-Pot at your Head. Go, send your Master to me.' 'Yes Madam,' answered Betty. As soon as he came in, she thus began: 'What the Devil do you mean by this, Mr. Tow-wouse? Am I to buy Shirts to lend to a sett of scabby Rascals?' 'My Dear,' said Mr. Tow-wouse, 'this is a poor Wretch.' 'Yes,' says she, 'I know it is a poor Wretch; but what the Devil have we to do with poor Wretches? The Law makes us provide, for too many already. We shall have thirty or forty poor Wretches in red Coats shortly.'[6]

---

[5] Colley Cibber, poet laureate since 1730, wrote fulsome odes to the king on his birthday and on new year's day. Fielding here alludes to his own facetious "Ode to the New Year" in his play *The Historical Register for the Year 1736* (I.i): "This is a Day, in Days of Yore, / Our Fathers never saw before: / This is a Day, tis one to ten, / Our Sons will never see again. / Then sing the day, / And sing the song, / And thus be merry / All day long."

[6] At this time innkeepers were legally required to supply soldiers with food, drink, and lodging for four pence per solider per day.

'My Dear,' cries Tow-wouse, 'this Man hath been robbed of all he has.' 'Well then,' says she, 'where's his Money to pay his Reckoning? Why does not such a Fellow go to an Ale-house? I shall send him packing as soon as I am up, I assure you.' 'My Dear,' said he, 'common Charity won't suffer you to do that.' 'Common Charity, a F—t!' says she, 'Common Charity teaches us to provide for ourselves, and our Families; and I and mine won't be ruined by your Charity, I assure you.' 'Well,' says he, 'my Dear, do as you will when you are up; you know I never contradict you.' 'No,' says she, 'if the Devil was to contradict me, I would make the House too hot to hold him.'

With such like Discourses they consumed near half an Hour, whilst Betty provided a Shirt from the Hostler, who was one of her Sweethearts, and put it on poor Joseph. The Surgeon had likewise at last visited him, had washed and drest his Wounds, and was now come to acquaint Mr. Tow-wouse, that his Guest was in such extreme danger of his Life, that he scarce saw any hopes of his Recovery.— 'Here's a pretty Kettle of Fish,' cries Mrs. Tow-wouse, 'you have brought upon us! We are like to have a Funeral at our own Expence.' Tow-wouse, (who notwithstanding his Charity, would have given his Vote as freely as he ever did at an Election, that any other House in the Kingdom should have had quiet Possession of his Guest) answered, 'My Dear, I am not to blame: he was brought hither by the Stage-Coach; and Betty had put him to bed before I was stirring.' 'I'll Betty her,' says she—At which, with half her Garments on, the other half under her Arm, she sallied out in quest of the unfortunate Betty, whilst Tow-wouse and the Surgeon went to pay a Visit to poor Joseph, and enquire into the Circumstance of this melancholy Affair.

CHAP. XIII.

What happened to Joseph *during his Sickness at the Inn, with the curious Discourse between him and Mr.* Barnabas *the Parson of the Parish.*

As soon as Joseph had communicated a particular History of the Robbery, together with a short Account of himself and his intended Journey, he asked the Surgeon, If he apprehended him to be in any Danger: To which the Surgeon very honestly answered, 'He feared he was; for that his Pulse was very exalted and feverish, and if his Fever should prove more than Symptomatic, it would be impossible to save him.' Joseph, fetching a deep Sigh, cried, 'Poor Fanny, I would I could have lived to see thee! but G—'s Will be done.'

The Surgeon then advised him, If he had any worldly Affairs to settle, that he would do it as soon as possible; for though he hoped he might recover, yet he thought himself obliged to acquaint him he was in great Danger; and if the malign Concoction of his Humours should cause a Suscitation of his Fever, he might soon grow delirious, and incapable to make his Will. Joseph answered, 'That it was impossible for any Creature in the Universe to be in a poorer Condition than himself: for since the Robbery, he had not one thing of any kind whatever, which he could call his own.' *I had,* said he, *a poor little Piece of Gold which they-took away, that would be a Comfort to me in all my Afflictions; but surely, Fanny, I want nothing to remind me of thee. I have thy dear Image in my Heart, and no Villain can ever tear it thence.*

Joseph desired Paper and Pens to write a Letter, but they were refused him; and he was advised to use all his Endeavours to compose himself. They then left him; and Mr. Tow-wouse sent to a Clergyman to come and administer his good Offices to the Soul of poor Joseph, since the Surgeon despaired of making any successful Applications to his Body.

Mr. Barnabas (for that was the Clergyman's Name) came as soon as sent for; and having first drank a Dish of Tea with the Landlady, and afterwards a Bowl of Punch with the Landlord, he walked up to the Room where Joseph lay: but, finding him asleep, returned to take the other Sneaker;[1] which when he had finished, he again crept softly up to the Chamber-Door, and, having opened it, heard the Sick Man talking to himself in the following manner:

'O most adorable Pamela! most virtuous Sister! whose Example could alone enable me to withstand all the Temptations of Riches and Beauty, and to preserve my Virtue pure and chaste, for the Arms of my dear Fanny, if it had pleased Heaven that I should ever have come unto them. What Riches, or Honours, or Pleasures can make us amends for the Loss of Innocence? Doth not that alone afford us more Consolation, than all worldly Acquisitions? What but Innocence and Virtue could give any Comfort to such a miserable Wretch as I am? Yet these can make me prefer this sick and painful Bed to all the Pleasures I should have found in my Lady's. These can make me face Death without Fear; and though I love my Fanny more than ever Man loved a Woman, these can teach me to resign myself to the Divine Will without repining. O, thou delightful

---

[1] A small bowl, usually of (alcoholic) punch.

charming Creature! If Heaven had indulged thee to my Arms, the poorest, humblest State would have been a Paradise; I could have lived with thee in the lowest Cottage, without envying the Palaces, the Dainties, or the Riches of any Man breathing. But I must leave thee, leave thee for ever, my dearest Angel! I must think of another World, and I heartily pray thou may'st meet Comfort in this.'— Barnabas thought he had heard enough; so down Stairs he went, and told Tow-wouse he could do his Guest no Service: for that he was very light-headed, and had uttered nothing but a Rhapsody of Nonsense all the time he stayed in the Room.

The Surgeon returned in the Afternoon, and found his Patient in a higher Fever, as he said, than when he left him, though not delirious: for notwithstanding Mr. Barnabas's Opinion, he had not been once out of his Senses since his arrival at the Inn.

Mr. Barnabas was again sent for, and with much difficulty prevailed on to make another Visit. As soon as he entered the Room, he told Joseph, 'He was come to pray by him, and to prepare him for another World: In the first place therefore, he hoped he had repented of all his Sins.' Joseph answered, 'He hoped he had: but there was one thing which he knew not whether he should call a Sin; if it was, he feared he should die in the Commission of it; and that was the Regret of parting with a young Woman, whom he loved as tenderly as he did his Heartstrings.' Barnabas bad him be assured, that 'any Repining at the Divine Will was one of the greatest Sins he could commit; that he ought to forget all carnal Affections, and think of better things.' Joseph said, 'That neither in this World nor the next, he could forget his Fanny; and that the Thought, however grievous, of parting from her for ever, was not half so tormenting, as the Fear of what she would suffer when she knew his Misfortune.' Barnabas said, 'That such Fears argued a Diffidence and Despondence very criminal; that he must divest himself of all human Passions, and fix his Heart above.' Joseph answered, 'That was what he desired to do, and should be obliged to him, if he would enable him to accomplish it.' Barnabas replied, 'That must be done by Grace.' Joseph besought him to discover how he might attain it. Barnabas answered, 'By Prayer and Faith.' He then questioned him concerning his Forgiveness of the Thieves. Joseph answered, 'He feared that was more than he could do: for nothing would give him more Pleasure than to hear they were taken.' 'That,' cries Barnabas, 'is for the sake of Justice.' 'Yes,' said Joseph, 'but if I was to meet them again, I am afraid I should attack them, and kill them too, if I could.' 'Doubtless,' answered Barnabas, 'it is lawful to kill a Thief: but can you say, you forgive them as a Christian ought?' Joseph desired to know what that Forgiveness was. 'That is' answered Barnabas, 'to forgive them as—as—it is to forgive them as—in short, it is to forgive them as a Christian.' Joseph replied, 'He forgave them as much as he could.' 'Well, well,' said Barnabas, 'that will do.' He then demanded of him, if he remembered any more Sins unrepented of; and if he did, he desired him to make haste and repent of them as fast as he could: that they might repeat over a few Prayers together. Joseph answered, 'He could not recollect any great Crimes he had been guilty of, and that those he had committed he was sincerely sorry for.' Barnabas said that was enough, and then proceeded to Prayer with all the expedition he was master of; some Company then waiting for him below in the Parlour, where the Ingredients for Punch were all in Readiness; but no one would squeeze the Oranges 'till he came.

Joseph complained he was dry, and desired a little Tea; which Barnabas reported to Mrs. Tow-wouse, who answered, 'She had just done drinking it, and could not be slopping[2] all day;' but ordered Betty to carry him up some Small Beer.

Betty obeyed her Mistress's Commands; but Joseph, as soon as he had tasted it, said, he feared it would encrease his Fever, and that he longed very much for Tea: To which the good-natured Betty answered, he should have Tea, if there was any in the Land; she accordingly went and bought him some herself, and attended him with it; where we will leave her and Joseph together for some time, to entertain the Reader with other Matters.

CHAP. XIV.

Being very full of Adventures, which succeeded each other at the Inn.

IT was now the Dusk of the Evening, when a grave Person rode into the Inn, and committing his Horse to the Hostler, went directly into the Kitchin, and having called for a Pipe of Tobacco took his place by the Fire-side; where several other Persons were likewise assembled.

The Discourse ran altogether on the Robbery which was committed the Night before, and on the poor Wretch, who lay above in the dreadful Condition, in which we have already seen him.

---

[2] Probably from "to slop," "to spill or splash liquid" (*OED*).

Mrs. Tow-wouse said, 'She wondered what the devil Tom Whipwell meant by bringing such Guests to her House, when there were so many Ale-houses on the Road proper for their Reception.' But she assured him, if he died, the Parish should be at the Expence of the Funeral. She added, 'Nothing would serve the Fellow's Turn but Tea, she would assure him.' Betty, who was just returned from her charitable Office, answered, she believed he was a Gentleman, for she never saw a finer Skin in her Life. 'Pox on his Skin,' replied Mrs. Tow-wouse, 'I suppose, that is all we are like to have for the Reckoning. I desire no such Gentlemen should ever call at the Dragon,' (which it seems was the Sign of the Inn.)

The Gentleman lately arrived discovered a great deal of Emotion at the Distress of this poor Creature, whom he observed not to be fallen into the most compassionate Hands. And indeed, if Mrs. Tow-wouse had given no Utterance to the Sweetness of her Temper, Nature had taken such Pains in her Countenance, that Hogarth himself never gave more Expression to a Picture.

Her Person was short, thin, and crooked. Her Forehead projected in the middle, and thence descended in a Declivity to the Top of her Nose, which was sharp and red, and would have hung over her Lips, had not Nature turned up the end of it. Her Lips were two Bits of Skin, which, whenever she spoke, she drew together in a Purse. Her Chin was picked;[1] and at the upper end of that Skin, which composed her Cheeks, stood two Bones, that almost hid a Pair of small red Eyes. Add to this, a Voice most wonderfully adapted to the Sentiments it was to convey, being both loud and hoarse.

It is not easy to say; whether the Gentleman had conceived a greater Dislike for his Landlady, or Compassion for her unhappy Guest. He enquired very earnestly of the Surgeon, who was now come into the Kitchin, Whether he had any hopes of his Recovery? He begged him to use all possible means towards it, telling him, 'it was the duty of Men of all Professions, to apply their Skill *gratis* for the Relief of the Poor and Necessitous.' The Surgeon answered, 'he should take proper care: but he defied all the Surgeons in London to do him any good.' 'Pray, Sir,' said the Gentleman, 'What are his Wounds?'—'Why, do you know any thing of Wounds?' says the Surgeon (winking upon Mrs. Tow-wouse.) 'Sir, I have a small smattering

---

[1] Johnson defines "picked" as "sharp," in the sense of "pointed"; he illustrates the word with a quotation from a farming manual: "Let the stake be made picked at the top, that the jay may not settle on it."

in Surgery,' answered the Gentleman. 'A smattering,—ho, ho, ho!' said the Surgeon, 'I believe it is a smattering indeed.'

The Company were all attentive, expecting to hear the Doctor, who was what they call a dry Fellow, expose the Gentleman.

He began therefore with an Air of Triumph: 'I suppose, Sir, you have traveled.' 'Not really, Sir,' said the Gentleman. 'Ho! then you have practised in the Hospitals, perhaps.'—'No, Sir.' 'Hum! not that neither?' 'Whence, Sir, then, if I may be so bold to enquire, have you got your Knowledge in Surgery?' 'Sir,' answered the Gentleman, 'I do not pretend to much; but, the little I know I have from Books.' 'Books!' cries the Doctor.—'What, I suppose you have read Galen and Hippocrates!' 'No, Sir,' said the Gentleman. 'How! you understand Surgery,' answers the Doctor, 'and not read Galen and Hippocrates!' 'Sir,' cries the other, 'I believe there are many Surgeons who never read these Authors.' 'I believe so too,' says the Doctor, 'more shame for them: but thanks to my Education, I have them by heart, and very seldom go without them both in my Pocket.' 'They are pretty large Books,' said the Gentleman. 'Aye,' said the Doctor, 'I believe I know how large they are better than you.' (At which he fell a winking, and the whole Company burst into a Laugh.)[2]

The Doctor pursuing his Triumph asked the Gentleman, 'if he did not understand Physic as well as Surgery.' 'Rather better,' answered the Gentleman. 'Aye, like enough,' cries the Doctor, with a wink. 'Why, I know a little of Physic too.' 'I wish I knew half so much,' said Tow-wouse, 'I'd never wear an Apron again.' 'Why, I believe, Landlord,' cries the Doctor, 'there are few Men, tho' I say it, within twelve Miles of the Place, that handle a Fever better.— *Veniente occurrite Morbo:*[3] That is my Method.—I suppose Brother, you understand Latin?' 'A little,' says the Gentleman. 'Aye, and Greek now I'll warrant you: *Ton dapomibominos poluflosboio Thalasses.*[4] But I have almost forgot these things, I could have repeated Homer by heart once.'—'Ifags! the Gentleman has caught a *Traytor,*'[5] says Mrs. Tow-wouse; at which they all fell a laughing.

---

[2] Hippocrates (c. 470–370 BCE) and Galen (129–99 CE) were the chief medical authorities of antiquity, but surgeons trained as practical apprentices rather than studying at universities and so in general would not know their works.

[3] "Counteract the oncoming illness," misquoted from Persius, *Satires* 3.64.

[4] Two unconnected phrases from *The Iliad*, nonsensical in combination ("answering him of the loud-sounding sea").

[5] Mrs. Tow-wouse likely mangles the expression "catch a tartar," that is, "to tackle one who unexpectedly proves to be too formidable" (*OED*). "Ifags" is a mild oath derived from "in faith."

The Gentleman, who had not the least affection for joking, very contentedly suffered the Doctor to enjoy his Victory; which he did with no small Satisfaction: and having sufficiently sounded his Depth, told him, 'he was thoroughly convinced of his great Learning and Abilities; and that he would be obliged to him, if he would let him know his opinion of his Patient's Case above Stairs.' 'Sir,' says the Doctor, 'his Case is that of a dead Man—The Contusion on his Head has *perforated* the *internal Membrane* of the *Occiput,* and *divellicated* that *radical* small *minute* invisible *Nerve,* which *coheres* to the *Pericranium;* and this was attended with a Fever at first *symptomatic,* then *pneumatic;* and is at length *grown deliruus,* or delirious, as the Vulgar express it.'

He was proceeding in this learned manner, when a mighty Noise interrupted him. Some young Fellows in the Neighbourhood had taken one of the Thieves, and were bringing him into the Inn. Betty ran up Stairs with this News to Joseph; who begged they might search for a little piece of broken Gold, which had a Ribband tied on it, and which he could swear to amongst all the Hoards of the richest Man in the Universe.

Notwithstanding the Fellow's persisting in his Innocence, the Mob were very busy in searching him, and presently among other things pulled out the Piece of Gold just mentioned; which Betty no sooner saw than she laid violent hands on it, and conveyed it up to Joseph, who received it with raptures of Joy, and hugging it in his Bosom declared, he could now die contented.

Within a few Minutes afterwards, came in some other Fellows, with a Bundle which they had found in a Ditch, and which was indeed the Clothes which had been stripped off from Joseph, and the other things they had taken from him.

The Gentleman no sooner saw the Coat, than he declared he knew the Livery; and, if it had been taken from the poor Creature above stairs, he desired he might see him: for that he was very well acquainted with the Family to whom that Livery belonged.

He was accordingly conducted up by Betty: But what, Reader, was the surprize on both sides, when he saw Joseph was the Person in Bed; and when Joseph discovered the Face of his good Friend Mr. Abraham Adams!

It would be impertinent to insert a Discourse which chiefly turned on the relation of Matters already well known to the Reader: for as soon as the Curate had satisfied Joseph concerning the perfect Health of his Fanny, he was on his side very inquisitive into all the Particulars which had produced this unfortunate Accident.

To return therefore to the Kitchin, where a great variety of Company were now assembled from all the Rooms of the House, as well as the Neighbourhood: so much delight do Men take in contemplating the Countenance of a Thief:

Mr. Tow-wouse began to rub his Hands with pleasure, at seeing so large an Assembly; who would, he hoped, shortly adjourn into several Apartments, in order to discourse over the Robbery; and drink a Health to all honest Men: But Mrs. Tow-wouse, whose Misfortune it was commonly to see things a little perversly, began to rail at those who brought the Fellow into her House; telling her Husband, 'they were very likely to thrive, who kept a House of Entertainment for Beggars and Thieves.'

The Mob had now finished their search; and could find nothing about the Captive likely to prove any Evidence: for as to the Clothes, tho' the Mob were very well satisfied with that Proof; yet, as the Surgeon observed, they could not convict him, because they were not found in his Custody; to which Barnabas agreed, and added, that these were *Bona Waviata*,[6] and belonged to the Lord of the Manor.

'How,' says the Surgeon, 'do you say these Goods belong to the Lord of the Manor?' 'I do,' cried Barnabas. 'Then I deny it,' says the Surgeon. 'What can the Lord of the Manor have to do in the Case? Will any one attempt to persuade me that what a Man finds is not his own?' 'I have heard,' (says an old Fellow in the Corner) 'Justice Wise-one say, that if every Man had his Right, whatever is found belongs to the King of London.' 'That may be true,' says Barnabas, 'in some sense: for the Law makes a difference between things stolen, and things found: for a thing may be stolen that never is found; and a thing may be found that never was stolen. Now Goods that are both stolen and found are *Waviata*; and they belong to the Lord of the Manor.' 'So the Lord of the Manor is the Receiver of stolen Goods:' (says the Doctor) at which there was a universal Laugh, being first begun by himself.

While the Prisoner, by persisting in his Innocence, had almost (as there was no Evidence against him) brought over Barnabas, the Surgeon, Tow-wouse, and several others to his side; Betty informed them, that they had over-looked a little Piece of Gold, which she had carried up to the Man in bed; and which he offered to swear to amongst a Million, aye, amongst ten Thousand. This immediately

---

[6] The legal term for stolen goods discarded ("waived") by a felon on the run.

turned the Scale against the Prisoner; and every one now concluded him guilty. It was resolved therefore, to keep him secured that Night, and early in the Morning to carry him before a Justice.

CHAP. XV.

Shewing how Mrs. Tow-wouse was a little mollified; and how officious Mr. Barnabas and the Surgeon were to prosecute the Thief: With a Dissertation accounting for their Zeal, and that of many other Persons not mentioned in this History.

BETTY told her Mistress, she believed the Man in Bed was a greater Man than they took him for: for besides the extreme Whiteness of his Skin, and the Softness of his Hands, she observed a very great Familiarity between the Gentleman and him; and added, she was certain they were intimate Acquaintance, if not Relations.

This somewhat abated the severity of Mrs. Tow-wouse's Countenance. She said, 'G—forbid she should not discharge the duty of a Christian, since the poor Gentleman was brought to her House. She had a natural Antipathy to Vagabonds: but could pity the Misfortunes of a Christian as soon as another.' Tow-wouse said, 'If the Traveller be a Gentleman, tho' he hath no Money about him now, we shall most likely be paid hereafter; so you may begin to score whenever you will.' Mrs. Tow-wouse answered, 'Hold your simple Tongue, and don't instruct me in my business. I am sure I am sorry for the Gentleman's Misfortune with all my Heart; and I hope the Villain who hath used him so barbarously, will be hanged. Betty, go see what he wants. G—forbid he should want anything in my house.'

Barnabas and the Surgeon went up to Joseph, to satisfy themselves concerning the piece of Gold. Joseph was with difficulty prevailed upon to shew it them; but would by no Entreaties be brought to deliver it out of his own Possession. He however attested this to be the same which had been taken from him; and Betty was ready to swear to the finding it on the Thief.

The only Difficulty that remained, was how to produce this Gold before the Justice: for as to carrying Joseph himself, it seemed impossible; nor was there any greater likelihood of obtaining it from him: for he had fastened it with a Ribband to his Arm, and solemnly vowed, that nothing but irresistible Force should ever separate them; which Resolution, Mr. Adams, clenching a Fist rather less than the Knuckle of an Ox, declared he would support him.

A Dispute arose on this Occasion concerning Evidence, not very necessary to be related here; after which the Surgeon dress'd Mr. Joseph's Head; still persisting in the imminent Danger in which his Patient lay: but concluding with a very important Look, 'that he began to have some Hopes; that he should send him a *Sanative soporiferous* Draught,[1] and would see him in the Morning.' After which Barnabas and he departed, and left Mr. Joseph and Mr. Adams together.

Adams informed Joseph of the occasion of this Journey which he was making to London, namely to publish three Volumes of Sermons; being encouraged, he said, by an Advertisement lately set forth by a Society of Booksellers, who proposed to purchase any Copies offered to them at a Price to be settled by two Persons:[2] but tho' he imagined he should get a considerable Sum of Money on this occasion, which his Family were in urgent need of, he protested he would not leave Joseph in his present Condition: finally, he told him, 'he had nine Shillings and three-pence half-penny in his Pocket, which he was welcome to use as he pleased.'

This Goodness of Parson Adams brought Tears into Joseph's Eyes; he declared 'he had now a second Reason to desire Life, that he might shew his Gratitude to such a Friend.' Adams bid him 'be chearful; for that he plainly saw the Surgeon, besides his Ignorance, desired to make a Merit of curing him, tho' the Wounds in his Head, he perceived, were by no means dangerous; that he was convinced he had no Fever, and doubted not but he would be able to travel in a day or two.'

These Words infused a Spirit into Joseph; he said, 'he found himself very sore from the Bruises, but had no reason to think any of his Bones injured, or that he had received any Harm in his Inside; unless that he felt something very odd in his Stomach: but knew not whether that might not arise from not having eaten one Morsel for above twenty-four Hours.' Being then asked, if he had any Inclination to eat, he answered in the Affirmative. Then Parson Adams desired him to name what he had the greatest Fancy for; whether a poached Egg, or Chicken-broth: he answered, 'he could eat both very well; but that he seemed to have the greatest Appetite for a piece of boiled Beef and Cabbage.'

---

[1] A healing, sleep-inducing medicine.

[2] This advertisement actually appeared in Fielding's periodical *The Champion* from March to August 1741, but the "two Persons"—one to be named by the Booksellers, the other by the author—also had the authority to reject any manuscript submission.

Adams was pleased with so perfect a Confirmation that he had not the least Fever: but advised him to a lighter Diet, for that Evening. He accordingly eat[3] either a Rabbit or a Fowl, I never could with any tolerable Certainty discover which; was by Mrs. Tow-wouse's Order conveyed into a better Bed, and equipped with one of her Husband's Shirts.

In the Morning early, Barnabas and the Surgeon came to the Inn, in order to see the Thief conveyed before the Justice. They had consumed the whole Night in debating what Measures they should take to produce the Piece of Gold in Evidence against him: for they were both extremely zealous in the Business, tho' neither of them were in the least interested in the Prosecution; neither of them had ever received any private Injury from the Fellow, nor had either of them ever been suspected of loving the Public well enough, to give them a Sermon or a Dose of Physic for nothing.

To help our Reader therefore as much as possible to account for this Zeal, we must inform him, that as this Parish was so unfortunate to have no Lawyer in it; there had been a constant Contention between the two Doctors, spiritual and physical, concerning their Abilities in a Science, in which, as neither of them professed it, they had equal Pretensions to dispute each other's Opinions. These Disputes were carried on with great Contempt on both sides, and had almost divided the Parish; Mr. Tow-wouse and one half of the Neighbours inclining to the Surgeon, and Mrs. Tow-wouse with the other half to the Parson. The Surgeon drew his Knowledge from those inestimable Fountains, called the *Attorney's Pocket-Companion*, and *Mr. Jacob's Law-Tables;* Barnabas trusted entirely to *Wood's Institutes.*[4] It happened on this Occasion, as was pretty frequently the Case, that these two learned Men differed about the Sufficiency of Evidence: the Doctor being of opinion, that the Maid's Oath would convict the Prisoner without producing the Gold; the Parson, *è contra, totis viribus.*[5] To display their Parts therefore before the Justice and the Parish was the sole Motive, which we can discover, to this Zeal, which both of them pretended to be for public Justice.

---

[3] Pronounced. "et," an archaic past-tense form of "eat."

[4] John Mallory, *The Attorney's Pocket Companion* (1733); Giles Jacob, *The Statute-Law Common-plac'd: or a General Table to the Statutes* (1719); Thomas Wood, *An Institute of the Laws of England* (1720).

[5] That is, the parson argued "to the contrary, with all his strength."

O Vanity! How little is thy Force acknowledged, or thy Operations discerned! How wantonly dost thou deceive Mankind under
different Disguises! Sometimes thou dost wear the Face of Pity, sometimes of Generosity: nay, thou hast the Assurance even to put on those
glorious Ornaments which belong only to heroic Virtue. Thou odious, deformed Monster! whom Priests have railed at, Philosophers
despised, and Poets ridiculed: Is there a Wretch so abandoned as to
own thee for an Acquaintance in public? yet, how few will refuse to
enjoy thee in private? nay, thou art the Pursuit of most Men through
their Lives. The greatest Villanies are daily practised to please thee:
nor is the meanest Thief below, or the greatest Hero above thy Notice.
Thy Embraces are often the sole Aim and sole Reward of the private
Robbery, and the plundered Province. It is to pamper up thee, thou
Harlot, that we attempt to withdraw from others what we do not
want, or to withhold from them what they do. All our Passions are
thy Slaves. Avarice itself is often no more than thy Hand-maid, and
even Lust thy Pimp. The Bully Fear, like a Coward, flies before thee,
and Joy and Grief hide their Heads in thy Presence.

I Know thou wilt think, that whilst I abuse thee, I court thee;
and that thy Love hath inspired me to write this sarcastical Panegyric on thee: but thou art deceived, I value thee not of a farthing;
nor will it give me any Pain, if thou should'st prevail on the Reader
to censure this Digression as errant Nonsense: for know to thy Confusion, that I have introduced thee for no other Purpose than to
lengthen out a short Chapter; and so I return to my History.

CHAP. XVI.

*The escape of the Thief. Mr. Adams's Disappointment. The Arrival of
two very extraordinary Personages, and the Introduction of Parson
Adams to Parson Barnabas.*

BARNABAS and the Surgeon being returned, as we have said, to the
Inn, in order to convey the Thief before the Justice, were greatly
concerned to find a small Accident had happened, which somewhat
disconcerted them; and this was no other than the Thief's Escape,
who had modestly withdrawn himself by Night, declining all
Ostentation, and not chusing, in imitation of some great Men, to
distinguish himself at the Expence of being pointed at.

When the Company had retired the Evening before, the Thief
was detained in a Room where the Constable, and one of the young

Fellows who took him, were planted as his Guard. About the second Watch, a general Complaint of Drowth[1] was made both by the Prisoner and his Keepers. Among whom it was at last agreed, that the Constable should remain on Duty, and the young Fellow should call up the Tapster; in which Disposition the young Fellow apprehended not the least Danger, as the Constable was well armed, and could besides easily summon him back to his Assistance, if the Prisoner made the least Attempt to gain his Liberty.

The young Fellow had not long left the Room, before it came into the Constable's Head, that the Prisoner might leap on him by surprize, and thereby, preventing him of the use of his Weapons, especially the long Staff in which he chiefly confided, might reduce the Success of a Struggle to an equal Chance. He wisely therefore, to prevent this Inconvenience, slipt out of the Room himself and locked the Door, waiting without with his Staff in his Hand, ready lifted to fell the unhappy Prisoner, if by ill Fortune he should attempt to break out.

But human Life, as it hath been discovered by some great Man or other, (for I would by no means be he understood to affect the Honour of making any such Discovery) very much resembles a Game at Chess: for as in the latter, while a Gamester is too attentive to secure himself very strongly on one side the Board, he is apt to leave an unguarded Opening on the other; so doth it often happen in Life; and so did it happen on this Occasion: for whilst the cautious Constable with such wonderful Sagacity had possessed himself of the Door, he most unhappily forgot the Window.

The Thief, who played on the other side, no sooner perceived this Opening, than he began to move that way; and finding the Passage easy, he took with him the young Fellow's Hat; and without any Ceremony stepped into the Street, and made the best of his Way.

The young Fellow returning with a double Mug of Strong Beer was a little surprized to find the Constable at the Door; but much more so, when, the Door being opened, he perceived the Prisoner had made his Escape, and which way. He threw down the Beer, and without uttering any thing to the Constable, except a hearty Curse or two, he nimbly leapt out at the Window, and went again in pursuit of his Prey; being very unwilling to lose the Reward which he had assured himself of.

The Constable hath not been discharged of Suspicion on this account: It hath been said, that not being concerned in the taking

[1] Thirst.

the Thief, he could not have been entitled to any part of the Reward, if he had been convicted; that the Thief had several Guineas in his Pocket; that it was very unlikely he should have been guilty of such an Oversight; that his Pretence for leaving the Room was absurd: that it was his constant Maxim, that a wise Man never refused Money on any Conditions; that at every Election he always had sold his Vote to both Parties, &c.

But notwithstanding these and many other such Allegations, I am sufficiently convinced of his Innocence; having been positively assured of it, by those who received their Informations from his own Mouth; which, in the Opinion of some Moderns, is the best and indeed the only Evidence.

All the Family were now up, and with many others assembled in the Kitchin, where Mr. Tow-wouse was in some Tribulation; the Surgeon having declared, that by Law, he was liable to be indicted for the Thief's Escape, as it was out of his House: He was a little comforted however by Mr. Barnabas's Opinion, that as the Escape was by Night, the Indictment would not lie.

Mrs. Tow-wouse delivered herself in the following Words: 'Sure never was such a Fool as my Husband! would any other Person living have left a Man in the Custody of such a drunken, drowsy Block-head as Tom Suckbribe;' (which was the Constable's Name) 'and if he could be indicted without any harm to his Wife and Children, I should be glad of it.' (Then the Bell rung in Joseph's Room.) 'Why Betty, John Chamberlain, where the Devil are you all? Have you no Ears, or no Conscience, not to tend the Sick better?—See what the Gentleman wants; why don't you go yourself, Mr. Tow-wouse? but any one may die for you; you have no more feeling than a Deal-Board.[2] If a Man lived a Fortnight in your House without spending a Penny, you would never put him in mind of it. See whether he drinks Tea or Coffee for Breakfast.' 'Yes, my Dear,' cry'd Tow-wouse. She then asked the Doctor and Mr. Barnabas what Morning's Draught they chose, who answered, they had a Pot of Syder-and[3] at the Fire; which we will leave them merry over, and return to Joseph.

He had rose pretty early this Morning: but tho' his Wounds were far from threatening any danger, he was so sore with the Bruises, that it was impossible for him to think of undertaking a Journey yet; Mr. Adams therefore, whose Stock was visibly decreased with the

---

[2] "Deal" here refers to "firwood; or the wood of pines" (Johnson).

[3] "Cider-and" is "cider mixed with spirits or some other ingredients" (OED).

Expences of Supper and Breakfast, and which could not survive that Day's Scoring, began to consider how it was possible to recruit it. At last he cry'd, 'He had luckily hit on a sure Method, and though it would oblige him to return himself home together with Joseph, it mattered not much.' He then sent for Tow-wouse, and taking him into another Room, told him, 'He wanted to borrow three Guineas, for which he would put ample Security in his Hands.' Tow-wouse, who expected a Watch, or Ring, or something of double the Value, answered, 'He believed he could furnish him.' Upon which Adams, pointing to his Saddle-Bag, told him with a Face and Voice full of Solemnity, 'that there were in that Bag no less than nine Volumes of Manuscript Sermons,[4] as well worth a hundred Pound as a Shilling was worth twelve Pence, and that he would deposite one of the Volumes in his Hands by way of Pledge; not doubting but that he would have the Honesty to return it on his Repayment of the Money: for otherwise he must be a very great loser, seeing that every Volume would at least bring him ten Pounds, as he had been informed by a neighbouring Clergyman in the Country: for, said he, as to my own part, having never yet dealt in Printing, I do not pretend to ascertain the exact Value of such things.'

Tow-wouse, who was a little surprized at the Pawn, said (and not without some Truth) 'That he was no Judge of the Price of such kind of Goods: and as for Money, he really was very short.' Adams answered, 'Certainly he would not scruple to lend him three Guineas, on what was undoubtedly worth at least ten.' The Landlord replied, 'He did not believe he had so much Money in the House, and besides he was to make up a Sum. He was very confident the Books were of much higher Value, and heartily sorry it did not suit him.' He then cry'd out, *Coming Sir!* though no body called; and ran down Stairs without any Fear of breaking his Neck.

Poor Adams was extremely dejected at this Disappointment, nor knew he what farther Stratagem to try. He immediately applied to his Pipe, his constant Friend and Comfort in his Afflictions; and leaning over the Rails, he devoted himself to Meditation, assisted by the inspiring Fumes of Tobacco.

---

[4]An inconsistency—Fielding attributes *three* volumes of sermons to Adams in Chaper 15 (p. 68) and again later in Chapter 16 (p. 75). In Book II, Chapter 2, Adams once more has nine volumes (p. 90). In the fourth edition, Fielding changed the second reference in I.16 to "nine volumes," but retained the original reference to "three volumes" in I.15.

He had on a Night-Cap drawn over his Wig, and a short great Coat, which half covered his Cassock;[5] a Dress which, added to something comical enough in his Countenance, composed a Figure likely to attract the Eyes of those who were not over-given to Observation.

Whilst he was smoking his Pipe in this Posture, a Coach and Six, with a numerous Attendance, drove into the Inn. There alighted from the Coach a young Fellow, and a Brace of Pointers, after which another young Fellow leapt from the Box, and shook the former by the hand, and both, together with the Dogs, were instantly conducted by Mr. Tow- wouse into an Apartment; whither as they passed, they entertained themselves with the following short facetious Dialogue.

'You are a pretty Fellow for a Coachman, Jack!' says he from the Coach, 'you had almost overturned us just now.' 'Pox take you,' says the Coachman, 'if I had only broke your Neck, it would have been saving somebody else the trouble: but I should have been sorry for the Pointers.' 'Why, you Son of a B—,' answered the other, 'if no body could shoot better than you, the Pointers would be of no use.' 'D—n me,' says the Coachman, 'I will shoot with you, five Guineas a Shot.' 'You be hang'd,' says the other, 'for five Guineas you shall shoot at my A—.' 'Done,' says the Coachman, 'I'll pepper you better than ever you was peppered by Jenny Bouncer.'[6] 'Pepper your Grandmother,' says the other, 'here's Tow-wouse will let you shoot at him for a Shilling a time.' 'I know his Honour better,' cries Tow-wouse, 'I never saw a surer shoot at a Partridge. Every Man misses now and then; but if I could shoot half as well as his Honour, I would desire no better Livelihood than I could get by my Gun.' 'Pox on you,' said the Coachman, 'you demolish more Game now than your Head's worth. There's a Bitch, Tow-wouse, by G— she never blinked* a Bird in her Life.' 'I have a Puppy, not a Year old, shall hunt with her for a hundred,' cries the other Gentleman. 'Done,' says the Coachman, 'but you will be pox'd before you make the Bett. If you have a mind for a Bett, cries the Coachman, I will match my spotted Dog with your white Bitch for a hundred, play or

---

[5] "A long close-fitting frock or tunic worn by Anglican clergymen, originally along with and under the gown" (*OED*). It is the long black garment seen in Hullett's depiction of Adams, Illustration 6 p. 227.

[6] The coachman plays on two meanings of "pepper": "to beat; to mangle with shots or blows" (Johnson), and "infect with venereal disease" (Grose).

* *Fielding's note*: To blink is a Term used to signify the Dog's passing by a Bird without pointing at it.

pay.' 'Done,' says the other, 'and I'll run Baldface against Slouch with you for another.' 'No,' cries he from the Box, 'but I'll venture Miss Jenny against Baldface, or Hannibal either.' 'Go to the Devil,' cries he from the Coach, 'I will make every Bett your own way, to be sure! I will match Hannibal with Slouch for a thousand, if you dare, and I say done first.'

They were now arrived, and the Reader will be very contented to leave them, and repair to the Kitchin, where Barnabas, the Surgeon, and an Exciseman were smoking their Pipes over some Syder-and, and where the Servants, who attended the two noble Gentlemen we have just seen alight, were now arrived.

'Tom,' cries of the Footmen, 'there's Parson Adams smoking his Pipe in the Gallery.' 'Yes,' says Tom, 'I pulled off my Hat to him, and the Parson spoke to me.'

'Is the Gentleman a Clergyman then?' says Barnabas, (for his Cassock had been tied up when first he arrived.) 'Yes, Sir,' answered the Footman, 'and one there be but few like.' 'Aye,' said Barnabas, 'if I had known it sooner, I should have desired his Company; I would always shew a proper Respect for the Cloth; but what say you, Doctor, shall we adjourn into a Room, and invite him to take part of a Bowl of Punch?'

This Proposal was immediately agreed to, and executed; and Parson Adams accepting the Invitation, much Civility passed between the two Clergymen, who both declared the great Honour they had for the Cloth. They had not been long together, before they entered into a Discourse on small Tithes, which continued a full Hour, without the Doctor or the Exciseman's having one Opportunity to offer a Word.

It was then proposed to begin a general Conversation, and the Exciseman opened on foreign Affairs: but a Word unluckily dropping from one of them introduced a Dissertation on the Hardships suffered by the inferiour Clergy; which after a long Duration, concluded with bringing the three Volumes of Sermons on the Carpet.

Barnabas greatly discouraged poor Adams; he said, 'The Age was so wicked, that no body read Sermons: Would you think it, Mr. Adams, (said he) I once intended to print a Volume of Sermons myself, and they had the Approbation of two or three Bishops: but what do you think a Bookseller offered me?' 'Twelve Guineas perhaps (cried Adams.)' 'Not Twelve Pence, I assure you,' answered Barnabas, 'nay the Dog refused me a Concordance in Exchange.—At last, I offered to give him the printing them, for the sake of dedicating them to that very Gentleman who just now drove his own Coach into the Inn, and I assure you he had the Impudence to refuse my Offer: by which means I lost a good Living, that was afterwards given away in Exchange for a Pointer, to one who—but I will not say any thing against the Cloth. So you may guess, Mr. Adams, what you are to expect; for if Sermons would have gone down,[7] I believe—I will not be vain: but to be concise with you, three Bishops said, they were the best that ever were writ: but indeed there are a pretty moderate Number printed already, and not all sold yet.'— 'Pray, Sir,' says Adams, 'to what do you think the Numbers may amount?' 'Sir,' answered Barnabas, 'a Bookseller told me he believed five thousand Volumes at least.' 'Five thousand!' quoth the Surgeon, 'what can they be writ upon? I remember, when I was a Boy, I used to read one Tillotson's Sermons;[8] and I am sure, if a Man practised half so much as is in one of those Sermons, he will go to Heaven.' 'Doctor,' cried Barnabas, 'you have a profane way of talking, for which I must reprove you. A Man can never have his Duty too frequently inculcated into him. And as for Tillotson, to be sure he was a good Writer, and said things very well: but Comparisons are odious; another Man may write as well as he—I believe there are some of my Sermons,'—and then he apply'd the Candle to his Pipe.—'And I believe there are some of my Discourses,' cries Adams, 'which the Bishops would not think totally unworthy of being printed; and I have been informed, I might procure a very large Sum (indeed an immense one) on them.' 'I doubt that;' answered Barnabas: 'however, if you desire to make some Money of them, perhaps you may sell them by advertising *the Manuscript Sermons of a Clergyman lately deceased, all warranted Originals, and never printed*. And now I think of it, I should be obliged to you, if there be ever a Funeral one among them, to lend it me: for I am this very day to preach a Funeral Sermon; for which I have not penned a Line, though I am to have a double Price.' Adams answered, 'He had but one, which he feared would not serve his purpose, being sacred to the Memory of a Magistrate, who had exerted himself very singularly in the Preservation of the Morality of his Neighbours, insomuch that he had neither Alehouse, nor lewd Women in the Parish where he lived'.—'No,' replied Barnabas, 'that will not do quite so well; for the Deceased upon whose Virtues I am to

---

[7] Found acceptance.
[8] For Tillotson, see Contexts, pp. 341–43.

harangue, was a little too much addicted to Liquor, and publickly kept a Mistress.—I believe I must take a common Sermon, and trust to my Memory to introduce something handsome on him.' '—To your Invention rather,' (said the Doctor) 'your Memory will be apter to put you out: for no Man living remembers any thing good of him.'

With such kind of spiritual Discourse, they emptied the Bowl of Punch, paid their Reckoning, and separated: Adams and the Doctor went up to Joseph; Parson Barnabas departed to celebrate the aforesaid Deceased, and the Exciseman descended into the Cellar to gage the Vessels.[9]

Joseph was now ready to sit down to a Loin of Mutton, and waited for Mr. Adams, when he and the Doctor came in. The Doctor having felt his Pulse, and examined his Wounds, declared him much better, which he imputed to *that sanative soporiferous Draught,* a Medicine, 'whose Virtues,' he said, 'were never to be sufficiently extolled:' And great indeed they must be, if Joseph was so much indebted to them as the Doctor imagined; since nothing more than those Effluvia, which escaped the Cork, could have contributed to his Recovery: for the Medicine had stood untouched in the Window ever since its arrival.

Joseph passed that day and the three following with his Friend Adams, in which nothing so remarkable happened as the swift Progress of his Recovery. As he had an excellent Habit of Body, his Wounds were now almost healed; and his Bruises gave him so little Uneasiness, that he pressed Mr. Adams to let him depart, told him he should never be able to return sufficient Thanks for all his Favours; but begged that he might no longer delay his Journey to London.

Adams, notwithstanding the Ignorance, as he conceived it, of Mr. Tow-wouse, and the Envy (for such he thought it) of Mr. Barnabas, had great Expectations from his Sermons: seeing therefore Joseph in so good a way, he told him he would agree to his setting out the next Morning in the Stage-Coach, that he believed he should have sufficient after the Reckoning paid, to procure him one Day's Conveyance in it, and afterwards he would be able to get on, on Foot, or might be favoured with a lift in some Neighbour's Waggon, especially as there was then to be a Fair in the Town whither the Coach would carry him, to which Numbers from his Parish resorted.—And as to himself, he agreed to proceed to the great City.

---

[9] That is, to determine the quantity of beer and ale on the premises for purposes of taxation.

They were now walking in the Inn Yard, when a fat, fair, short Person rode in, and alighting from his Horse went directly up to Barnabas, who was smoaking his Pipe on a Bench. The Parson and the Stranger shook one another very lovingly by the Hand, and went into a Room together.

The Evening now coming on, Joseph retired to his Chamber, whither the good Adams accompanied him; and took this Opportunity to expatiate on the great Mercies God had lately shewn him, of which he ought not only to have the deepest inward Sense; but likewise to express outward Thankfulness for them. They therefore fell both on their Knees, and spent a considerable time in Prayer and Thanksgiving.

They had just finished, when Betty came in and told Mr. Adams, Mr. Barnabas desired to speak to him on some Business of Consequence below Stairs. Joseph desired, if it was likely to detain him long, he would let him know it, that he might go to Bed, which Adams promised, and in that Case, they wished one another good Night.

CHAP. XVII.

A pleasant Discourse between the two Parsons and the Bookseller, which was broke off by an unlucky Accident happening in the Inn, which produced a Dialogue between Mrs. Tow-wouse and her Maid of no gentle kind.

As soon as Adams came into the Room, Mr. Barnabas introduced him to the Stranger, who was, he told him, a Bookseller, and would be as likely to deal with him for his Sermons as any Man whatever. Adams, saluting the Stranger, answered Barnabas, that he was very much obliged to him, that nothing could be more convenient; for he had no other Business to the great City, and was heartily desirous of returning with the young Man who was just recovered of his Misfortune. He then snapt his Fingers (as was usual with him) and took two or three turns about the Room in an Extasy.—And to induce the Bookseller to be as expeditious as possible, as likewise to offer him a better Price for his Commodity, he assured him, their meeting was extremely lucky to himself: for that he had the most pressing Occasion for Money at that time, his own being almost spent, and having a Friend then in the same Inn who was just recovered from some Wounds he had received from Robbers, and was in a most indigent Condition. 'So that nothing,' says he, 'could be so opportune, for the supplying both of our Necessities, as my making an immediate Bargain with you.'

As soon as he had seated himself, the Stranger began in these Words; 'Sir, I do not care absolutely to deny engaging in what my Friend Mr. Barnabas recommends: but Sermons are mere Drugs.[1] The Trade is so vastly stocked with them, that really unless they come out with the Name of Whitfield or Westley,[2] or some other such great Man, as a Bishop, or those sort of People, I don't care to touch, unless now it was a Sermon preached on the 30th of January,[3] or we could say in the Title Page, published at the *earnest Request* of the Congregation, or the Inhabitants: but truly for a dry Piece of Sermons, I had rather be excused; especially as my Hands are so full at present. However, Sir, as Mr. Barnabas mentioned them to me, I will, if you please, take the Manuscript with me to Town, and send you my Opinion of it in a very short time.'

'O,' said Adams, 'if you desire it, I will read two or three Discourses as a Specimen.' This Barnabas, who loved Sermons no better than a Grocer doth Figs, immediately objected to, and advised Adams to let the Bookseller have his Sermons; telling him, if he gave him a Direction, he might be certain of a speedy Answer: Adding, he need not scruple trusting them in his Possession. 'No,' said the Bookseller, 'if it was a Play that had been acted twenty Nights together, I believe it would be safe.'

Adams did not at all relish the last Expression; he said, he was sorry to hear Sermons compared to Plays. 'Not by me, I assure you,' cry'd the Bookseller, 'though I don't know whether the licensing Act[4] may not shortly bring them to the same Footing: but I have formerly known a hundred Guineas given for a Play——.' 'More shame for those who gave it,' cry'd Barnabas. 'Why so?' said the Bookseller, 'for they got hundreds by it.' 'But is there no Difference between conveying good or ill Instructions to Mankind?' said Adams; 'would not

---

[1] "Any thing without worth or value" (Johnson).

[2] John Wesley (1703–91) and George Whitefield (1714–70) were leaders of the evangelical movement known as Methodism; for Whitefield, see Contexts, pp. 351–52.

[3] The anniversary of the execution of Charles I (1649), a popular occasion for sermons on loyalty to the crown. See, for example, John Taylor, John, Vicar of Lambourne, *The Evil Nature of Rebellious Principles and Practices, and the Fatal Consequences of them. A sermon preach'd on the 30th of January 1716, Being the Fast for the Martyrdom of King Charles I, of Blessed Memory* (Oxford, 1716).

[4] On the licensing act of 1737, see Table of Dates, p. xxiii.

an honest Mind rather lose Money by the one, than gain it by the other?' 'If you can find any such, I will not be their Hinderance,' answered the Bookseller, 'but I think those Persons who get by preaching Sermons, are the properest to lose by printing them: for my part, the Copy that sells best, will be always the best Copy in my Opinion; I am no Enemy to Sermons but because they don't sell: for I would as soon print one of Whitfield's, as any Farce whatever.'

'Whoever prints such Heterodox Stuff ought to be hanged,' says Barnabas. 'Sir,' said he, turning to Adams, 'this Fellow's Writings (I know not whether you have seen them) are levelled at the Clergy. He would reduce us to the Example of the primitive Ages, forsooth! and would insinuate to the People, that a Clergyman ought to be always preaching and praying. He pretends to understand the Scripture literally, and would make Mankind believe, that the Poverty and low Estate, which was recommended to the Church in its Infancy, and was only temporary Doctrine adapted to her under Persecution, was to be preserved in her flourishing and established State. Sir, the Principles of Toland, Woolston, and all the Free-Thinkers, are not calculated to do half the Mischief, as those professed by this Fellow and his Followers.'[5]

'Sir,' answered Adams, 'if Mr. Whitfield had carried his Doctrine no farther than you mention, I should have remained, as I once was, his Well-Wisher. I am myself as great an Enemy to the Luxury and Splendour of the Clergy as he can be. I do not, more than he, by the flourishing Estate of the Church, understand the Palaces, Equipages, Dress, Furniture, rich Dainties, and vast Fortunes of her Ministers. Surely those, which savour so strongly of this World, become not the Servants of one who professed his Kingdom was not of it: but when he began to call Nonsense and Enthusiasm[6] in to his Aid, and to set up the detestable Doctrine of Faith against good Works, I was his Friend no longer; for surely, that Doctrine was coined in Hell, and one would think none but the Devil himself could have the Confidence to preach it. For can any thing be more derogatory to the Honour of God, than for Men to imagine that the All-wise Being will hereafter say to the Good and Virtuous, *Notwithstanding the Purity of thy Life, notwithstanding that constant Rule of Virtue and*

---

[5] "Free-Thinker" was a title adopted by various religious skeptics including John Toland (1670–1722) and Thomas Woolston (1670–1733).

[6] "A vain belief of private revelation; a vain confidence of divine favour or communication" (Johnson).

Goodness in which you walked upon Earth, still as thou did'st not believe every thing in the true Orthodox manner, thy want of Faith shall condemn thee? Or on the other side, can any Doctrine have a more pernicious Influence on Society, than a Persuasion, that it will be a good Plea for the Villain at the last day; *Lord, it is true I never obeyed one of thy Commandments, yet punish me not, for I believe them all?*' 'I suppose, Sir,' said the Bookseller, 'your Sermons are of a different Kind.' 'Ay, Sir,' said Adams, 'the contrary, I thank Heaven, is inculcated in almost every Page, or I should belye my own Opinion, which hath always been, that a virtuous and good Turk, or Heathen, are more acceptable in the sight of their Creator, than a vicious and wicked Christian, tho' his Faith was as perfectly orthodox as St. Paul's himself.'—'I wish you Success,' says the Bookseller, 'but must beg to be excused, as my Hands are so very full at present; and indeed I am afraid, you will find a Backwardness in the Trade, to engage in a Book which the Clergy would be certain to cry down.' 'God forbid,' says Adams, 'any Books should be propagated which the Clergy would cry down: but if you mean by the Clergy, some few designing factious Men, who have it at Heart to establish some favourite Schemes at the Price of the Liberty of Mankind, and the very Essence of Religion, it is not in the power of such Persons to decry any Book they please; witness that excellent Book called, *A Plain Account of the Nature and End of the Sacrament;* a Book written (if I may venture on the Expression) with the Pen of an Angel, and calculated to restore the true Use of Christianity, and of that sacred Institution: for what could tend more to the noble Purposes of Religion, than frequent cheerful Meetings among the Members of a Society, in which they should, in the Presence of one another, and in the Service of the supreme Being, make Promises of being good, friendly and benevolent to each other? Now this excellent Book was attacked by a Party, but unsuccessfully.'[7] At these Words Barnabas fell a ringing with all the Violence imaginable; upon which a Servant attending, he bid him 'bring a Bill immediately: for that he was in Company, for aught he knew, with the Devil himself; and he expected to hear the *Alcoran,* the

---

[7] In *A Plain Account of the Nature and End of the Sacrament of the Lord's Supper* (1735), Benjamin Hoadly (1676–1761), bishop of Winchester, argued that the true point of the Eucharist was to commemorate Christ's sacrifice and "to revive and enlarge our affectionate Union and Sympathy" with other communicants (105). Hoadly's ethical emphasis was criticized on theological grounds by other churchmen, including George Whitefield.

Leviathan,[8] or Woolston commended, if he staid a few Minutes longer.' Adams desired, 'as he was so much moved at his mentioning a Book, which he did without apprehending any possibility of Offence, that he would be so kind to propose any Objections he had to it, which he would endeavour to answer.' 'I propose Objections!' said Barnabas, 'I never read a Syllable in any such wicked Book; I never saw it in my Life, I assure you.'—Adams was going to answer, when a most hideous Uproar began in the Inn, Mrs. Tow-wouse, Mr. Tow-wouse, and Betty all lifting up their Voices together: but Mrs. Tow-wouse's Voice, like a Bass Viol in a Concert, was clearly and distinctly distinguished among the rest, and was heard to articulate the following Sounds.—'O you damn'd Villain, is this the Return to all the Care I have taken of your Family? This the Reward of my Virtue? Is this the manner in which you behave to one who brought you a Fortune, and preferred you to so many Matches, all your Betters? To abuse my Bed, my own Bed, with my own Servant: but I'll maul the Slut, I'll tear her nasty Eyes out; was ever such a pitiful Dog, to take up with such a mean Trollop? If she had been a Gentlewoman like my self, it had been some excuse; but a beggarly saucy dirty Servant- Maid. Get you out of my House, you Whore.' To which, she added another Name, which we do not care to stain our Paper with.—It was a monosyllable, beginning with a B—, and indeed was the same, as if she had pronounced the Words, *She Dog.* Which Term, we shall, to avoid Offence, use on this Occasion, tho' indeed both the Mistress and Maid uttered above-mentioned B—, a word eternally disgustful to Females of the lower sort. Betty had borne all hitherto with Patience, and had uttered only Lamentations: but the last Appellation stung her to the Quick, 'I am a Woman as well as yourself,' she roared out, 'and no She-Dog, and if I have been a little naughty, I am not the first; if I have been no better than I should be,' cries she sobbing, 'that's no Reason you should call me out of my Name. My Be-Betters are wo-worse than me.' 'Huzzy, huzzy,' says Mrs. Tow-wouse, 'have you the Impudence to answer me? Did I not catch you, you saucy—' and then again repeated the terrible Word so odious to female Ears. 'I can't bear that Name,' answered Betty, 'if I have been wicked, I am to answer for it myself in the other World; but I have done nothing that's unnatural; and

---

[8] The *Alcoran* or *Koran* is the sacred book of Islam. In *The Leviathan* (1651), Thomas Hobbes (1588–1679) asserted the unlimited power of the civil state, denying any independent authority to the church.

I will go out of your House this Moment: for I will never be called *She Dog,* by any Mistress in England.' Mrs. Tow-wouse then armed herself with the Spit; but was prevented from executing any dreadful Purpose by Mr. Adams, who confined her Arms with the Strength of a Wrist which Hercules would not have been ashamed of. Mr. Tow-wouse being caught, as our Lawyers express it, with the Manner,[9] and having no Defence to make, very prudently withdrew himself, and Betty committed herself to the Protection of the Hostler, who, though she could not conceive him pleased with what had happened, was in her Opinion rather a gentler Beast than her Mistress.

Mrs. Tow-wouse, at the Intercession of Mr. Adams, and finding the Enemy vanished, began to compose herself, and at length recovered the usual serenity of her Temper, in which we will leave her, to open to the Reader the Steps which led to a Catastrophe, common enough, and comical enough too, perhaps in modern History, yet often fatal to the Repose and Well-being of Families, and the Subject of many Tragedies, both in Life and on the Stage.

CHAP. XVIII.

The History of Betty *the Chambermaid, and an Account of what occasioned the violent Scene in the preceding Chapter.*

BETTY, who was the Occasion of all this Hurry, had some good Qualities. She had Good-nature, Generosity and Compassion, but unfortunately her Constitution was composed of those warm Ingredients, which, though the Purity of Courts or Nunneries might have happily controuled them, were by no means able to endure the ticklish Situation of a Chamber-maid at an Inn, who is daily liable to the Solicitations of Lovers of all Complexions, to the dangerous Addresses of fine Gentlemen of the Army, who sometimes are obliged to reside with them a whole Year together; and above all are exposed to the Caresses of Footmen, Stage-Coachmen, Drawers;[1] all of whom employ the whole Artillery of kissing, flattering, bribing, and every other Weapon which is to be found in the whole Armory of Love, against them.

[9] "A Thief taken with the Manner, i.e., surprized in the Fact with the Goods upon him" (Fielding, *The Covent Garden Journal,* October 28, 1752).
[1] Bartenders.

Betty, who was about one and twenty, had now lived three Years in this dangerous Situation, during which she had escaped pretty well. An Ensign of Foot was the first Person who made any Impression on her Heart; he did indeed raise a Flame in her, which required the Care of a Surgeon to cool.[2]

While she burnt for him, several others burnt for her. Officers of the Army, young Gentlemen travelling the Western Circuit,[3] inoffensive Squires, and some of graver Character were set afire by her Charms!

At length, having perfectly recovered the Effects of her first unhappy Passion, she seemed to have vowed a State of perpetual Chastity. She was long deaf to all the Sufferings of her Lovers, till one day at a neighbouring Fair, the Rhetoric of John the Hostler, with a new Straw Hat, and a Pint of Wine, made a second Conquest over her.

She did not however feel any of those Flames on this Occasion, which had been the Consequence of her former Amour; nor indeed those other ill Effects, which prudent young Women very justly apprehend from too absolute an Indulgence to the pressing Endearments of their Lovers. This latter, perhaps, was a little owing to her not being entirely constant to John, with whom she permitted Tom Whipwell the Stage-Coachman, and now and then a handsome young Traveller, to share her Favours.[4]

Mr. Tow-wouse had for some time cast the languishing Eyes of Affection on this young Maiden. He had laid hold on every Opportunity of saying tender things to her, squeezing her by the Hand, and sometimes of kissing her Lips: for as the Violence of his Passion had considerably abated to Mrs. Tow-wouse; so like Water, which it stopt from its usual Current in one Place, it naturally sought a Vent in another. Mrs. Tow-wouse is thought to have perceived this Abatement, and probably it added very little to the natural Sweetness of her Temper: for tho' she was as true to her Husband, as the Dial to the Sun, she was rather more desirous of being shone on, as being more capable of feeling his Warmth.

Ever since Joseph's arrival, Betty had conceived an extraordinary Liking to him, which discovered itself more and more, as he grew

[2] That is, he infected her with venereal disease, which was treated with mercury compounds.

[3] The semiannual itinerary of southwestern England made by judges and barristers (including Fielding) to conduct the county assizes (superior criminal and civil courts).

[4] Alludes to the folk belief that a woman might avoid pregnancy through promiscuity.

better and better; till that fatal Evening when, as she was warming his Bed, her Passion grew to such a Height, and so perfectly mastered both her Modesty and her Reason, that after many fruitless Hints, and sly Insinuations, she at last threw down the Warming-Pan, and embracing him with great Eagerness swore he was the handsomest Creature she had ever seen.

Joseph in great Confusion leapt from her, and told her, he was sorry to see a young Woman cast off all Regard to Modesty: but she had gone too far to recede, and grew so very indecent, that Joseph was obliged, contrary to his Inclination, to use some Violence to her, and taking her in his Arms, he shut her out of the Room, and locked the Door.

How ought Man to rejoice, that his Chastity is always in his own power, that if he hath sufficient Strength of Mind, he hath always a competent Strength of Body to defend himself: and cannot, like a poor weak Woman, be ravished against his Will.

Betty was in the most violent Agitation at this Disappointment. Rage and Lust pulled her Heart, as with two Strings, two different Ways; one Moment she thought of stabbing Joseph, the next, of taking him in her Arms, and devouring him with Kisses; but the latter Passion was far more prevalent. Then she thought of revenging his Refusal on herself: but whilst she was engaged in this Meditation, happily Death presented himself to her in so many Shapes of drowning, hanging, poisoning, &c. that her distracted Mind could resolve on none. In this Perturbation of Spirit, it accidentally occurred to her Memory, that her Master's Bed was not made; she therefore went directly to his Room; where he happened at that time to be engaged at his Bureau. As soon as she saw him, she attempted to retire: but he called her back, and taking her by the hand squeezed her so tenderly, at the same time whispered so many soft things into her Ears, and, then pressed her so closely with his Kisses, that the vanquished Fair-One, whose Passions were already raised, and which were not so whimsically capricious that one Man only could lay them, though perhaps, she would have rather preferred that one: The vanquished Fair-One quietly submitted, I say, to her Master's Will, who had just attained the Accomplishment of his Bliss, when Mrs. Tow-wouse unexpectedly entered the Room, and caused all that Confusion which we have before seen, and which it is not necessary at present to take any farther Notice of: since without the Assistance of a single hint from us, every Reader of any Speculation, or Experience, though not married himself, may easily conjecture, that it concluded with the Discharge of Betty, the Submission of Mr. Tow-worse, with some things to be performed on his side by way of Gratitude for his Wife's Goodness in being reconciled to him, with many hearty Promises never to offend any more in the like manner: and lastly, his quietly and contentedly bearing to be reminded of his Transgressions, as a kind of Penance, once or twice a Day, during the Residue of his Life.

THE
HISTORY
OF THE
ADVENTURES
OF
Joſeph Andrews, and his Friend
Mr. *Abraham Adams.*

BOOK II.

CHAP. I.

Of Divisions in Authors.

THERE are certain Mysteries or Secrets in all Trades from the highest
to the lowest, from that of *Prime Ministring* to this of *Authoring,*
which are seldom discovered, unless to Members of the same Calling. Among those used by us Gentlemen of the latter Occupation,
I take this of dividing our Works into Books and Chapters to be
none of the least considerable. Now for want of being truly
acquainted with this Secret, common Readers imagine, that by this
Art of dividing, we mean only to swell our Works to a much larger
Bulk than they would otherwise be extended to. These several
Places therefore in our Paper, which are filled with our Books and
Chapters, are understood as so much Buckram, Stays, and Stay-tape

in a Taylor's Bill, serving only to make up the Sum Total, commonly found at the Bottom of our first Page,[1] and of his last.

But in reality the Case is otherwise, and in this, as well as all other Instances, we consult the Advantage of our Reader, and not our own; and indeed many notable Uses arise to him from this Method: for first, those little Spaces between our Chapters may be looked upon as an Inn or Resting-Place, where he may stop and take a Glass, or any other Refreshment, as it pleases him. Nay, our fine Readers will, perhaps, be scarce able to travel farther than through one of them in a Day. As to those vacant Pages which are placed between our Books, they are to be regarded as those Stages, where, in long Journeys, the Traveller stays some time to repose himself, and consider of what he hath seen in the Parts he hath already past through; a Consideration which I take the Liberty to recommend a little to the Reader: for however swift his Capacity may be, I would not advise him to travel through these Pages too fast: for if he doth, he may probably miss the seeing some curious Productions of Nature which will be observed by the slower and more accurate Reader. A Volume without any such Places of Rest resembles the Opening of Wilds or Seas, which tires the Eye and fatigues the Spirit when entered upon.

Secondly, What are the Contents prefixed to every Chapter, but so many Inscriptions over the Gates of Inns (to continue the same Metaphor) informing the Reader what Entertainment he is to expect, which if he likes not, he may travel on to the next: for in Biography, as we are not tied down to an exact Concatenation equally with other Historians; so a Chapter or two (for Instance this I am now writing) may be often passed over without any Injury to the Whole. And in these Inscriptions I have been as faithful as possible, not imitating the celebrated Montagne, who promises you one thing and gives you another;[2] nor some Title-Page Authors, who promise a great deal, and produce nothing at all.

There are, besides these more obvious Benefits, several others which our Readers enjoy from this Art of dividing; tho' perhaps most of them too mysterious to be presently understood by any who are not initiated into the Science of *Authoring*. To mention thereof but one which is most obvious, it prevents spoiling the Beauty of a Book by turning down its Leaves, a Method otherwise necessary to those Readers, who, (tho' they read with great

[1] A book's price sometimes appeared on the bottom of its title page.
[2] The frequently digressive *Essais* (1580–88) of Michel de Montaigne.

Improvement and Advantage) are apt, when they return to their study, after half an Hour's Absence, to forget where they left off.

These Divisions have the Sanction of great Antiquity. Homer not only divided his great Work into twenty-four Books, (in Compliment perhaps to the twenty-four Letters to which he had very particular Obligations) but, according to the opinion of some very sagacious critics, hawked them all separately, delivering only one Book at a Time, (probably by Subscription).[3] He was the first Inventor of the Art which hath so long lay dormant, of publishing by Numbers; an Art now brought to such Perfection, that even Dictionaries are divided and exhibited piece-meal to the Publick; nay, one Bookseller hath (*to encourage Learning and ease the Public*) contrived to give them a Dictionary in this divided manner, for only fifteen Shillings more than it would have cost entire.

Virgil hath given us his Poem in twelve Books, an Argument of his Modesty; for by that doubtless he would insinuate that he pretends to no more than half the Merit of the Greek: for the same Reason, our Milton went originally no farther than ten; 'till being puffed up by the Praise of his Friends, he put himself on the same footing with the Roman Poet.[4]

I shall not however enter so deep into this Matter as some very learned Criticks have done; who have with infinite Labour and acute Discernment discovered what Books are proper for Embellishment, and what require Simplicity only, particularly with regard to Similies, which I think are now generally agreed to become any Book but the first.

I will dismiss this Chapter with the following Observation: That it becomes an Author generally to divide a Book, as it doth a Butcher to joint his Meat, for such Assistance is of great Help to both the Reader and the Carver. And now having indulged myself a little, I will endeavour to indulge the Curiosity of my Reader, who is no doubt impatient to know what he will find in the subsequent Chapters of this Book.

---

[3] Homer's epics were divided into 24 books; each book was designated by a letter of the 24-character Greek alphabet (*A* to *Ω*). The notion that Homer "hawked" his books separately alludes to a critical tradition (rejected by Fielding) that sees Homer's epics as later compilations of piece-meal materials. "By subscription" alludes to Alexander Pope's lucrative subscription publication of his verse translations of Homer's *Iliad* (1715–20) and *Odyssey* (1725–26).

[4] Virgil's *Aeneid* has twelve books. Milton first divided *Paradise Lost* (1667) into ten books; in 1674 he re-divided it into twelve books.

CHAP. II.

A surprizing Instance of Mr. Adams's *short Memory, with the unfortunate Consequences which it brought on Joseph.*

MR. Adams and Joseph were now ready to depart different Ways, when an Accident determined the former to return with his Friend, which Tow-wouse, Barnabas, and the Bookseller had not been able to do. This Accident was, that those Sermons, which the Parson was traveling to London to publish, were, O my good Reader, left behind; what he had mistaken for them in the Saddle-Bags being no other than three Shirts, a Pair of Shoes, and some other Necessaries, which Mrs. Adams, who thought her Husband would want Shirts more than Sermons on his Journey, had carefully provided him.

This Discovery was now luckily owing to the Presence of Joseph at the opening the Saddle-Bags, who having heard his Friend say, he carried with him nine Volumes of Sermons, and not being of that Sect of Philosophers, who can reduce all the Matter of the World into a Nutshell, seeing there was no room for them in the Bags, where the Parson had said they were deposited, had the Curiosity to cry out, 'Bless me, Sir, where are your Sermons?' The Parson answer'd, 'There, there, Child, there they are, under my Shirts.' Now it happened that he had taken forth his last Shirt, and the Vehicle remained visibly empty. 'Sure, Sir,' says Joseph, 'there is nothing in the Bags.' Upon which Adams starting, and testifying some surprise, cry'd, 'Hey! fie, fie upon it; they are not here sure enough. Ay, they are certainly left behind.'

Joseph was greatly concerned at the Uneasiness which he apprehended his Friend must feel from his Disappointment: he begged him to pursue his Journey, and promised he would himself return with the Books to him, with the utmost Expedition. 'No, thank you, Child,' answered Adams, 'it shall not be so. What would it avail me, to tarry in the Great City, unless I had my Discourses with me, which are, *ut ita dicam*, the sole Cause, the *Aitia monotate* of my Peregrination.[1] No, Child, as this accident hath happened, I am resolved to return back to my Cure, together with you; which indeed my Inclination sufficiently leads me to. This Disappointment may perhaps be intended for my Good.' He concluded that a Verse

---

[1] These italicized phrases are, respectively, Latin for "so to speak" and Greek for "sole cause."

out of Theocritus, which signifies no more than, *that sometimes it rains and sometimes the Sun shines*.

Joseph bowed with Obedience, and Thanksfulness for the Inclination which the Parson express'd of returning with him; and now the Bill was called for, which, on Examination, amounted within a Shilling to the Sum which Mr. Adams had in his Pocket. Perhaps the Reader may wonder how he was able to produce a sufficient Sum for so many Days: that he may not be too much surprized, therefore, it cannot be unnecessary to acquaint him, that he had borrowed a Guinea of a Servant belonging to the Coach and Six, who had been formerly one of his Parishioners, and whose Master, the Owner of the Coach, then lived within three Miles of him: for so good was the Credit of Mr. Adams, that even Mr. Peter the Lady Booby's Steward, would have lent him a Guinea with very little Security.

Mr. Adams discharged the Bill, and they were both setting out, having agreed *to ride and tie*: a Method of Travelling much used by two Persons who have but one Horse between them, and is thus performed. The two Travellers set out together, one on horseback, the other on foot: Now as it generally happens that he on horseback out-goes him on foot, the Custom is, that when he arrives at the Distance agreed on, he is to dismount, tie the Horse to some Gate, Tree, Post, or other thing, and then proceed on foot; when the other comes up to the Horse, he unties him, mounts and gallops on, 'till having passed by his Fellow-Traveller, he likewise arrives at the Place of tying. And this is that Method of Travelling so much in use among our prudent Ancestors, who knew that Horses had Mouths as well as Legs, and that they could not use the latter without being at the Expence of suffering the Beasts themselves to use the former. This was the Method in use in those Days: when, instead of a Coach and Six, a Member of Parliament's Lady used to mount a Pillion behind her Husband; and a grave Serjeant at Law condescended to amble to Westminster on an easy Pad,[2] with his Clerk kicking his Heels behind him.

Adams was now gone some Minutes, having insisted on Joseph's beginning the Journey on horseback, and Joseph had his Foot in the Stirrup, when the Hostler presented him a Bill for the Horse's Board during his Residence at the Inn. Joseph said Mr. Adams had paid all; but this Matter being referred to Mr. Tow-wouse was by him

---

[2] "An easy paced horse" (Johnson).

decided in favour of the Hostler, and indeed with Truth and Justice: for this was a fresh Instance of that shortness of Memory which did not arise from want of Parts, but that continual Hurry in which Parson Adams was always involved.

Joseph was now reduced to a Dilemma which extremely puzzled him. The Sum due for Horse-meat[3] was twelve Shillings, (for Adams, who had borrowed the Beast, had ordered him to be fed as well as they could feed him) and the Cash in his Pocket amounted to Sixpence, (for Adams had divided the last Shilling with him.) Now, tho' there have been some ingenious Persons who have contrived to pay twelve Shillings with Sixpence, Joseph was not one of them. He had never contracted a Debt in his Life, and was consequently the less ready at an Expedient to extricate himself. Tow-wouse was willing to give him Credit 'till next time, to which Mrs. Tow-wouse would probably have consented (for such was Joseph's Beauty, that it had made some Impression even on that Piece of Flint which that good Woman wore in her Bosom by way of Heart.) Joseph would have found therefore, very likely, the Passage free, had he not, when he honestly discovered the Nakedness of his Pockets, pulled out that little Piece of Gold which we have mentioned before. This caused Mrs. Tow-wouse's Eyes to water; she told Joseph, she did not conceive a Man could want Money whilst he had Gold in his Pocket. Joseph answered, he had such a Value for that little Piece of Gold, that he would not part with it for a hundred times the Riches which the greatest Esquire in the County was worth. 'A pretty Way indeed,' said Mrs. Tow-wouse, 'to run in debt, and then refuse to part with your Money, because you have a Value for it. I never knew any Piece of Gold of more Value than as many Shillings as it would change for.' 'Not to preserve my Life from starving, nor to redeem it from a Robber, would I part with this dear Piece,' answered Joseph. 'What (says Mrs. Tow-wouse) I suppose, it was given you by some vile Trollop, some Miss or other; if it had been the Present of a virtuous Woman, you would not have such a Value for it. My Husband is a Fool if he parts with the Horse without being paid for him.' 'No, no, I can't part with the Horse indeed, till I have the Money,' cry'd Tow-wouse. A Resolution highly commended by a Lawyer then in the Yard, who declared Mr. Tow-wouse might justify the Detainer[4]

---

[3] That is, horse-feed, "provender" (Johnson).

[4] Legal term (cf. "detainder") for holding another's person or possessions in custody.

As we cannot therefore at present get Mr. Joseph out of the Inn, we shall leave him in it, and carry our Reader on after Parson Adams, who, his Mind being perfectly at ease, fell into a Contemplation on a Passage in *Æschylus*,[5] which entertained him for three Miles together, without suffering him once to reflect on his Fellow-Traveller.

At length, having spun out this Thread, and being now at the Summit of a Hill, he cast his Eyes backwards, and wondered that he could not see any sign of Joseph. As he left him ready to mount the Horse, he could not apprehend any Mischief had happened, neither could he suspect that he had miss'd his Way, it being so broad and plain: the only Reason which presented itself to him, was, that he had met with an Acquaintance who had prevailed with him to delay some time in Discourse.

He therefore resolved to proceed slowly forwards, not doubting but that he should be shortly overtaken, and soon came to a large Water, which, filling the whole Road, he saw no Method of passing unless by wading through, which he accordingly did up to his Middle; but was no sooner got to the other Side than he perceived, if he had looked over the Hedge, he would have found a Foot-Path capable of conducting him without wetting his Shoes.

His Surprize at Joseph's not coming up grew now very troublesome: he began to fear he knew not what; and as he determined to move no farther, and, if he did not shortly overtake him, to return back, he wished to find a House of publick Entertainment where he might have dried his Clothes and refresh himself with a Pint: but seeing no such, (for no other Reason than because he did not cast his Eyes a hundred Yards forwards) he sat himself down on a Stile, and pulled out his *Æschylus*.

A Fellow passing presently by, Adams asked him, if he could direct him to an Alehouse. The Fellow who had just left it, and perceived the House and Sign to be within sight, thinking he had jeered him, and being of a morose Temper, bade him *follow his Nose and be d—n'd*. Adams told him he was a *saucy Jackanapes*; upon which the Fellow turned about angrily: but perceiving Adams clench his Fist, he thought proper to go on without taking any farther notice.

A Horseman following immediately after, and being asked the same Question, answered, 'Friend, there is one within a Stone's-Throw; I believe you may see it before you.' Adams, lifting up his

---

[5] Ancient Greek tragedian. His *Oresteia* trilogy, which recounts the mythical origins of judicature in Athens, may be an ironic point of reference for Book II's satire of incompetent judges and self-seeking lawyers in rural England.

Eyes, cry'd, 'I protest and so there is'; and, thanking his Informer, proceeded directly to it.

CHAP. III.

The Opinion of two Lawyers concerning the same Gentleman, with Mr. Adams's Enquiry into the Religion of his Host.

HE had just entered the House, had called for his Pint and seated himself, when two Horsemen came to the Door, and fastening their Horses to the Rails, alighted. They said there was a violent Shower of Rain coming on, which they intended to weather there, and went into a little Room by themselves, not perceiving Mr. Adams.

One of these immediately asked the other, if he had seen a more comical Adventure a great while? Upon which the other said, 'he doubted whether by Law, the Landlord could justify detaining the Horse for his Corn and Hay.' But the first answered, 'undoubtedly he can: it is an adjudged Case, and I have known it tried.'

Adams, who tho' he was, as the Reader may suspect, a little inclined to Forgetfulness, never wanted more than a Hint to remind him, over-hearing their Discourse, immediately suggested to himself that this was his own Horse, and that he had forgot to pay for him, which upon enquiry, he was certified of by the Gentlemen; who added, that the Horse was likely to have more Rest than Food, unless he was paid for.

The poor Parson resolved to return presently to the Inn, tho' he knew no more than Joseph, how to procure his Horse his Liberty: he was however prevailed on to stay under Covert, 'till the Shower, which was now very violent, was over.

The three Travellers now sat down together over a Mug of good Beer; when Adams, who had observed a Gentleman's House as he passed along the Road, enquired to whom it belonged: one of the Horsemen had no sooner mentioned the Owner's Name, than the other began to revile him in the most opprobrious Terms. The English Language scarce affords a single reproachful Word, which he did not vent on this Occasion. He charged him likewise with many particular Facts. He said,—'he no more regarded a Field of Wheat when he was hunting, than he did the High-way; that he had injured several poor Farmers by trampling their Corn under his Horse's Heels; and if any of them begged him with the utmost Submission to refrain, his Horse-whip was always ready to do them justice.' He said, 'that he was the greatest Tyrant to the Neighbours in every other Instance, and would not suffer a Farmer to keep a Gun, tho' he might justify it by Law; and in his own Family so cruel a Master, that he never kept a Servant a Twelve-month. In his Capacity as a Justice,' continued he, 'he behaves so partially, that he commits or acquits just as he is in the humour, without any regard to Truth or Evidence: The Devil may carry any one before him for me; I would rather be tried before some Judges than be a Prosecutor before him: If I had an Estate in the Neighbourhood, I would sell it for half the Value, rather than live near him.' Adams shook his Head, and said, 'he was sorry such Men were suffered to proceed with Impunity, and that Riches could set any Man above Law.' The Reviler a little after retiring into the Yard, the Gentleman, who had first mentioned his Name to Adams, began to assure him, 'that his Companion was a prejudiced Person. It is true,' says he, 'perhaps, that he may have sometimes pursued his Game over a Field of Corn, but he hath always made the Party ample Satisfaction; that so far from tyrannizing over his Neighbours, or taking away their Guns, he himself knew several Farmers not qualified, who not only kept Guns, but killed Game with them.[1] That he was the best Justice of Peace in the Kingdom, and to his certain knowledge had decided many difficult Points, which were referred to him, with the greatest Equity, and the highest Wisdom. And he verily believed, several Persons would give a Year's Purchase[2] more for an Estate near him, than under the Wings of any other great Man.' He had just finished his Encomium, when his Companion returned and acquainted him the Storm was over. Upon which, they presently mounted their Horses and departed.

Adams, who was in the utmost Anxiety at those different Characters of the same Person, asked his Host if he knew the Gentleman: for he began to imagine they had by mistake been speaking of two several Gentlemen. 'No, no, Master!' answered the Host, a shrewd cunning Fellow, 'I know the Gentleman very well of whom they have been speaking, as I do the Gentleman who spoke of him. As for riding over other Men's Corn, to my knowledge he hath not been on horseback these two Years. I never heard he did any Injury of that kind; and as to making Reparation, he is not so free of his

---

[1] Only men with considerable property holdings "qualified" to kill game; these substantial estate-holders were entitled to take guns away from unqualified persons.

[2] That is, the annual rent or return from land.

Money as that comes to neither. Nor did I ever hear of his taking away any Man's Gun; nay, I know several who have Guns in their Houses: but as for killing Game with them, no Man is stricter; and I believe he would ruin any who did. You heard one of the Gentlemen say, he was the worst Master in the World, and the other that he is the best: but as for my own part, I know all his Servants, and never heard from any of them that he was either one or the other.—' 'Aye! aye!' says Adams, 'and how doth he behave as a Justice, pray?' 'Faith, Friend,' answered the Host, 'I question whether he is in the Commission:[3] the only Cause I have heard he hath decided a great while, was one between those very two Persons who just went out of this House; and I am sure he determined that justly, for I heard the whole Matter.' 'Which did he decide it in favour of,' quoth Adams? 'I think I need not answer that Question,' cried the Host, 'after the different Characters you have heard of him. It is not my Business to contradict Gentlemen, while they are drinking in my House; but I knew neither of them spoke a Syllable of Truth.' 'God forbid!—(said Adams)—that Men should arrive at such a Pitch of Wickedness, to belye the Character of their Neighbour from a little private Affection, or what is infinitely worse, a private Spite. I rather believe we have mistaken them, and they mean two other Persons: for there are many Houses on the Road.' 'Why prithee, Friend—cries the Host,—dost thou pretend never to have told a Lye in thy Life?' 'Never a malicious one, I am certain,' answered Adams; 'nor with a Design to injure the Reputation of any Man living.' 'Pugh, malicious! no, no,' replied the Host; 'not malicious with a Design to hang a Man, or bring him into Trouble: but surely out of love to one's self, one must speak better of a Friend than an Enemy.' 'Out of love to yourself, you should confine yourself to Truth,' says Adams, 'for by doing otherwise, you injure the noblest Part of yourself, your immortal Soul. I can hardly believe any Man such an Idiot to risque the Loss of that by any trifling Gain, and the greatest Gain in this World is but Dirt in comparison of what shall be revealed hereafter.' Upon which the Host taking up the Cup, with a Smile drank a Health to Hereafter: adding, 'he was for something present.' 'Why,' says Adams very gravely, 'Do not you believe another World?' To which the Host answered, 'yes, he was no Atheist.' 'And you believe you have an immortal Soul,' cries

---

[3] Local magistrates were known as the "Commission of the Peace."

Adams. He answered, 'God forbid he should not.' 'And Heaven and Hell?' said the Parson. The Host then bid him 'not to profane: for those were Things not to be mentioned nor thought of but in Church.' Adams asked him, 'why he went to Church, if what he learned there had no Influence on his Conduct in Life?' 'I go to Church,' answered the Host, 'to say my Prayers and behave godly.' 'And dost not thou,' cry'd Adams, 'believe what thou hearest at Church?' 'Most part of it, Master,' returned the Host. 'And dost not thou then tremble,' cries Adams, 'at the Thought of eternal Punishment?' 'As for that, Master,' said he, 'I never once thought about it: but what signifies talking about Matters so far off? The Mug is out,[4] shall I draw another?'

Whilst he was gone for that purpose, a Stage-Coach drove up to the Door. The Coachman coming into the House, was asked by the Mistress, what passengers he had in his Coach? 'A Parcel of *Squinny-gut* B—s, (says he) I have a good mind to overturn them; you won't prevail upon them to drink any thing I assure you.' Adams asked him, if he had not seen a young Man on Horse-back on the Road, (describing Joseph.) 'Aye,' said the Coachman, 'a Gentlewoman in my Coach that is his Acquaintance redeemed him and his Horse; he would have been here before this time, had not the Storm driven him to shelter.' 'God bless her,' said Adams in a Rapture; nor could he delay walking out to satisfy himself who this charitable Woman was; but what was his surprize, when he saw his old Acquaintance, Madam Slipslop? Her's indeed was not so great, because she had been informed by Joseph, that he was on the Road. Very civil were the Salutations on both sides; and Mrs. Slipslop rebuked the Hostess for denying the Gentleman to be there when she asked for him: but indeed the poor Woman had not erred designedly; for Mrs. Slipslop asked for a Clergyman; and she had unhappily mistaken him for a Person travelling to a neighbouring Fair with the Thimble and Button,[5] or some other such Operation: for he marched in a swinging great, but short, white Coat with black Buttons, a short Wig, and a Hat, which so far from having a black Hatband, had nothing black about it.

[4] Empty.

[5] Mrs. Slip-slop mistakes Adams for a sharper at "thimblerig," "a swindling game usually played with three thimbles and a pea which was ostensibly placed under one of them; the sharper then challenging the bystanders to guess under which the pea has been placed, and to bet on their choice" (*OED*).

Joseph was now come up, and Mrs. Slipslop would have had him quit his Horse to the Parson, and come himself into the Coach: but he absolutely refused, saying he thanked Heaven he was well enough recovered to be very able to ride, and added, he hoped he knew his Duty better than to ride in a Coach while Mr. Adams was on horseback.

Mrs. Slipslop would have persisted longer, had not a Lady in the Coach put a short End to the Dispute, by refusing to suffer a Fellow in a Livery to ride in the same Coach with herself: so it was at length agreed that Adams should fill the vacant Place in the Coach, and Joseph should proceed on horseback.

They had not proceeded far before Mrs. Slipslop, addressing herself to the Parson, spoke thus: 'There hath been a strange Alteration in our Family, Mr. Adams, since Sir Thomas's Death.' 'A strange Alteration indeed!' says Adams, 'as I gather from some Hints which have dropped from Joseph.' 'Aye,' says she, 'I could never have believed it, but the longer one lives in the World, the more one sees. So Joseph hath given you Hints.' —'But of what Nature, will always remain a perfect Secret with me,' cries the Parson; 'he forced me to promise before he would communicate any thing. I am indeed concerned to find her ladyship behave in so unbecoming a manner. I always thought her in the main, a good Lady, and should never have suspected her of Thoughts so unworthy a Christian, and with a young Lad her own Servant.' 'These things are no Secrets to me, I assure you,' cries Slipslop; 'and I believe, they will none any where shortly: for ever since the Boy's Departure she hath behaved more like a mad Woman than any thing else.' 'Truly, I am heartily concerned,' says Adams, 'for she was a good sort of a Lady; indeed I have often wished she had attended a little more constantly at the Service, but she hath done a great deal of Good in the Parish.' 'O Mr. Adams!' says Slipslop, 'People that don't see all, often know nothing. Many Things have been given away in our Family, I do assure you, without her knowledge. I have heard you say in the Pulpit, we ought not to brag: but indeed I can't avoid saying, if she had kept the Keys herself, the Poor would have wanted many a Cordial which I have let them have. As for my late Master, he was as worthy a Man as ever lived, and would have done infinite Good if he had not been controlled: but he loved a quiet Life, Heavens rest his Soul! I am confident he is there, and enjoys a quiet Life, which some Folks would not allow him here.' Adams answered, 'he had never heard this before, and was mistaken, if she herself,' (for he remembered she used to commend her Mistress and blame her Master,) 'had not formerly been of another Opinion.' 'I don't know, (replied she) what I might once think: but now I am *confidous* Matters are as I tell you: The World will shortly see who hath been deceived; for my part I say nothing, but that it is *wondersome* how some People can carry all things with a grave Face.'

Thus Mr. Adams and she discoursed: 'till they came opposite to a great House which stood at some distance from the Road; a Lady in the Coach spying it, cry'd yonder lives the unfortunate Leonora, if one can justly call a Woman unfortunate, whom we must own at the same time guilty, and the Author of her own Calamity. This was abundantly sufficient to awaken the Curiosity of Mr. Adams, as indeed it did that of the whole Company, who jointly solicited the Lady to acquaint them with Leonora's History, since it seemed, by what she had said, to contain something remarkable.

The Lady, who was perfectly well bred, did not require many Entreaties, and having only wished this Entertainment might make amends for the Company's Attention, she began in the following manner.

CHAP. IV.

The History of Leonora, *or the Unfortunate Jilt.*

LEONORA was the Daughter of a Gentleman of Fortune; she was tall and well-shaped, with a Sprightliness in her Countenance, which often attracts beyond more regular Features joined with an insipid Air; nor is this kind of Beauty less apt to deceive than allure; the Good-Humour which it indicates, being often mistaken for Good-Nature, and the Vivacity for true Understanding.

Leonora, who was now at the Age of eighteen, lived with an Aunt of her's in a Town in the North of England. She was an extreme Lover of Gaiety, and very rarely missed a Ball, or any other public Assembly; where she had frequent Opportunities of satisfying a greedy Appetite of Vanity with the Preference which was given her by the Men to almost every other Woman present.

Among many young Fellows who were particular in their Gal-lantries towards her, Horatio soon distinguished himself in her Eyes beyond all his Competitors; she danced with more than ordinary Gaiety when he happened to be her Partner; neither the Fairness of the Evening, nor the Musick of the Nightingale, could lengthen her Walk like his Company. She affected no longer to understand the Civilities of others: whilst she inclined so attentive an Ear to every Compliment of Horatio, that she often smiled even when it was too delicate for her Comprehension.

'Pray, Madam,' says Adams, 'who was this Squire Horatio?'

Horatio, says the Lady, was a young Gentleman of a good Family, bred to the Law, and had been some few Years called to the Degree of a Barrister.[1] His Face and Person were such as the Generality allowed handsome: but he had a Dignity in his Air very rarely to be seen. His Temper was of the saturnine Complexion, but without the least Taint of Moroseness. He had Wit and Humour, with an Inclination to Satire, which he indulged rather too much.

This Gentleman, who had contracted the most violent Passion for Leonora, was the last Person who perceived the Probability of its Success. The whole Town had made the Match for him, before he himself had drawn a Confidence from her Actions sufficient to mention his Passion to her; for it was his Opinion, (and perhaps he was there in the right) that it is highly impolitick to talk seriously of Love to a Woman before you have made such a Progress in her Affections, that she herself expects and desires to hear it.

But whatever Diffidence the Fears of a Lover may create, which are apt to magnify every Favour conferred on a Rival, and to see the little Advances towards themselves through the other End of the Perspective;[2] it was impossible that Horatio's Passion should so blind his Discernment, as to prevent his conceiving Hopes from the Behaviour of Leonora; whose Fondness for him was now as visible to an indifferent Person in their Company, as his for her.

'I never knew any of these forward Sluts come to good,' (says the Lady, who refused Joseph's Entrance into the Coach,) 'nor shall I wonder at any thing she doth in the Sequel.'

The Lady proceeded in her Story thus: It was in the Midst of a gay Conversation in the Walks one Evening, when Horatio whispered Leonora, that he was desirous to take a Turn or two with her in private; for that he had something to communicate to her of

---

[1] A "counselor at law" who was "qualified to plead the causes of clients in the courts of justice" (Johnson). Fielding was a barrister.

[2] In the sense of "a magnifying glass, telescope, monocle" (*OED*), which magnifies objects from one side and diminishes them from the other.

great Consequence. 'Are you sure it is of Consequence?' said she, smiling. —'I hope,' answered he, 'you will think so too, since the whole future Happiness of my Life must depend on the Event.'

Leonora, who very much suspected what was coming, would have deferred it till another Time: but Horatio, who had more than half conquered the Difficulty of speaking, by the first Motion, was so very importunate, that she at last yielded, and leaving the rest of the Company, they turned aside into an unfrequented Walk.

They had retired far out of the sight of the Company, both maintaining a strict Silence. At last Horatio made a full Stop, and taking Leonora, who stood pale and trembling, gently by the Hand, he fetched a deep Sigh, and then looking on her Eyes with all the Tenderness imaginable, he cried out in a faltering Accent; 'O Leonora! is it necessary for me to declare to you on what the future Happiness of my Life must be founded! Must I say, there is something belonging to you which is a Bar to my Happiness, and which unless you will part with, I must be miserable?' 'What can that be,' replied Leonora? —'No wonder,' said he, 'you are sur-prized that I should make an Objection to any thing which is yours, yet sure you may guess, since it is the only one which the Riches of the World, if they were mine, should purchase of me. —O it is that which you must part with, to bestow all the rest! Can Leonora, or rather will she doubt longer? —Let me then whisper it in her Ears,—It is your Name, Madam. It is by parting with that, by your Condescension to be for ever mine, which must at once prevent me from being the most miserable, and will render me the happiest of Mankind.' Leonora, covered with Blushes, and with as angry a Look as she could possibly put on, told him, 'that had she suspected what his Declaration would have been, he should not have decoyed her from her Company; that he had so surprized and frighted her, that she begged him to convey her back as quick as possible;' which he, trembling very near as much as herself, did.

'More Fool he,' cried Slipslop, 'it is a sign he knew very little of our *Sect*.' 'Truly, Madam,' said Adams, 'I think you are in the right, I should have insisted to know a piece of her Mind, when I had car-ried matters so far.' But Mrs. Grave-airs desired the Lady to omit all such fulsome Stuff in her Story; for that it made her sick.

Well then, Madam, to be as concise as possible, said the Lady, many Weeks had not pass'd after this Interview, before Horatio and Leonora were what they call on a good footing together. All

Ceremonies except the last were now over; the Writings were now drawn,[3] and every thing was in the utmost forwardness preparative to the putting Horatio in possession of all his Wishes. I will, if you please, repeat you a Letter from each of them which I have got by heart, and which will give you no small Idea of their Passion on both sides.

Mrs. Grave-airs objected to hearing these Letters: but being put to the Vote, it was carried against her by all the rest in the Coach; Parson Adams contending for it with the utmost Vehemence.

HORATIO to LEONORA.

How vain, most adorable Creature, is the Pursuit of Pleasure in the Absence of an Object to which the Mind is entirely devoted, unless it have some Relation to that Object! I was last Night condemned to the Society of Men of Wit and Learning, which, however agreeable, it might have formerly been to me, now only gave me a Suspicion that they imputed my Absence in Conversation to the true Cause. For which Reason, when your Engagements forbid me the extatic Happiness of seeing you, I am always desirous to be alone; since my Sentiments for Leonora are so delicate, that I cannot bear the Apprehension of another's prying into those delightful Endearments with which the warm Imagination of a Lover will sometimes indulge him, and which I suspect my Eyes then betray. To fear this Discovery of our Thoughts, may perhaps appear too ridiculous a Nicety to Minds not susceptible of all the Tendernesses of this delicate Passion. And surely we shall suspect there are few such, when we consider that it requires every human Virtue to exert itself in its full Extent. Since the Beloved, whose Happiness it ultimately respects, may give us charming Opportunities of being brave in her Defence, generous to her Wants, compassionate to her Afflictions, grateful to her Kindness; and, in the same manner, of exercising every other Virtue, which he who would not do to any Degree, and that with the utmost Rapture, can never deserve the Name of a Lover: It is therefore with a View to the delicate Modesty of your Mind that I cultivate it so purely in my own; and it is that which will sufficiently suggest to you the Uneasiness I bear from those Liberties, which Men to whom the World allow Politeness, will sometimes give themselves on these Occasions.

---

[3] The necessary legal contracts had been prepared.

Can I tell you with what Eagerness I expect the Arrival of that blest Day, when I shall experience the Falshood of a common Assertion, that the greatest human Happiness consists in Hope? A Doctrine which no Person had ever stronger Reason to believe than myself at present, since none ever tasted such Bliss as fires my Bosom with the Thoughts of spending my future Days with such a Companion, and that every Action of my Life will have the glorious Satisfaction of conducing to your Happiness.

* LEONORA to HORATIO.

The Refinement of your Mind has been so evidently proved by every Word and Action ever since I had first the Pleasure of knowing you, that I thought it impossible my good Opinion of Horatio could have been heightened by any additional Proof of Merit. This very Thought was my Amusement when I received your last Letter, which, when I opened, I confess I was surprized to find the delicate Sentiments expressed there, so far exceeded what I thought could come even from you, (altho' I know all the generous Principles human Nature is capable of, are centered in your Breast) that Words cannot paint what I feel on the Reflection, that my Happiness shall be the ultimate End of all your Actions.

Oh Horatio! what a Life must that be, where the meanest domestic Cares are sweetened by the pleasing Consideration, that the Man on Earth who best deserves, and to whom you are most inclined to give your Affections, is to reap either Profit or Pleasure from all you do! In such a Case, Toils must be turned into Diversions, and nothing but the unavoidable Inconveniences of Life can make us remember that we are mortal.

If the solitary Turn of your Thoughts, and the Desire of keeping them undiscovered, makes even the Conversation of Men of Wit and Learning tedious to you, what anxious Hours must I spend who am condemned by Custom to the Conversation of Women, whose natural Curiosity leads them to pry into all my Thoughts, and whose Envy can never suffer Horatio's Heart to be possessed by any one without forcing them into malicious Designs against the Person who is so happy as to possess it: but indeed, if ever Envy can possibly have any Excuse, or even Alleviation, it is in this Case, where the Good is so great, that it must be equally natural to all to wish it for themselves, nor am I ashamed to own it: and to your Merit,

* *Fielding's note:* This Letter was written by a young Lady on reading the former.

Horatio, I am obliged, that prevents my being in that most uneasy of all the Situations I can figure in my Imagination, of being led by Inclination to love the Person whom my own Judgment forces me to condemn.

Matters were in so great forwardness between this fond Couple, that the Day was fixed for their Marriage, and was now within a Fortnight, when the Sessions chanced to be held for that County in a Town about twenty Miles Distance from that which is the Scene of our Story.[4] It seems it is usual for the young Gentlemen of the Bar to repair to these Sessions, not so much for the sake of Profit, as to shew their Parts, and learn the Law of the Justices of Peace: for which Purpose one of the wisest and gravest of all the Justices is appointed Speaker or Chairman, as they modestly call it, and he reads them a Lecture, and instructs them in the true Knowledge of the Law.

'You are here guilty of a little Mistake,' says Adams, 'which if you please I will correct; I have attended at one of these Quarter Sessions, where I observed the Counsel taught the Justices, instead of learning any thing of them.'

It is not very material, said the Lady. Hither repaired Horatio, who as he hoped by his Profession to advance his Fortune, which was not at present very large, for the sake of his dear Leonora, he resolved to spare no Pains, nor lose any Opportunity of improving or advancing himself in it.

The same Afternoon in which he left the Town, as Leonora stood at her Window, a Coach and Six passed by: which she declared to be the completest, genteelest, prettiest Equipage she ever saw; adding these remarkable Words, O I am in love with that Equipage! which, tho' her Friend Florella at that time did not greatly regard, she hath since remembered.

In the Evening an Assembly was held, which Leonora honoured with her Company: but intended to pay her dear Horatio the Compliment of refusing to dance in his Absence.

O Why have not Women as good Resolution to maintain their Vows, as they have often good Inclinations in making them!

The Gentleman who owned the Coach and Six came to the Assembly. His Clothes were as remarkably fine as his Equipage could be. He soon attracted the Eyes of the Company; all the Smarts,[5] all

---

[4] The Court of Quarter Sessions, the highest county court, met several times a year.

[5] "A fellow affecting briskness or vivacity" (Johnson).

the Silk Waistcoats with Silver and Gold Edgings, were eclipsed in an instant.

'Madam,' said Adams, 'if it be not impertinent, I should be glad to know how this Gentleman was drest.'

'Sir,' answered the Lady, 'I have been told, he had on a Cut-Velvet Coat of a Cinnamon Colour, lined with a Pink Satten, embroidered all over with Gold; his Waistcoat, which was Cloth of Silver, was embroidered with Gold likewise. I cannot be particular as to the rest of his Dress: but it was all in the French Fashion; for Bellarmine, (that was his Name) was just arrived from Paris.'

This fine Figure did not more entirely engage the Eyes of every Lady in the Assembly, than Leonora did his. He had scarce beheld her, but he stood motionless and fixed as a Statue, or at least would have done so, if Good-Breeding had permitted him. However, he carried it so far, before he had power to correct himself, that every Person in the Room easily discovered where his Admiration was settled. The other Ladies began to single out their former Partners, all perceiving who would be Bellarmine's Choice; which they however endeavoured, by all possible means, to prevent: Many of them saying to Lenora, 'O Madam, I suppose we shan't have the pleasure of seeing you dance To-Night;' and then crying out in Bellarmine's hearing, 'O Leonora will not dance, I assure you; her Partner is not here.' One maliciously attempted to prevent her, by sending a disagreeable Fellow to ask her, that so she might be obliged either to dance with him, or sit down: but this Scheme proved abortive.

Leonora saw herself admired by the fine Stranger, and envied by every Woman present. Her little Heart began to flutter within her, and her Head was agitated with a convulsive Motion; she seemed as if she would speak to several of her Acquaintance, but had nothing to say: for as she would not mention her present Triumph, so she could not disengage her Thoughts one Moment from the Contemplation of it: She had never tasted any thing like this Happiness. She had before known what it was to torment a single Woman; but to be hated and secretly cursed by a whole Assembly, was a Joy reserved for this blessed Moment. As this vast Profusion of Ecstasy had awaked her Understanding, so there was nothing so foolish as her Behaviour; she played a thousand childish Tricks, distorted her Person into several Shapes, and her Face into several Laughs, without any Reason. In a word, her Carriage was as absurd as her Desires, which were, to affect an Insensibility of the Stranger's

Admiration, and at the same time a Triumph from that Admiration over every Woman in the Room.

In this Temper of Mind, Bellarmine, having enquired who she was, advanced to her, and with a low Bow, begged the Honour of dancing with her, which she with as low a Curt'sy immediately granted. She danced with him all Night, and enjoyed perhaps the highest Pleasure, which she was capable of feeling.

At these Words, Adams fetched a deep Groan, which frighted the Ladies, who told him, 'they hoped he was not ill.' He answered, 'he groaned only for the Folly of Leonora.'

Leonora retired (continued the Lady) about Six in the Morning, but not to Rest. She tumbled and tossed in her Bed, with very short Intervals of Sleep, and those entirely filled with Dreams of the Equipage and fine Clothes she had seen, and the Balls, Operas and Ridottos,[6] which had been the Subject of their Conversation.

In the Afternoon Bellarmine, in the dear Coach and Six, came to wait on her. He was indeed charmed with her Person, and was, on Enquiry, so well pleased with the Circumstances of her Father, (for he himself, notwithstanding all this Finery, was not quite so rich as a *Croesus* or an *Attālus*. '*Attālus*,' says Mr. Adams: 'but pray how came you acquainted with these Names?'[7] The Lady smiled at the Question, and proceeded—He was so pleased, I say, that he resolved to make his Addresses to her directly. He did so accordingly, and that with so much Warmth and Briskness, that he quickly baffled her weak Repulses, and obliged the Lady to refer him to her Father, who, she knew, would quickly declare in favour of a Coach and Six.

Thus, what Horatio had by Sighs and Tears, Love and Tenderness, been so long obtaining, the *French-English* Bellarmine with Gaiety and Gallantry possessed himself of in an instant. In other words, what Modesty had employed a full Year in raising, Impudence demolished in twenty-four Hours.

Here Adams groaned a second time; but the Ladies, who began to smoke him,[8] took no Notice.

---

[6] "An entertainment or social assembly consisting of music and dancing" (*OED*).

[7] "Rich as Croesus" (a sixth-century BCE king of Lydia) was a common expression. The three Near Eastern monarchs named Attalus (third-second centuries BCE) "made themselves celebrated for their valuable libraries which they collected at Pergamus, and for the patronage which merit and virtue always found at their court" (Lemprière).

[8] "To smell out, find out" (Johnson): the ladies have come to think of Adams as too sympathetic, and so disregard his fervent responses to Leonora's tale.

From the Opening of the Assembly till the End of Bellarmine's Visit, Leonora had scarce once Thought of Horatio: but he now began, tho' an unwelcome Guest, to enter into her Mind. She wished she had seen the charming Bellarmine and his charming Equipage, before Matters had gone so far. 'Yet why (says she) should I wish to have seen him before; or what signifies it that I have seen him now? Is not Horatio my Lover? almost my Husband? Is he not as handsome, nay handsomer than Bellarmine? Aye, but Bellarmine is the genteeler and the finer Man; yes, that he must be allowed. Yes, yes, he is that certainly. But did not I no longer ago than yesterday love Horatio more than all the World? aye, but yesterday I had not seen Bellarmine. But doth not Horatio doat on me, and may he not in despair break his Heart if I abandon him? Well, and hath not Bellarmine a Heart to break too? Yes, but I promised Horatio first; but that was poor Bellarmine's Misfortune; if I had seen him first, I should certainly have preferred him. Did not the dear Creature prefer me to every Woman in the Assembly, when every She was laying out for him? When was it in Horatio's Power to give me such an Instance of Affection? Can he give me an Equipage or any of those Things which Bellarmine will make me Mistress of? How vast is the Difference between being the Wife of a poor Counsellor, and the Wife of one of Bellarmine's Fortune! If I marry Horatio, I shall triumph over no more than one Rival: but by marrying Bellarmine, I shall be the Envy of all my Acquaintance. What Happiness! —But can I suffer Horatio to die? for he hath sworn he cannot survive my Loss: but perhaps he may not die; if he should, can I prevent it? Must I sacrifice myself to him? besides, Bellarmine may be as miserable for me too.' She was thus arguing with herself, when some young Ladies called her to the Walks, and a little relieved her Anxiety for the present.

The next Morning Bellarmine breakfasted with her in presence of her Aunt, whom he sufficiently informed of his Passion for Leonora; he was no sooner withdrawn, than the old Lady began to advise her Niece on this Occasion. —'You see, Child (says she) what Fortune hath thrown in your way; and I hope you will not withstand your own Preferment.' Leonora sighing, 'begged her not to mention any such thing, when she knew her Engagements to Horatio.' 'Engagements to a Fig,' cry'd the Aunt; 'you should thank Heaven on your Knees, that you have it yet in your Power to break them. Will any Woman hesitate a Moment, whether she shall ride in a Coach, or walk on Foot all the Days of her Life? —But Bellarmine drives Six, and Horatio not even a Pair.' 'Yes, but, Madam, what will the World say?' answered Leonora; 'will not they condemn me?' 'The World is always on the side of Prudence,' cries the Aunt, 'and would surely condemn you, if you sacrificed your Interest to any Motive whatever. O, I know the World very well; and you shew your own Ignorance, my Dear, by your Objection. O' my Conscience! the World is wiser. I have lived longer in it than you; and I assure you there is not any thing worth our Regard besides Money: nor did I ever know one Person who married from other Considerations, who did not afterwards heartily repent it. Besides, if we examine the two Men, can you prefer a sneaking Fellow, who hath been bred at a University, to a fine Gentleman just come from his Travels? —All the World must allow Bellarmine to be a fine Gentleman, positively a fine Gentleman, and a handsome Man.—' 'Perhaps, Madam, I should not doubt, if I knew how to be handsomely off with the other.' 'O leave that to me,' says the Aunt. 'You know your Father hath not been acquainted with the Affair. Indeed, for my part, I thought it might do well enough, not dreaming of such an Offer: but I'll disengage you; leave me to give the Fellow an Answer. I warrant you shall have no farther Trouble.'

Leonora was at length satisfied with her Aunt's Reasoning; and, Bellarmine supping with her that Evening, it was agreed he should the next Morning go to her Father and propose the Match, which she consented should be consummated at his Return.

The Aunt retired soon after Supper; and the Lovers being left together, Bellarmine began in the following manner: 'Yes, Madam, this Coat I assure you was made at Paris, and I defy the best English Taylor even to imitate it. There is not one of them can cut, Madam, they can't cut. If you observe how this Skirt is turned, and this Sleeve, a clumsy English Rascal can do nothing like it. —Pray how do you like my Liveries?' Leonora answered, 'she thought them very pretty.' 'All French,' says he, 'I assure you, except the Great Coats; I never trust any thing more than a Great Coat to an Englishman; you know one must encourage our own People what one can, especially as, before I had a Place, I was in the Country Interest, he, he, he!⁹ but for myself, I would see the dirty Island at the bottom of the Sea, rather

---

⁹ A "place" is a government office (or sinecure); the "Country Interest" was the vocal opposition party, composed of Tories and disaffected Whigs, to the "Court" party of prime minister Robert Walpole (April 1721–February 1742). Among the Country party's charges against Walpole were an alleged neglect of England's woolen industry and the encouraging of Parisian fashions at court.

than wear a single Rag of English Work about me; and I am sure after you have made one Tour to Paris, you will be of the same Opinion with regard to your own Clothes. You can't conceive what an Addition a French Dress would be to your Beauty; I positively assure you, at the first Opera I saw since I came over, I mistook the English Ladies for Chamber-maids, he, he, he!'

With such sort of polite Discourse did the gay Bellarmine entertain his beloved Leonora, when the Door opened on a sudden, and Horatio entered the Room. Here 'tis impossible to express the Surprize of Leonora.

'Poor Woman,' says Mrs. Slipslop, 'what a terrible *Quandary* she must be in!' 'Not at all,' says Miss Grave-airs, 'such Sluts can never be confounded.' 'She must have them more than *Corinthian* Assurance,' said Adams, 'ay more than *Lais* herself.'[10]

A long Silence, continued the Lady, prevailed in the whole Company: If the familiar Entrance of Horatio struck the greatest Astonishment into Bellarmine, the unexpected Presence of Bellarmine no less surprized Horatio. At length Leonora collecting all the Spirits she was Mistress of, addressed herself to the latter, and pretended to wonder at the Reason of so late a Visit. 'I should, indeed,' answered he, 'have made some Apology for disturbing you at this Hour, had not my finding you in Company assured me I do not break in on your Repose.' Bellarmine rose from his Chair, traversed the Room in a Minuet Step, and humm'd an Opera Tune, while Horatio advancing to Leonora ask'd her in a Whisper, if that Gentleman was not a Relation of her's; to which she answered with a Smile, or rather Sneer, 'No, he is no Relation of mine yet;' adding, 'she could not guess the Meaning of his Question.' Horatio told her softly, 'it did not arise from Jealousy.' 'Jealousy!' cries she, 'I assure you;—it would be very strange in a common Acquaintance to give himself any of those Airs.' These Words a little surprized Horatio; but before he had time to answer, Bellarmine danced up to the Lady, and told her, 'he feared he interrupted some Business between her and the Gentleman.' 'I can have no Business,' said she, 'with the Gentleman, nor any other, which need be any Secret to you.'

'You'll pardon me,' said Horatio, 'if I desire to know who this Gentleman is, who is to be intrusted with all our Secrets.' 'You'll

[10] "Corinthian brass," originally a fine metal from the ancient Greek city of Corinth, referred in Fielding's day to "an impudent, brazen-faced fellow" (Grose). Lais was a legendary Corinthian prostitute of the fourth century BCE (Lemprière).

know soon enough," cries Leonora; 'but I can't guess what Secrets can ever pass between us of such mighty Consequence.' 'No Madam!' cries Horatio, 'I'm sure you would not have me understand you in earnest.' ''Tis indifferent to me,' says she, 'how you understand me; but I think so unseasonable a Visit as difficult to be understood at all, at least when People find one engaged, though one's Servants do not deny one, one may expect a well-bred Person should soon take the Hint.' 'Madam,' said Horatio, 'I did not imagine any Engagement with a Stranger, as it seems this Gentleman is, would have made my Visit impertinent, or that any such Ceremonies were to be preserved between Persons in our Situation.' 'Sure you are in a Dream,' says she, 'or would persuade me that I am in one. I know no pretensions a common Acquaintance can have to lay aside the Ceremonies of Good-Breeding.' 'Sure,' said he, 'I am in a Dream; for it is impossible I should be really esteemed a common Acquaintance by Leonora, after what has passed between us!' 'Passed between us! Do you intend to affront me before this Gentleman?' 'D—n me, affront the Lady,' says Bellarmine, cocking his Hat and strutting up to Horatio, 'does any Man dare affront this Lady before me, d—n me?' 'Harkee, Sir,' says Horatio, 'I would advise you to lay aside that fierce Air; for I am mightily deceived, if this Lady has not a violent Desire to get your Worship a good Drubbing.' 'Sir,' said Bellarmine, 'I have the Honour to be her Protector, and d—n me, if I understand your Meaning.' 'Sir,' answered Horatio, 'she is rather your Protectress: but give yourself no more Airs, for you see I am prepared for you,' (shaking his Whip at him.) 'Oh! *Serviteur tres humble*,' says Bellarmine, '*Je vous entend parfaitment bien*.'[11] At which time the Aunt, who had heard of Horatio's Visit, entered the Room, and soon satisfied all his Doubts. She convinced him that he was never more awake in his Life, and that nothing more extraordinary had happened in his three days Absence, than a small Alteration in the Affections of Leonora; who now burst into Tears, and wondered what Reason she had given him to use her in so barbarous a manner. Horatio desired Bellarmine to withdraw with him: but the Ladies prevented it, by laying violent Hands on the latter; upon which, the former took his Leave without any great Ceremony, and departed, leaving the Lady with his Rival to consult for his Safety, which Leonora feared her Indiscretion might have endangered: but the Aunt comforted her with Assurances, that

---

[11] French for "[your] very humble servant. I understand you perfectly well."

Horatio would not venture his Person against so accomplished a Cavalier as Bellarmine, and that being a Lawyer, he would seek Revenge in his own way, and the most they had to apprehend from him was an Action.[12]

They at length therefore agreed to permit Bellarmine to retire to his Lodgings, having first settled all Matters relating to the Journey which he was to undertake in the Morning, and their Preparations for the Nuptials at his return.

But alas! as wife Men have observed, the Seat of Valour is not the Countenance; and many a grave and plain Man, will, on a just Provocation, betake himself to that mischievous Metal, cold Iron; while Men of a fiercer Brow, and sometimes with that Emblem of Courage, a Cockade, will more prudently decline it.

Leonora was waked in the Morning, from a Visionary Coach and Six, with the dismal Account, that Bellarmine was run through the Body by Horatio; that he lay languishing at an Inn, and the Surgeons had declared the Wound mortal. She immediately leap'd out of the Bed, danced about the Room in a frantic manner, tore her Hair and beat her Breast in all the Agonies of Despair; in which sad Condition her Aunt, who likewise arose at the News, found her. The good old Lady applied her utmost Art to comfort her Niece. She told her, 'while there was Life, there was Hope: but that if he should die, her Affliction would be of no service to Bellarmine, and would only expose herself, which might probably keep her some time without any future Offer; that as Matters had happened, her wisest way would be to think no more of Bellarmine, but to endeavour to regain the affections of Horatio.' 'Speak not to me,' cry'd the disconsolate Leonora; 'is it not owing to me, that poor Bellarmine has lost his Life? have not these cursed Charms' (at which Words she looked stedfastly in the Glass) 'been the Ruin of the most charming Man of this Age? Can I ever bear to contemplate my own Face again?' (with her Eyes still fixed on the Glass.) 'Am I not the Murderess of the finest Gentleman? No other Woman in the Town could have made any Impression on him.' 'Never think of Things past,' cries the Aunt, 'think of regaining the affections of Horatio.' 'What Reason,' said the Niece, 'have I to hope he would forgive me? No, I have lost him as well as the other, and it was your wicked Advice which was the Occasion of all; you seduced me, contrary to my Inclinations, to abandon poor Horatio,' at which Words she

[12] Lawsuit.

burst into Tears; 'you prevailed upon me, whether I would or no, to give up my Affections for him; had it not been for you, Bellarmine never would have entered into my Thoughts; had not his Addresses been backed by your Persuasions, they never would have made any Impression on me; I should have defied all the Fortune and Equipage in the World; but it was you, it was you, who got the better of my Youth and Simplicity, and forced me to lose my dear Horatio for ever.'

The Aunt was almost borne down with this Torrent of Words; she however rallied all the Strength she could, and drawing her Mouth up in a Purse, began: 'I am not surprized, Niece, at this Ingratitude. Those who advise young Women for their Interest, must always expect such a Return: I am convinced my Brother will thank me for breaking off your Match with Horatio at any Rate.' 'That may not be in your power yet,' answered Leonora; 'tho' it is very ungrateful in you to desire or attempt it, after the Presents you have received from him.' (For indeed true it is, that many Presents, and some pretty valuable ones, had passed from Horatio to the old Lady: but as true it is, that Bellarmine when he breakfasted with her and her Niece, had complimented her with a Brilliant from his Finger, of much greater Value than all she had touched of the other.)

The Aunt's Gall was on float to reply, when a Servant brought a Letter into the Room; which Leonora, hearing it came from Bellarmine, with great Eagerness opened, and read as follows:

> Most Divine Creature,
>   The Wound which I fear you have heard I received from my Rival, is not like to be so fatal as those shot into my Heart, which have been fired from your Eyes, *tout-brilliant*. Those are the only Cannons by which I am to fall: for my Surgeon gives me Hopes of being soon able to attend your *Ruelle*; till when, unless you would do me an Honour which I have scarce the *Hardiesse* to think of,[13] your Absence will be the greatest Anguish which can be felt by,
>
>   MADAM,
>   Avec tout le respecte in the World,
>   Your most Obedient, most Absolute
>   Devoté,
>   BELLARMINE'

---

[13] Bellarmine's three French phrases mean, respectively, "all shining," "a morning reception in a fashionable lady's bedchamber," and "boldness." The phrases in his salutation mean "with all the respect" and "devoted [person]."

As soon as Leonora perceived such Hopes of Bellarmine's Recovery, and that the Gossip Fame had, according to Custom, so enlarged his Danger, she presently abandoned all further Thoughts of Horatio, and was soon reconciled to her Aunt, who received her again into Favour, with a more Christian Forgiveness than we generally meet with. Indeed it is possible she might be a little alarmed at the Hints which her Niece had given her concerning the Presents. She might apprehend such Rumours, should they get abroad, might injure a Reputation, which by frequenting Church twice a day, and preserving the utmost Rigour and Strictness in her Countenance and Behaviour for many Years, she had established.

Leonora's Passion returned now for Bellarmine with greater Force after its small Relaxation than ever. She proposed to her Aunt to make him a Visit in his Confinement, which the old Lady, with great and commendable Prudence, advised her to decline: 'For,' says she, 'should any Accident intervene to prevent your intended Match, too forward a Behaviour with this Lover may injure you in the Eyes of others. Every Woman, till she is married, ought to consider of and provide against the Possibility of the Affair's breaking off.' Leonora said, 'she should be indifferent to whatever might happen in such a Case: for she had now so absolutely placed her Affections on this dear Man (so she called him) that, if it was her Misfortune to lose him, she should for ever abandon all Thoughts of Mankind.' She therefore resolved to visit him, notwithstanding all the prudent Advice of her Aunt to the contrary, and that very Afternoon executed her Resolution.

The Lady was proceeding in her Story, when the Coach drove into the Inn where the Company were to dine, sorely to the Dissatisfaction of Mr. Adams, whose Ears were the most hungry Part about him; he being, as the Reader may perhaps guess, of an insatiable Curiosity, and heartily desirous of hearing the End of this Amour, tho' he professed he could scarce with Success to a Lady of so inconstant a Disposition.

CHAP. V.

A dreadful Quarrel which happened at the Inn where the Company dined, with its bloody Consequences to Mr. Adams.

As soon as the Passengers had alighted from the Coach, Mr. Adams, as was his Custom, made directly to the Kitchin, where he found

Joseph sitting by the Fire, and the Hostess anointing his Leg: for the Horse which Mr. Adams had borrowed of his Clerk, had so violent a Propensity to kneeling, that one would have thought it had been his Trade as well as his Master's: Nor would he always give any notice of such his Intention; he was often found on his Knees, when the Rider least expected it. This Foible, however, was of no great Inconvenience to the Parson, who was accustomed to it, and, as his Legs almost touched the Ground when he bestrode the Beast, had but little way to fall and threw himself forward on such Occasions with so much Dexterity, that he never received any Mischief; the Horse and he frequently rolling many Paces Distance, and afterwards both getting up and meeting as good Friends as ever.

Poor Joseph, who had not been used to such kind of Cattle, tho' an excellent Horseman, did not so happily disengage himself: but falling with his Leg under the Beast, received a violent Contusion, to which the good Woman was, as we have said, applying a warm Hand, with some camphorated Spirits just at the time when the Parson entered the Kitchin.

He had scarce express'd his Concern for Joseph's Misfortune, before the Host likewise entered. He was by no means of Mr. Towwouse's gentle Disposition, and was indeed perfect Master of his House, and every thing in it but his Guests.

This surly Fellow, who always proportioned his Respect to the Appearance of a Traveller, from *God bless your Honour*, down to plain *Coming presently*, observing his Wife on her Knees to a Footman, cried out, without considering his Circumstances, 'What a Pox is the Woman about? why don't you mind the Company in the Coach? Go and ask them what they will have for Dinner?' 'My Dear,' says she, 'you know they can have nothing but what is at the Fire, which will be ready presently; and really the poor young Man's Leg is very much bruised.' At which Words, she fell to chafing more violently than before: the Bell then happening to ring, he damn'd his Wife, and bid her go in to the Company, and not stand rubbing there all Day: for he did not believe the young Fellow's Leg was so bad as he pretended; and if it was, within twenty Miles he would find a Surgeon to cut it off. Upon these Words, Adams fetched two Strides across the Room; and snapping his Fingers over his Head, muttered aloud, He would excommunicate such a Wretch for a Farthing: for he believed the Devil had more Humanity. These Words occasioned a Dialogue between Adams and the Host, in which there were two or three sharp Replies, till Joseph bade the latter know how to behave himself to his Betters. At which the Host (having first strictly surveyed Adams) scornfully repeating the word *Betters*, flew into a Rage, and telling Joseph he was as able to walk out of his House as he had been to walk into it, offered to lay violent Hands on him; which perceiving, Adams dealt him so sound a Compliment over his Face with his Fist, that the Blood immediately gushed out of his Nose in a Stream. The Host being unwilling to be out-done in Courtesy, especially by a Person of Adams's Figure, returned the Favour with so much Gratitude, that the Parson's Nostrils likewise began to look a little redder than usual. Upon which he again assailed his Antagonist, and with another stroke laid him sprawling on the Floor.

The Hostess, who was a better Wife than so surly a Husband deserved, seeing her Husband all bloody and stretched along, hastened presently to his Assistance, or rather to revenge the Blow which, to all appearance, was the last he would ever receive; when, lo! a Pan full of Hog's-Blood, which unluckily stood on the Dresser,[1] presented itself first to her Hands. She seized it in her Fury, and without any Reflection discharged it into the Parson's Face, and with so good an Aim, that much the greater part first saluting his Countenance, and trickled thence in so large a Current down his Beard, and over his Garments, that a more horrible Spectacle was hardly to be seen, or even imagined. All which was perceived by Mrs. Slipslop, who entered the Kitchin at that Instant. This good Gentlewoman, not being of a Temper so extremely cool and patient as perhaps was required to ask many Questions on this Occasion, flew with great Impetuosity at the Hostess's Cap, which, together with some of her Hair, she plucked from her Head in a Moment, giving her at the same time several hearty Cuffs in the Face, which, by frequent Practice on the inferiour Servants, she had learned an excellent Knack of delivering with a good Grace. Poor Joseph could hardly rise from his Chair; the Parson was employed in wiping the Blood from his Eyes, which had intirely blinded him, and the Landlord was but just beginning to stir, whilst Mrs. Slipslop holding down the Landlady's Face with her Left Hand, made so dextrous a use of her Right, that the poor Woman began to roar in a Key, which alarmed all the Company in the Inn.

There happened to be in the Inn at this time, besides the Ladies who arrived in the Stage-Coach, the two Gentlemen who were present

[1] "The bench in a kitchen on which meat is drest or prepared for the table" (Johnson).

at Mr. Tow-wouse's when Joseph was detained for his Horse's Meat, and whom we have before mentioned to have stopt at the Alehouse with Adams. There was likewise a Gentleman just returned from his Travels to Italy; all whom the horrid Outcry of Murder presently brought into the Kitchin, where the several Combatants were found in the Postures already described.

It was now no Difficulty to put an end to the Fray, the Conquerors being satisfied with the Vengeance they had taken, and the Conquered having no Appetite to renew the Fight. The principal Figure, and which engaged the Eyes of all, was Adams, who was all over covered with Blood, which the whole Company concluded to be his own; and consequently imagined him no longer for this World. But the Host, who had now recovered from his Blow, and was risen from the Ground, soon delivered them from this Apprehension, by damning his Wife for wasting the Hog's Puddings,[2] and telling her all would have been very well if she had not intermeddled like a B— as she was; adding he was very glad the Gentlewoman had paid her, tho' not half what she deserved. The poor Woman had indeed fared much the worst, having, besides the unmerciful Cuffs received, lost a Quantity of Hair which Mrs. Slipslop in Triumph held in her left Hand.

The Traveller, addressing himself to Miss Grave-airs, desired her not to be frighten'd: for here had been only a little Boxing, which he said to their *Disgracia* the English were *accustomata* to: Adding; it must be however a Sight somewhat strange to him, who was just come from Italy, the Italians not being addicted to the *Cuffardo*, but *Bastonza*, says he.[3] He then went up to Adams, and telling him he looked like the Ghost of Othello, bid him *not shake his gory Locks at him, for he could not say he did it*.[4] Adams very innocently answered, *Sir, I am far from accusing you*. He then returned to the Lady, and cried, 'find the bloody Gentleman is *uno insipido del nullo senso. Damnata di me*, if I have seen such a *spectaculo* on my way from *Viterbo*.'[5]

One of the Gentlemen having learnt from the Host the Occasion of this Bustle, and being assured by him that Adams had struck

---

[2] Hog's blood was used in "black pudding," "a kind of sausage made of blood and suet, sometimes with the addition of flour or meal" (*OED*).

[3] The traveler's phrases are chiefly Italianized English: "disgrace," "accustomed," "[fisty-]cuffs"; *bastonza* is a corruption of the Italian *bastone* or cudgel.

[4] Misquoted from *Macbeth* 3.4.

[5] Viterbo is a city in the middle of the Italian peninsula.

the first Blow, whispered in his Ear: He'd warrant he would *recover*. 'Recover! Master,' said the Host, smiling: 'Yes, yes, I am not afraid of dying with a Blow or two neither; I am not such a Chicken as that.' 'Pugh!' said the Gentleman, 'I mean you will recover Damages in that Action which undoubtedly you intend to bring, as soon as a Writ can be returned from London; for you look like a Man of too much Spirit and Courage to suffer any one to beat you without bringing your Action against him: He must be a scandalous Fellow indeed, who would put up a Drubbing, whilst the Law is open to revenge it; besides, he hath drawn Blood from you and spoiled your Coat, and the Jury will give Damages for that too. An excellent new Coat upon my Word, and now not worth a Shilling!'

'I don't care,' continued he, 'to intermeddle in these Cases: but you have a Right to my Evidence; and if I am sworn, I must speak the Truth. I saw you sprawling on the Floor, and the Blood gushing from your Nostrils. You may take your own Opinion; but was I in your Circumstances, every Drop of my Blood should convey an Ounce of Gold into my Pocket: Remember I don't advise you to go to Law; but if your Jury were Christians, they must give swinging Damages, that's all.' 'Master,' cry'd the Host, scratching his Head, 'I have no Stomach to Law, I thank you. I have seen enough of that in the Parish, where two of my Neighbours have been at Law about a House, 'till they have both lawed themselves into a Goal.'[6] At which Words he turned about, and began to enquire again after his Hog's Puddings; nor would it probably have been a sufficient Excuse for his Wife that she spilt them in his Defence, had not some Awe of the Company, especially of the Italian Traveller, who was a Person of great Dignity, with-held his Rage. Whilst one of the above-mentioned Gentlemen was employed, as we have seen him, on the behalf of the Landlord, the other was no less hearty on the side of Mr. Adams, whom he advised to bring his Action immediately. He said the Assault of the Wife was in Law the Assault of the Husband; for they were but one Person; and he was liable to pay Damages, which he said must be considerable, where so bloody a Disposition appeared. Adams answered, if it was true that they were but one Person, he had assaulted the Wife; for he was sorry to own he had struck the Husband the first Blow. 'I am sorry you own it too,' cries the Gentleman; 'for it could not possibly appear to the Court: for here was no Evidence present but the lame Man in the

---

[6] Alternative spelling for "gaol" or "jail."

Chair, whom I supposed to be your Friend, and would consequently say nothing but what made for you.' 'How, Sir,' says Adams, 'do you take me for a Villain, who would prosecute Revenge in cold Blood, and use unjustifiable Means to obtain it? If you knew me and my Order, I should think you affronted both.' At the word Order, the Gentleman stared, (for he was too bloody to be of any modern Order of Knights) and turning hastily about, said, 'Every Man knew his own Business.'

Matters being now composed, the Company retired to their several Apartments, the two Gentlemen congratulating each other on the Success of their good Offices, in procuring a perfect Reconciliation between the contending Parties; and the Traveller went to his Repast, crying, as the Italian Poet says,

> 'Je voi very well, que tutta e Pace;
> So send up Dinner, good Boniface.'[7]

The Coachman began now to grow importunate with his Passengers, whose Entrance into the Coach was retarded by Miss Grave-airs insisting, against the Remonstrances of all the rest, that she would not admit a Footman into the Coach; for poor Joseph was too lame to mount a Horse. A young Lady, who was, as it seems, an Earl's Grand-Daughter, begged it with almost Tears in her Eyes. Mr. Adams prayed, and Mrs. Slipslop scolded, but all to no Purpose. She said, 'she would not demean herself to ride with a Footman: that there were Waggons on the Road: that if the Master of the Coach desired it, she would pay for two Places: but would suffer no such Fellow to come in.' 'Madam,' says Slipslop, 'I am sure no one can refuse another coming into a Stage-Coach.' 'I don't know, Madam,' says the Lady, 'I am not much used to Stage-Coaches, I seldom travel in them.' 'That may be, Madam,' replied Slipslop, 'very good People do, and some People's Betters, for aught I know.' Miss Grave-airs said, 'some Folks might sometimes give their Tongues a Liberty, to some People that were their Betters, which did not become them: for her Part, she was not used to converse with Servants.' Slipslop returned, 'some People kept no Servants to converse with: for her part, she thanked Heaven she lived in a Family where there were a

---

[7] *Je voi* is close to the French "I see," and the following phrase is substandard Italian for "that all is peace." If the "Italian Poet" is Dante, then "Boniface" may refer in part to Pope Bonifacio VIII, whose politics he opposed; "Boniface" was also the name of an innkeeper in the Farquhar play *Beaux' Strategem* (1707).

great many; and had more under her own Command, than any paultry little Gentlewoman in the Kingdom.' Miss Grave-airs cry'd, 'she believed her Mistress would not encourage such Sauciness to her Betters.' 'My Betters,' says Slipslop, 'who is my Betters, pray?' 'I am your Betters,' answered Miss Grave-airs, 'and I'll acquaint your Mistress.' —At which Mrs. Slipslop laughed aloud, and told her, 'her Lady was one of the great Gentry, and such little paultry Gentle-women, as some Folks who travelled in Stage-Coaches, would not easily come at her.'

This smart Dialogue between some People, and some Folks, was going on at the Coach-Door, when a solemn Person riding into the Inn, and seeing Miss Grave-airs, immediately accosted her with 'Dear Child, how do you?' She presently answered, 'O! Papa, I am glad you have overtaken me.' 'So am I,' answered he: 'for one of our Coaches is just at hand; and there being room for you in it, you shall go no farther in the Stage, unless you desire it.' 'How can you imagine I should desire it?' says she; so bidding Slipslop, 'ride with her Fellow, if she pleased;' she took her Father by the Hand, who was just alighted, and walked with him into a Room.

Adams instantly asked the Coachman in a Whisper, if he knew who the Gentleman was? The Coachman answered, 'he was now a Gentleman, and kept his Horse and Man: but Times are altered, Master,' said he; 'I remember when he was no better born than myself.' 'Aye! Aye!' says Adams. 'My Father drove the Squire's Coach,' answered he, 'when that very Man rode Postilion: but he is now his Steward, and a great Gentleman.' Adams then snapped his Fingers, and cry'd, *he thought she was some such Trollop.*

Adams made haste to acquaint Mrs. Slipslop with this good News, as he imagined it; but it found a Reception different from what he expected. That prudent Gentlewoman, who despised the Anger of Miss Grave-airs, whilst she conceived her the Daughter of a Gentleman of small Fortune, now she heard her Alliance with the upper Servants of a great Family in her Neighbourhood, began to fear her Interest with the Mistress. She wished she had not carried the Dispute so far, and began to think of endeavouring to reconcile herself to the young Lady before she left the Inn; when luckily the Scene at London, which the Reader can scarce have forgotten, pre-sented itself to her Mind, and comforted her with such Assurance, that she no longer apprehended any Enemy with her Mistress.

Every thing being now adjusted, the Company entered the Coach, which was just on its Departure, when one Lady recollected she had left her Fan, a second her Gloves, a third a Snuff-Box, and a fourth a Smelling-Bottle behind her; to find all which occasioned some Delay, and much Swearing, to the Coachman.

As soon as the Coach had left the Inn, the Women all together fell to the Character of Miss Grave-airs, whom one of them declared she had suspected to be some low Creature, from the Beginning of their Journey; and another affirmed had not even the Looks of a Gentlewoman; a third warranted she was no better than she should be, and turning to the Lady who had related the Story in the Coach, said, 'Did you ever hear, Madam, any thing so prudish as her Remarks? Well, deliver me from the Censoriousness of such a Prude.' The fourth added, 'O Madam! all these Creatures are censorious: but for my part, I wonder where the Wretch was bred; indeed I must own I have seldom conversed with these mean kind of People, so that it may appear stranger to me; but to refuse the general Desire of a whole Company, hath something in it so astonishing, that, for my Part, I own I should hardly believe it, if my own Ears had not been Witnesses to it.' 'Yes, and so handsome a young Fellow,' cries Slipslop: 'the Woman must have no Compassion in her, I believe she is more of a Turk than a Christian; I am certain if she had any Christian Woman's Blood in her Veins, the Sight of such a young Fellow must have warm'd it. Indeed there are some wretched, miserable old Objects, that turn one's Stomach; I should not wonder if she had refused such a one; I am as nice as herself, and should have cared no more than herself for the Company of *stinking* old Fellows: but hold up thy Head, Joseph, thou art none of those; and she who hath no *Compulsion* for thee is a *Myhummetman*, and I will maintain it.' This Conversation made Joseph uneasy, as well as the Ladies; who, perceiving the Spirits which Mrs. Slipslop was in, (for indeed she was not a Cup too low) began to fear the Consequence; one of them therefore desired the Lady to conclude the Story—'Aye Madam,' said Slipslop, 'I beg your Ladyship to give us that Story you *commencated* in the Morning,' which Request that well-bred Woman immediately complied with.

CHAP. VI.

Conclusion of the Unfortunate Jilt.

LEONORA having once broke through the Bounds which Custom and Modesty impose on her Sex, soon gave an unbridled Indulgence to her Passion. Her Visits to Bellarmine were more constant, as well as longer, than his Surgeon's; in a Word, she became absolutely his Nurse, made his Water-gruel, administred him his Medicines, and, notwithstanding the prudent Advice of her Aunt to the contrary, almost intirely resided in her wounded Lover's Apartment.

The Ladies of the Town began to take her Conduct under consideration; it was the chief Topic of Discourse at their Tea-Tables, and was very severely censured by the most part; especially by Lindamira, a Lady whose discreet and starch Carriage, together with a constant Attendance at Church three times a day, had utterly defeated many malicious Attacks on her own Reputation: for such was the Envy that Lindamira's Virtue had attracted, that, notwithstanding her own strict Behaviour and strict Enquiry into the Lives of others, she had not been able to escape being the Mark of some Arrows herself, which however did her no Injury; a Blessing perhaps owed by her to the Clergy, who were her chief male Companions, and with two or three of whom she had been barbarously and unjustly calumniated.

'Not so unjustly neither perhaps,' says Slipslop, 'for the Clergy are Men as well as other Folks.'

The extreme Delicacy of Lindamira's Virtue was cruelly hurt by these Freedoms which Leonora allowed herself: She said, 'it was an Affront to her Sex, that she did not imagine it consistent with any Woman's Honour to speak to the Creature, or to be seen in her Company; and that, for her part, she should always refuse to dance at an Assembly with her, for fear of Contamination, by taking her by the Hand.'

But to return to my Story: As soon as Bellarmine was recovered, which was somewhat within a Month from his receiving the Wound, he set out, according to Agreement, for Leonora's Father's, in order to propose the Match, and settle all Matters with him touching Settlements, and the like.

A little before his Arrival, the old Gentleman had received an Intimation of the Affair by the following Letter; which I can repeat *verbatim*, and which they say was written neither by Leonora nor her Aunt, tho' it was in a Woman's Hand. The Letter was in these Words:

SIR,
I am sorry to acquaint you that your Daughter Leonora hath acted one of the basest, as well as most simple[1] Parts with a

---

[1] Foolish.

young Gentleman to whom she had engaged herself, and whom
she hath (pardon the Word) jilted for another of inferiour Fortune, notwithstanding his superiour Figure. You may take what
Measures you please on this Occasion; I have performed what I
thought my Duty; as I have, tho' unknown to you, a very great
Respect for your Family.

The old Gentleman did not give himself the trouble to answer this
kind Epistle; nor did he take any notice of it after he had read it, 'till
he saw Bellarmine. He was, to say the Truth, one of those Fathers
who look on Children as an unhappy Consequence of their youth-
ful Pleasures; which as he would have been delighted not to have
had attended them, so was he no less pleased with any Opportunity
to rid himself of the Incumbrance. He passed, in the World's Language, as an exceeding good Father, being not only so rapacious as
to rob and plunder all Mankind to the utmost of his power, but
even to deny himself the Conveniencies and almost Necessaries of
Life; which his Neighbours attributed to a Desire of raising
immense Fortunes for his Children: but in fact it was not so; he
heaped up Money for its own sake only, and looked on his Children
as his Rivals, who were to enjoy his beloved Mistress, when he was
incapable of possessing her, and which he would have been much
more charmed with the Power of carrying along with him: nor had
his Children any other Security of being his Heirs, than that the
Law would constitute them such without a Will, and that he had
not Affection enough for any one living to take the trouble of
writing one.

To this Gentleman came Bellarmine on the Errand I have mentioned. His Person, his Equipage, his Family and his Estate, seemed
to the Father to make him an advantageous Match for his Daughter; he therefore very readily accepted his Proposals: but when Bellarmine imagined the principal Affair concluded, and began to open
the incidental Matters of Fortune; the old Gentleman presently
changed his Countenance, saying, 'he resolved never to marry his
Daughter on a *Smithfield* Match;[2] that whoever had Love for her to
take her, would, when he died, find her Share of his Fortune in his
Coffers: but he had seen such Examples of Undutifulness happen

---

[2] Smithfield, an area in the north-west part of London, was the site of a livestock
market. A "Smithfield bargain" is a phrase "used to express matches or marriages
contracted solely on the score of [financial] interest," in which "the fair sex are
bought and sold like the cattle in Smithfield" (Grose).

from the too early Generosity of Parents, that he had made a Vow never to part with a Shilling whilst he lived. He commended the Saying of Solomon,[3] *he that spareth the Rod, spoileth the Child*: but added, he might have likewise asserted, that *he that spareth the Purse, saveth the Child*.' He then ran into a Discourse on the Extravagance of the Youth of the Age; whence he launched into a Dissertation on Horses, and came at length to commend those Bellarmine drove. That fine Gentleman, who at another Season would have been well enough pleased to dwell a little on that Subject, was now very eager to resume the Circumstance of Fortune. He said, 'he had a very high Value for the young Lady, and would receive her with less than he would any other whatever; but that even his Love to her made some Regard to worldly Matters necessary; for it would be a most distracting Sight for him to see her, when he had the Honour to be her Husband, in less than a Coach and Six.' The old Gentleman answered, 'Four will do, Four will do'; and then took a turn from Horses to Extravagance, and from Extravagance to Horses, till he came round to the Equipage again, whither he was no sooner arrived, than Bellarmine brought him back to the Point; but all to no purpose; he made his Escape from that Subject in a Minute; till at last the Lover declared, 'that in the present Situation of his Affairs it was impossible for him, though he loved Leonora more than *tout le monde*,[4] to marry her without any Fortune.' To which the Father answered, 'he was sorry then his Daughter must lose so valuable a Match; that if he had an Inclination, at present it was not in his power to advance a Shilling: that he had had great Losses, and been at great Expences on Projects; which, though he had great Expectation from them, had yet produced him nothing: that he did not know what might happen hereafter, as on the Birth of a Son, or such Accident; but he would make no Promise, or enter into any Article: for he would not break his Vow for all the Daughters in the World.'

In short, Ladies, to keep you no longer in suspense; Bellarmine having tried every Argument and Persuasion which he could invent, and finding them all ineffectual, at length took his leave, but not in order to return to Leonora; he proceeded directly to his own Seat, whence, after a few Days stay, he returned to Paris, to the great Delight of the French, and the Honour of the English Nation.

[3] Proverbs 13:24.
[4] "All the world."

But as soon as he arrived at his home, he presently dispatched a Messenger with the following Epistle to Leonora.

Adorable and Charmante,
I am sorry to have the Honour to tell you I am not the *heureux*[5] Person destined for your divine Arms. Your Papa hath told me so with a *Politesse* not often seen on this side Paris. You may perhaps guess his manner of refusing me—*Ah mon Dieu!* You will certainly believe me, Madam, incapable of my self delivering this *triste* Message, which I intend to try the French Air to cure the Consequences of—*Ah jamais! Coeur! Ange —Au Diable!*—If your Papa obliges you to a Marriage, I hope we shall see you at Paris, till when the Wind that flows from thence will be the warmest *dans le Monde*: for it will consist almost entirely of my Sighs. *Adieu, ma Princesse! Ah L'Amour!*
BELLARMINE.

I shall not attempt, Ladies, to describe Leonora's Condition when she received this Letter. It is a Picture of Horror, which I should have as little Pleasure in drawing, as you in beholding. She immediately left the Place, where she was the Subject of Conversation and Ridicule, and retired to that House I shewed you, when I began the Story; where she hath ever since led a disconsolate Life, and deserves perhaps Pity for her Misfortunes more than our Censure, for a Behaviour to which the Artifices of her Aunt very probably contributed, and to which very young Women are often rendered too liable by that blameable Levity in the Education of our Sex.

'If I was inclined to pity her,' said a young Lady in the Coach, 'it would be for the Loss of Horatio; for I cannot discern any Misfortune in her missing such a Husband as Bellarmine.'

'Why I must own,' says Slipslop, 'the Gentleman was a little false-hearted: but *howsumever* it was hard to have two Lovers, and get never a Husband at all— But pray, Madam, what became of *Our-asho?*'

He remains, said the Lady, still unmarried, and hath applied himself so strictly to his Business, that he hath raised, I hear, a very considerable Fortune. And what is remarkable, they say, he never hears the name of Leonora without a Sigh, or hath ever uttered one Syllable to charge her with her ill Conduct towards him.

---

[5] "Happy." *Triste* is "sad." Bellarmine's string of interjections translate "Oh my God!" "Ah never! Heart! Angel! To the devil!"

CHAP. VII.

A very short Chapter, in which Parson Adams *went a great Way.*

THE Lady having finished her Story, received the Thanks of the
Company; and now Joseph putting his Head out of the Coach,
cried out, 'Never believe me, if yonder be not our Parson Adams
walking along without his Horse.' 'On my Word, and so he is,' says
Slipslop; 'and as sure as Two-pence, he hath left him behind at the
Inn.' Indeed, true it is, the Parson had exhibited a fresh Instance of
his Absence of Mind: for he was so pleased with having got Joseph
into the Coach, that he never once thought of the Beast in the
Stable; and finding his Legs as nimble as he desired, he sallied out
brandishing a Crabstick, and had kept on before the Coach, mend-
ing and slackening his Pace occasionally, so that he had never been
much more or less than a Quarter of a Mile distant from it.

Mrs. Slipslop desired the Coachman to overtake him, which he
attempted, but in vain: for the faster he drove, the faster ran the
Parson, often crying out, *Aye aye, catch me if you can*: till at length
the Coachman swore he would as soon attempt to drive after a
Greyhound; and giving the Parson two or three hearty Curses, he
cry'd, 'Softly, softly Boys,' to his Horses, which the civil Beasts
immediately obeyed.

But we will be more courteous to our Reader than he was to
Mrs. Slipslop; and leaving the Coach and its Company to pursue
their Journey, we will carry our Reader on after Parson Adams,
who stretched on without once looking behind him; till having left
the Coach full three Miles in his Rear, he came to a Place, where, by
keeping the extremest Track to the Right, it was just barely possible
for a human Creature to miss his Way. This Track however did he
keep, as indeed he had a wonderful Capacity at these kinds of bare
Possibilities; and travelling in it about three Miles over the Plain, he
arrived at the Summit of a Hill, whence looking a great way backwards, and perceiving no Coach in Sight, he sat himself down on
the Turf, and pulling out his *Æschylus* determined to wait here for
its Arrival.

He had not sat long here, before a Gun going off very near a
little startled him; he looked up, and saw a Gentleman within a
hundred Paces taking up a Partridge, which he had just shot.

Adams stood up, and presented a Figure to the Gentleman
which would have moved Laughter in many; for his Cassock had

just again fallen down below his great Coat, that is to say, it reached his Knees; whereas, the Skirts of his great Coat descended no lower than half way down his Thighs: but the Gentleman's Mirth gave way to his Surprize, at beholding such a Personage in such a Place.

Adams advancing to the Gentleman, told him he hoped he had good Sport; to which the other answered, very little. 'I see, Sir,' says Adams, 'you have smote one Partridge:' to which the Sportsman made no Reply, but proceeded to charge his Piece.

Whilst the Gun was charging, Adams remained in Silence, which he at last broke, by observing that it was a delightful Evening. The Gentleman, who had at first sight conceived a very distasteful Opinion of the Parson, began, on perceiving a Book in his Hand, and smoking likewise the Information of the Cassock, to change his Thoughts, and made a small Advance to Conversation on his side, by saying, *Sir, I suppose you are not one of these Parts?*

Adams immediately told him, No; that he was a Traveller, and invited by the Beauty of the Evening and the Place to repose a little, and amuse himself with reading. 'I may as well repose myself too,' said the Sportsman; 'for I have been out this whole Afternoon, and the Devil a Bird have I seen 'till I came hither.'

'Perhaps then the Game is not very plenty hereabouts,' cries Adams. 'No, Sir,' said the Gentleman, 'the Soldiers, who are quartered in the Neighbourhood, have killed it all.' 'It is very probable,' cries Adams; 'for Shooting is their Profession.' 'Ay, shooting the Game,' answered the other, 'but I don't see they are so forward to shoot our Enemies. I don't like that Affair of Carthagena;[1] if I had been there, I believe I should have done otherguess Things, d—n me; what's a Man's Life when his Country demands it? a Man who won't sacrifice his Life for his Country, deserves to be hanged, d—n me.' Which Words he spoke with so violent a Gesture, so loud a Voice, so strong an Accent, and so fierce a Countenance, that he might have frightened a Captain of Trained-Bands[2] at the Head of his Company; but Mr. Adams was not greatly subject to Fear: he

---

[1] A Spanish stronghold in the Caribbean, which English warships attempted but failed to take in March and April of 1741, during the war with Spain (1739–48), initially called the War of Jenkins' Ear. The war took its name from Robert Jenkins, captain of the ship Rebecca, who claimed Spanish coast guards in the Caribbean had cut off his ear in 1731.

[2] Civilian militia.

told him intrepidly that he very much approved his Virtue, but disliked his Swearing, and begged him not to addict himself to so bad a Custom, without which he said he might fight as bravely as Achilles did. Indeed he was charm'd with this Discourse; he told the Gentleman he would willingly have gone many Miles to have met a Man of his generous Way of thinking; that if he pleased to sit down, he should be greatly delighted to commune with him: for tho' he was a Clergyman, he would himself be ready, if thereto called, to lay down his Life for his Country.

The Gentleman sat down, and Adams by him; and then the latter began, as in the following Chapter, a Discourse which we have placed by itself, as it is not only the most curious in this, but perhaps in any other Book.

CHAP. VIII.

A notable Dissertation by Mr. Abraham Adams; *wherein that Gentleman appears in a political Light.*

'I do assure you, Sir,' says he, taking the Gentleman by the Hand, 'I am heartily glad to meet with a Man of your Kidney: for tho' I am a poor Parson, I will be bold to say, I am an honest Man, and would not do an ill Thing to be made a Bishop: Nay, tho' it hath not fallen in my way to offer so noble a Sacrifice, I have not been without Opportunities of suffering for the Sake of my Conscience, I thank Heaven for them; for I have had Relations, tho' I say it, who made some Figure in the World; particularly a Nephew, who was a Shop-keeper, and an Alderman of a Corporation.[1] He was a good Lad, and was under my Care when a Boy, and I believe would do what I bid him to his dying Day. Indeed, it looks like extreme Vanity in me, to affect being a Man of such Consequence, as to have so great an Interest in an Alderman; but others have thought so too, as mani-festly appeared by the Rector, whose Curate I formerly was, send-ing for me on the Approach of an Election, and telling me, if I expected to continue in his Cure, that I must bring my Nephew to vote for one Colonel Courtley, a Gentleman whom I had never heard Tidings of 'till that Instant. I told the Rector, I had no power over my Nephew's Vote, (God forgive me for such Prevarication!)

---

[1] Town or borough government.

that I supposed he would give it according to his Conscience, that I would by no means endeavour to influence him to give it otherwise. He told me it was in vain to equivocate; that he knew I had already spoke to him in favour of Esquire Fickle my Neighbour, and indeed it was true I had: for it was at a Season when the *Church was in Danger*,[2] and when all good Men expected they knew not what would happen to us all. I then answered boldly, If he thought I had given my Promise, he affronted me, in proposing any Breach of it. Not to be prolix: I persevered, and so did my Nephew, in the Esquire's Interest, who was chose chiefly through his Means; and so I lost my Curacy. Well, Sir, but do you think the Esquire ever mentioned a Word of the Church? *Ne verbum quidem, ut ita dicam*;[3] within two Years he got a Place, and hath ever since lived in London; where I have been informed, (but G— forbid I should believe that) that he never so much as goeth to Church. I remained, Sir, a considerable Time without any Cure, and lived a full Month on one Funeral Sermon, which I preached on the Indisposition of a Clergyman: but this by the Bye. At last, when Mr. Fickle got his Place, Colonel Courtly stood again; and who should make Interest for him, but Mr. Fickle himself? That very identical Mr. Fickle, who had formerly told me, the Colonel was an Enemy to both the Church and State, had the Confidence to sollicite my Nephew for him, and the Colonel himself offered me to make me Chaplain to his Regiment, which I refused in favour of Sir Oliver Hearty, who told us, he would sacrifice every thing to his Country: and I believe he would, except his Hunting, which he stuck so close to, that in five Years together he went but twice up to Parliament; and one of those Times, I have been told, never was within sight of the House. However, he was a worthy Man, and the best Friend I ever had: for by his Interest with a Bishop he got me replaced into my Curacy, and gave me eight Pounds out of his own Pocket to buy me a Gown and Cassock, and furnish my House. He had our Interest while he lived, which was not many Years. On his Death, I had fresh Applications made to me; for all the World knew the Interest I had in my

---

[2] "The Church in Danger" was a slogan associated with Henry Sacheverell (1674–1724), a preacher who gave two famous sermons in 1709 charging the Whig ministry with a failure to protect the interests of the Church of England. It became a rallying cry for "high Churchmen" who opposed toleration of dissenting Protestant sects, or any detraction from the authority of the established Church.

[3] "Not even a word, if I may say so."

good Nephew, who now was a leading Man in the Corporation; and Sir Thomas Booby buying the Estate which had been Sir Oliver's, proposed himself a Candidate. He was then a young Gentleman just come from his Travels; and it did me good to hear him discourse on Affairs, which for my Part I knew nothing of. If I had been Master of a thousand Votes, he should have had them all. I engaged my Nephew in his Interest and he was elected, and a very fine Parliament-Man he was. They tell me he made Speeches of an Hour long; and I have been told very fine ones: but he could never persuade the Parliament to be of his Opinion. —*Non omnia possumus omnes*.[4] He promised me a Living, poor Man; and I believe I should have had it, but an Accident happened; which was, that my Lady had promised it before, unknown to him. This indeed I never heard till afterwards: for my Nephew, who died about a Month before the Incumbent, always told me I might be assured of it. Since that Time, Sir Thomas, poor Man, had always so much Business, that he never could find Leisure to see me. I believe it was partly my Lady's fault too: who did not think my Dress good enough for the Gentry at her Table. However, I must do him the Justice to say, he never was ungrateful; and I have always found his Kitchin, and his Cellar too, open to me; many a time after Service on a *Sunday*, for I preach at four Churches, have I recruited my Spirits with a Glass of his Ale. Since my Nephew's Death the Corporation is in other hands; and I am not a Man of that Consequence I was formerly. I have now no longer any Talents to lay out in the Service of my Country; and to whom nothing is given, of him can nothing be required. However, on all proper Seasons, such as the Approach of an Election, I throw a suitable Dash or two into my Sermons; which I have the Pleasure to hear is not disagreeable to Sir Thomas, and the other honest Gentlemen my Neighbours, who have all promised me these five Years, to procure an Ordination for a Son of mine, who is now near thirty, hath an infinite Stock of Learning, and is, I thank Heaven, of an unexceptionable Life; tho', as he was never at an University, the Bishop refuses to ordain him. Too much Care cannot indeed be taken in admitting any to the sacred Office; tho' I hope he will never act so as to be a Disgrace to any Order: but will serve his God and his Country to the utmost of his Power, as I have endeavoured to do before him; nay, and will lay down his Life

---

[4] "We cannot all do all" (Virgil, *Eclogues* 8.63); one of Fielding's favorite Latin tags, it reappears frequently in *Tom Jones*.

whenever called to that Purpose. I am sure I have educated him in those Principles; so that I have acquitted my Duty, and shall have nothing to answer for on that account: but I do not distrust him; for he is a good Boy; and, if Providence should throw it in his way to be of much consequence in a public Light, as his Father once was; I can answer for him, he will use his Talents as honestly as I have done.'

CHAP. IX.

In which the Gentleman descants on Bravery and heroic Virtue, 'till an unlucky Accident puts an end to the Discourse.

THE Gentleman highly commended Mr. Adams for his good Resolutions, and told him, 'he hoped his Son would tread in his Steps;' adding, 'that if he would not die for his Country, he would not be worthy to live in it. I'd make no more of shooting a Man that would not die for his Country, than—

Sir,' said he, 'I have disinherited a Nephew who is in the Army, because he would not exchange his Commission, and go to the West-Indies.[1] I believe the Rascal is a Coward, tho' he pretends to be in Love forsooth. I would have all such Fellows hanged, Sir, I would have them hanged.' Adams answered, 'that would be too severe: That Men did not make themselves; and if Fear had too much Ascendance in the Mind, the Man was rather to be pitied than abhorred: That Reason and Time might teach him to subdue it.' He said, 'a Man might be a Coward at one time, and brave at another. Homer,' says he, 'who so well understood and copied Nature, hath taught us this Lesson; for Paris fights, and Hector runs away:[2] nay, we have a mighty Instance of this in the History of later Ages, no longer ago than the 705th Year of Rome, when the Great Pompey, who had won so many Battles, and been honoured with so many Triumphs, and of whose Valour several Authors, especially Cicero and Paterculus, have formed such Elogiums; this very Pompey left the Battle of Pharsalia before he had lost it, and retreated to his Tent, where he sat like the most pusillanimous Rascal in a Fit of

---

[1] That is, to fight against Spain in the War of Jenkins' Ear.

[2] In the *Iliad*, Paris, although he is sometimes berated for cowardice, fights fiercely against Diomedes (Book 11); conversely, the great warrior Hector finally flees from Achilles (Book 22). Adams draws his next example from Julius Caesar's triumph over Pompey at the battle of Pharsalia (48 BCE).

Despair, and yielded a Victory, which was to determine the Empire
of the World, to Caesar. I am not much travelled in the History of
modern Times, that is to say, these last thousand Years: but those
who are, can, I make no question, furnish you with parallel
Instances.' He concluded therefore, that had he taken any such
hasty Resolutions against his Nephew, he hoped he would consider
better, and retract them. The Gentleman answered with great
Warmth, and talked much of Courage and his Country, 'till perceiving it grew late, he asked Adams, 'what Place he intended for that
Night?' He told him, 'he waited there for the Stage-Coach.' 'The
Stage-Coach! Sir,' said the Gentleman, 'they are all past by long
ago. You may see the last yourself almost three Miles before us.'
'I protest and so they are,' cries Adams, 'then I must make haste and
follow them.' The Gentleman told him, 'he would hardly be able to
overtake them; and that if he did not know his Way, he would be in
danger of losing himself on the Downs; for it would be presently
dark; and he might ramble about all Night, and perhaps find himself farther from his Journey's End in the Morning than he was
now.' He advised him therefore to accompany him to his House,
which was very little out of his Way, assuring him, 'that he would
find some Country-Fellow in his Parish, who would conduct him
for Sixpence to the City where he was going.' Adams accepted this
Proposal, and on they travelled, the Gentleman renewing his Discourse on Courage, and the Infamy of not being ready at all times
to sacrifice our Lives to our Country. Night overtook them much
about the same time as they arrived near some Bushes: whence, on a
sudden, they heard the most violent Shrieks imaginable in a female
Voice. Adams offered to snatch the Gun out of his Companion's
Hand. 'What are you doing?' said he. 'Doing!" says Adams, 'I am
hastening to the Assistance of the poor Creature whom some Villains are murdering.' 'You are not mad enough, I hope,' says the
Gentleman, trembling: 'Do you consider this Gun is only charged
with Shot, and that the Robbers are most probably furnished with
Pistols loaded with Bullets? This is no Business of ours; let us make
as much haste as possible out of the way, or we may fall into their
Hands ourselves.' The Shrieks now encreasing, Adams made no
Answer, but snapt his Fingers, and brandishing his Crabstick, made
directly to the Place whence the Voice issued; and the Man of
Courage made as much Expedition towards his own Home, whither
he escaped in a very short time without once looking behind him:
where we will leave him, to contemplate his own Bravery, and to

censure the want of it in others; and return to the good Adams, who, on coming up to the Place whence the Noise proceeded, found a Woman struggling with a Man, who had thrown her on the Ground, and had almost overpowered her. The great Abilities of Mr. Adams were not necessary to have formed a right Judgment of this Affair on the first sight. He did not therefore want the Entreaties of the poor Wretch to assist her; but lifting up his Crabstick, he immediately levelled a Blow at that Part of the Ravisher's Head, where, according to the Opinion of the Ancients, the Brains of some Persons are deposited, and which he had undoubtedly let forth, had not Nature, (who, as wise Men have observed, equips all Creatures with what is most expedient for them) taken a provident Care, (as she always doth with those she intends for Encounters) to make this part of the Head three times as thick as those of ordinary Men, who are designed to exercise Talents which are vulgarly called rational, and for whom as Brains are necessary, she is obliged to leave some room for them in the Cavity of the Skull: whereas, those Ingredients being entirely useless to Persons of the heroic Calling, she hath an Opportunity of thickening the Bone, so as to make it less subject to any Impression, or liable to be cracked or broken; and indeed, in some who are predestined to the Command of Armies and Empires, she is supposed sometimes to make that Part perfectly solid.

As a Game-Cock, when engaged in amorous Toying with a Hen, if perchance he espies another Cock at hand, immediately quits his Female, and opposes himself to his Rival; so did the Ravisher, on the Information of the Crabstick, immediately leap from the Woman, and hastened to assail the Man. He had no Weapons but what Nature had furnished him with. However, he clenched his Fist, and presently darted it at that Part of Adam's Breast where the Heart is lodged. Adams staggered at the Violence of the Blow, when, throwing away his Staff, he likewise clenched that Fist which we have before commemorated, and would have discharged it full in the Breast of his Antagonist, had he not dexterously caught it with his left Hand, at the same time darting his Head, (which some modern Heroes, of the lower Class, use, like the Battering-Ram of the Ancients, for a Weapon of Offence; another Reason to admire the Cunningness of Nature, in composing it of those impenetrable Materials) dashing his Head, I say, into the Stomach of Adams, he tumbled him on his Back, and not having any regard to the Laws of Heroism, which would have restrained him from any farther Attack on his

Enemy 'till he was again on his Legs, he threw himself upon him, and laying hold on the Ground with his left Hand, he with his right belaboured the Body of Adams 'till he was weary, and indeed, 'till he concluded (to use the Language of fighting) *that he had done his Business*; or, in the Language of Poetry, that *he had sent him to the Shades below*; in plain English, *that he was dead.*

But Adams, who was no Chicken, and could bear a Drubbing as well as any boxing Champion in the Universe, lay still only to watch his Opportunity; and now perceiving his Antagonist to pant with his Labours, he exerted his utmost Force at once, and with such Success, that he overturned him, and became his Superior; when fixing one of his Knees in his Breast, he cried out in an exulting Voice, *It is my turn now*: and after a few Minutes constant Application, he gave him so dextrous a Blow just under his Chin, that the Fellow no longer retained any Motion, and Adams began to fear he had struck him once too often; for he often asserted, 'he should be concerned to have the Blood of even the Wicked upon him.'

Adams got up, and called aloud to the young Woman,—'Be of good cheer, Damsel, said he, you are no longer in danger of your Ravisher, who, I am terribly afraid, lies dead at my Feet; but God forgive me what I have done in defence of Innocence.' The poor Wretch, who had been some time in recovering Strength enough to rise, and had afterwards, during the Engagement, stood trembling, being disabled by Fear, even from running away, hearing her Champion was victorious, came up to him, but not without Apprehensions, even of her Deliverer; which, however, she was soon relieved from, by his courteous Behaviour and gentle Words. They were both standing by the Body, which lay Motionless on the Ground, and which Adams wished to see stir much more than the Woman did, when he earnestly begged her to tell him 'by what Misfortune she came, at such a time of Night, into so lonely a Place?' She acquainted him, 'she was travelling towards London, and had accidentally met with the Person from whom he had delivered her, who told her he was likewise on his Journey to the same Place, and would keep her Company; an Offer which, suspecting no Harm, she had accepted; that he told her, they were at a small Distance from an Inn where she might take up her Lodging that Evening, and he would show her a nearer way to it than by following the Road. That if she had suspected him, (which she did not, he spoke so kindly to her,) being alone on these Downs in the dark, she had no human Means to avoid him; that therefore she put her whole Trust in Providence, and walk'd on, expecting every Moment to arrive at the Inn; when, on a sudden, being come to those Bushes, he desired her to stop, and after some rude Kisses, which she resisted, and some Entreaties, which she rejected, he laid violent Hands on her, and was attempting to execute his wicked Will, when, she thanked G—, he timely came up and prevented him.' Adams encouraged her for saying she had put her whole Trust in Providence, and told her 'He doubted not but Providence had sent him to her Deliverance, as a Reward for that Trust. He wished indeed he had not deprived the wicked Wretch of Life, but G—'s Will be done; he said, he hoped the Goodness of his Intention would excuse him in the next World, and he trusted in her Evidence to acquit him in this.' He was then silent, and began to consider with himself, whether it would be properer to make his Escape, or to deliver himself into the Hands of Justice; which Meditation ended, as the Reader will see in the next Chapter.

CHAP. X.

Giving an Account of the strange Catastrophe of the preceding Adventure, which drew poor Adams into fresh Calamities; and who the Woman was who owed the Preservation of her Chastity to his victorious Arm.

THE Silence of Adams, added to the Darkness of the Night and the Loneliness of the Place, struck dreadful Apprehensions into the poor Woman's Mind: She began to fear as great an Enemy in her Deliverer, as he had delivered her from; and as she had not Light enough to discover the Age of Adams, and the Benevolence visible in his Countenance, she suspected he had used her as some very honest Men have used their Country; and had rescued her out of the hands of one Rifler, in order to Rifle her himself. Such were the Suspicions she drew from his Silence: but indeed they were ill-grounded. He stood over his vanquished Enemy, wisely weighing in his Mind the Objections which might be made to either of these two Methods of proceeding mentioned in the last Chapter, his Judgment sometimes inclining to the one, and sometimes to the other; for both seemed to him so equally adviseable, and so equally dangerous, that probably he would have ended his Days, at least two or three of them, on that very Spot, before he had taken any Resolution: At length he lifted up his Eyes, and spied a Light at a Distance, to which he instantly addressed himself with *Heus tu, Traveller, heus tu!*[1] He presently heard several Voices, and perceived the Light approaching toward him. The Persons who attended the Light began some to laugh, others to sing, and others to hollow, at which the Woman testified some Fear (for she had concealed her Suspicions of the Parson himself,) but Adams said, 'Be of good Cheer, Damsel, and repose thy Trust in the same Providence, which hath hitherto protected thee, and never will forsake the Innocent.' These People who now approached were no other, Reader, than a Set of young Fellows, who came to these Bushes in pursuit of a Diversion which they call *Bird-batting*. This, if thou art ignorant of it (as perhaps if thou hast never travelled beyond Kensington, Islington, Hackney, or the Borough,[2] thou mayst be) I will inform thee, is performed by holding a large Clap-Net[3] before a Lantern, and at the same time beating the Bushes: for the Birds, when they are disturbed from their Places of Rest, or Roost, immediately make to the Light, and so are enticed within the Net. Adams immediately told them what had happened, and desired them, 'to hold the Lantern to the Face of the Man on the Ground, for he feared he had *smote* him fatally.' But indeed his Fears were frivolous; for the Fellow, tho' he had been stunned by the last Blow he received, had long since recovered his Senses, and finding himself quit of Adams, had listened attentively to the Discourse between him and the young Woman; for whose Departure he had patiently waited, that he might likewise withdraw himself, having no longer Hopes of succeeding in his Desires, which were moreover almost as well cooled by Mr. Adams, as they could have been by the young Woman herself, had he obtained his utmost Wish. This Fellow, who had a Readiness at improving any Accident, thought he might now play a better part than that of a dead Man; and accordingly, the Moment the Candle was held to his Face, he leapt up, and laying hold on Adams, cried out, 'No, Villain, I am not dead, though you and your wicked Whore might well think me so, after the barbarous Cruelties

---

[1] "Hey, you!" (Latin).

[2] The Borough of Southwark. In Fielding's day the places mentioned here were all suburbs or rural villages outside London; they have since been incorporated into the city.

[3] "A kind of net so constructed that it can be suddenly shut by pulling a string. Forms of it are used by fowlers, and by entomologists" (*OED*).

you have exercised on me. Gentlemen,' said he, 'you are luckily come to the Assistance of a poor Traveller, who would otherwise have been robbed and murdered by this vile Man and Woman, who led me hither out of my Way from the High-Road, and both falling on me have used me as you see.' Adams was going to answer, when one of the young Fellows cry'd, 'D—n them, let's carry them both before the Justice.' The poor woman began to tremble, and Adams lifted up his Voice, but in vain. Three or four of them laid Hands on him, and one holding the Lantern to his Face, they all agreed, *he had the most villainous Countenance* they ever beheld; and an Attorney's Clerk who was of the Company declared, *he was sure he had remembered him at the Bar.* As to the Woman, her Hair was dishevelled in the Struggle, and her Nose had bled, so that they could not perceive whether she was handsome or ugly: but they said her Fright plainly discovered her Guilt. And searching her Pockets, as they did those of Adams for Money, which the Fellow said he had lost, they found in her Pocket a Purse with some Gold in it, which abundantly convinced them, especially as the Fellow offered to swear to it. Mr. Adams was found to have no more than one Halfpenny about him. This the Clerk said, 'was a great Presumption that he was an old Offender, by cunningly giving all the Booty to the Woman.' To which all the rest readily assented.

This Accident promising them better Sport, than what they had proposed, they quitted their Intention of catching Birds, and unanimously resolved to proceed to the Justice with the Offenders. Being informed what a desperate Fellow Adams was, they tied his Hands behind him; and having hid their Nets among the Bushes, and the Lantern being carried before them, they placed the two Prisoners in their Front, and then began their March: Adams not only submitting patiently to his own Fate, but comforting and encouraging his Companion under her Sufferings.

Whilst they were on their way, the Clerk informed the rest, that this Adventure would prove a very beneficial one: for that they would be all entitled to their Proportions of 80£. for apprehending the Robbers. This occasioned a Contention concerning the Parts which they had severally borne in taking them; one insisting, he ought to have the greatest Share, for he had first laid his Hands on Adams; another claiming a superior Part, for having first held the Lantern to the Man's Face, on the Ground, by which, he said, 'the whole was discovered.' The Clerk claimed four fifths of the Reward, for having proposed to search the Prisoners; and likewise the carrying them before the Justice: he said indeed, 'in strict Justice he ought to have the whole.' These Claims, however, they at last consented to refer to a future Decision, but seem'd all to agree that the Clerk was intitled to a Moiety. They then debated what Money should be allotted to the young Fellow, who had been employed only in holding the Nets. He very modestly said, 'That he did not apprehend any large Proportion would fall to his Share; but hoped they would allow him something: he desired them to consider, that they had assigned their Nets to his Care, which prevented him from being as forward as any in laying hold of the Robbers, (for so these innocent People were called;) that if he had not occupied the Nets, some other must; concluding however, that he should be contented with the smallest Share imaginable, and should think that rather their Bounty than his Merit.' But they were all unanimous in excluding him from any Part whatever, the Clerk particularly swearing, 'if they gave him a Shilling, they might do what they pleased with the rest; for he would not concern himself with the Affair.' This Contention was so hot, and so totally engaged the Attention of all the Parties, that a dextrous nimble Thief, had he been in Mr. Adams's situation, would have taken care to have given the Justice no Trouble that Evening. Indeed it required not the Art of a *Shepherd*[4] to escape, especially as the Darkness of the Night would have so much befriended him: but Adams trusted rather to his Innocence than his Heels, and without thinking of Flight, which was easy, or Resistance (which was impossible, as there were six lusty young Fellows, besides the Villain himself, present) he walked with perfect Resignation the Way they thought proper to conduct him.

Adams frequently vented himself in Ejaculations during their Journey; at last poor Joseph Andrews occurring to his Mind, he could not refrain sighing forth his Name, which being heard by his Companion in Affliction, she cried, with some Vehemence, 'Sure I should know that Voice; you cannot certainly, Sir, be Mr. Abraham Adams?' 'Indeed Damsel,' says he, 'that is my Name; there is something also in your Voice, which persuades me I have heard it before.' 'La, Sir,' says she, 'don't you remember poor Fanny?' 'How Fanny!' answered Adams, 'indeed I very well remember you; what can have brought you hither?' 'I have told you Sir,' replied she, 'I was travelling towards London; but I thought you mentioned

---

[4] The thief Jack Sheppard (1702–24), famed for his jail-breaks.

Joseph Andrews, pray what is become of him?' 'I left him, Child, this Afternoon,' said Adams, 'in the Stage-Coach, in his way towards our Parish, whither he is going to see you.' 'To see me? La, Sir,' answered Fanny, 'sure you jeer me; what should he be going to see me for?' 'Can you ask that?' replied Adams. 'I hope Fanny you are not inconstant; I assure you he deserves much better of you.' 'La! Mr. Adams,' said she, 'what is Mr. Joseph to me? I am sure I never had any thing to say to him, but as one Fellow-Servant might to another.' 'I am sorry to hear this,' said Adams; 'a virtuous Passion for a young Man, is what no Woman need be ashamed of. You either do not tell me Truth, or you are false to a very worthy Man.' Adams then told her what had happened at the Inn, to which she listened very attentively; and a Sigh often escaped from her, notwithstanding her utmost Endeavours to the contrary, nor could she prevent herself from asking a thousand Questions, which would have assured any one but Adams, who never saw farther into People than they desired to let him, of the Truth of a Passion she endeavoured to conceal. Indeed the Fact was, that this poor Girl having heard of Joseph's Misfortune by some of the Servants belonging to that Coach, which we have formerly mentioned to have stopt at the Inn while the poor Youth was confined to his Bed, that instant abandoned the Cow she was milking, and taking with her a little Bundle of Clothes under her Arm, and all the Money she was worth in her own Purse, without consulting any one, immediately set forward, in pursuit of One, whom, notwithstanding her Shyness to the Parson, she loved with inexpressible Violence, though with the purest and most delicate Passion. This Shyness therefore, as we trust it will recommend her Character to all our Female Readers, and not greatly surprize such of our Males as are well acquainted with the younger part of the other Sex, we shall not give our selves any trouble to vindicate.

CHAP. XI.

What happened to them while before the Justice. A Chapter very full of Learning.

THEIR Fellow-Travellers were so engaged in the hot Dispute concerning the Division of the Reward for apprehending these innocent People, that they attended very little to their Discourse. They were now arrived at the Justice's House, and sent one of his Servants in to acquaint his Worship, that they had taken two Robbers, and brought them before him. The Justice, who was just returned from a Fox-Chace, and had not yet finished his Dinner, ordered them to carry the Prisoners into the Stable, whither they were attended by all the Servants in the House, and all the People of the Neighbour-hood, who flocked together to see them with as much Curiosity as if there was something uncommon to be seen, or that a Rogue did not look like other People.

The Justice being now in the height of his Mirth and his Cups, bethought himself of the Prisoners; and telling his Company he believed they should have good Sport in their Examination, he ordered them into his Presence. They had no sooner entered the Room, than he began to revile them, saying, 'that Robberies on the Highway were now grown so frequent, that People could not sleep safely in their Beds, and assured them they both should be made Examples of at the ensuing Assizes.' After he had gone on some time in this manner, he was reminded by his Clerk, 'that it would be proper to take the Deposition of the Witnesses against them.' Which he bid him do, and he would light his Pipe in the mean time. Whilst the Clerk was employed in writing down the Deposi-tions of the Fellow who had pretended to be robbed, the Justice employed himself in cracking Jests on poor Fanny, in which he was seconded by all the Company at Table. One asked, 'whether she was to be indicted for a *Highwayman?*' Another whispered in her Ear, 'if she had not provided herself a great Belly, he was at her service.'[1] A third said, 'he warranted she was a Relation of Turpin.'[2] To which one of the Company, a great Wit, shaking his Head, and then his Sides, answered, 'he believed she was nearer related to *Turpis;*' at which there was an universal Laugh. They were proceeding thus with the poor Girl, when somebody smoking the Cassock peeping forth from under the Great Coat of Adams, cried out, 'What have we here, a Parson?' 'How, Sirrah,' says the Justice, 'do you go a rob-bing in the Dress of a Clergyman? let me tell you, your Habit will not entitle you to the *Benefit of the Clergy.*'[3] 'Yes,' said the witty

[1] Pregnancy was a ground for postponing or commuting capital punishment, and thus a valuable asset for female offenders.

[2] Dick Turpin, a highwayman hung in 1739. *Turpis* is Latin for "wicked" or "dis-graceful" (cf. the English 'turpitude').

[3] Originally the exemption of Christian clerics from criminal prosecution in the secu-lar courts, "benefit of the clergy" was extended in first felony offenses to all those who could read; it was abolished in 1827.

Fellow, 'he will have one Benefit of Clergy, he will be exalted above the Heads of the People;' at which there was a second Laugh. And now the witty Spark, seeing his Jokes take, began to rise in Spirits; and, turning to Adams, challenged him to *cap* Verses,[4] and provoking him by giving the first Blow, he repeated,

Molle meum levibus cord est vilebile Telis.[5]

Upon which Adams, with a Look full of ineffable Contempt, told him, he deserved scourging for his Pronunciation. The witty Fellow answered, 'What do you deserve, Doctor, for not being able to answer the first time? Why I'll give you one you Blockhead—with an *S*.

Si licet, ut fulvum spectatur in igdibus haurum.

What can'st not with an *M* neither? Thou art a pretty Fellow for a Parson—. Why did'st not steal some of the Parson's Latin as well as his Gown?' Another at the Table then answered, 'if he had, you would have been too hard for him; I remember you at the College a very Devil at this Sport; I have seen you catch a fresh Man: for no body that knew you, would engage with you.' 'I have forgot those things now,' cried the Wit, 'I believe I could have done pretty well formerly. —Let's see, what did I end with—an *M* again—ay—

Mars, Bacchus, Apollo, virorum.[6]

I could have done it once.'—'Ah! Evil betide you, and so you can now,' said the other, 'no body in this County will undertake you.' Adams could hold no longer; 'Friend,' said he, 'I have a Boy

---

[4] "To name alternately verses beginning with a particular letter" (Johnson); here, to use the last letter of a quotation as the first letter of the next quotation.

[5] This, like with the wit's subsequent quotations, is a mangled version of an example used in William Lily's *A Short Introduction of Grammar* (London, 1720 ed.), the standard Latin textbook in England from its 1527 publication through the early nineteenth century. The wit here garbles (substituting *vilebile* for the correct *violabile*) a line from Ovid's *Heroides* 15.79 used to illustrate a principle of Latin meter (Lily, p. 205): "tender is my heart, and easily pierced by the light shaft" (Loeb Classical Library translation). His next quotation garbles Ovid, *Tristia* 1.5.25, "certainly [*scilicet*] as deep-yellow gold [*aurum*] is tested in fires [*ignibus*]," quoted in Lily, p. 170.

[6] From Lily: "*Propria quae maribus tribuuntur, mascula dicas: / Ut sunt Divorum; Mars, Bacchus, Apollo: virorum: / Ut Cato, Virgilius . . .*" (p. 76); "Proper names that are assigned to males you may call masculines, / As are those of Gods: Mars, Bacchus, Apollo; and of men, / Like Cato, Virgil . . ."

not above eight Years old, who would instruct thee, that the last
Verse runs thus:

Ut sunt Divorum, Mars, Bacchus, Apollo, virorum.'

'I'll hold thee a Guinea of that,' said the Wit, throwing the Money
on the Table. —'And I'll go your halves,' cries the other. 'Done,'
answered Adams; but upon applying to his Pocket, he was forced to
retract, and own he had no Money about him; which set them all a
laughing, and confirmed the Triumph of his Adversary, which was
not moderate, any more than the Approbation he met with from the
whole Company, who told Adams he must go a little longer to
School, before he attempted to attack that Gentleman in Latin.

The Clerk having finished the Depositions, as well of the Fellow
himself, as of those who apprehended the Prisoners, delivered them
to the Justice; who having sworn the several Witnesses, without
reading a Syllable, ordered his Clerk to make the *Mittimus*.[7]

Adams then said, 'he hoped he should not be condemned
unheard.' 'No, no,' cries the Justice, 'you will be asked what you
have to say for yourself, when you come on your Trial: we are not
trying you now; I shall only commit you to Goal: if you can prove
your Innocence at *Size*, you will be found *Ignoramus*,[8] and so no
Harm done.' 'Is it no Punishment, Sir, for an innocent Man to lie
several Months in Goal?' cries Adams: 'I beg you would at least
hear me before you sign the *Mittimus*.' 'What signifies all you can
say?' says the Justice, 'is it not here in black and white against you?
I must tell you, you are a very impertinent Fellow, to take up so
much of my time. —So make haste with his *Mittimus*.'

The Clerk now acquainted the Justice, that among other suspicious Things, as a Penknife, etc. found in Adams's Pocket, they had
discovered a Book written, as he apprehended, in Cyphers: for no
one could read a Word in it. 'Ay,' says the Justice, 'this fellow may be
more than a common Robber, he may be in a Plot against the Government.— Produce the Book.' Upon which the poor Manuscript of
Æschylus, which Adams had transcribed with his own Hand, was

---

[7] "We send" (Latin): a writ committing a suspect to jail.

[8] "Size" is the Justice's colloquial version of the "assizes," "the sessions held period-
ically in each county of England, for the purpose of administering civil and criminal
justice, by judges acting under certain special commissions" (*OED*). *Ignoramus*,
"we do not know" (Latin), is the writ delivered when a grand jury finds insufficient
evidence for prosecution.

brought forth; and the Justice looking at it, shook his Head, and turning to the Prisoner asked the meaning of these Cyphers. 'Cyphers!' answered Adams, 'it is a Manuscript of *Æschylus*.' 'Who? who?' said the Justice. Adams repeated, '*Æschylus*.' 'That is an outlandish Name,' cried the Clerk. 'A fictitious Name rather, I believe,' said the Justice. One of the Company declared it looked very much like Greek. 'Greek?' said the Justice, 'why 'tis all Writing.' 'Nay,' says the other, 'I don't positively say it is so: for it is a very long time since I have seen any Greek. There's one,' says he, turning to the Parson of the Parish, who was present, 'will tell us immediately.' The Parson taking up the Book, and putting on his Spectacles and Gravity together, muttered some Words to himself, and then pronounced aloud —'Ay indeed it is a Greek manuscript, a very fine piece of Antiquity. I make no doubt but it was stolen from the same Clergyman from whom the Rogue took the Cassock.' 'What did the Rascal mean by this *Æschylus*?' says the Justice. 'Pooh!' answered the Doctor with a contemptuous Grin, 'do you think that Fellow knows anything of this Book? *Æschylus!* ho! ho! ho! I see now what it is. —A Manuscript of one of the Fathers.[9] I know a Nobleman who would give a great deal of Money for such a Piece of Antiquity. —Ay, ay, Question and Answer. The Beginning is the Catechism in Greek. —Ay, —Ay,—*Pollaki toi*—What's your Name?'[10] 'Ay, what's your Name?' says the Justice to Adams, who answered, 'it is *Æschylus*, and I will maintain it.' —'O it is,' says the Justice, 'make Mr. *Æschylus* his *Mittimus*. I will teach you to banter me with a false Name.'

One of the Company having looked stedfastly at Adams asked him, 'if he did not know Lady Booby?' Upon which Adams presently calling him to mind, answered in a Rapture, 'O Squire, are you there? I believe you will inform his Worship I am innocent.' 'I can indeed say,' replied the Squire, 'that I am very much surprized to see you in this Situation;' and then addressing himself to the Justice, he said, 'Sir, I assure you Mr. Adams is a Clergyman as he appears, and a Gentleman of a very good Character. I wish you would enquire a little farther into this Affair; for I am convinced of his Innocence.' 'Nay,' says the Justice, 'if he is a Gentleman, and you are sure he is

---

[9] That is, the Fathers of the Church, "the early Christian writers; usually applied to those of the first five centuries" (*OED*).

[10] The Greek phrase quoted here actually means "often [to or for] you," and does not commence any catechism.

innocent, I don't desire to commit him, not I; I will commit the Woman by herself, and take your Bail for the Gentleman; look into the Book, Clerk, and see how it is to take Bail; come—and make the *Mittimus* for the Woman as fast as you can.' 'Sir,' cries Adams, 'I assure you she is as innocent as myself.' 'Perhaps,' said the Squire, 'there may be some Mistake; pray let us hear Mr. Adams's Relation.' 'With all my Heart,' answered the Justice, 'and give the Gentleman a Glass to whet his Whistle before he begins. I know how to behave myself to Gentlemen as well as another. No body can say I have committed a Gentleman since I have been in the Commission.' Adams then began the Narrative, in which, though he was very pro-lix, he was uninterrupted, unless by several *Hums* and *Ha's* of the Justice, and his Desire to repeat those Parts which seemed to him most material. When he had finished, the Justice, who, on what the Squire had said, believed every Syllable of his Story on his bare Affir-mation, notwithstanding the Depositions on Oath to the contrary, began to let loose several *Rogues and Rascals* against the Witness, whom he ordered to stand forth, but in vain: the said Witness, long since finding what Turn Matters were like to take, had privily with-drawn, without attending the Issue. The Justice now flew into a vio-lent Passion, and was hardly prevailed with not to commit the innocent Fellows, who had been imposed on as well as himself. He swore, 'they had best find out the Fellow who was guilty of Perjury, and bring him before him within two Days, or he would bind them all over to their good Behaviour.' They all promised to use their best Endeavours to that Purpose, and were dismissed. Then the Justice insisted, that Mr. Adams should sit down and take a Glass with him; and the Parson of the Parish delivered him back the Manuscript without saying a Word; nor would Adams, who plainly discerned his Ignorance, expose it. As for Fanny, she was, at her own Request, rec-ommended to the Care of a Maid-Servant of the House, who helped her to new dress, and clean herself.

The Company in the Parlour had not been long seated, before they were alarmed with a horrible Uproar from without, where the Persons who had apprehended Adams and Fanny, had been regal-ing, according to the Custom of the House, with the Justice's Strong Beer. These were all fallen together by the Ears, and were cuffing each other without any Mercy. The Justice himself sallied out, and with the Dignity of his Presence, soon put an End to the Fray. On his return into the Parlour, he reported, 'That the Occasion of the Quarrel, was no other than a Dispute, to whom, if Adams had been convicted, the greater Share of the Reward for apprehending him had belonged.' All the Company laughed at this, except Adams, who, taking his Pipe from his Mouth, fetched a deep Groan, and said, he was concerned to see so litigious a Temper in Men. That he remembered a Story something like it in one of the Parishes where his Cure lay: 'There was,' continued he, 'a Competition between three young Fellows for the Place of the Clerk, which I disposed of, to the best of my Abilities, according to Merit: that is, I gave it to him who had the happiest Knack at setting a Psalm. The Clerk was no sooner established in his Place than a Contention began between the two disappointed Candidates concerning their Excellence, each contending, on whom, had they two been the only Competitors, my Election would have fallen. This Dispute frequently disturbed the Congregation, and introduced a Discord into the Psalmody, 'till I was forced to silence them both. But alas, the litigious Spirit could not be stifled; and being no longer able to vent itself in singing, it now broke forth in fighting. It produced many Battles, (for they were very near a Match;) and, I believe, would have ended fatally, had not the Death of the Clerk given me an Opportunity to promote one of them to his Place; which presently put an end to the Dispute, and entirely reconciled the contending Parties.' Adams then proceeded to make some philosophical Observations on the Folly of growing warm in Disputes, in which neither Party is interested.[11] He then applied himself vigorously to smoaking; and a long Silence ensued, which was at length broken by the Justice; who began to sing forth his own Praises, and to value himself exceedingly on his nice Discernment in the Cause which had lately been before him. He was quickly interrupted by Mr. Adams, between whom and his Worship a Dispute now arose, whether he ought not, in strictness of Law, to have committed him, the said Adams; in which the latter maintained he ought to have been committed, and the Justice as vehemently held he ought not. This had most probably produced a Quarrel, (for both were very violent and positive in their Opinions) had not Fanny accidentally heard, that a young Fellow was going from the Justice's House to the very Inn where the Stage-Coach in which Joseph was, put up. Upon this News, she immediately sent for the Parson out of the Parlour. Adams, when he found her resolute to go, (tho' she would not own the Reason, but

---

[11] Has anything at stake.

pretended she could not bear to see the Faces of those who had suspected her of such a Crime) was as fully determined to go with her; he accordingly took leave of the Justice and Company, and so ended a Dispute, in which the Law seemed shamefully to intend to set a Magistrate and a Divine together by the Ears.

CHAP. XII.

A very delightful Adventure, as well to the Persons concerned as to the good-natur'd Reader.

ADAMS, Fanny, and the Guide, set out together, about one in the Morning, the Moon being then just risen. They had not gone above a Mile, before a most violent Storm of Rain obliged them to take Shelter in an Inn, or rather Alehouse; where Adams immediately procured himself a good Fire, a Toast and Ale, and a Pipe, and began to smoke with great Content, utterly forgetting every thing that had happened.

Fanny sat likewise down by the Fire; but was much more impatient at the Storm. She presently engaged the Eyes of the Host, his Wife, the Maid of the House, and the young Fellow who was their Guide; they all conceived they had never seen any thing half so handsome: and indeed, Reader, if thou art of an amorous Hue, I advise thee to skip over the next Paragraph; which, to render our History perfect, we are obliged to set down, humbly hoping, that we may escape the Fate of *Pygmalion:*[1] for if it should happen to us or to thee to be struck with this Picture, we should be perhaps in as helpless a Condition as *Narcissus*; and might say to ourselves, *Quod petis est nusquam.*[2] Or if the finest Features in it should set Lady —'s Image before our Eyes, we should be still in as bad Situation, and might say to our Desires, *Caelum ipsum petimus stultitia.*[3]

Fanny was now in the nineteenth Year of her Age; she was tall, and delicately shaped; but not one of those slender young Women, who seem rather intended to hang up in the Hall of an

---

[1] A legendary sculptor who fell in love with the statue of a woman he created (Ovid, *Metamorphoses* Book 10).

[2] Narcissus falls in love with his own reflection in *Metamorphoses* Book 3; the Latin quotation from 1. 433 explains his frustration: "what you seek is nowhere."

[3] Heaven itself we seek in our foolishness" (Horace, *Odes* 1.3.38).

Anatomist, than for any other Purpose. On the contrary she was so plump, that she seemed bursting through her tight Stays, especially in the Part which confined her swelling Breasts. Nor did her Hips want the Assistance of a Hoop to extend them. The exact Shape of her Arms denoted the Form of those Limbs which she concealed; and tho' they were a little redden'd by her Labour; yet if her Sleeve slipt above her Elbow, or her Handkerchief discovered any part of her Neck, a Whiteness appeared which the finest Italian Paint would be unable to reach. Her Hair was of a Chesnut Brown, and Nature had been extremely lavish to her of it, which she had cut, and on Sundays used to curl down her Neck in the modern Fashion. Her Forehead was high, her Eye-brows arched, and rather full than otherwise. Her Eyes black and sparkling; her Nose just inclining to the Roman; her Lips red and moist, and her Under-Lip, according to the Opinion of the Ladies, too pouting. Her Teeth were white, but not exactly even. The Small-Pox had left one only Mark on her Chin, which was so large, it might have been mistaken for a Dimple, had not her left Cheek produced one so near a Neighbour to it, that the former served only for a Foil to the latter. Her Complexion was fair, a little injured by the Sun, but overspread with such a Bloom, that the finest Ladies would have exchanged all their White for it: add to these a Countenance, in which tho' she was extremely bashful, a Sensibility appeared almost incredible; and a Sweetness, whenever she smiled, beyond either Imitation or Description. To conclude all, she had a natural Gentility, superior to the Acquisition of Art, and which surprized all who beheld her.

This lovely Creature was sitting by the Fire with Adams, when her Attention was suddenly engaged by a Voice from an inner Room, which sung the following Song:

The Song[4]

Say, Chloe, where must the Swain stray
Who is by thy Beauties undone,
To wash their Remembrance away,
To what distant Lethe must run?
The Wretch who is sentenc'd to die,
May escape, and leave Justice behind;

---

[4] A bawdy pastoral song. Cf. Fielding's poem "The Question" in his *Miscellanies* (1743).

From his Country perhaps he may fly:
But O can he fly from his Mind!

O Rapture! unthought of before,
To be thus of Chloe possest;
Nor she, nor no Tyrant's hard Power,
Her Image can tear from my Breast.
But felt not Narcissus more Joy,
With his Eyes he beheld his lov'd Charms?
Yet what he beheld, the fond Boy
More eagerly wish'd in his Arms.

How can it thy dear Image be,
Which fills thus my Bosom with Woe?
Can aught bear Resemblance to thee,
Which Grief and not Joy can bestow?
This Counterfeit snatch from my Heart,
Ye Pow'rs, tho' with Torment I rave,
Tho' mortal will prove the fell Smart,
I then shall find rest in my Grave.

Ah! see the dear Nymph o'er the Plain
Comes smiling and tripping along,
A thousand Loves dance in her Train;
The Graces around her all throng.
To meet her soft Zephyrus flies,
And wafts all the Sweets from the Flow'rs;
Ah Rogue! whilst he kisses her Eyes,
More Sweets from her Breath he devours.

My Soul, whilst I gaze, is on fire,
But her Looks were so tender and kind;
My Hope almost reach'd my Desire,
And left lame Despair far behind.
Transported with Madness I flew,
And eagerly seiz'd on my Bliss;
Her Bosom but half she withdrew,
But half she refus'd my fond Kiss.

Advances like these made me bold,
I whisper'd her, *Love,—we're alone,*
The rest let Immortals unfold,
No Language can tell but their own.
Ah! Chloe, expiring, I cry'd,
How long I thy Cruelty bore?
Ah! Strephon, she blushing reply'd,
You ne'er was so pressing before.

Adams had been ruminating all this Time on a Passage in *Æschylus*, without attending in the least to the Voice, tho' one of the most melodious that ever was heard; when casting his Eyes on Fanny, he cried out, 'Bless us, you look extremely pale.' 'Pale! Mr. Adams,' says she, 'O Jesus!' and fell backwards in her Chair. Adams jumped up, flung his *Æschylus* into the Fire, and fell a roaring to the People of the House for Help. He soon summoned every one into the Room, and the Songster among the rest: But, O Reader, when this Nightingale, who was no other than Joseph Andrews himself, saw his beloved Fanny in the Situation we have described her, canst thou conceive the Agitations of his Mind? If thou canst not, wave that Meditation to behold his Happiness, when, clasping her in his Arms, he found Life and Blood returning into her Cheeks; when he saw her open her beloved Eyes, and heard her with the softest Accent whisper, 'Are you Joseph Andrews?' 'Art thou my Fanny?' he answered eagerly, and pulling her to his Heart, he imprinted numberless Kisses on her Lips, without considering who were present.

If Prudes are offended at the Lusciousness of this Picture, they may take their Eyes off from it, and survey Parson Adams dancing about the Room in a Rapture of Joy. Some Philosophers may perhaps doubt, whether he was not the happiest of the three; for the Goodness of his Heart enjoyed the Blessings which were exulting in the Breasts of both the other two, together with his own.[5] But we shall leave such Disquisitions as too deep for us, to those who are building some favourite Hypotheses, which they will refuse no Metaphysical Rubbish to erect and support: for our Part, we give it clearly on the Side of Joseph, whose Happiness was not only greater than the Parson's, but of longer Duration: for as soon as the first Tumults of Adams's Rapture were over, he cast his Eyes towards the Fire, where *Æschylus* lay expiring; and immediately rescued the poor Remains, to wit, the Sheep-skin Covering of his dear Friend, who had been his inseparable Companion for upwards of thirty Years.

Fanny had no sooner perfectly recovered herself, than she began to restrain the Impetuosity of her Transports; and reflecting on what she had done and suffered in the Presence of so many, she was immediately covered with Confusion; and pushing Joseph gently from her, she begged him to be quiet: nor would admit of either Kiss

---

[5] The philosopher Fielding chiefly has in mind is the third earl of Shaftesbury, who argued that "the pleasures of sympathy" constitutes an essential part of human happiness: see Contexts, pp. 348–49.

or Embrace any longer. Then seeing Mrs. Slipslop she curt'sied, and offered to advance to her; but that high Woman would not return her Curt'sies; but casting her Eyes another way, immediately withdrew into another Room, muttering as she went, she wondered *who the Creature was.*

CHAP. XIII.

A Dissertation concerning high People and low People, with Mrs. Slipslop's Departure in no very good Temper of Mind, and the evil Plight in which she left Adams *and his Company.*

IT will doubtless seem extremely odd to many Readers, that Mrs. Slipslop, who had lived several Years in the same House with Fanny, should in a short Separation utterly forget her. And indeed the Truth is, that she remembered her very well. As we would not willingly therefore, that any Thing should appear unnatural in this our History, we will endeavour to explain the Reasons of her Conduct; nor do we doubt being able to satisfy the most curious Reader, that Mrs. Slipslop did not in the least deviate from the common Road in this Behaviour; and indeed, had she done otherwise, she must have descended below herself, and would have very justly been liable to Censure.

Be it known then, that the human Species are divided into two sorts of People, to wit, *High* People and *Low* People. As by High People, I would not be understood to mean Persons literally born higher in their Dimensions than the rest of the Species, nor metaphorically those of exalted Characters or Abilities; so by Low People I cannot be construed to intend the Reverse. High People signify no other than People of Fashion, and low People those of no Fashion. Now this word *Fashion* hath by long Use lost its original Meaning, from which at present it gives us a very different Idea: for I am deceived, if by Persons of Fashion, we do not generally include a Conception of Birth and Accomplishments superior to the Herd of Mankind; whereas in reality, nothing more was originally meant by a Person of Fashion, than a Person who drest himself in the Fashion of the Times; and the Word really and truly signifies no more at this Day. Now the World being thus divided into People of Fashion, and People of no Fashion, a fierce Contention arose between them, nor would those of one Party, to avoid Suspicion, be seen publicly to speak to those of the other, tho' they often held a very good Correspondence in private. In this Contention, it is difficult to say which Party succeeded: for whilst the People of Fashion seized several Places to their own Use, such as Courts, Assemblies, Operas, Balls, &c. the People of no Fashion, besides one Royal Place, called his Majesty's Bear-Garden, have been in constant Possession of all Hops,[1] Fairs, Revels, &c. Two Places have been agreed to be divided between them, namely the Church and the Play-House; where they segregate themselves from each other in a remarkable Manner: for as the People of Fashion exalt themselves at Church over the Heads of the People of no Fashion; so in the Play-House they abase themselves in the same Degree under their Feet.[2] This Distinction I have never met with any one able to account for: It is sufficient, that so far from looking on each other as Brethren in the Christian Language, they seem scarce to regard each other as of the same Species. This the Terms *strange Persons, People one does not know, the Creature, Wretches, Beasts, Brutes,* and many other Appellations evidently demonstrate; which Mrs. Slipslop having often heard her Mistress use, thought she had also a Right to use in her Turn: and perhaps she was not mistaken; for these two Parties, especially those bordering nearly on each other, to wit, the lowest of the High, and the highest of the Low, often change their Parties according to Place and Time; for those who are People of Fashion in one place, are often People of no Fashion in another. And with regard to Time, it may not be unpleasant to survey the Picture of Dependance like a kind of Ladder: as for instance; early in the Morning arises the Postillion, or some other Boy, which great Families, no more than great Ships, are without, and falls to brushing the Clothes, and cleaning the Shoes of John the Footman, who being drest himself, applies his Hands to the same Labours for Mr. Second-hand the Squire's Gentleman; the Gentleman in the like manner, a little later in the Day, attends the Squire; the Squire is no sooner equipped, than he attends the Levee of my Lord; which is no sooner over, than my Lord himself is seen at the Levee of the Favourite, who, after his Hour of Homage is at an End, appears himself to pay Homage to the Levee of his Sovereign. Nor is there,

---

[1] "A place where meaner people dance" (Johnson).

[2] In church, the gentry sat in enclosed pews elevated on a platform above the church floor; in the theater, they sat in boxes or in the pit, beneath the inexpensive seats of the upper gallery.

perhaps, in this whole Ladder of Dependance, any one Step at a greater Distance from the other, than the first from the second: so that to a Philosopher the Question might only seem, whether you would chuse to be a great Man at six in the Morning, or at two in the Afternoon. And yet there are scarce two of these, who do not think the least Familiarity with the Persons below them a Condescension, and if they were to go one Step farther, a Degradation.

And now, Reader, I hope thou wilt pardon this long Digression, which seemed to me necessary to vindicate the great Character of Mrs. Slipslop, from what low People, who have never seen high People, might think an Absurdity: but we who know them, must have daily found very high Persons know us in one Place and not in another, To-day, and not To-morrow; all which it is difficult to account for, otherwise than I have here endeavoured; and perhaps, if the Gods, according to the Opinion of some, made Men only to laugh at them, there is no part of our Behaviour which answers the End of our Creation better than this.

But to return to our History: Adams, who knew no more of all this than the Cat which sat on the Table, imagining Mrs. Slipslop's Memory had been much worse than it really was, followed her into the next Room, crying out, 'Madam Slipslop, here is one of your old Acquaintance: Do but see what a fine Woman she is grown since she left Lady Booby's Service.' 'I think I *reflect* something of her,' answered she with great Dignity, 'but I can't remember all the inferior Servants in our Family.' She then proceeded to satisfy Adams's Curiosity, by telling him, 'when she arrived at the Inn, she found a Chaise ready for her; that her Lady being expected very shortly in the Country, she was obliged to make the utmost Haste, and in *Commensuration* of Joseph's Lameness, she had taken him with her;' and lastly, 'that the excessive *Virulence* of the Storm had driven them into the House where he found them.' After which, she acquainted Adams with his having left his Horse, and exprest some Wonder at his having strayed so far out of his Way, and at meeting him, as she said, 'in the Company of that Wench, who she feared was no better than she should be.'

The Horse was no sooner put into Adams's Head, but he was immediately driven out by this Reflection on the Character of Fanny. He protested, 'he believed there was not a chaster Damsel in the Universe. I heartily wish, I heartily wish,' cry'd he, (snapping his Fingers) 'that all her Betters were as good.' He then proceeded to inform her of the Accident of their meeting; but when he came to mention the Circumstance of delivering her from the Rape, she said, 'she thought him properer for the Army than the Clergy: that it did not become a Clergyman to lay violent Hands on any one; that he should have rather prayed that she might be strengthened.' Adams said, 'he was very far from being ashamed of what he had done;' she replied, 'want of Shame was not the *Currycuristick* of a Clergyman.' This Dialogue might have probably grown warmer, had not Joseph opportunely entered the Room, to ask leave of Madam Slipslop to introduce Fanny: but she positively refused to admit any such Trollops; and told him, 'she would have been burnt, before she would have suffered him to get into a Chaise with her, if she had once *respected* him of having his Sluts way-laid on the Road for him;' adding, 'that Mr. Adams acted a very pretty Part, and she did not doubt but to see him a Bishop.' He made the best Bow he could, and cried out, 'I thank you, Madam, for that Right Reverend Appellation, which I shall take all honest Means to deserve.' 'Very honest Means,' returned she with a Sneer, 'to bring good People together.' At these Words, Adams took two or three Strides a-cross the Room, when the Coachman came to inform Mrs. Slipslop, 'that the Storm was over, and the Moon shone very bright.' She then sent for Joseph, who was sitting without with his Fanny, and would have had him gone with her: but he peremptorily refused to leave Fanny behind; which threw the good Woman into a violent Rage. She said, 'she would inform her Lady what Doings were carrying on, and did not doubt but she would rid the Parish of all such People;' and concluded a long Speech full of Bitterness and very hard Words, with some Reflections on the Clergy, not decent to repeat: at last finding Joseph unmoveable, she flung herself into the Chaise, casting a Look at Fanny as she went, not unlike that which Cleopatra gives Octavia in the Play.[3] To say the truth, she was most disagreeably disappointed by the Presence of Fanny; she had, from her first seeing Joseph at the Inn, conceived Hopes of something which might have been accomplished at an Alehouse as well as a Palace. Indeed it is probable Mr. Adams had rescued more than Fanny from the Danger of a Rape that Evening.

When the Chaise had carried off the enraged Slipslop; Adams, Joseph, and Fanny assembled over the Fire; where they had a great deal of innocent Chat, pretty enough; but as possibly it would not

[3] Cleopatra, the lover of Mark Antony, confronts Antony's wife Octavia in the third Act of Dryden, *All for Love* (1677).

be very entertaining to the Reader, we shall hasten to the Morning; only observing that none of them went to bed that Night. Adams, when he had smoked three Pipes, took a comfortable Nap in a great Chair, and left the Lovers, whose Eyes were too well employed to permit any Desire of shutting them, to enjoy by themselves, during some Hours, an Happiness which none of my Readers, who have never been in love, are capable of the least Conception of, tho' we had as many Tongues as Homer desired,[4] to describe it with, and which all true Lovers will represent to their own Minds without the least Assistance from us.

Let it suffice then to say, that Fanny, after a thousand Entreaties, at last gave up her whole Soul to Joseph, and almost fainting in his Arms, with a Sigh infinitely softer and sweeter too than any Arabian Breeze, she whispered to his Lips, which were then close to hers, 'O Joseph, you have won me; I will be yours for ever.' Joseph, having thanked her on his Knees, and embraced her with an Eagerness, which she now almost returned, leapt up in a Rapture, and awakened the Parson, earnestly begging him, 'that he would that Instant join their Hands together.' Adams rebuked him for his Request, and told him, 'he would by no means consent to any thing contrary to the Forms of the Church, that he had no Licence, nor indeed would he advise him to obtain one. That the Church had prescribed a Form, namely the Publication of Banns, with which all good Christians ought to comply, and to the Omission of which he attributed the many Miseries which befel great Folks in Marriage; concluding, *As many as are joined together otherwise than G—'s Word doth allow, are not joined together by G—, neither is their Matrimony lawful.'* Fanny agreed with the Parson saying to Joseph with a Blush, 'she assured him she would not consent to any such thing, and that she wondered at his offering it.' In which Resolution she was comforted, and commended by Adams; and Joseph was obliged to wait patiently till after the third Publication of the Banns, which however he obtained the Consent of Fanny, in the presence of Adams, to put in at their Arrival.

The Sun had been now risen some Hours, when Joseph, finding his Leg surprisingly recovered, proposed to walk forwards; but when they were all ready to set out, an Accident a little retarded

---

[4] In *Iliad* 2.489–92, Homer claims that he could not without the Muses' assistance name all the Greek soldiers on the fields of Troy "even if ten tongues were mine and ten mouths and a voice untiring."

them. This was no other than the Reckoning, which amounted to seven Shillings; no great Sum, if we consider the immense Quantity of Ale which Mr. Adams poured in. Indeed they had no Objection to the Reasonableness of the Bill, but many to the Probability of paying it; for the Fellow who had taken poor Fanny's Purse, had unluckily forgot to return it. So that the Account stood thus:

Mr. Adams and Company Dr.[5]	0 7 0
In Mr. Adams's Pocket,	0 0 6½
In Mr. Joseph's,	0 0 0
In Mrs. Fanny's,	0 0 0
Balance	0 6 5½

They stood silent some few Minutes, staring at each other, when Adams whipt out on his Toes, and asked the Hostess 'if there was no Clergyman in that Parish?' She answered, 'there was.' 'Is he wealthy?' replied he; to which she likewise answered in the Affirmative. Adams then snapping his Fingers returned overjoyed to his Companions, crying out, '*Heureka, Heureka;*'[6] which not being understood, he told them in plain *English*, 'they need give themselves no trouble; for he had a Brother in the Parish, who would defray the Reckoning, and that he would just step to his House and fetch the Money, and return to them instantly.'

CHAP. XIV.

An Interview between Parson Adams and Parson Trulliber.

PARSON Adams came to the House of Parson Trulliber, whom he found stript into his Waistcoat, with an Apron on, and a Pail in his Hand, just come from serving his Hogs; for Mr. Trulliber was a Parson on Sundays, but all the other six might more properly be called a Farmer. He occupied a small piece of Land of his own, besides which he rented a considerable deal more. His Wife milked his Cows, waited in his Dairy, and followed the Markets with Butter

---

[5] "Debtor." The columns are for pounds, shillings, and pence.

[6] "I have found it," usually rendered in English without aspiration, "Eureka": Archimedes' exclamation at discovering the principle of specific gravity, "hence *allusively*, an exulting exclamation at having made a discovery" (*OED*). The word appears in the first edition of *Joseph Andrews* in Greek characters; in the second edition, as "Eureka."

and Eggs. The Hogs fell chiefly to his Care, which he carefully waited on at home, and attended to Fairs; on which occasion he was liable to many Jokes, his own Size being with much Ale rendered little inferiour to that of the Beasts he sold. He was indeed one of the largest Men you should see, and could have acted the part of Sir John Falstaff without stuffing. Add to this, that the Rotundity of his Belly was considerably increased by the shortness of his Stature, his Shadow ascending very near as far in height when he lay on his Back, as when he stood on his Legs. His Voice was loud and hoarse, and his Accents extremely broad; to complete the whole, he had a Stateliness in his Gate, when he walked, not unlike that of a Goose, only he stalked slower.

Mr. Trulliber being informed that somebody wanted to speak with him, immediately slipt off his Apron, and clothed himself in an old Night-Gown, being the Dress in which he always saw his Company at home. His Wife, who informed him of Mr. Adams's Arrival, had made a small Mistake; for she had told her Husband, 'she believed he was a Man come for some of his Hogs.' This Supposition made Mr. Trulliber hasten with the utmost expedition to attend his Guest. He no sooner saw Adams, than not in the least doubting the cause of his Errand to be what his Wife had imagined, he told him, 'he was come in very good time; that he expected a Dealer that very Afternoon;' and added, 'they were all pure and fat, and upwards of 20 Score a-piece.'[1] Adams answered, 'he believed he did not know him.' 'Yes, yes,' cried Trulliber, 'I have seen you often at *Fair*; why, we have dealt before now mun, I warrant you; yes, yes,' cries he, 'I remember thy Face very well, but won't mention a Word more till you have seen them, tho' I have never sold thee a Flitch of such Bacon as is now in the Stye.' Upon which he laid violent Hands on Adams, and dragged him into the Hogs-Stye, which was indeed but two Steps from his Parlour Window. They were no sooner arrived there than he cry'd out, 'Do but handle them; step in, Friend, art welcome to handle them whether dost buy or no.' At which Words opening the Gate, he pushed Adams into the Pig-Stye, insisting on it, that he should handle them, before he would talk one Word with him. Adams, whose natural Complacence was beyond any artificial, was obliged to comply before he was suffered to explain himself; and laying hold on one of their Tails, the unruly Beast gave such a sudden Spring, that he threw

---

[1] That is, over 400 pounds each.

poor Adams all along in the Mire. Trulliber instead of assisting him to get up, burst into a Laughter, and entering the Stye, said to Adams with some contempt, *Why, dost not know how to handle a Hog?* and was going to lay hold of one himself; but Adams, who thought he had carried his Complacence far enough, was no sooner on his Legs, than he escaped out of the Reach of the Animals, and cried out, *nihil habeo cum Porcis:*[2] 'I am a Clergyman, Sir, and am not come to buy Hogs.' Trulliber answered, 'he was sorry for the Mistake; but that he must blame his Wife;' adding, 'she was a Fool, and always committed Blunders.' He then desired him to walk in and clean himself; that he would only fasten up the Stye and follow him. Adams desired leave to dry his Great Coat, Wig, and Hat by the Fire, which Trulliber granted. Mrs. Trulliber would have brought him a Bason of Water to wash his Face; but her Husband bid her be quiet like a Fool as she was, or she would commit more Blunders, and then directed Adams to the Pump. While Adams was thus employed, Trulliber conceiving no great Respect for the Appearance of his Guest, fastened the Parlour-Door, and now con-ducted him into the Kitchin; telling him, he believed a Cup of Drink would do him no Harm, and whispered his Wife to draw a little of the worst Ale. After a short Silence, Adams said, 'I fancy, Sir, you already perceive me to be a Clergyman.' 'Ay, ay,' cries Trulliber grinning; 'I perceive you have some Cassock; I will not venture to *caale* it a whole one.' Adams answered, 'it was indeed none of the best; but he had the Misfortune to tear it about ten Years ago in passing over a Stile.' Mrs. Trulliber returning with the Drink, told her Husband, 'she fancied the Gentleman was a Traveller, and that he would be glad to eat a bit.' Trulliber bid her 'hold her imperti-nent Tongue;' and asked her 'if Parsons used to travel without Horses?' adding, 'he supposed the Gentleman had none by his hav-ing no Boots on.' 'Yes, Sir, yes,' says Adams, 'I have a Horse, but I have left him behind me.' 'I am glad to hear you have one,' says Trubiller; 'for I assure you, I don't love to see Clergymen on Foot; it is not seemly nor suiting the Dignity of the Cloth.' Here Trulliber made a long Oration on the Dignity of the Cloth (or rather Gown) not much worth relating, till his Wife had spread the Table and set a Mess of Porridge on it for his Breakfast. He then said to Adams, 'I don't know, Friend, how you came to *caale* on me; however, as you are here, if you think proper to eat a Morsel, you may.' Adams

---

[2] "I have nothing [to do] with pigs."

accepted the Invitation, and the two Parsons sat down together, Mrs. Trulliber waiting behind her Husband's Chair, as was, it seems, her Custom. Trulliber eat heartily, but scarce put any thing in his Mouth without finding Fault with his Wife's Cookery. All which the poor Woman bore patiently. Indeed she was so absolute an Admirer of her Husband's Greatness and Importance, of which she had frequent Hints from his own Mouth, that she almost carried her Adoration to an opinion of his Infallibility. To say the Truth, the Parson had exercised her more ways than one; and the pious Woman had so well edified by her Husband's Sermons, that she had resolved to receive the bad things of this World together with the good. She had indeed been at first a little contentious; but he had long since got the better, partly by her love for *this,* partly by her fear of *that,* partly by her Religion, partly by the Respect he paid himself, and partly by that which he received from the Parish: She had, in short, absolutely submitted, and now worshipped her Husband as Sarah did Abraham, calling him (not Lord but) Master.[3] Whilst they were at Table, her Husband gave her a fresh Example of his Greatness; for as she had just delivered a Cup of Ale to Adams, he snatched it out of his Hand, and crying out, *I caal'd vurst,* swallowed down the Ale. Adams denied it; it was referred to the Wife, who tho' her Conscience was on the side of Adams, durst not give it against her Husband. Upon which he said, 'No, Sir, no, I should not have been so rude to have taken it from you, if you had *caal'd vurst;* but I'd have you know I'm a better Man than to suffer the best He in the Kingdom to drink before me in my own House, when I *caale vurst.'*

As soon as their Breakfast was ended, Adams began in the following Manner: 'I think, Sir, it is high time to inform you of the business of my Embassy. I am a Traveller, and am passing this way in company with two young People, a Lad and a Damsel, my Parishioners, towards my own Cure: we stopt at a House of Hospitality in the Parish, where they directed me to you, as having the Cure.'— 'Tho' I am but a Curate,' says Trulliber, 'I believe I am as warm[4] as the Vicar himself, or perhaps the Rector of the next Parish too; I believe I could buy them both.' 'Sir,' cries Adams, 'I rejoice thereat.

---

[3] Fielding alludes to 1 Peter 3:6, "even as Sara obeyed Abraham, calling him lord" (King James Version). The Greek word translated here as "lord," *kurios,* can also be translated "master."

[4] "Rich; in good circumstances" (Grose).

Now, Sir, my Business is, that we are by various Accidents stript of our Money, and are not able to pay our Reckoning, being seven Shillings. I therefore request you to assist me with the Loan of those seven Shillings, and also seven Shillings more, which peradventure I shall return to you; but if not, I am convinced you will joyfully embrace such an Opportunity of laying up a Treasure in a better Place than any this World affords.'

Suppose a Stranger, who entered the Chambers of a Lawyer, being imagined a Client, when the Lawyer was preparing his Palm for the Fee, should pull out a Writ against him. Suppose an Apothecary, at the Door of a Chariot containing some great Doctor of eminent Skill, should, instead of Directions to a Patient, present him with a Potion for himself. Suppose a Minister should, instead of a good round Sum, treat my Lord—or Sir—or Esq;—with a good Broomstick. Suppose a civil Companion, or a led Captain should, instead of Virtue, and Honour, and Beauty, and Parts, and Admiration, thunder Vice and Infamy, and Ugliness, and Folly, and Contempt, in his Patron's Ears. Suppose when a Tradesman first carries in his Bill the Man of Fashion should pay it; or suppose, if he did so, the Tradesman should abate what he had overcharged on the Supposition of waiting. In short—suppose what you will, you never can, nor will suppose any thing equal to the Astonishment which seized on Trulliber, as soon as Adams had ended his Speech. A while he rolled his Eyes in Silence, some times surveying Adams, then his Wife, then casting them on the Ground, then lifting them to Heaven. At last, he burst forth in the following Accents. 'Sir, I believe I know where to lay up my little Treasure as well as another; I thank G— if I am not so warm as some, I am content; that is a Blessing greater than Riches; and he to whom that is given need ask no more. To be content with a little is greater than to possess the World, which a Man may possess without being so. Lay up my Treasure! what matters where a Man's Treasure is, whose Heart is in the Scriptures? there is the Treasure of a Christian.' At these Words the Water ran from Adams's Eyes; and catching Trulliber by the Hand in a Rapture, 'Brother,' says he, 'Heavens bless the Accident by which I came to see you; I would have walked many a Mile to have communed with you, and, believe me, I will shortly pay you a second Visit: but my Friends, I fancy, by this time, wonder at my stay; so let me have the Money immediately.' Trulliber then put on a stern Look, and cried out, 'Thou dost not intend to rob me?' At which the Wife, bursting into Tears, fell on her Knees, and roared out, 'O dear Sir, for Heaven's sake don't rob my Master, we are but poor People.' 'Get up for a Fool as thou art, and go about thy Business,' said Trulliber, 'dost think the Man will venture his Life? he is a Beggar, and no Robber.' 'Very true indeed,' answered Adams. 'I wish, with all my Heart, the Tithing-Man[5] was here,' cries Trulliber, 'I would have thee punished as a Vagabond for thy Impudence. Fourteen Shillings indeed! I won't give thee a Farthing. I believe thou art no more a Clergyman than the Woman there, (pointing to his Wife) but if thou art, dost deserve to have thy Gown stript over thy Shoulders, for running about the Country in such a manner.' 'I forgive your Suspicions,' says Adams, 'but suppose I am not a Clergyman, I am nevertheless thy Brother; and thou, as a Christian, much more as a Clergyman, art obliged to relieve my Distress.' 'Dost preach to me?' replied Trulliber, 'dost pretend to instruct me in my Duty?' 'Ifacks, a good Story,' cries Mrs. Trulliber, 'to preach to my Master.' 'Silence, Woman,' cries Trulliber, 'I would have thee know, Friend, (addressing himself to Adams) I shall not learn my Duty from such as thee; I know what Charity is, better than to give to Vagabonds.' 'Besides, if we were inclined, the Poors Rate[6] obliges us to give so much Charity,' cries the Wife. —'Pugh! thou art a Fool. Poors Reate! hold thy Nonsense,' answered Trulliber, and then turning to Adams, he told him, he would give him nothing. 'I am sorry,' answered Adams, 'that you do know what Charity is, since you practise it no better; I must tell you, if you trust to your Knowledge for your Justification, you will find yourself deceived, though you should add Faith to it without good Works.' 'Fellow,' cries Trulliber, 'Dost thou speak against Faith in my House? Get out of my Doors, I will no longer remain under the same Roof with a Wretch who speaks wantonly of Faith and the Scriptures.' 'Name not the Scriptures,' says Adams. 'How, not name the Scriptures! Do you disbelieve the Scriptures?' cries Trulliber. 'No, but you do,' answered Adams, 'if I may reason from your Practice: for their Commands are so explicite, and their Rewards and Punishments so immense, that it is impossible a Man should stedfastly believe without obeying. Now, there is no Command more express, no Duty more frequently enjoined, than Charity. Whoever therefore is void of Charity, I make no scruple of pronouncing that he is no Christian.' 'I would not advise thee, (says Trulliber) to say that I am no

---

[5] "A petty peace officer; the under-constable" (Johnson).

[6] A tax for the relief or support of the poor.

Christian; I won't take it of you: for I believe I am as good a Man as thyself;' (and indeed, though he was now rather too corpulent for athletic Exercises, he had in his Youth been one of the best Boxers and Cudgel-players in the County.) His Wife, seeing him clench his Fist, interposed, and begged him not to fight, but shew himself the true Christian, and take the Law of him. As nothing could provoke Adams to strike, but an absolute Assault on himself or his Friend, he smiled at the angry Look and Gestures of Trulliber; and telling him, he was sorry to see such Men in Orders, departed without further Ceremony.

CHAP. XV.

An Adventure, the Consequence of a new Instance which Parson Adams gave of his Forgetfulness.

WHEN he came back to the Inn, he found Joseph and Fanny sitting together. They were so far from thinking his Absence long, as he had feared they would, that they never once miss'd or thought of him. Indeed I have been often assured by both, that they spent these Hours in a most delightful Conversation: But as I never could prevail on either to relate it; so I cannot communicate it to the Reader.

Adams acquainted the Lovers with the ill Success of his Enterprize. They were all greatly confounded, none being able to propose any Method of departing, till Joseph at last advised calling in the Hostess, and desiring her to trust them; which Fanny said she despaired of her doing, as she was one of the sourest-fac'd Women she had ever beheld.

But she was agreebly disappointed; for the Hostess was no sooner asked the Question than she readily agreed; and with a Curt'sy and Smile, wished them a good Journey. However, lest Fanny's Skill in Physiognomy should be called in question, we will venture to assign one Reason, which might probably incline her to this Confidence and Good-Humour. When Adams said he was going to visit his Brother, he had unwittingly imposed on Joseph and Fanny; who both believed he had meant his natural Brother, and not his Brother in Divinity; and had so informed the Hostess on her Enquiry after him. Now Mr. Trulliber had by his Professions of Piety, by his Gravity, Austerity, Reserve, and the Opinion of his great Wealth, so great an Authority in his Parish, that they all lived in the utmost Fear and Apprehension of him. It was therefore no Wonder that the Hostess, who knew it was in his Option whether she should ever sell another Mug of Drink, did not dare affront his supposed Brother by denying him Credit.

They were now just on their Departure, when Adams recollected he had left his Great Coat and Hat at Mr. Trulliber's. As he was not desirous of renewing his Visit, the Hostess herself, having no Servant at home, offered to fetch it.

This was an unfortunate Expedient: for the Hostess was soon undeceived in the Opinion she had entertained of Adams, whom Trulliber abused in the grossest Terms, especially when he heard he had had the Assurance to pretend to be his near Relation.

At her Return therefore, she entirely changed her Note. She said, 'Folks might be ashamed of travelling about, and pretending to be what they were not. That Taxes were high, and for her Part, she was obliged to pay for what she had; she could not therefore possibly, nor she would not trust any body, no not her own Father. That Money was never scarcer, and she wanted to make up a Sum. That she expected therefore they should pay their Reckoning before they left the House.'

Adams was now greatly perplexed: but as he knew that he could easily have borrowed such a Sum at his own Parish, and as he knew he would have lent it himself to any Mortal in Distress; so he took fresh Courage, and sallied out all round the Parish, but to no Purpose; he returned as pennyless as he went, groaning and lamenting, that it was possible, in a Country professing Christianity, for a Wretch to starve in the midst of his Fellow-Creatures who abounded.

Whilst he was gone, the Hostess who stayed as a sort of Guard with Joseph and Fanny, entertained them with the Goodness of Parson Trulliber. And indeed he had not only a very good Character, as to other Qualities, in the Neighbourhood, but was reputed a Man of great Charity: for tho' he never gave a Farthing, he had always that Word in his Mouth.

Adams was no sooner returned the second time, than the Storm grew exceeding high, the Hostess declaring among other things, that if they offered to stir without paying her, she would soon overtake them with a Warrant.

Plato or Aristotle, or some body else hath said, THAT WHEN THE MOST EXQUISITE CUNNING FAILS, CHANCE OFTEN

Joseph Andrews, Fanny Goodwill and Parson Adams outside an Inn, Thomas Hearne, c. 1777. (Courtesy of the Cecil Higgins Art Gallery, Bedford, England.)

HITS THE MARK, AND THAT BY MEANS THE LEAST EXPECTED. Virgil expresses this very boldly:

> Turne quod optanti Divûm promittere nemo
> Auderet, volvenda Dies, en! attulit ultro.[1]

I would quote more great Men if I could: but my Memory not permitting me, I will proceed to exemplify these Observations by the following Instance.

There chanced (for Adams had not Cunning enough to contrive it) to be at that time in the Alehouse, a Fellow, who had been formerly a Drummer in an Irish Regiment, and now travelled the Country as a Pedlar. This Man having attentively listened to the Discourse of the Hostess, at last took Adams aside, and asked him what the Sum was

---

[1] "What none of all the Gods could grant thy Vows; / That, Turnus, this auspicious Day bestows." (*Aeneid* 9.6–7, translated freely by Dryden.)

for which they were detained. As soon as he was informed, he sighed, and said, 'he was sorry it was so much: for that he had no more than six Shillings and Sixpence in his Pocket, which he would lend them with all his heart.' Adams gave a Caper, and cry'd out, 'It would do: for that he had Sixpence himself.' And thus these poor People, who could not engage the Compassion of Riches and Piety, were at length delivered out of their Distress by the Charity of a poor Pedlar.

I shall refer it to my Reader to make what Observations he pleases on this Incident: it is sufficient for me to inform him, that after Adams and his Companions had returned him a thousand Thanks, and told him where he might call to be repaid, they all sallied out of the House without any Compliments from their Hostess, or indeed without paying her any; Adams declaring, he would take particular Care never to call there again, and she on her side assuring them she wanted no such Guests.

CHAP. XVI.

A very curious Adventure, in which Mr. Adams gave a much greater Instance of the honest Simplicity of his Heart than of his Experience in the Ways of this World.

OUR Travellers had walked about two Miles from that Inn, which they had more reason to have mistaken for a Castle, than Don Quixote ever had any of those in which he sojourned;[1] seeing they had met with such Difficulty in escaping out of its Walls; when they came to a Parish, and beheld a Sign of Invitation hanging out. A Gentleman sat smoking a Pipe at the Door; of whom Adams enquired the Road, and received so courteous and obliging an Answer, accompanied with so smiling a Countenance, that the good Parson, whose Heart was naturally disposed to Love and Affection, began to ask several other Questions; particularly the Name of the Parish, and who was the Owner of a large House whose Front they then had in prospect. The Gentleman answered as obligingly as before; and as to the House, acquainted him it was his own. He then proceeded in the following manner: 'Sir, I presume by your Habit you are a Clergyman: and as you are travelling on foot, I suppose a Glass of good Beer will not be disagreeable to you; and I can recommend my Landlord's within, as some of the best in all

---

[1] For Quixote, see Contexts, pp. 329–32.

this County. What say you, will you halt a little and let us take a Pipe together? there is no better Tobacco in the Kingdom.' This Proposal was not displeasing to Adams, who had allayed his Thirst that Day with no better Liquor than what Mrs. Trulliber's Cellar had produced; and which was indeed little superior either in Richness or Flavour to that which distilled from those Grains her generous Husband bestowed on his Hogs. Having therefore abundantly thanked the Gentleman for his kind Invitation, and bid Joseph and Fanny follow him, he entered the Ale-House, where a large Loaf and Cheese, and a Pitcher of Beer, which truly answered the Character given of it, being set before them, the three Travellers fell to eating with Appetites infinitely more voracious than are to be found at the most exquisite Eating-Houses in the Parish of St. James's.[2]

The Gentleman expressed great Delight in the hearty and chearful Behaviour of Adams; and particularly in the Familiarity with which he conversed with Joseph and Fanny, whom he often called his Children, a Term he explained to mean no more than his Parishioners; saying, he looked on all those whom God had entrusted to his Cure, to stand to him in that Relation. The Gentleman, shaking him by the Hand, highly applauded those Sentiments. 'They are indeed,' says he, 'the true Principles of a Christian Divine; and I heartily wish they were universal: but on the contrary, I am sorry to say the Parson of our Parish, instead of esteeming his poor Parishioners as a part of his Family, seems rather to consider them as not of the same Species with himself. He seldom speaks to any unless some few of the richest of us; nay, indeed he will not move his Hat to the others. I often laugh when I behold him on *Sundays* strutting along the Church-Yard like a Turky-Cock, through Rows of his Parishioners; who bow to him with as much Submission, and are as unregarded as a Sett of servile Courtiers by the proudest Prince in *Christendom*. But if such temporal Pride is ridiculous, surely the spiritual is odious and detestable: if such a puffed up empty human Bladder, strutting in princely Robes, justly moves one's Derision; surely in the Habit of a Priest it must raise our Scorn.'

'Doubtless,' answer'd Adams, 'your Opinion is right; but I hope such Examples are rare. The Clergy whom I have the Honour to know, maintain a different Behaviour; and you will allow me, Sir, that the Readiness which too many of the Laity show to condemn the Order, may be one Reason of their avoiding too much Humility.'

---

[2] A fashionable district of London.

'Very true indeed,' says the Gentleman; 'I find, Sir, you are a Man of excellent Sense, and am happy in this Opportunity of knowing you: perhaps our accidental Meeting may not be disadvantageous to you neither. At present, I shall only say to you, that the Incumbent of this Living is old and infirm; and that it is in my Gift. Doctor, give me your Hand; and assure yourself of it at his Decease.' Adams told him, 'he was never more confounded in his Life, than at his utter Incapacity to make any Return to such noble and unmerited Generosity.' 'A mere Trifle, Sir,' cries the Gentleman, 'scarce worth your Acceptance; a little more than three hundred a Year. I wish it was double the Value for your Sake.' Adams bowed, and cried from the Emotions of his Gratitude; when the other asked him, 'if he was married, or had any Children, besides those in the spiritual Sense he had mentioned.' 'Sir,' replied the Parson, 'I have a Wife and six at your service.' 'That is unlucky,' says the Gentleman; 'for I would otherwise have taken you into my own House as my Chaplain: however, I have another in the Parish, (for the Parsonage-House is not good enough) which I will furnish for you. Pray does your Wife understand a Dairy?' 'I can't profess she does,' says Adams. 'I am sorry for it,' quoth the Gentleman; 'I would have given you half a dozen Cows, and very good Grounds to have maintained them.' 'Sir,' says Adams, in an Ecstacy, 'you are too liberal; indeed you are.' 'Not at all,' cries the Gentleman, 'I esteem Riches only as they give me an Opportunity of doing good; and I never saw one whom I had greater Inclination to serve.' At which Words he shook him heartily by the Hand, and told him he had sufficient Room in his House to entertain him and his Friends. Adams begged he might give him no such Trouble, that they could be very well accommodated in the House where they were; forgetting they had not a Six-penny Piece among them. The Gentleman would not be denied; and informing himself how far they were travelling, he said it was too long a Journey to take on Foot, and begged that they would favour him, by suffering him to lend them a Servant and Horses; adding withal, that if they would do him the Pleasure of their Company only two Days, he would furnish them with his Coach and six. Adams turning to Joseph, said, 'how lucky is this Gentleman's Goodness to you, who I am afraid would be scarce able to hold out on your lame Leg;' and then addressing the Person who made him these liberal Promises, after much bowing, he cried out, 'Blessed be the Hour which first introduced me to a Man of your Charity: you are indeed a Christian of the true primitive kind, and an Honour to the Country wherein you live. I would willingly have taken a Pilgrimage to the Holy Land to to have beheld you: For the Advantages which we draw from your Goodness, give me little Pleasure, in Comparison of what I enjoy for your own Sake; when I consider the Treasures you are by these Means laying up for your self in a Country that passeth not away. We will therefore, most generous Sir, accept your Goodness, as well the Entertainment you have so kindly offered us at your House this Evening, as the Accommodation of your Horses To-morrow Morning.' He then began to search for his Hat, as did Joseph for his; and both they and Fanny were in Order of Departure, when the Gentleman stopping short, and seeming to meditate by himself for the space of about a Minute, exclaimed thus: 'Sure never any thing was so unlucky; I have forgot that my House-Keeper was gone abroad, and has locked up all my Rooms; indeed I would break them open for you, but shall not be able to furnish you with a Bed; for she has likewise put away all my Linnen. I am glad it entered into my Head, before I had given you the Trouble of walking there; besides, I believe you will find better Accommodations here than you expect. Landlord, you can provide good Beds for these People, can't you?' 'Yes and please your Worship,' cries the Host, 'and such as no Lord or Justice of the Peace in the Kingdom need be ashamed to lie in.' 'I am heartily sorry,' says the Gentleman, 'for this Disappointment. I am resolved I will never suffer her to carry away the Keys again.' 'Pray, Sir, let it not make you uneasy,' cries Adams, 'we shall do very well here; and the Loan of your Horses is a Favour we shall be incapable of making any Return to.' 'Ay!' said the Squire, 'the Horses shall attend you here, at what Hour in the Morning you please.' And now after many Civilities too tedious to enumerate, many Squeezes by the Hand, with most affectionate Looks and Smiles on each other, and after appointing the Horses at seven the next Morning, the Gentleman took his Leave of them, and departed to his own House. Adams and his Companions returned to the Table, where the Parson smoaked another Pipe, and then they all retired to Rest.

Mr. Adams rose very early and called Joseph out of his Bed, between whom a very fierce Dispute ensued, whether Fanny should ride behind Joseph, or behind the Gentleman's Servant; Joseph insisting on it, that he was perfectly recovered, and was as capable of taking care of Fanny as any other Person could be. But Adams would not agree to it, and declared he would not trust her behind him; for that he was weaker than he imagined himself to be.

This Dispute continued a long time, and had begun to be very hot, when a Servant arrived from their good Friend, to acquaint them, that he was unfortunately prevented from lending them any Horses; for that his Groom had, unknown to him, put his whole Stable under a Course of Physick.

This Advice presently struck the two Disputants dumb; Adams cried out, 'Was ever any Thing so unlucky as this poor Gentleman? I protest I am more sorry on his Account than my own. You see, Joseph, how this good-natur'd Man is treated by his Servants; one locks up his Linen, another physicks his Horses; and I suppose by his being at this House last Night, the Butler had locked up his Cellar. Bless us! how Good-nature is used in this World! I protest I am more concerned on his Account than my own.' 'So am not I,' cries Joseph; 'not that I am much troubled about walking on foot; all my Concern is, how we shall get out of the House; unless God sends another Pedlar to redeem us. But certainly, this Gentleman has such an Affection for you, that he would lend you a larger Sum than we owe here; which is not above four or five Shillings.' 'Very true, Child,' answered Adams; 'I will write a Letter to him, and will even venture to sollicit him for three Half-Crowns; there will be no harm in having two or three Shillings in our Pockets; as we have full forty Miles to travel, we may possibly have occasion for them.'

Fanny being now risen, Joseph paid her a Visit, and left Adams to write his Letter, which having finished, he dispatched a Boy with it to the Gentleman, and then seated himself by the Door, lighted his Pipe, and betook himself to Meditation.

The Boy staying longer than seemed to be necessary, Joseph who with Fanny was now returned to the Parson, expressed some Apprehensions, that the Gentleman's Steward had locked up his Purse too. To which Adams answered, 'It might very possibly be; and he should wonder at no Liberties, which the Devil might put into the Head of a wicked Servant to take with so worthy a Master:' but added, 'that as the Sum was so small, so noble a Gentleman would be easily able to procure it in the Parish; tho' he had it not in his own Pocket. Indeed,' says he, 'if it was four or five Guineas, or any such large Quantity of Money, it might be a different Matter.'

They were now sat down to Breakfast over some Toast and Ale, when the Boy returned, and informed them, that the Gentleman was not at home. 'Very well!' cries Adams; 'but why, Child, did you not stay 'till his Return? Go back again, my good Boy, and wait for his coming home: he cannot be gone far, as his Horses are all sick; and besides, he had no Intention to go abroad; for he invited us to spend this Day and To-morrow at his House. Therefore go back, Child, and tarry 'till his return home.' The Messenger departed, and was back again with great Expedition; bringing an Account, that the Gentleman was gone a long Journey, and would not be at home again this Month. At these Words Adams seemed greatly confounded, saying, 'This must be a sudden Accident, as the Sickness or Death of a Relation, or some such unforeseen Misfortune;' and then turning to Joseph, cried, 'I wish you had reminded me to have borrowed this Money last Night.' Joseph smiling, answered, 'he was very much deceived, if the Gentleman would not have found some Excuse to avoid lending it. I own,' says he, 'I was never much pleased with his professing so much Kindness for you at first sight: for I have heard the Gentlemen of our Cloth in London tell many such Stories of their Masters. But when the Boy brought the Message back of his not being at home, I presently knew what would follow; for whenever a Man of Fashion doth not care to fulfil his Promises, the Custom is, to order his Servants that he will never be at home to the Person so promised. In London they call it *denying him*. I have my self denied Sir Thomas Booby above a hundred times; and when the Man hath danced Attendance for about a Month, or sometimes longer, he is acquainted in the end, that the Gentleman is gone out of Town, and could do nothing in the Business.' 'Good Lord!' says Adams, 'what Wickedness is there in the Christian World? I profess, almost equal to what I have read of the Heathens. But surely, Joseph, your Suspicions of this Gentleman must be unjust; for, what a silly Fellow must he be, who would do the Devil's Work for nothing? and can'st thou tell me any Interest he could possibly propose to himself by deceiving us in his Professions?' 'It is not for me,' answered Joseph, 'to give Reasons for what Men do, to a Gentleman of your Learning.' 'You say right,' quoth Adams; 'Knowledge of Men is only to be learnt from Books, Plato and Seneca for that; and those are Authors, I am afraid Child, you never read.' 'Not I, Sir, truly,' answered Joseph; 'all I know is, it is a Maxim among the Gentlemen of our Cloth, that those Masters who promise the most, perform the least; and I have often heard them say, they have found the largest Vails[3] in those Families where they were not promised any. But, Sir, instead of considering any farther these Matters, it would be our wisest way to contrive some Method of getting out of

---

[3] "Money given to servants" (Johnson); tips.

this House: for the generous Gentleman, instead of doing us any Service, hath left us the whole Reckoning to pay.' Adams was going to answer, when their Host came in and, with a kind of jeering Smile, said, 'Well, Masters! the Squire hath not sent his Horses for you yet. Laud help me! how easily some Folks make Promises!' 'How!' says Adams, 'have you ever known him do any thing of this kind before?' 'Aye marry have I,' answered the Host; 'it is no business of mine, you know, Sir, to say any thing to a Gentleman to his face: but now he is not here, I will assure you, he has not his Fellow within the three next Market-Towns. I own, I could not help laughing, when I heard him offer you the Living; for thereby hangs a good Jest. I thought he would have offered you my House next; for one is no more his to dispose of than the other.' At these Words, Adams blessing himself declared, 'he had never read of such a Monster; but what vexes me most,' says he, 'is, that he hath decoyed us into running up a long Debt with you, which we are not able to pay; for we have no Money about us; and, what is worse, live at such a Distance, that, if you should trust us, I am afraid you would lose your Money, for want of our finding any Conveniency of sending it.' 'Trust you, Master!' says the Host, 'that I will with all my heart; I honour the Clergy too much to deny trusting one of them for such a Trifle; besides, I like your fear of never paying me. I have lost many a Debt in my Life-time; but was promised to be paid them all in a very short time. I will score this Reckoning for the Novelty of it. It is the first I do assure you of its kind. But what say you, Master, shall we have t'other Pot before we part? It will waste but a little Chalk more;[4] and if you never pay me a Shilling, the Loss will not ruin me.' Adams liked the Invitation very well; especially as it was delivered with so hearty an Accent. —He shook his Host by the Hand, and, thanking him, said, 'he would tarry another Pot, rather for the Pleasure of such worthy Company, than for the Liquor;' adding, 'he was glad to find some Christians left in the Kingdom; for that he almost began to suspect that he was sojourning in a Country inhabited only by *Jews* and *Turks*.'

The kind Host produced the Liquor, and Joseph with Fanny retired into the Garden; where while they solaced themselves with amorous Discourse, Adams sat down with his Host; and both filling their Glasses, and lighting their Pipes, they began that Dialogue which the Reader will find in the next Chapter.

---

[4] Innkeepers kept tabs by writing with chalk on slate.

CHAP. XVII.

A Dialogue between Mr. Abraham Adams *and his Host, which, by the Disagreement in their Opinions, seemed to threaten an unlucky Catastrophe, had it not been timely prevented by the Return of the Lovers.*

'SIR,' said the Host, 'I assure you, you are not the first to whom our Squire hath promised more than he hath performed. He is so famous for this Practice, that his Word will not be taken for much by those who know him. I remember a young Fellow whom he promised his Parents to make an Exciseman. The poor People, who could ill afford it, bred their Son to Writing and Accounts, and other Learning, to qualify him for the Place; and the Boy held up his Head above his Condition with these Hopes; nor would he go to plough, nor do any other kind of Work; and went constantly drest as fine as could be, with two clean *Holland*[1] Shirts a Week, and this for several Years; 'till at last he followed the Squire up to London, thinking there to mind him of his Promises: but he could never get sight of him. So that being out of Money and Business, he fell into evil Company, and wicked Courses; and in the end came to a Sentence of Transportation, the News of which broke the Mother's Heart. I will tell you another true Story of him: There was a Neighbour of mine, a Farmer, who had two Sons whom he bred up to the Business. Pretty Lads they were; nothing would serve the Squire, but that the youngest must be made a Parson. Upon which he persuaded the Father to send him to School, promising, that he would afterwards maintain him at the University; and when he was of proper Age, give him a Living. But after the Lad had been seven Years at School, and his Father brought him to the Squire with a Letter from his Master, that he was fit for the University; the Squire, instead of minding his Promise, or sending him thither at his Expence, only told his Father, that the young Man was a fine Scholar; and it was Pity he could not afford to keep him at Oxford for four or five Years more, by which Time, if he could get him a Curacy, he might have him ordained. The Farmer said, he was not a Man sufficient to do any such thing. Why then, answered the Squire, I am very sorry you have given him so much Learning; for if he cannot get his living by that, it will rather spoil him for any thing

[1] Linen.

else; and your other Son, who can hardly write his Name, will do more at plowing and sowing, and is in a better Condition than he: and indeed so it proved; for the poor Lad, not finding Friends to maintain him in his Learning as he had expected, and being unwilling to work, fell to drinking, though he was a very sober Lad before; and in a short time, partly with Grief, and partly with good Liquor, fell into a Consumption and died. Nay, I can tell you more still: There was another, a young Woman, and the handsomest in all this Neighbourhood, whom he enticed up to London, promising to make her a Gentlewoman to one of your Women of Quality: but instead of keeping his Word, we have since heard, after having a Child by her himself, she became a common Whore; then kept a Coffee-House in *Covent-Garden*, and a little after died of the French Distemper[2] in a Goal. I could tell you many more Stories: but how do you imagine he served me myself? You must know, Sir, I was bred a Sea-faring Man and have been many Voyages; 'till at last I came to be Master of a Ship myself, and was in a fair Way of making a Fortune, when I was attacked by one of those cursed *Guarda-Costas*, who took our Ships before the Beginning of the War;[3] and after a Fight, wherein I lost the greater part of my Crew, my Rigging being all demolished, and two Shots received between Wind and Water, I was forced to strike. The Villains carried off my Ship, a Brigantine of 150 Tons, a pretty Creature she was, and put me, a Man, and a Boy, into a little bad Pink,[4] in which, with much ado, we at last made Falmouth; tho' I believe the Spaniards did not imagine she could possibly live a Day at Sea. Upon my return hither, where my Wife, who was of this Country, then lived, the Squire told me, he was so pleased with the Defence I had made against the Enemy, that he did not fear getting me promoted to a Lieutenancy of a Man of War, if I would accept of it, which I thankfully assured him I would. Well, Sir, two or three Years past, during which, I had many repeated Promises, not only from the Squire, but (as he told me) from the Lords of the Admiralty. He never returned from London, but I was assured I might be satisfied now, for I was certain of the first Vacancy; and what surprizes me still, when I reflect on it, these Assurances were given me with no less Confidence, after so many Disappointments, than at first. At last, Sir, growing going weary

---

[2] Venereal disease, which the English often associated with the French.
[3] The War of Jenkins' Ear (see Chap. 7, n. 1).
[4] "A kind of heavy narrow-sterned ship" (Johnson).

and somewhat suspicious after so much Delay, I wrote to a Friend in London, who I knew had some Acquaintance at the best House in the Admiralty, and desired him to back the Squire's Interest: for indeed I feared he had sollicited the Affair with more Coldness than he pretended. —And what Answer do you think my Friend sent me? — Truly, Sir, he acquainted me, that the Squire had never mentioned my Name at the Admiralty in his Life; and unless I had much faithfuller Interest, advised me to give over my Pretensions, which I immediately did; and, with the Concurrence of my Wife, resolved to set up an Alehouse, where you are heartily welcome: and so my Service to you; and may the Squire, and all such sneaking Rascals, go to the Devil together.' 'Oh fie!' says Adams; 'Oh fie! He is indeed a wicked Man; but G— will, I hope, turn his Heart to Repentance. Nay, if he could but once see the Meanness of this detestable Vice; would he but once reflect that he is one of the most scandalous as well as pernicious Lyars; sure he must despise himself to so intolerable a Degree, that it would be impossible for him to continue a Moment in such a Course. And, to confess the Truth, notwithstanding the Baseness of this Character, which he hath too well deserved, he hath in his Countenance sufficient Symptoms of that *bona Indoles*,[5] that Sweetness of Disposition which furnishes out a good Christian.' 'Ah! Master, Master, (says the Host) if you had travelled as far as I have, and conversed with the many Nations where I have traded, you would not give any Credit to a Man's Countenance. Symptoms in his Countenance, quotha! I would look there perhaps to see whether a Man had had the Small-Pox, but for nothing else!' He spoke this with so little Regard to the Parson's Observation, that it a good deal nettled him; and, taking the Pipe hastily from his Mouth, he thus answered: 'Master of mine, perhaps I have travelled a great deal farther than you without the Assistance of a Ship. Do you imagine sailing by different Cities or Countries is travelling? No.

Coelum non Animum mutant qui trans mare currunt.[6]

I can go farther in an Afternoon than you in a Twelve-Month. What, I suppose you have seen the Pillars of Hercules, and perhaps the Walls of Carthage. Nay, you may have heard Scylla, and seen

---

[5] "Good nature" (Latin).

[6] "They change their sky, not their mind, who hasten across the sea" (Horace, *Epistles* 1.11.27). In what follows, Adams shows off his knowledge of classical Greek place names.

Charybdis; you may have entered the Closet where Archimedes was found at the taking Syracuse. I suppose you have sailed among the Cyclades, and passed the famous Streights which take their name from the unfortunate Helle, whose Fate is sweetly described by Apollonius Rhodius;[7] you have passed the very Spot, I conceive, where Daedalus fell into that Sea, his waxen Wings being melted by the Sun; you have traversed the Euxine Sea, I make no doubt; nay, you may have been on the Banks of the Caspian, and called at Colchis, to see if there is ever another Golden Fleece.'—'Not I truly, Master,' answered the Host, 'I never touched at any of these Places.' 'But I have been at all these,' replied Adams. 'Then I suppose,' cries the Host, 'you have been at the East Indies? for there are no such, I will be sworn either in the West or the Levant.'[8] 'Pray where's the Levant?' quoth Adams, 'that should be in the East Indies by right.' —'Oh ho! you are a pretty Traveller,' cries the Host, 'and not know the Levant. My service to you, Master; you must not talk of these things with me! you must not tip us the Traveller;[9] it won't go here.' 'Since thou art so dull to misunderstand me still,' quoth Adams, 'I will inform thee; the travelling I mean is in Books, the only way of travelling by which any Knowledge is to be acquired. From them I learn what I asserted just now, that Nature generally imprints such a Portraiture of the Mind in the Countenance, that a skilful Physiognomist will rarely be deceived. I presume you have never read the Story of Socrates to this purpose, and therefore I will tell it you. A certain Physiognomist asserted of Socrates, that he plainly discovered by his Features that he was a Rogue in his Nature. A Character so contrary to the Tenour of all this great Man's Actions, and the generally received Opinion concerning him, incensed the Boys of Athens so that they threw Stones at the Physiognomist, and would have demolished him for his Ignorance, had not Socrates

---

[7] Apollonios Rhodios, in *Argonautika* (third-century BCE), tells of Jason and the Argonauts' quest for the golden fleece of the winged ram that had earlier carried the princess Helle away from her murderous step-mother. According to Lemprière, "Helle was carried through the air on a golden ram . . . and in her passage she became giddy, and fell from her seat into that part of the sea which from her received the name of Hellespont." Fielding's next sentence mistakes the artificer Daedalus for his son Icarus, whose waxen wings melted when he flew too near the sun.

[8] "Levant," from the French "rising" (of the sun), referred to "The east, particularly those coasts of the Mediterranean east of Italy" (Johnson), although Adams takes it to mean the far east of India.

[9] "To tell wonderful stories" (Grose).

himself prevented them by confessing the Truth of his Observations, and acknowledging, that tho' he corrected his Disposition by Philosophy, he was indeed naturally as inclined to Vice as had been predicated of him.[10] Now, pray resolve me,—How should a Man know this Story, if he had not read it?' 'Well Master,' said the Host, 'and what signifies it whether a Man knows it or no? He who goes abroad as I have done, will always have Opportunities enough of knowing the World, without troubling his head with Socrates, or any such Fellows.' —'Friend,' cries Adams, 'if a Man would sail round the World, and anchor in every Harbour of it, without Learning, he would return home as ignorant as he went out.' 'Lord help you,' answered the Host, 'there was my Boatswain, poor Fellow! he could scarce either write or read; and yet he would navigate a Ship with any Master of a Man of War; and a very pretty Knowledge of Trade he had too.' 'Trade,' answered Adams, 'as Aristotle proves in his first Chapter of Politics, is below a Philosopher, and unnatural as it is managed now.' The Host look'd stedfastly at Adams, and after a Minute's silence asked him 'if he was one of the Writers of the *Gazetteers*? for I have heard,' says he, 'they are writ by Parsons.' '*Gazetteers*!' answered Adams, 'What is that?' 'It is a dirty News-Paper,' replied the Host, 'which hath been given away all over the Nation for these many Years, to abuse Trade and honest Men, which I would not suffer to lie on my Table, tho' it hath been offered me for nothing.'[11] 'Not I truly,' said Adams, 'I never write any thing but Sermons; and I assure you I am no Enemy to Trade, whilst it is consistent with Honesty; nay, I have always looked on the Tradesman as a very valuable Member of Society, and perhaps inferior to none but the Man of Learning.' 'No, I believe he is not, nor to him neither,' answered the Host. 'Of what use would Learning be in a Country without Trade! What would all you Parsons do to clothe your Backs and feed your Bellies? Who fetches you your Silks and your Linens, and your Wines, and all the other Necessaries of Life? I speak chiefly with regard to the Sailors.' 'You should say the Extravagancies of Life,' replied the Parson; 'but admit they were the Necessaries, there is something more necessary than Life itself, which is provided by Learning; I mean the Learning

---

[10] A story from Cicero, *Tusculan Disputations* 4.37.80.

[11] *The Daily Gazetteer*, the official newspaper of Walpole's Whig ministry, was distributed free throughout the kingdom. It had supported Walpole's (unsuccessful) efforts in the late 1730s to avoid war with Spain.

of the Clergy. Who clothes you with Piety, Meekness, Humility, Charity, Patience, and all the other Christian Virtues? Who feeds your Souls with the Milk of brotherly Love, and diets them with all the dainty Food of Holiness, which at once cleanses them of all impure carnal Affections, and fattens them with the truly rich Spirit of Grace? —Who doth this?' 'Ay, who indeed!' cries the Host; 'for I do not remember ever to have seen any such Clothing or such Feeding. And so in the mean time, Master, my service to you.' Adams was going to answer with some Severity, when Joseph and Fanny returned, and pressed his Departure so eagerly, that he would not refuse them; and so, grasping his Crabstick, he took leave of his Host, (neither of them being so well pleased with each other as they had been at their first sitting down together) and with Joseph and Fanny, who both expressed much Impatience, departed, and now all together renewed their Journey.

THE

HISTORY

OF THE

ADVENTURES

OF

Joseph Andrews, and his Friend
Mr. *Abraham Adams.*

BOOK III.

CHAP. I.

Matter prefatory in Praise of Biography.

NOTWITHSTANDING the Preference which may be vulgarly given to
the Authority of those Romance-Writers, who intitle their Books,
the History of England, the History of France, of Spain, &c. it is
most certain, that Truth is to be found only in the Works of those
who celebrate the Lives of Great Men, and are commonly called
Biographers, as the others should indeed be termed Topographers
or Chorographers: Words which might well mark the Distinction
between them; it being the Business of the latter chiefly to describe
Countries and Cities, which, with the Assistance of Maps, they do
pretty justly, and may be depended upon: But as to the Actions and
Characters of Men, their Writings are not quite so authentic, of
which there needs no other Proof than those eternal Contradictions
occurring between two Topographers who undertake the History of

the same Country: For instance, between my Lord Clarendon and Mr. Whitlock, between Mr. Echard and Rapin, and many others;[1] where, Facts being set forth in a different Light, every Reader believes as he pleases; and indeed the more judicious and suspicious very justly esteem the whole as no other than a Romance, in which the Writer hath indulged a happy and fertile Invention. But tho' these widely differ in the Narrative of Facts; some ascribing Victory to the one, and others to the other Party: Some representing the same Man as a Rogue, to whom the others give a great and honest Character, yet all agree in the Scene where the Fact is supposed to have happened; and where the Person, who is both a Rogue, and an honest Man, lived. Now with us Biographers the Case is different; the Facts we deliver may be relied on, tho' we often mistake the Age and Country wherein they happened: For tho' it may be worth the Examination of Critics, whether the Shepherd *Chrysostom*, who, as Cervantes informs us, died for Love of the fair *Marcella*, who hated him, was ever in Spain, will any one doubt but that such a silly Fellow hath really existed? Is there in the World such a Sceptic as to disbelieve the Madness of *Cardenio*, the Perfidy of *Ferdinand*, the impertinent Curiosity of *Anselmo*, the Weakness of *Camilla*, the irresolute Friendship of *Lothario*;[2] tho' perhaps as to the Time and Place where those several Persons lived, that good Historian may be deplorably deficient: But the most known Instance of this kind is in the true History of *Gil-Blas*,[3] where the inimitable Biographer hath made a notorious Blunder in the Country of Dr. *Sanglardo*, who used his Patients as a Vintner doth his Wine-Vessels, by letting out their Blood, and filling them up with Water. Doth not every one, who is the least versed in Physical History, know that Spain was not the Country in which this Doctor lived? The same Writer hath likewise erred in the Country of his Archbishop, as well as that of those great Personages whose Understandings were too sublime to taste

---

[1] Historians with conflicting opinions about the turbulent period of the English Civil Wars, Interregnum, and Stuart Restoration, 1642–1660.

[2] Characters in interpolated tales of love and intrigue in *Don Quixote* 1.2.4–6 and 1.4.6–8.

[3] The French novel *Histoire de Gil Blas de Santillane* was published by Alian-René Lesage (1668–1747) in three installments (1715, 1724, 1735), each of which was quickly translated into English. The novel's protagonist, Gil Blas, rises from lowly origins as a country boy to high service in the Spanish court; Dr. Sangrado and the Archbishop of Granada are two of his masters along the way.

any thing but Tragedy, and in many others. The same Mistakes may likewise be observed in *Scarron*, the *Arabian Nights*, the History of *Marianne* and *Le Paisan Parvenu*,[4] and perhaps some few other Writers of this Class, whom I have not read, or do not at present recollect; for I would by no means be thought to comprehend those Persons of surprizing Genius, the Authors of immense Romances, or the modern Novel and *Atalantis* Writers;[5] who, without any Assistance from Nature or History, record Persons who never were, or will be, and Facts which never did, nor possibly can happen: Whose Heroes are of their own Creation, and their Brains the Chaos whence all their Materials are collected. Not that such Writers deserve no Honour; so far otherwise, that perhaps they merit the highest: for what can be nobler than to be as an Example of the wonderful Extent of human Genius! One may apply to them what Balzac[6] says of Aristotle, that they are a *second Nature* (for they have no Communication with the first); by which Authors of an inferiour Class, who cannot stand alone, are obliged to support themselves as with Crutches; but these of whom I am now speaking, seem to be possessed of *those Stilts,* which the excellent Voltaire tells us in his Letters *carry the Genius far off, but with an irregular Pace.*[7] Indeed far out of the Sight of the Reader,

> Beyond the Realm of Chaos and old Night.[8]

But, to return to the former Class, who are contented to copy Nature, instead of forming Originals from the confused heap of Matter in their own Brains; is not such a Book as that which records the Achievements of the renowned Don Quixote, more worthy the Name of a History than even Mariana's:[9] for whereas the latter is

---

[4] *Arabian Nights Entertainment: Consisting of One Thousand and One Stories* (1705–1708) was translated from Antoine Galland's French edition (1704–1708), the first collection of these Oriental tales to appear in Europe. *La Vie de Marianne* (1731–41) and *Le Paysan Parvenu* (1735–36) are novels by Pierre Carlet de Chamblain de Marivaux (1688–1763).

[5] *The New Atalantis* (1709) is a scandal novel by Mary de la Rivière Manley (1663–1724); on Manley, see Introduction p. xvi.

[6] Jean-Louis Guez de Balzac (1594–1654), French academician.

[7] Voltaire, *Letters Concerning the English Nation*, trans. J. Lockman (1733), Letter 18.

[8] Milton, *Paradise Lost* 1.541–43.

[9] Juan de Mariana (1536–1623), *Historia general de España* (1601), English translation 1699.

confined to a particular Period of Time, and to a particular Nation; the former is the History of the World in general, at least that Part which is polished by Laws, Arts and Sciences; and of that from the Time it was first polished to this Day; nay and forwards, as long as it shall so remain.

I shall now proceed to apply these Observations to the Work before us; for indeed I have set them down principally to obviate some Constructions, which the Good-nature of Mankind, who are always forward to see their Friends Virtues recorded, may put to particular parts. I question not but several of my Readers will know the Lawyer in the Stage-Coach, the Moment they hear his Voice. It is likewise odds, but the Wit and the Prude meet with some of their Acquaintance, as well as all the rest of my Characters. To prevent therefore any such malicious Applications, I declare here once for all, I describe not Men, but Manners;[10] not an Individual, but a Species. Perhaps it will be answered, Are not the Characters then taken from Life? To which I answer in the Affirmative; nay, I believe I might aver, that I have writ little more than I have seen. The Lawyer is not only alive, but hath been so these 4000 Years; and I hope G— will indulge his Life as many yet to come. He hath not indeed confined himself to one Profession, one Religion, or one Country; but when the first mean selfish Creature appeared on the human Stage, who made Self the Centre of the whole Creation, would give himself no Pain, incur no Danger, advance no Money to assist or preserve his Fellow-Creatures; then was our Lawyer born; and whilst such a Person as I have described exists on Earth, so long shall he remain upon it. It is therefore doing him little Honour, to imagine he endeavours to mimick some little obscure Fellow, because he happens to resemble him in one particular Feature, or perhaps in his Profession; whereas his Appearance in the World is calculated for much more general and noble Purposes; not to expose one pitiful Wretch to the small and contemptible Circle of his Acquaintance; but to hold the Glass to thousands in their Closets, that they may contemplate their Deformity, and endeavour to reduce it, and thus by suffering private Mortification may avoid public Shame. This places the Boundary between, and distinguishes

---

[10] Johnson defines "manners" as "general way of life; morals; habits." Fielding contrasts knowledge of *particular* "men" with the general study of character types or moral dispositions (the selfish personality, the lustful personality, etc.).

the Satirist from the Libeller; for the former privately corrects the Fault for the Benefit of the Person, like a Parent; the latter publicly exposes the Person himself, as an Example to others, like an Executioner.

There are besides little Circumstances to be considered; as the Drapery of a Picture, which tho' Fashion varies at different Times, the Resemblance of the Countenance is not by those means diminished. Thus, I believe, we may venture to say, Mrs. Tow-wouse is coeval with our Lawyer; and tho' perhaps during the Changes which so long an Existence must have passed through, she may in her Turn have stood behind the Bar at an Inn; I will not scruple to affirm, she hath likewise in the Revolution of Ages sat on a Throne. In short, where extreme Turbulency of Temper, Avarice, and an Insensibility of human Misery, with a Degree of Hypocrisy, have united in a female Composition, Mrs. Tow-wouse was that Woman; and where a good Inclination, eclipsed by a Poverty of Spirit and Understanding, hath glimmered forth in a Man, that Man hath been no other than her sneaking Husband.

I shall detain my Reader no longer than to give him one Caution more of an opposite kind: For as in most of our particular Characters we mean not to lash Individuals, but all of that like sort; so in our general Descriptions, we mean not Universals, but would be understood with many Exceptions: For instance, in our Description of high People, we cannot be intended to include such, as whilst they are an Honour to their high Rank, by a well-guided Condescension, make their Superiority as easy as possible, to those whom Fortune hath chiefly placed below them. Of this number I could name a Peer[11] no less elevated by Nature than by Fortune, who, whilst he wears the noblest Ensigns of Honour on his Person, bears the truest Stamp of Dignity on his Mind, adorned with Greatness, enriched with Knowledge, and embellished with Genius. I have seen this Man relieve with Generosity, while he hath conversed with Freedom, and be to the same Person a Patron and a Companion. I could name a Commoner[12] raised higher above the Multitude by superiour Talents, than is in the Power of his Prince to exalt him;

---

[11] Probably Fielding's early patron Philip Dormer Stanhope, fourth earl of Chesterfield (1694–1773).

[12] Ralph Allen (1693–1764), entrepreneur and philanthropist, Fielding's patron during the writing of *Joseph Andrews*.

whose Behaviour to those he hath obliged is more amiable than
the Obligation itself, and who is so great a Master of Affability, that
if he could divest himself of an inherent Greatness in his Manner,
would often make the lowest of his Acquaintance forget who
was the Master of that Palace in which they are so courteously
entertained. These are Pictures which must be, I believe, known:
I declare they are taken from the Life, and not intended to exceed it.
By those high People therefore whom I have described, I mean a Set
of Wretches, who, while they are a Disgrace to their Ancestors,
whose Honours and Fortunes they inherit, (or perhaps a greater to
their Mother, for such Degeneracy is scarce credible) have the Inso-
lence to treat those with Disregard, who are at least equal to the
Founders of their own Splendor. It is, I fancy, impossible to conceive
a Spectacle more worthy of our Indignation, than that of a Fellow
who is not only a Blot in the Escutcheon of a great Family, but a
Scandal to the human Species, maintaining a supercilious Behaviour to Men who are an Honour to their Nature, and a Disgrace to
their Fortune.

And now, Reader, taking these Hints along with you, you may,
if you please, proceed to the Sequel of this our true History.

CHAP. II.

A Night-Scene, wherein several wonderful Adventures befel **Adams**
and his Fellow-Travellers.

IT was so late when our Travellers left the Inn or Ale-house, (for it
might be called either) that they had not travelled many Miles,
before Night overtook them, or met them, which you please. The
Reader must excuse me if I am not particular as to the Way they
took; for as we are now drawing near the Seat of the Boobies; and
as that is a ticklish Name, which malicious Persons may apply
according to their evil Inclinations, to several worthy Country
'Squires, a Race of Men whom we look upon as entirely inoffensive,
and for whom we have an adequate Regard, we shall lend no Assistance to any such malicious Purposes.

Darkness had now overspread the Hemisphere, when Fanny
whispered Joseph, 'that she begged to rest herself a little; for that
she was so tired, she could walk no farther.' Joseph immediately
prevailed with Parson Adams, who was as brisk as a Bee, to stop.
He had no sooner seated himself, than he lamented the Loss of his

dear *Æschylus;* but was a little comforted, when reminded, that if he had it in his Possession, he could not see to read.

The Sky was so clouded, that not a Star appeared. It was indeed, according to Milton, Darkness visible.[1] This was a Circumstance, however, very favourable to Joseph; for Fanny, not suspicious of being overseen by Adams, gave a loose to her Passion, which she had never done before; and reclining her Head on his Bosom, threw her Arm carelessly round him, and suffered him to lay his Cheek close to hers. All this infused such Happiness into Joseph, that he would not have changed his Turf for the finest Down in the finest Palace in the Universe.

Adams sat at some Distance from the Lovers, and being unwilling to disturb them, applied himself to Meditation; in which he had not spent much time, before he discovered a Light at some Distance, that seemed approaching towards him. He immediately hailed it; but, to his Sorrow and Surprize, it stopped for a moment and then disappeared. He then called to Joseph, asking him, 'if he had not seen the Light.' Joseph answered, he had. 'And did you not mark how it vanished?' (returned he) tho' I am not afraid of Ghosts, I do not absolutely disbelieve them.'

He then entered into a Meditation on those unsubstantial Beings, which was soon interrupted, by several Voices which he thought almost at his Elbow, tho' in Fact they were not so extremely near. However, he could distinctly hear them agree on the Murder of any one they met. And a little after heard one of them say, 'he had killed a Dozen since that day Fortnight.'

Adams now fell on his Knees, and committed himself to the care of Providence; and poor Fanny, who likewise heard those terrible Words, embraced Joseph so closely, that had not he, whose Ears were also open, been apprehensive on her Account, he would have thought no Danger which threatened only himself, too dear a Price for such Embraces.

Joseph now drew forth his Penknife, and Adams having finished his Ejaculations, grasped his Crabstick, his only Weapon, and coming up to Joseph, would have had him quit Fanny, and place her in their Rear: But his Advice was fruitless, she clung closer to him, not at all regarding the Presence of Adams, and in a soothing Voice declared, 'she would die in his Arms.' Joseph clasping her with

---

[1] *Paradise Lost* 1.63 (a description of the lighting in Hell).

inexpressible Eagerness, whispered her, 'that he preferred Death in hers to Life out of them.' Adams brandishing his Crabstick, said, 'he despised Death as much as any Man,' and then repeated aloud,

'Est hic, est animus lucis contemptor, & illum,
Qui vita bene credat emi quo tendis, honorem.'[2]

Upon this the Voices ceased for a Moment, and then one of them called out, 'D—n you, who is there?' To which Adams was prudent enough to make no Reply; and of a sudden he observed half a dozen Lights, which seemed to rise all at once from the Ground, and advance briskly towards him. This he immediately concluded to be an Apparition, and now beginning to conceive that the Voices were of the same kind, he called out, 'In the Name of the L—d, what would'st thou have?' He had no sooner spoke than he heard one of the Voices cry out, 'D—n them, here they come;' and soon after heard several hearty Blows, as if a number of Men had been engaged at Quarterstaff. He was just advancing towards the Place of Combat, when Joseph catching him by the Skirts, begged him that they might take the Opportunity of the dark to convey away Fanny from the Danger which threatned her. He presently complied, and Joseph lifting up Fanny, they all three made the best of their Way; and without looking behind them or being overtaken, they had travelled full two Miles, poor Fanny not once complaining of being tired, when they saw far off several Lights scattered at a small Distance from each other, and at the same time found themselves on the Descent of a very steep Hill. Adams's Foot slipping, he instantly disappeared, which greatly frightned both Joseph and Fanny; indeed, if the Light had permitted them to see it, they would scarce have refrained laughing to see the Parson rolling down the Hill, which he did from Top to Bottom, without receiving any Harm. He then hollowed as loud as he could, to inform them of his Safety, and relieve them from the Fears which they had conceived for him. Joseph and Fanny halted some time, considering what to do; at last they advanced a few Paces, where the Declivity seemed least steep; and then Joseph taking his Fanny in his Arms, walked firmly down the Hill, without making a false Step, and at length landed her at the Bottom, where Adams soon came to them.

---

[2] "The thing call'd Life, with ease I can disclaim, / And think it oversold to purchase Fame" (Dryden, *Aeneis* 9.264–65).

Learn hence, my fair Countrywomen, to consider your own Weakness, and the many Occasions on which the strength of a Man may be useful to you; and duly weighing this, take care, that you match not yourselves with the spindle-shanked Beaus and Petit Maîtres[3] of the Age, who, instead of being able, like Joseph Andrews, to carry you in lusty Arms through the rugged Ways and downhill Steeps of Life, will rather want to support their feeble Limbs with your Strength and Assistance.

Our Travellers now moved forwards, where the nearest Light presented itself, and having crossed a common Field, they came to a Meadow, whence they seemed to be at a very little Distance from the Light, when, to their Grief, they arrived at the Banks of a River. Adams here made a full Stop, and declared he could swim, but doubted how it was possible to get Fanny over; to which Joseph answered, 'if they walked along its Banks, they might be certain of soon finding a Bridge, especially as by the Number of Lights they might be assured a Parish was near.' 'Odso, that's true indeed,' said Adams, 'I did not think of that.' Accordingly Joseph's Advice being taken, they passed over two Meadows, and came to a little Orchard, which led them to a House. Fanny begged of Joseph to knock at the Door, assuring him, 'she was so weary that she could hardly stand on her Feet.' Adams, who was foremost, performed this Ceremony, and the Door being immediately opened, a plain kind of a Man appeared at it; Adams acquainted him, 'that they had a young Woman with them, who was so tired with her Journey, that he should be much obliged to him, if he would suffer her to come in and rest herself.' The Man, who saw Fanny by the Light of the Candle which he held in his Hand, perceiving her innocent and modest Look, and having no Apprehensions from the civil Behaviour of Adams, presently answer'd, that the young Woman was very welcome to rest herself in his House, and so were her Company. He then ushered them into a very decent Room, where his Wife was sitting at a Table; she immediately rose up, and assisted them in setting forth Chairs, and desired them to sit down, which they had no sooner done, than the Man of the House asked them if they would have any thing to refresh themselves with? Adams thanked him, and answered, he should be obliged to him for a Cup of his Ale, which was likewise chosen by Joseph and Fanny. Whilst he was

---

[3] Fops.

gone to fill a very large Jugg with this Liquor, his Wife told Fanny she seemed greatly fatigued, and desired her to take something stronger than Ale; but she refused, with many Thanks, saying it was true, she was very much tired, but a little Rest she hoped would restore her. As soon as the Company were all seated, Mr. Adams, who had filled himself with Ale, and by public Permission had lighted his Pipe, turned to the Master of the House, asking him, 'if evil Spirits did not use to walk in that Neighbourhood?' To which receiving no Answer, he began to inform him of the Adventure which they had met with on the Downs; nor had he proceeded far in his Story, when somebody knocked very hard at the Door. The Company expressed some Amazement, and Fanny and the good Woman turned pale; her Husband went forth, and whilst he was absent, which was some time, they all remained silent looking at one another, and heard several Voices discoursing pretty loudly. Adams was fully persuaded that Spirits were abroad, and began to meditate some Exorcisms; Joseph a little inclined to the same Opinion: Fanny was more afraid of Men, and the good Woman herself began to suspect her Guests, and imagined those without were Rogues belonging to their Gang. At length the Master of the House returned, and laughing, told Adams he had discovered his Apparition; that the Murderers were Sheep-stealers, and the twelve Persons murdered were no other than twelve Sheep. Adding, that the Shepherds had got the better of them, had secured two, and were proceeding with them to a Justice of Peace. This Account greatly relieved the Fears of the whole Company; but Adams muttered to himself, 'He was convinced of the Truth of Apparitions for all that.'

They now sat chearfully round the Fire, till the Master of the House having surveyed his Guests, and conceiving that the Cassock, which having fallen down, appeared under Adams's Great-Coat, and the shabby Livery on Joseph Andrews did not well suit with the Familiarity between them, began to entertain some Suspicions, not much to their Advantage: addressing himself therefore to Adams, he said, 'he perceived he was a Clergyman by his Dress, and supposed that honest Man was his Footman.' 'Sir,' answer'd Adams, 'I am a Clergyman at your Service; but as to that young Man, whom you have rightly termed honest, he is at present in no body's Service; he never lived in any other Family than that of Lady Booby, from whence he was discharged, I assure you, for no Crime.' Joseph said, 'he did not wonder the Gentleman was surprized to see one of Mr. Adams's Character condescend to so much Goodness with a

poor Man.' 'Child,' said Adams, 'I should be ashamed of my Cloth,
if I thought a poor Man, who is honest, below my Notice or my
familiarity. I know not how those who think otherwise, can profess
themselves Followers and Servants of him who made no distinction,
unless, peradventure, by preferring the Poor to the Rich. Sir,' said
he, addressing himself to the Gentleman, 'these two poor young
People are my Parishioners, and I look on them and love them as
my Children. There is something singular enough in their History,
but I have not now time to recount it.' The Master of the House,
notwithstanding the Simplicity which discovered itself in Adams,
knew too much of the World to give a hasty Belief to Professions.
He was not yet quite certain that Adams had any more of the Clergyman in him than his Cassock. To try him therefore further, he
asked him, 'if Mr. Pope had lately published any thing new?' Adams
answer'd, 'he had heard great Commendations of that Poet, but
that he had never read, nor knew any of his Works.' 'Ho! ho!' says
the Gentleman to himself, 'have I caught you?' 'What,' said he,
'have you never seen his Homer?' Adams answer'd, 'he had never
read any Translation of the Classicks.' 'Why truly,' reply'd the Gentleman, 'there is a Dignity in the Greek Language which I think no
modern Tongue can reach.' 'Do you understand Greek, Sir,' said
Adams hastily. 'A little, Sir,' answered the Gentleman. 'Do you
know, Sir,' cry'd Adams, 'where I can buy an *Æschylus;* an unlucky
Misfortune lately happened to mine.' *Æschylus* was beyond the
Gentleman, tho' he knew him very well by Name; he therefore
returning back to *Homer,* asked Adams 'what Part of the *Iliad* he
thought most excellent.' Adams return'd, 'His Question would be
properer, what kind of Beauty was the chief in Poetry; for that
Homer was equally excellent in them all.'

'And indeed,' continued he, 'what Cicero says of a complete
Orator, may well be applied to a great Poet; *He ought to comprehend all Perfections.*[4] Homer did this in the most excellent Degree;
it is not without Reason therefore, that the Philosopher,[5] in the 22d
Chap. of his Poeticks, mentions him by no other Appellation than
that of *The Poet:* He was the Father of the Drama, as well as the
Epic: Not of Tragedy only, but of Comedy also; for his *Margites,*
which is deplorably lost, bore, says Aristotle, the same Analogy to

[4] Cicero, *De Oratore* 1.6.
[5] That is, Aristotle, in his *Poetics.*

Comedy, as his Odyssey and Iliad to Tragedy. To him therefore we
owe Aristophanes, as well as Euripides, Sophocles, and my poor
Æschylus. But if you please we will confine ourselves (at least for
the present) to the *Iliad,* his noblest Work; tho' neither Aristotle,
nor Horace give it the Preference, as I remember, to the *Odyssey.*
First then as to his Subject, can any thing be more simple, and at the
same time more noble? He is rightly praised by the first of those
judicious Critics, for not chusing the whole War, which, tho' he says
it hath a complete Beginning and End, would have been too great
for the Understanding to comprehend at one View. I have therefore
often wondered why so correct a Writer as Horace should, in his
Epistle to Lollius, call him the *Trojani Belli Scriptorem.*[6] Secondly,
his Action, termed by Aristotle *Pragmaton Systasis;*[7] is it possible
for the Mind of Man to conceive an Idea of such perfect Unity, and
at the same time so replete with Greatness? And here I must observe
what I do not remember to have seen noted by any, the
Harmotton,[8] that Agreement of his Action to his Subject: For as the
Subject is Anger, how agreeable is his Action, which is War? from
which every Incident arises, and to which every Episode immediately relates. Thirdly, his Manners, which Aristotle places second in
his Description of the several Parts of Tragedy, and which he says
are included in the Action; I am at a Loss whether I should rather
admire the Exactness of his Judgment in the nice Distinction, or the
Immensity of his Imagination in their Variety. For, as to the former
of these, how accurately is the sedate, injured Resentment of
Achilles distinguished from the hot insulting Passion of Agamemnon? How widely doth the brutal Courage of Ajax differ from the
amiable Bravery of Diomedes; and the Wisdom of Nestor, which is
the Result of long Reflection and Experience, from the Cunning of
Ulysses, the Effect of Art and Subtilty only? If we consider their
Variety, we may cry out with Aristotle in his 24th Chapter, that no
Part of this divine Poem is destitute of Manners. Indeed I might
affirm, that there is scarce a Character in human Nature untouched
in some part or other. And as there is no Passion which he is not
able to describe, so is there none in his Reader which he cannot
raise. If he hath any superior Excellence to the rest, I have been

---

[6] "Author of the Trojan War" (Horace, *Epistles* 1.2).
[7] "Arrangement of the incidents," or plot (*Poetics* 6).
[8] "The fitting" or "the suitable" (*Poetics* 15, 22).

inclined to fancy it is in the Pathetic.⁹ I am sure I never read with
dry Eyes the two Episodes, where Andromache is introduced, in the
former lamenting the Danger, and in the latter the Death of
Hector.¹⁰ The Images are so extremely tender in these, that I am
convinced, the Poet had the worthiest and best Heart imaginable.
Nor can I help observing how Sophocles falls short of the Beauties
of the Original, in that Imitation of the dissuasive Speech of Andromache, which he hath put into the Mouth of Tecmessa.¹¹ And yet
Sophocles was the greatest Genius who ever wrote Tragedy, nor
have any of his Successors in that Art, that is to say, neither Euripides nor Seneca the Tragedian, been able to come near him. As to his
Sentiments and Diction, I need say nothing; the former are particularly remarkable for the utmost Perfection on that Head, namely
Propriety; and as to the latter, Aristotle, whom doubtless you have
read over and over, is very diffuse. I shall mention but one thing
more, which that great Critic in his Division of Tragedy calls *Opsis*,
or the Scenery, and which is as proper to the Epic as to the Drama,
with this Difference, that in the former it falls to the share of the
Poet, and in the latter to that of the Painter. But did ever Painter
imagine a Scene like that in the 13th and 14th *Iliads*? where the
Reader sees at one View the Prospect of Troy, with the Army drawn
up before it; the Grecian Army, Camp, and Fleet, Jupiter sitting on
Mount Ida, with his Head wrapt in a Cloud, and a Thunderbolt in
his Hand looking towards Thrace; Neptune driving through the
Sea, which divides on each side to permit his Passage, and then seating himself on Mount Samos: The Heavens opened, and the Deities
all seated on their Thrones. This is Sublime! This is Poetry!' Adams
then rapt out a hundred Greek Verses, and with such a Voice,
Emphasis and Action,¹² that he almost frighten'd the Women; and
as for the Gentleman, he was so far from entertaining any further
Suspicion of Adams, that he now doubted whether he had not a
Bishop in his House. He ran into the most extravagant Encomiums
on his Learning; and the Goodness of his Heart began to dilate to
all the Strangers. He said he had great Compassion for the poor

---

⁹ "Affecting the passions; passionate; moving" (Johnson).

¹⁰ *Iliad* 6.405–39, 22.475–514.

¹¹ Sophocles, *Ajax* 485–524; Tecmessa is the captive wife of the hero Ajax.

¹² "Action" in the oratorical sense of "gesticulation; the accordance of the motions
of the body with the words spoken" (Johnson).

young Woman, who looked pale and faint with her Journey; and in Truth he conceived a much higher Opinion of her Quality than it deserved. He said, he was sorry he could not accommodate them all: But if they were contented with his Fire-side, he would sit up with the Men; and the young Woman might, if she pleased, partake his Wife's Bed, which he advised her to; for that they must walk upwards of a Mile to any House of Entertainment, and that not very good neither. Adams, who liked his Seat, his Ale, his Tobacco, and his Company, persuaded Fanny to accept this kind Proposal, in which Sollicitation he was seconded by Joseph. Nor was she very difficultly prevailed on; for she had slept little the last Night, and not at all the preceding, so that Love itself was scarce able to keep her Eyes open any longer. The Offer therefore being kindly accepted, the good Woman produced every thing eatable in her House on the Table, and the Guests being heartily invited, as heartily regaled themselves, especially Parson Adams. As to the other two, they were Examples of the Truth of that physical Observation, that Love, like other sweet Things, is no Whetter of the Stomach.

Supper was no sooner ended, than Fanny, at her own Request, retired, and the good Woman bore her Company. The Man of the House, Adams, and Joseph, who would modestly have withdrawn, had not the Gentleman insisted on the contrary, drew round the Fire-side, where Adams, (to use his own Words) replenished his Pipe, and the Gentleman produced a Bottle of excellent Beer, being the best Liquor in his House.

The modest Behaviour of Joseph, with the Gracefulness of his Person, the Character which Adams gave of him, and the Friendship he seemed to entertain for him, began to work on the Gentleman's Affections and raised in him a Curiosity to know the Singularity which Adams had mentioned in his History. This Curiosity Adams was no sooner informed of, than with Joseph's Consent, he agreed to gratify it, and accordingly related all he knew, with as much Tenderness as was possible for the Character of Lady Booby; and concluded with the long, faithful and mutual Passion between him and Fanny, not concealing the Meanness of her Birth and Education. These latter Circumstances entirely cured a Jealousy[13] which had lately risen in the Gentleman's Mind, that

---

[13] In the sense of "suspicious fear" (Johnson).

Fanny was the Daughter of some Person of Fashion, and that Joseph had run away with her, and Adams was concerned in the Plot. He was now enamour'd of his Guests, drank their Healths with great Cheerfulness, and returned many Thanks to Adams, who had spent much Breath; for he was a circumstantial Teller of a Story.

Adams told him it was now in his Power to return that Favour; for his extraordinary Goodness, as well as that Fund of Literature he was Master of,* which he did not expect to find under such a Roof, had raised in him more Curiosity than he had ever known. Therefore, said he, if it be not too troublesome, Sir, your History, if you please.

The Gentleman answered, he could not refuse him what he had so much right to insist on; and after some of the common Apologies, which are the usual Preface to a Story, he thus began.

CHAP. III.

In which the Gentleman relates the History of his Life.

SIR, I am descended of a good Family, and was born a Gentleman. My Education was liberal, and at a public School,¹ in which I proceeded

---

* *Fielding's note*: The Author hath by some been represented to have made a Blunder here: For Adams had indeed shewn some Learning, (say they) perhaps all the Author had; but the Gentleman hath shewn none, unless his Approbation of Mr. Adams be such: But surely it would be preposterous in him to call it so. I have, however, notwithstanding this Criticism, which I am told came from the Mouth of a great Orator in a public Coffee-House, left this Blunder as it stood in the First Edition. I will not have the Vanity to apply to any thing in this Work, the Observation which M. Dacier [Anne Lefevere Dacier, 1654–1720, French translator of the classics] makes in her Preface to her Aristophanes: *Je tiens pour une Maxime constante qu'une Beauté mediocre plait plus generalement qu'une Beauté sans défaut* [I hold as an invariable maxim that a middling beauty pleases more generally than a faultless beauty]. Mr. Congreve hath made such another Blunder in his *Love for Love* [stage-comedy, 1695], where Tattle tells Miss Prue, *She should admire him as much for the Beauty he commends in her, as if he himself was possest of it.*

¹ "Public schools" or "great schools" were private boarding schools for boys that offered instruction in Latin and Greek and served as conduits to Cambridge and Oxford Universities: chief among them were Eton, Winchester, Westminster, and Harrow. They were "public" in the sense of being royally chartered and endowed for the public benefit rather than run for entrepreneurial profit. They were also "public" in relation to the educational alternatives that Adams endorses below in Chapter 5: being tutored in one's own home, or taught in small groups in the home of an instructor such as Adams.

so far as to become Master of the Latin, and to be tolerably versed in the Greek Language. My Father died when I was sixteen, and left me Master of myself. He bequeathed me a moderate Fortune, which he intended I should not receive till I attained the Age of twenty-five: For he constantly asserted that was full early enough, to give up any Man entirely to the Guidance of his own Discretion. However, as this Intention was so obscurely worded in his Will, that the Lawyers advised me to contest the Point with my Trustees; I own I paid so little Regard to the Inclinations of my dead Father, which were sufficiently certain to me, that I followed their Advice, and soon succeeded: For the Trustees did not contest the Matter very obstinately on their side. 'Sir,' said Adams, 'May I crave the Favour of your Name?' The Gentleman answered, 'his Name was Wilson,' and then proceeded.

I stay'd a very little while at School after his Death; for, being a forward Youth, I was extremely impatient to be in the World: For which I thought my Parts, Knowledge, and Manhood, thoroughly qualified me. And to this early Introduction into Life, without a Guide, I impute all my future Misfortunes; for besides the obvious Mischiefs which attend this, there is one which hath not been so generally observed. The first Impression which Mankind receives of you, will be very difficult to eradicate. How unhappy, therefore, must it be to fix your Character in Life, before you can possibly know its Value, or weigh the Consequences of those Actions which are to establish your future Reputation?

A little under seventeen I left my School, and went to London, with no more than six Pounds in my Pocket. A great Sum as I then conceived; and which I was afterwards surprized to find so soon consumed.

The Character I was ambitious of attaining, was that of a fine Gentleman; the first Requisites to which I apprehended were to be supplied by a Taylor, a Periwig-maker, and some few more Tradesmen, who deal in furnishing out the human Body. Notwithstanding the Lowness of my Purse, I found Credit with them more easily than I expected, and was soon equipped to my Wish. This I own then agreeably surprized me; but I have since learned, that it is a Maxim among many Tradesmen at the polite End of the Town to deal as largely as they can, reckon[2] as high as they can, and arrest as soon as they can.

---

[2] Charge.

The next Qualifications, namely Dancing, Fencing, Riding the great Horse, and Music, came into my Head: But as they required Expence and Time, I comforted myself with regard to Dancing, that I had learned a little in my Youth, and could walk a Minuet genteelly enough; as to Fencing, I thought my Good-Humour would preserve me from the Danger of a Quarrel; as to the Horse, I hoped it would not be thought of; and for Music, I imagined I could easily acquire the Reputation of it; for I had heard some of my Schoolfellows pretend to Knowledge in Operas, without being able to sing or play on the Fiddle.

Knowledge of the Town seemed another Ingredient; this I thought I should arrive at by frequenting public Places. Accordingly I paid constant Attendance to them all; by which means I was soon Master of the fashionable Phrases, learned to cry up the fashionable Diversions, and knew the Names and Faces of the most fashionable Men and Women.

Nothing now seemed to remain but an Intrigue, which I was resolved to have immediately; I mean the Reputation of it; and indeed I was so successful, that in a very short time I had half a dozen with the finest Women in Town.

At these Words Adams fetched a deep Groan, and then, blessing himself, cry'd out, *Good Lord! What wicked Times these are?*

Not so wicked as you imagine, continued the Gentleman; for I assure you, they were all Vestal Virgins for any thing which I knew to the contrary. The Reputation of Intriguing with them was all I sought, and was what I arrived at: and perhaps I only flattered myself even in that; for very probably the Persons to whom I shewed their Billets, knew as well as I, that they were Counterfeits, and that I had written them to myself.

'*Write Letters to yourself!*' said Adams staring!

O sir, answered the Gentleman, *It is the very Error of the Times.* Half our modern Plays have one of these Characters in them. It is incredible the Pains I have taken, and the absurd Methods I employed to traduce the Character of Women of Distinction. When another had spoken in Raptures of any one, I have answered, 'D—n her, she! We shall have her at H—d's[3] very soon.' When he hath replied, 'he thought her virtuous,' I have answered, 'Ay, thou wilt always think a Woman virtuous, till she is in the Streets; but you and I, Jack or Tom,

---

[3] "Mother Haywood's," a fashionable brothel in Covent Garden.

(turning to another in Company) know better.' At which I have drawn a Paper out of my Pocket, perhaps a Taylor's Bill, and kissed it, crying at the same time, *By Gad I was once fond of her.*

'Proceed, if you please, but do not swear any more,' said Adams.

Sir, said the Gentleman, I ask your Pardon. Well, Sir, in this Course of Life I continued full three Years.— 'What Course of Life?' answered Adams; 'I do not remember you have yet mentioned any.' —Your Remark is just, said the Gentleman smiling, I should rather have said, in this Course of doing nothing. I remember some time afterwards I wrote the Journal of one Day, which would serve, I believe, as well for any other, during the whole Time. I will endeavour to repeat it to you.

In the Morning I arose, took my great Stick, and walked out in my green Frock with my Hair in Papers, (*a Groan from Adams*) and sauntered about till ten.

Went to the Auction; told Lady — she had a dirty Face; laughed heartily at something Captain — said; I can't remember what; for I did not very well hear it; whispered Lord — ; bowed to the Duke of — ; and was going to bid for a Snuff-box; but did not, for fear I should have had it.

From 2 to 4, drest myself.	A Groan.
4 to 6, dined.	A Groan.
6 to 8, Coffee-house.	
8 to 9, Drury-Lane Play-house.	
9 to 10, Lincoln's-Inn-Fields.	
10 to 12, Drawing-Room.	A great Groan.

At all which Places nothing happened worth Remark. At which Adams said with some Vehemence, 'Sir, this is below the Life of an Animal, hardly above Vegetation; and I am surprized what could lead a Man of your Sense into it.' What leads us into more Follies than you imagine, Doctor, answered the Gentleman, Vanity: For as contemptible a Creature as I was, and I assure you, yourself cannot have more Contempt for such a Wretch than I now have, I then admired myself, and should have despised a Person of your present Appearance (you will pardon me) with all your Learning, and those excellent Qualities which I have remarked in you. Adams bowed, and begged him to proceed. After I had continued two Years in this Course of Life, said the Gentleman, an Accident happened which obliged me to change the Scene. As I was one day at St. James's

Coffee-house, making very free with the Character of a young Lady of Quality, an Officer of the Guards, who was present, thought proper to give me the lye.[4] I answered, I might possibly be mistaken; but I intended to tell no more than the Truth. To which he made no Reply, but by a scornful Sneer. After this I observed a strange Coldness in all my Acquaintance; none of them spoke to me first, and very few returned me even the Civility of a Bow. The Company I used to dine with, left me out, and within a Week I found myself in as much Solitude at St. James's, as if I had been in a Desart. An honest elderly Man, with a great Hat and long Sword, at last told me, he had a Compassion for my Youth, and therefore advised me to shew the World I was not such a Rascal as they thought me to be. I did not at first understand him: But he explained himself, and ended with telling me, if I would write a Challenge to the Captain, he would, out of pure Charity, go to him with it. 'A very charitable Person truly!' cried Adams. I desired till the next Day, continued the Gentleman, to consider on it, and retiring to my Lodgings, I weighed the Consequences on both sides as fairly as I could. On the one, I saw the Risk of this Alternative, either losing my own Life, or having on my hands the Blood of a Man with whom I was not in the least angry. I soon determined that the Good which appeared on the other, was not worth this Hazard. I therefore resolved to quit the Scene, and presently retired to the Temple,[5] where I took Chambers. Here I soon got a fresh Set of Acquaintance, who knew nothing of what had happened to me. Indeed they were not greatly to my Approbation; for the Beaus of the Temple are only the Shadows of the others. They are the Affectation of Affectation. The Vanity of these is still more ridiculous, if possible, than of the others. Here I met with smart Fellows, who drank with Lords they did not know, and intrigued with Women they never saw. Covent-Garden[6] was now the farthest Stretch of my Ambition, where I shone forth in the Balconies at the Play-houses, visited Whores, made Love to Orange-Wenches, and damned Plays. This

---

[4] A gentleman accused of lying was expected to challenge his accuser to a duel (this is the "challenge" referred to below). Fielding, as a novelist and later as a magistrate, disapproved of the practice of dueling.

[5] A complex of buildings near the center of the old City of London inhabited by law students, many of whom were interested more in theater-going than in their studies.

[6] The district of London known for its playhouses, fruit-vendors ("orange-wenches") and prostitutes.

Career was soon put a stop to by my Surgeon, who convinced me of the Necessity of confining myself to my Room for a Month.[7] At the End of which, having had Leisure to reflect, I resolved to quit all further Conversation with Beaus and Smarts of every kind, and to avoid, if possible, any Occasion of returning to this Place of Confinement. 'I think,' said Adams, 'the Advice of a Month's Retirement and Reflection was very proper; but I should rather have expected it from a Divine than a Surgeon.' The Gentleman smiled at Adams's Simplicity, and without explaining himself farther on such an odious Subject, went on thus: I was no sooner perfectly restored to Health, than I found my Passion for Women, which I was afraid to satisfy as I had done, made me very uneasy; I determined therefore to keep a Mistress. Nor was I long before I fixed my Choice on a young Woman, who had before been kept by two Gentlemen, and to whom I was recommended by a celebrated Bawd. I took her home to my Chambers, and made her a Settlement during Cohabitation. This would perhaps have been very ill paid: However, she did not suffer me to be perplexed on this account; for before Quarter-day,[8] I found her at my Chambers in too familiar Conversation with a young Fellow who was drest like an Officer, but was indeed a City Apprentice. Instead of excusing her Inconstancy, she rapped out half a dozen Oaths, and, snapping her Fingers at me, swore she scorned to confine herself to the best Man in England. Upon this we parted, and the same Bawd presently provided her another Keeper. I was not so much concerned at our Separation, as I found within a Day or two I had Reason to be for our Meeting: For I was obliged to pay a second Visit to my Surgeon. I was now forced to do Penance for some Weeks, during which Time I contracted an Acquaintance with a beautiful young Girl, the Daughter of a Gentleman, who, after having been 40 Years in the Army, and in all the Campaigns under the Duke of Marlborough, died a Lieutenant on Half-Pay; and had left a Widow with this only Child, in very distrest Circumstances: They had only a small Pension from the Government, with what little the Daughter could add to it by her Work; for she had great Excellence at her Needle. This Girl was, at my first Acquaintance with her, sollicited in Marriage by a young Fellow in good Circumstances. He was Apprentice to a Linen-draper, and had a

---

[7] That is, as part of a cure for a sexually transmitted disease.

[8] "One of the four days in the year on which rent or interest is paid" (Johnson).

little Fortune sufficient to set up his Trade. The Mother was greatly pleased with this Match, as indeed she had sufficient Reason. However, I soon prevented it. I represented him in so low a Light to his Mistress, and made so good an Use of Flattery, Promises, and Presents, that, not to dwell longer on this Subject than is necessary, I prevailed with the poor Girl, and conveyed her away from her Mother! In a word, I debauched her. —(At which Words Adams started up, fetched three Strides cross the Room, and then replaced himself in his Chair.) You are not more affected with this Part of my Story than myself: I assure you it will never be sufficiently repented of in my own Opinion: But if you already detest it, how much more will your Indignation be raised when you hear the fatal Consequences of this barbarous, this villainous Action? If you please therefore, I will here desist.—'By no means,' cries Adams, 'Go on, I beseech you; and Heaven grant you may sincerely repent of this and many other things you have related.' —I was now, continued the Gentleman, as happy as the Possession of a fine young Creature, who had a good Education, and was endued with many agreeable Qualities, could make me. We lived some Months with vast Fondness together, without any Company or Conversation more than we found in one another: But this could not continue always; and tho' I still preserved a great Affection for her, I began more and more to want the Relief of other Company, and consequently to leave her by Degrees, at last, whole Days to herself. She failed not to testify some Uneasiness on these Occasions, and complained of the melancholy Life she led; to remedy which, I introduced her into the Acquaintance of some other kept Mistresses, with whom she used to play at Cards, and frequent Plays and other Diversions. She had not lived long in this Intimacy, before I perceived a visible Alteration in her Behaviour; all her Modesty and Innocence vanished by Degrees, till her Mind became thoroughly tainted. She affected the Company of Rakes, gave herself all manner of Airs, was never easy but abroad, or when she had a Party at my Chambers. She was rapacious of Money, extravagant to Excess, loose in her Conversation; and if ever I demurred to any of her Demands, Oaths, Tears, and Fits were the immediate Consequences. As the first Raptures of Fondness were long since over, this Behaviour soon estranged my Affections from her; I began to reflect with Pleasure that she was not my Wife, and to conceive an Intention of parting with her; of which having given her a Hint, she took care to prevent me the Pains of turning her out of doors, and accordingly departed herself, having first broken open my Escrutore, and taken with her all she could find, to the Amount of about 200 £. In the first Heat of my Resentment, I resolved to pursue her with all the Vengeance of the Law: But as she had the good Luck to escape me during that Ferment, my Passion afterwards cooled; and having reflected that I had been the first Aggressor, and had done her an Injury for which I could make her no Reparation, by robbing her of the Innocence of her Mind; and hearing at the same time that the poor old Woman her Mother had broke her Heart on her Daughter's Elopement from her, I, concluding myself her Murderer, ('As you very well might,' cries Adams, with a Groan;) was pleased, that God Almighty had taken this Method of punishing me, and resolved quietly to submit to the Loss. Indeed I could wish I had never heard more of the poor Creature, who became in the end an abandoned Profligate; and, after being some Years a common Prostitute, at last ended her miserable Life in Newgate.[9] —Here the Gentleman fetched a deep Sigh, which Mr. Adams echoed very loudly; and both continued silent, looking on each other, for some Minutes. At last the Gentleman proceeded thus: I had been perfectly constant to this Girl during the whole Time I kept her: But she had scarce departed before I discovered more Marks of her Infidelity to me than the Loss of my Money. In short, I was forced to make a third Visit to my Surgeon, out of whose Hands I did not get a hasty Discharge.

I now forswore all future Dealings with the Sex, complained loudly that the Pleasure did not compensate the Pain, and railed at the beautiful Creatures, in as gross Language as Juvenal himself formerly reviled them in.[10] I looked on all the Town-Harlots with a Detestation not easy to be conceived; their Persons appeared to me as painted Palaces inhabited by Disease and Death: Nor could their Beauty make them more desirable Objects in my Eyes, than Gilding could make me covet a Pill, or golden Plates a Coffin. But tho' I was no longer the absolute Slave, I found some Reasons to own myself still the Subject of Love. My Hatred for Women decreased daily; and I am not positive but Time might have betrayed me again to some common Harlot, had I not been secured by a Passion for the charming Sapphira; which having once entered upon, made a

---

[9] London's principal prison.

[10] The 6th Satire of the Latin poet Juvenal, which Dryden translated in 1693, calling it "a bitter invective against the fair sex," but reassuring his readers: "Whatever his Roman ladies were, the English are free from all his imputations."

violent Progress in my Heart. Sapphira was Wife to a Man of Fashion and Gallantry, and one who seemed, I own, every way worthy of her Affections, which however he had not the Reputation of having. She was indeed a *Coquette achevée*.[11] 'Pray Sir,' says Adams, 'What is a Coquette? I have met with the Word in French Authors, but never could assign any Idea to it. I believe it is the same with *une Sotte,* Anglicé, *a Fool.*' Sir, answer'd the Gentleman, perhaps you are not much mistaken: but as it is a particular kind of Folly, I will endeavour to describe it. Were all Creatures to be ranked in the Order of Creation, according to their Usefulness, I know few Animals that would not take Place of a Coquette; nor indeed hath this Creature much Pretence to any thing beyond Instinct: for tho' sometimes we might imagine it was animated by the Passion of Vanity, yet far the greater part of its Actions fall beneath even that low Motive; for instance, several absurd Gestures and Tricks, infinitely more foolish than what can be observed in the most ridiculous Birds and Beasts, and which would persuade the Beholder, that the silly Wretch was aiming at our Contempt. Indeed its Characteristic is Affectation, and this led and governed by Whim only: for as Beauty, Wisdom, Wit, Good-nature, Politeness and Health are sometimes affected by this Creature; so are Ugliness, Folly, Nonsense, Ill-nature, Ill-breeding and Sickness likewise put on by it in their Turn. Its Life is one constant Lye, and the only Rule by which you can form any Judgment of them is, that they are never what they seem. If it was possible for a Coquette to love (as it is not, for if ever it attains this Passion, the Coquette ceases instantly) it would wear the Face of Indifference, if not of Hatred, to the beloved Object; you may therefore be assured, when they endeavour to persuade you of their Liking, that they are indifferent to you at least. And indeed this was the Case of my Sapphira, who no sooner saw me in the number of her Admirers, than she gave me what is commonly called Encouragement; she would often look at me, and, when she perceived me meet her Eyes, would instantly take them off, discovering at the same time as much Surprize and Emotion as possible. These Arts failed not of the Success she intended; and as I grew more particular to her than the rest of her Admirers, she advanced, in Proportion, more directly to me than to the others. She affected the low Voice, Whisper, Lisp, Sigh, Start, Laugh, and

[11] "An accomplished flirt."

many other Indications of Passion, which daily deceive Thousands. When I play'd at Whisk[12] with her, she would look earnestly at me, and at the same time lose Deal or revoke; then burst into a ridiculous Laugh, and cry, 'La! I can't imagine what I was thinking of.' To detain you no longer, after I had gone through a sufficient Course of Gallantry, as I thought, and was thoroughly convinced I had raised a violent Passion in my Mistress; I sought an Opportunity of coming to an *Eclaircissement*[13] with her. She avoided this as much as possible; however great Assiduity at length presented me one. I will not describe all the Particulars of this Interview; let it suffice, that till she could no longer pretend not to see my Drift, she first affected a violent Surprize, and immediately after as violent a Passion: She wondered what I had seen in her Conduct, which could induce me to affront her in this manner: And breaking from me the first Moment she could, told me, I had no other way to escape the Consequence of her Resentment, than by never seeing, or at least speaking to her more. I was not contented with this Answer; I still pursued her, but to no Purpose, and was at length convinced that her Husband had the sole Possession of her Person, and that neither he nor any other had made any Impression on her Heart. I was taken off from following this *Ignis Fatuus*[14] by some Advances which were made me by the Wife of a Citizen,[15] who, tho' neither very young nor handsome, was yet too agreeable to be rejected by my amorous Constitution. I accordingly soon satisfied her, that she had not cast away her Hints on a barren or cold Soil; on the contrary, they instantly produced her an eager and desiring Lover. Nor did she give me any Reason to complain; she met the Warmth she had raised, with equal Ardour. I had no longer a Coquette to deal with, but one who was wiser than to prostitute the noble Passion of Love to the ridiculous Lust of Vanity. We presently understood one another; and as the Pleasures we sought lay in a mutual Gratification, we soon found and enjoyed them. I thought myself at first greatly happy in the possession of this new Mistress, whose Fondness would have quickly surfeited a more sickly Appetite, but it had

---

[12] Or "whist," a card game.

[13] An open understanding.

[14] "Foolish fire," a phosphorescent light that sometimes appears over marshlands (perhaps the result of rotting organic materials) and misleads travelers; thus, anything misleading or delusive.

[15] "A man of trade, not a gentleman" (Johnson).

a different Effect on mine; she carried my Passion higher by it than Youth or Beauty had been able: But my Happiness could not long continue uninterrupted. The Apprehensions we lay under from the Jealousy of her Husband, gave us great Uneasiness. 'Poor Wretch! I pity him,' cry'd Adams. He did indeed deserve it, said the Gentleman, for he loved his Wife with great Tenderness; and I assure you it is a great Satisfaction to me that I was not the Man who first seduced her Affections from him. These Apprehensions appeared also too well grounded; for in the End he discovered us, and procured Witnesses of our Caresses. He then prosecuted me at Law, and recovered 3000 £. Damages,[16] which much distressed my Fortune to pay: and what was worse, his Wife being divorced came upon my hands. I led a very uneasy Life with her; for besides that my Passion was now much abated, her excessive Jealousy was very troublesome. At length Death rid me of an Inconvenience, which the Consideration of my having been the Author of her Misfortunes would never suffer me to take any other Method of discarding.

I now bade adieu to Love, and resolved to pursue other less dangerous and expensive Pleasures. I fell into the Acquaintance of a Set of jolly Companions, who slept all Day and drank all Night: Fellows who might rather be said to consume Time than to live. Their best Conversation was nothing but Noise: Singing, Hollowing, Wrangling, Drinking, Toasting, Sp—wing, Smoking, were the chief Ingredients of our Entertainment. And yet bad as these were, they were more tolerable than our graver Scenes, which were either excessive tedious Narratives of dull common Matters of Fact, or hot Disputes about trifling Matters, which commonly ended in a Wager. This Way of Life the first serious Reflection put a Period to; and I became Member of a Club frequented by young Men of great Abilities. The Bottle was now only called in to the Assistance of our Conversation, which rolled on the deepest Points of Philosophy. These Gentlemen were engaged in a Search after Truth, in the Pursuit of which they threw aside all the Prejudices of Education, and governed themselves only by the infallible Guide of Human Reason. This great Guide, after having shewn them the Falshood of that very antient but simple Tenet, that there is such a Being as a Deity in the Universe, helped them to establish in his stead a certain Rule of Right, by adhering to which they all arrived at the utmost Purity of Morals. Reflection

---

[16] That is, the husband's award in a civil suit against Wilson for adultery.

made me as much delighted with this Society, as it had taught me to despise and detest the former. I began now to esteem myself a Being of a higher Order than I had ever before conceived, and was the more charmed with this *Rule of Right,* as I really found in my own Nature nothing repugnant to it. I held in utter Contempt all Persons who wanted any other Inducement to Virtue besides her intrinsic Beauty and Excellence;[17] and had so high an Opinion of my present Companions, with regard to their Morality, that I would have trusted them with whatever was nearest and dearest to me. Whilst I was engaged in this delightful Dream, two or three Accidents happened successively, which at first much surprized me. For, one of our greatest Philosophers, or *Rule of Right-men,* withdrew himself from us, taking with him the Wife of one of his most intimate Friends. Secondly, Another of the same Society left the Club without remembring to take leave of his Bail. A third having borrowed a Sum of Money of me, for which I received no Security, when I asked him to repay it, absolutely denied the Loan. These several Practices, so inconsistent with our golden Rule, made me begin to suspect its Infallibility; but when I communicated my Thoughts to one of the Club, he said, 'there was nothing absolutely good or evil in itself; that Actions were denominated good or bad by the Circumstances of the Agent. That possibly the Man who ran away with his Neighbour's Wife, might be one of very good Inclinations, but overprevailed on by the Violence of an unruly Passion, and, in other Particulars, might be a very worthy Member of Society: That if the Beauty of any Woman created in him an Uneasiness, he had a Right from Nature to relieve himself;' with many other Things, which I then detested so much, that I took Leave of the Society that very Evening, and never returned to it again. Being now reduced to a State of Solitude which I did not like, I became a great Frequenter of the Play-houses, which indeed was always my favourite Diversion, and most Evenings past away two or three Hours behind the Scenes, where I met with several Poets,[18] with whom I made Engagements at the Taverns. Some of the Players were likewise of our Parties.

---

[17] The "rule of right-men" are influenced by the third earl of Shaftesbury, who held "a beautiful . . . Action" to be the best and most pleasing object of contemplation: see Contexts, p. 348. In *The Moralists* 2.3, Shaftesbury asked, "Is it not still for the Good of Mankind and of the World, that Obedience to the *Rule of Right* should . . . be paid?"

[18] That is, playwrights.

At these Meetings we were generally entertain'd by the Poets with reading their Performances, and by the Players with repeating their Parts: Upon which Occasions, I observed the Gentleman who furnished our Entertainment, was commonly the best pleased of the Company; who, tho' they were pretty civil to him to his Face, seldom failed to take the first Opportunity of his Absence to ridicule him. Now I made some Remarks, which probably are too obvious to be worth relating. 'Sir,' says Adams, 'your Remarks, if you please.' First then, says he, I concluded that the general Observation, that Wits are most inclined to Vanity, is not true. Men are equally vain of Riches, Strength, Beauty, Honours, &c. But these appear of themselves to the Eyes of the Beholders, whereas the poor Wit is obliged to produce his Performance to shew you his Perfection; and on his Readiness to do this, that vulgar Opinion I have before mentioned is grounded: But doth not the Person who expends vast Sums in the Furniture of his House, or the Ornaments of his Person, who consumes much Time, and employs great Pains in dressing himself, or who thinks himself paid for Self-Denial, Labour, or even Villany, by a Title or a Ribbon, sacrifice as much to Vanity as the poor Wit, who is desirous to read you his Poem or his Play? My second Remark was, that Vanity is the worst of Passions, and more apt to contaminate the Mind than any other: For as Selfishness is much more general than we please to allow it; so it is natural to hate and envy those who stand between us and the Good we desire. Now in Lust and Ambition these are few; and even in Avarice we find many who are no Obstacles to our Pursuits; but the Vain man seeks Pre-eminence; and every Thing which is excellent or praise-worthy in another, renders him the Mark of his Antipathy. Adams now began to fumble in his Pockets, and soon cried out, 'O la! I have it not about me'— Upon this the Gentleman asking him what he was searching for, he said he searched after a Sermon, which he thought his Master-piece, against Vanity. 'Fie upon it, fie upon it,' cries he, 'why do I ever leave that Sermon out of my Pocket? I wish it was within five Miles; I would willingly fetch it, to read it to you.' The Gentleman answered, that there was no Need, for he was cured of the Passion. 'And for that very Reason,' quoth Adams, 'I would read it, for I am confident you would admire it: Indeed, I have never been a greater Enemy to any Passion than that silly one of Vanity.' The Gentleman smiled, and proceeded— From this Society I easily past to that of the Gamesters, where nothing remarkable happened, but the finishing my Fortune, which those Gentlemen soon helped me to the End of.

This opened Scenes of Life hitherto unknown; Poverty and Distress, with their horrid Train of Duns, Attorneys, Bailiffs, haunted me Day and Night. My Clothes grew shabby, my Credit bad, my Friends and Acquaintance of all kinds cold. In this Situation, the strangest Thought imaginable came into my Head; and what was this, but to write a Play? for I had sufficient Leisure; Fear of Bailiffs confined me every Day to my Room; and having always had a little Inclination, and something of a Genius that Way, I set myself to work, and within few Months produced a Piece of five Acts, which was accepted of at the Theatre. I remembered to have formerly taken Tickets of other Poets for their Benefits, long before the Appearance of their Performances;[19] and resolving to follow a Precedent which was so well suited to my present Circumstances, I immediately provided myself with a large Number of little Papers. Happy indeed would be the State of Poetry, would these Tickets pass current at the Bakehouse, the Ale-House, and the Chandler's-Shop: But alas! far otherwise; no Taylor will take them in Payment for Buckram, Stays, Stay-tape; nor no Bailiff for Civility-Money.[20] They are indeed no more than a Passport to beg with, a Certificate that the Owner wants five Shillings, which induces well-disposed Christians to Charity. I now experienced what is worse than Poverty, or rather what is the worst Consequence of Poverty, I mean Attendance and Dependance on the Great. Many a Morning have I waited Hours in the cold Parlours of Men of Quality, where after seeing the lowest Rascals in Lace and Embroidery, the Pimps and Buffoons in Fashion admitted, I have been sometimes told, on sending in my Name, that my Lord could not possibly see me this Morning: A sufficient Assurance that I should never more get Entrance into that House. Sometimes I have been at last admitted; and the great Man hath thought proper to excuse himself, by telling me he was *tied up.* 'Tied up,' says Adams, 'pray what's that?' Sir, says the Gentleman, the Profit which Booksellers allowed Authors for the best Works, was so very small, that certain Men of Birth and Fortune some Years ago, who were the Patrons of Wit and Learning, thought fit to encourage them farther, by entering into voluntary Subscriptions for their Encouragement. Thus Prior, Rowe, Pope, and some other Men of Genius, received large Sums for their Labours from the Public. This seemed so easy a

---

[19] Playwrights often sold tickets in advance for their first "benefit night"—that is, their play's third performance—on which the theater's profits went directly to them.

[20] Money given to a jailer in exchange for preferential treatment.

Method of getting Money, that many of the lowest Scriblers of the Times ventured to publish their Works in the same Way; and many had even the Assurance to take in Subscriptions for what was never writ, nor even intended. Subscriptions in this Manner growing infinite, and a kind of Tax on the Publick; some Persons finding it not so easy a Task to discern good from bad Authors, or to know what Genius was worthy Encouragement, and what was not, to prevent the Expence of Subscribing to so many, invented a Method to excuse themselves from all Subscriptions whatever; and this was to receive a small Sum of Money in Consideration of giving a large one if ever they subscribed; which many have done, and many more have pretended to have done, in order to silence all Sollicitation. The same Method was likewise taken with Play-house Tickets, which were no less a public Grievance; and this is what they call being *tied up* from subscribing. 'I can't say but the Term is apt enough, and somewhat typical, said Adams; for a Man of large Fortune, who ties himself up, as you call it, from the Encouragement of Men of Merit, ought to be tied up in reality.' Well, Sir, says the Gentlemen, to return to my Story. Sometimes I have received a Guinea from a Man of Quality, given with as ill a Grace as Alms are generally to the meanest Beggar, and purchased too with as much Time spent in Attendance, as, if it had been spent in honest Industry, might have brought me more Profit with infinitely more Satisfaction. After about two Months spent in this disagreeable Way with the utmost Mortification, when I was pluming my Hopes on the Prospect of a plentiful Harvest from my Play, upon applying to the Prompter to know when it came into Rehearsal, he informed me he had received Orders from the Managers to return me the Play again; for that they could not possibly act it that Season; but if I would take it and revise it against the next, they would be glad to see it again. I snatch'd it from him with great Indignation, and retired to my Room, where I threw myself on the Bed in a Fit of Despair—'You should rather have thrown yourself on your Knees,' says Adams; 'for Despair is sinful.' As soon, continued the Gentleman, as I had indulged the first Tumult of my Passion, I began to consider coolly what Course I should take, in a Situation without Friends, Money, Credit or Reputation of any kind. After revolving many things in my Mind, I could see no other Possibility of furnishing myself with the miserable Necessaries of Life than to retire to a Garret near the Temple, and commence Hackney-writer to the Lawyers; for which I was well qualified, being an excellent Penman. This Purpose I resolved on, and immediately put it in execution. I had an Acquaintance with an Attorney who had formerly transacted Affairs for me, and to him I applied: But instead of furnishing me with any Business, he laughed at my Undertaking, and told me, 'he was afraid I should turn his Deeds into Plays, and he should expect to see them on the Stage.' Not to tire you with Instances of this kind from others, I found that Plato himself did not hold Poets in greater Abhorrence[21] than these Men of Business do. Whenever I durst venture to a Coffee-house, which was on Sundays only,[22] a Whisper ran round the Room, which was constantly attended with a Sneer—*That's Poet Wilson:* for I know not whether you have observed it, but there is a Malignity in the Nature of Man, which, when not weeded out, or at least covered by a good Education and Politeness, delights in making another uneasy or dissatisfied with himself. This abundantly appears in all Assemblies, except those which are filled by People of Fashion, and especially among the younger People of both Sexes, whose Birth and Fortunes place them just without the polite Circles; I mean the lower Class of the Gentry, and the higher of the mercantile World, who are in reality the worst bred part of Mankind. Well, Sir, whilst I continued in this miserable State, with scarce sufficient Business to keep me from starving, the Reputation of a Poet being my Bane, I accidentally became acquainted with a Bookseller, who told me, 'it was a Pity a Man of my Learning and Genius should be obliged to such a Method of getting his Livelihood; that he had a Compassion for me, and if I would engage with him, he would undertake to provide handsomely for me.' A Man in my Circumstances, as he very well knew, had no Choice. I accordingly accepted his Proposal with his Conditions, which were none of the most favourable, and fell to translating with all my Might. I had no longer Reason to lament the want of Business; for he furnished me with so much, that in half a Year I almost writ myself blind. I likewise contracted a Distemper by my sedentary Life, in which no Part of my Body was exercised but my right Arm, which rendered me incapable of writing for a long time. This unluckily happening to delay the Publication of the Work, and my last Performance not having sold well, the Bookseller declined any further Engagement, and aspersed me to his Brethren as a careless, idle Fellow. I had however, by having half-worked and

---

[21] For Plato's distrust of poets, see *The Republic* Books 2, 3, and 10.
[22] The one day of the week on which debtors like Wilson could not be arrested.

half-starved myself to Death, during the Time I was in his Service, amassed a few Guineas, with which I bought a Lottery-Ticket, resolving to throw myself into Fortune's Lap, and try if she would make me amends for the Injuries she had done me at the Gaming-Table. This Purchase being made left me almost pennyless; when, as if I had not been sufficiently miserable, a Bailiff in Woman's Clothes got Admittance to my Chamber, whither he was directed by the Bookseller. He arrested me at my Taylor's Suit for thirty-five Pounds; a Sum for which I could not procure Bail, and was therefore conveyed to his House, where I was locked up in an upper Chamber.[23] I had now neither Health (for I was scarce recovered from my Indisposition), Liberty, Money, or Friends; and had abandoned all Hopes, and even the Desire of Life. 'But this could not last long,' said Adams; 'for doubtless the Taylor released you the Moment he was truly acquainted with your Affairs; and knew that your Circumstances would not permit you to pay him.' Oh, Sir, answered the Gentleman, he knew that, before he arrested me; nay, he knew that nothing but Incapacity could prevent me paying my Debts; for I had been his Customer many Years, had spent vast Sums of Money with him, and had always paid most punctually in my prosperous Days: But when I reminded him of this, with Assurance, that, if he would not molest my Endeavours, I would pay him all the Money I could, by my utmost Labour and Industry, procure, reserving only what was sufficient to preserve me alive. He answered, His Patience was worn out; that I had put him off from time to time; that he wanted the Money; that he had put it into a Lawyer's Hands; and if I did not pay him immediately, or find Security, I must lie in Goal, and expect no Mercy. 'He may expect Mercy,' cries Adams, starting from his Chair, 'where he will find none. How can such a Wretch repeat the Lord's Prayer, where the Word, which is translated, I know not for what Reason, *Trespasses,* is in the Original *Debts?*[24] And as surely as we do not forgive others their Debts when they are unable to pay them; so surely shall we ourselves be unforgiven, when we are in no

---

[23] A bailiff is an under-officer employed by a sheriff; among his duties is the arrest of debtors. Wilson's first place of confinement is the bailiff's house (or "sponging house"), where debtors were kept before being taken to jail or until they compromised with their creditors. At these houses extortionate charges were commonly made for food, drink, and lodging.

[24] In the Lord's Prayer as it appears in the King James Version of the Bible, Matthew 6:9–15, Jesus says "forgive us our debts," but in the Church of England's *Book of Common Prayer* the line appears (as in Catholic liturgy) "forgive us our trespasses."

Condition of paying.' He ceased, and the Gentleman proceeded. While I was in this deplorable Situation, a former Acquaintance, to whom I had communicated my Lottery-Ticket, found me out, and, making me a Visit, with great Delight in his Countenance, shook me heartily by the Hand, and wished me Joy of my good Fortune: For, says he, your Ticket is come up a Prize of 3000 £. Adams snapt his Fingers at these Words in an Ecstasy of Joy; which however did not continue long: For the Gentleman thus proceeded. Alas! Sir, this was only the Trick of Fortune to sink me the deeper: For I had disposed of this Lottery-Ticket two Days before to a Relation, who refused lending me a Shilling without it, in order to procure myself Bread. As soon as my Friend was acquainted with my unfortunate Sale, he began to revile me, and remind me of all the ill Conduct and Miscarriages of my Life. He said, 'I was one whom Fortune could not save, if she would; that I was now ruined without any Hopes of Retrieval, nor must expect any Pity from my Friends; that it would be extreme Weakness to compassionate the Misfortunes of a Man who ran headlong to his own Destruction.' He then painted to me, in as lively Colours as he was able, the Happiness I should have now enjoyed, had I not foolishly disposed of my Ticket. I urged the Plea of Necessity: But he made no Answer to that, and began again to revile me, till I could bear it no longer, and desired him to finish his Visit. I soon exchanged the Bailiff's House for a Prison; where, as I had not Money sufficient to procure me a separate Apartment, I was crouded in with a great Number of miserable Wretches, in common with whom I was destitute of every Convenience of Life, even that which all the Brutes enjoy, wholesome Air. In these dreadful Circumstances I applied by Letter to several of my old Acquaintance, and such to whom I had formerly lent Money without any great Prospect of its being returned, for their Assistance; but in vain. An Excuse instead of a Denial was the gentlest Answer I received. —Whilst I languished in a Condition too horrible to be described, and which in a Land of Humanity, and, what is much more, Christianity, seems a strange Punishment for a little Inadvertency and Indiscretion; whilst I was in this Condition, a Fellow came one day into the Prison, and enquiring me out, delivered me the following Letter:

SIR,

My Father, to whom you sold your Ticket in the last Lottery, died the same Day in which it came up a Prize, as you have possibly heard, and left me sole Heiress of all his Fortune. I am so much touched with your present Circumstances, and the Uneasiness you must feel at having been driven to dispose of what might have made you happy, that I must desire your Acceptance of the inclosed, and am

Your humble Servant, HARRIET HEARTY.

And what do you think was inclosed? 'I don't know,' cried Adams: 'Not less than a Guinea, I hope.' —Sir, it was a Bank-Note for 200 £—'200 £' says Adams, in a Rapture! —No less, I assure you, answered the Gentleman; a Sum I was not half so delighted with, as with the dear Name of the generous Girl that sent it me; and who was not only the best, but the handsomest Creature in the Universe; and for whom I had long had a Passion, which I never durst disclose to her. I kissed her Name a thousand times, my Eyes overflowing with Tenderness and Gratitude, I repeated—But not to detain you with these Raptures, I immediately acquired my Liberty, and, having paid all my Debts, departed, with upwards of fifty Pounds in my Pocket, to thank my kind Deliverer. She happened to be then out of Town, a Circumstance which, upon Reflection, pleased me; for by that means I had an Opportunity to appear before her in a more decent Dress. At her Return to Town within a Day or two, I threw myself at her Feet with the most ardent Acknowledgments, which she rejected with an unfeigned Greatness of Mind, and told me, I could not oblige her more than by never mentioning, or, if possible, thinking on a Circumstance which must bring to my Mind an Accident that might be grievous to me to think on. She proceeded thus: 'What I have done is in my own Eyes a Trifle, and perhaps infinitely less than would have become me to do. And if you think of engaging in any Business, where a larger Sum may be serviceable to you, I shall not be over-rigid, either as to the Security or Interest.' I endeavoured to express all the Gratitude in my Power to this Profusion of Goodness, tho' perhaps it was my Enemy, and began to afflict my Mind with more Agonies than all the Miseries I had underwent; it affected me with severer Reflections than Poverty, Distress, and Prisons united, had been able to make me feel: For, Sir, these Acts and Professions of Kindness, which were sufficient to have raised in a good Heart the most violent Passion of Friendship to one of the same, or to Age and Ugliness in a different Sex, came to me from a Woman, a young and beautiful Woman, one whose Perfections I had long known; and for whom I had long conceived a violent Passion, tho' with a Despair, which made me endeavour rather to curb and conceal, than to nourish or acquaint her with it. In short, they came upon me united with Beauty, Softness, and Tenderness, such bewitching Smiles—O Mr. Adams, in that Moment I lost myself, and forgetting our different Situations, nor considering what Return I was making to her Goodness, by desiring her, who had given me so much, to bestow her All, I laid gently hold on her Hand, and, conveying it to my Lips, I prest it with inconceivable Ardour; then, lifting up my swimming Eyes, I saw her Face and Neck overspread with one Blush; she offered to withdraw her Hand, yet not so as to deliver it from mine, tho' I held it with the gentlest Force. We both stood trembling, her Eyes cast on the Ground, and mine stedfastly fixed on her. Good G—, what was then the Condition of my Soul! burning with Love, Desire, Admiration, Gratitude, and every tender Passion, all bent on one charming Object. Passion at last got the better of both Reason and Respect, and softly letting go her Hand, I offered madly to clasp her in my Arms; when a little recovering herself, she started from me, asking me, with some Shew of Anger, 'If she had any Reason to expect this Treatment from me.' I then fell prostrate before her, and told her, 'If I had offended, my Life was absolutely in her Power, which I would in any manner lose for her sake. Nay, Madam, said I, you shall not be so ready to punish me, as I to suffer. I own my Guilt. I detest the Reflection that I would have sacrificed your Happiness to mine. Believe me, I sincerely repent my Ingratitude; yet, believe me too, it was my Passion, my unbounded Passion for you, which hurried me so far; I have loved you long and tenderly; and the Goodness you have shewn me, hath innocently weighed down a Wretch undone before. Acquit me of all mean, mercenary Views; and, before I take my Leave of you for ever, which I am resolved instantly to do, believe me, that Fortune could have raised me to no height to which I could not have gladly lifted you. O curst be Fortune.'—'Do not,' says she, interrupting me with the sweetest Voice, 'Do not curse Fortune, since she hath made me happy; and, if she hath put your Happiness in my Power, I have told you, you shall ask nothing in Reason which I will refuse.' 'Madam,' said I, 'you mistake me, if you imagine, as you seem, my Happiness is in the Power of Fortune now. You have obliged me too much already; if I have any Wish, it is for some blest Accident, by which I may contribute with my Life to the least Augmentation of your Felicity. As for myself, the only Happiness I can ever have, will be hearing of yours; and if Fortune will make that complete, I will forgive her all her Wrongs to me.' 'You may, indeed,' answered she, smiling, 'For your own happiness must be included in mine. I have long known your Worth; nay, I must confess,' said she blushing, 'I have long discovered that Passion for me you profess, notwithstanding those Endeavours which I am convinced were unaffected, to conceal it; and if all I can give with Reason will not suffice,—take Reason away,—and now I believe you cannot ask me what I will deny.' —She uttered these Words with a Sweetness not to be imagined. I immediately started; my Blood, which lay freezing at my Heart, rushed tumultuously through every Vein. I stood for a Moment silent; then, flying to her, I caught her in my Arms, no longer resisting,—and softly told her, she must give me then herself.—O Sir,— Can I describe her Look? She remained silent, and almost motionless, several Minutes. At last, recovering herself a little, she insisted on my leaving her, and in such a manner, that I instantly obeyed: You may imagine, however, I soon saw her again.—But I ask Pardon, I fear I have detained you too long in relating the Particulars of the former Interview. 'So far otherwise,' said Adams, licking his Lips, 'that I could willingly hear it over again.' Well, Sir, continued the Gentleman, to be as concise as possible, within a Week she consented to make me the happiest of Mankind. We were married shortly after; and when I came to examine the Circumstances of my Wife's Fortune, (which I do assure you I was not presently at Leisure enough to do) I found it amounted to about six thousand Pounds, most part of which lay in Effects; for her Father had been a Wine-Merchant, and she seemed willing, if I liked it, that I should carry on the same Trade. I readily, and too inconsiderately, undertook it: For, not having been bred up to the Secrets of the Business, and endeavouring to deal with the utmost Honesty and Uprightness, I soon found out Fortune in a declining Way, and my Trade decreasing by little and little: For my Wines, which I never adulterated after their Importation, and were sold as neat as they came over, were universally decried by the Vintners,[25] to whom I could not allow them quite as cheap as those who gained double the Profit by a less Price. I soon began to despair of improving our Fortune by these means; nor was I at all easy at the Visits and Familiarity of many who had been my Acquaintance in my Prosperity, but denied and shunned me in my Adversity, and now very forwardly renewed their Acquaintance with me. In short, I had sufficiently seen, that the Pleasures of the World

---

[25] Wine-selling tavern-keepers. Wilson did not dilute his wines, and so could not compete with wine merchants who did so and could thus sell wine cheaper by volume.

are chiefly Folly, and the Business of it mostly Knavery; and both, nothing better than Vanity: The Men of Pleasure tearing one another to Pieces, from the Emulation of spending Money, and the Men of Business, from Envy in getting it. My Happiness consisted entirely in my Wife, whom I loved with an inexpressible Fondness, which was perfectly returned; and my Prospects were no other than to provide for our growing Family; for she was now big of her second Child: I therefore took an Opportunity to ask her Opinion of entering into a retired Life, which, after hearing my Reasons, and perceiving my Affection for it, she readily embraced. We soon put our small Fortune, now reduced under three thousand Pounds, into Money, with part of which we purchased this little Place, whither we retired soon after her Delivery, from a World full of Bustle, Noise, Hatred, Envy and Ingratitude, to Ease, Quiet and Love. We have here lived almost twenty Years, with little other Conversation than our own, most of the Neighbourhood taking us for very strange People; the Squire of the Parish representing me as a Madman, and the Parson as a Presbyterian; because I will not hunt with the one, nor drink with the other.[26] 'Sir,' says Adams, 'Fortune hath, I think, paid you all her Debts in this sweet Retirement.' Sir, replied the Gentleman, I am thankful to the great Author of all Things for the Blessings I here enjoy. I have the best of Wives, and three pretty Children, for whom I have the true Tenderness of a Parent; but no Blessings are pure in this World. Within three Years of my Arrival here I lost my eldest Son. (*Here he sighed bitterly.*) 'Sir,' says Adams, 'we must submit to Providence, and consider Death is common to all.' We must submit, indeed, answered the Gentleman; and if he had died, I could have borne the Loss with Patience: But alas! Sir, he was stolen away from my Door by some wicked travelling People whom they call *Gipsies;* nor could I ever with the most diligent Search recover him. Poor Child! he had the sweetest Look, the exact Picture of his Mother; at which some Tears unwittingly dropt from his Eyes, as did likewise from those of Adams, who always sympathized with his Friends on those Occasions. Thus, Sir, said the Gentleman, I have finished my Story, in which, if I have been too particular, I ask your Pardon; and now, if you please, I will fetch you another Bottle; which Proposal the Parson thankfully accepted.

---

[26] Presbyterians were reputedly less prone to, or at least more censorious of, drunkenness than were members of the Church of England (including the punch and ale-loving curates we meet in this novel).

CHAP. IV.

A Description of Mr. Wilson's Way of Living. The tragical Adventure of the Dog, and other grave Matters.

THE Gentleman returned with the Bottle; and Adams and he sat some time silent, when the former started up, and cried, 'No, *that won't do.*' The Gentleman enquired into his Meaning; he answered, 'He had been considering that it was possible the late famous King Theodore[1] might have been that very Son whom he lost;' but added, 'that his Age could not answer that Imagination. However,' says he, 'G— disposes all things for the best, and very probably he may be some Great Man, or Duke, and may, one day or other, revisit you in that Capacity.' The Gentleman answered, he should know him amongst ten thousand; for he had a Mark on his left Breast of a Strawberry, which his Mother had given him by longing for that Fruit.[2]

That beautiful young Lady, the Morning, now rose from her Bed, and with a Countenance blooming with fresh Youth and Sprightliness, like Miss ——,* with soft Dews hanging on her pouting Lips, began to take her early Walk over the eastern Hills; and presently after, that gallant Person the Sun stole softly from his Wife's Chamber to pay his Addresses to her; when the Gentleman ask'd his Guest if he would walk forth and survey his little Garden, which he readily agreed to, and Joseph at the same time awaking from a Sleep in which he had been two Hours buried, went with them. No Parterres, no Fountains, no Statues, embellished this little Garden. Its only Ornament was a short Walk, shaded on each Side by a Filbert Hedge, with a small Alcove at one End, whither in hot Weather the Gentleman and his Wife used to retire and divert themselves with their Children, who played in the Walk before them: But tho' Vanity had no Votary in this little Spot, here was variety of Fruit, and every thing useful for the Kitchin, which was abundantly sufficient to catch the Admiration of Adams, who told the Gentleman he had certainly a good Gardener. Sir, answered he, that Gardener is now before you; whatever you see here, is the Work solely of my own Hands. Whilst I am providing Necessaries for my Table, I likewise procure myself an Appetite for them.

---

[1] Theodore Etienne von Neuhof (1686–1756), an international adventurer whose bid to be the King of an independent Corsica was supported by Fielding.

[2] On "maternal impression," see contexts section on Heliodorus and my note, p. 328.

Fielding's note: Whoever the Reader pleases.

In fair Seasons, I seldom pass less than six Hours of the twenty-four in this Place, where I am not idle; and by these means I have been able to preserve my Health ever since my Arrival here without Assistance from Physic. Hither I generally repair at the Dawn, and exercise myself whilst my Wife dresses her Children, and prepares our Breakfast; after which we are seldom asunder during the Residue of the Day; for when the Weather will not permit them to accompany me here, I am usually within with them; for I am neither ashamed of conversing with my Wife, nor of playing with my Children: to say the Truth, I do not perceive that Inferiority of Understanding which the Levity of Rakes, the Dulness of Men of Business, or the Austerity of the Learned would persuade us of in Women. As for my Woman, I declare I have found none of my own Sex capable of making juster Observations on Life, or of delivering them more agreeably; nor do I believe any one possessed of a faithfuller or braver Friend. And sure as this Friendship is sweetened with more Delicacy and Tenderness; so is it confirmed by dearer Pledges than can attend the closest male Alliance: For what Union can be so fast, as our common Interest in the Fruits of our Embraces? Perhaps, Sir, you are not yourself a Father; if you are not, be assured you cannot conceive the Delight I have in my Little-Ones. Would you not despise me, if you saw me stretched on the Ground, and my Children playing round me? 'I should reverence the Sight,' quoth Adams, 'I myself am now the Father of six, and have been of eleven, and I can say I never scourged a Child of my own, unless as his School-master, and then have felt every Stroke on my own Posteriors. And as to what you say concerning Women, I have often lamented my own Wife did not understand Greek.' —The Gentleman smiled, and answered, he would not be apprehended to insinuate that his own had an Understanding above the Care of her Family; on the contrary, says he, my Harriet, I assure you, is a notable Housewife, and few Gentlemen's House-keepers understand Cookery or Confectionary better; but these are Arts which she hath no great Occasion for now: however, the Wine you commended so much last Night at Supper, was of her own making, as is indeed all the Liquor in my House, except my Beer, which falls to my Province. (And I assure you it is as excellent, quoth Adams, as ever I tasted.) We formerly kept a Maid-Servant, but since my Girls have been growing up, she is unwilling to indulge them in Idleness; for as the Fortunes I shall give them will be very small, we intend not to breed them above the Rank they are likely to fill hereafter, nor to teach them to despise, or ruin a plain Husband. Indeed I could wish a Man of my own Temper, and a retired Life might fall to their Lot: for I have experienced that calm serene Happiness which is seated in Content, is inconsistent with the Hurry and Bustle of the World. He was proceeding thus, when the Little Things, being just risen, ran eagerly towards him, and asked him Blessing: They were shy to the Strangers; but the eldest acquainted her Father, that her Mother and the young Gentlewoman were up, and that Breakfast was ready. They all went in, where the Gentleman was surprized at the Beauty of Fanny, who had now recovered herself from her Fatigue, and was entirely clean drest; for the Rogues who had taken away her Purse, had left her her Bundle. But if he was so much amazed at the Beauty of this young Creature, his Guests were no less charmed at the Tenderness which appeared in the Behaviour of Husband and Wife to each other, and to their Children, and the dutiful and affectionate Behaviour of these to their Parents. These Instances pleased the well-disposed Mind of Adams equally with the Readiness which they exprest to oblige their Guests, and their Forwardness to offer them the best of every thing in their House; and what delighted him still more, was an Instance or two of their Charity: for whilst they were at Breakfast, the good Woman was called forth to assist her sick Neighbour, which she did with some Cordials made for the public Use; and the good Man went into his Garden at the same time, to supply another with something which he wanted thence; for they had nothing which those who wanted it were not welcome to. These good People were in the utmost Cheerfulness, when they heard the Report of a Gun; and immediately afterwards a little Dog, the Favourite of the eldest Daughter, came limping in all bloody, and laid himself at his Mistress's Feet: The poor Girl, who was about eleven Years old, burst into Tears at the Sight; and presently one of the Neighbours came in and informed them, that the young 'Squire, the Son of the Lord of the Manor, had shot him as he past by, swearing at the same time he would prosecute the Master of him for keeping a Spaniel; for that he had given Notice he would not suffer one in the Parish.[3] The Dog, whom his Mistress had taken into her Lap, died in a few Minutes, licking her Hand. She exprest great Agony at his Loss, and the other Children began to cry for their Sister's Misfortune, nor could Fanny herself refrain. Whilst the Father and Mother attempted to comfort her, Adams grasped his Crab-stick, and would have sallied out after the Squire, had not Joseph with-held

---

[3] Hunting dogs as well as guns could be confiscated from persons unqualified to hunt, but Wilson, although he does not hunt, is presumably qualified to do so by his property holding. In any event, his daughter's dog is a lap-dog, not a hunting dog.

him. He could not however bridle his Tongue—He pronounced the Word *Rascal* with great Emphasis; said he deserved to be hanged more than a Highwayman, and wish'd he had the scourging him. The Mother took her Child lamenting and carrying the dead Favourite in her Arms out of the Room, when the Gentleman said, this was the second time this Squire had endeavoured to kill the little Wretch, and had wounded him smartly once before, adding, he could have no Motive but Ill-nature; for the little Thing, which was not near as big as one's Fist, had never been twenty Yards from the House in the six Years his Daughter had had it. He said he had done nothing to deserve this Usage: but his Father had too great a Fortune to contend with. That he was as absolute as any Tyrant in the Universe, and had killed all the Dogs, and taken away all the Guns in the Neighbourhood, and not only that, but he trampled down Hedges, and rode over Corn and Gardens, with no more Regard than if they were the Highway. 'I wish I could catch him in my Garden,' said Adams; 'tho' I would rather forgive him riding through my House than such an ill-natur'd Act as this.'

The Cheerfulness of their Conversation being interrupted by this Accident, in which the Guests could be of no Service to their kind Entertainer, and as the Mother was taken up in administring Consolation to the poor Girl, whose Disposition was too good hastily to forget the sudden Loss of her little Favourite, which had been fondling with her a few Minutes before; and as Joseph and Fanny were impatient to get home and begin those previous Ceremonies to their Happiness which Adams had insisted on, they now offered to take their Leave. The Gentleman importuned them much to stay for Dinner: but when he found their Eagerness to depart, he summoned his Wife, and accordingly having performed all the usual Ceremonies of Bows and Curtsies, more pleasant to be seen than to be related, they took their Leave, the Gentleman and his Wife heartily wishing them a good Journey, and they as heartily thanking them for their kind Entertainment. They then departed, Adams declaring that this was the Manner in which the People had lived in the Golden Age.

CHAP. V.

A Disputation on Schools, held on the Road between Mr. Abraham Adams *and* Joseph; *and a Discovery not unwelcome to them both.*

OUR Travellers having well refreshed themselves at the Gentleman's House, Joseph and Fanny with Sleep, and Mr. Abraham Adams with Ale and Tobacco, renewed their Journey with great Alacrity; and, pursuing the Road in which they were directed, travelled many Miles before they met with any Adventure worth relating. In this Interval, we shall present our Readers with a very curious Discourse, as we apprehend it, concerning public Schools, which pass'd between Mr. Joseph Andrews and Mr. Abraham Adams.

They had not gone far, before Adams calling to Joseph, asked him if he had attended to the Gentleman's Story; he answered, to all the former Parts. 'And don't you think,' says he, 'he was a very unhappy Man in his Youth?' 'A very unhappy Man indeed,' answered the other. 'Joseph,' cries Adams, screwing up his Mouth, 'I have found it; I have discovered the Cause of all the Misfortunes which befel him. A public School, Joseph, was the Cause of all the Calamities which he afterwards suffered. Public Schools are the Nurseries of all Vice and Immorality.[1] All the wicked Fellows whom I remember at the University were bred at them. —Ah Lord! I can remember as well as if it was but Yesterday, a Knot of them; they called them King's Scholars, I forget why—very wicked Fellows! Joseph, you may thank the Lord you were not bred at a public School, you would never have preserved your Virtue as you have. The first Care I always take, is of a Boy's Morals; I had rather he should be a Blockhead than an Atheist or a Presbyterian. What is all the Learning of the World compared to his immortal Soul? What shall a Man take in exchange for his Soul? But the Masters of great Schools trouble themselves about no such Thing. I have known a Lad of eighteen at the University, who hath not been able to say his Catechism; but for my own part, I always scourged a Lad sooner for missing that than any other Lesson. Believe me, Child, all that Gentleman's Misfortunes arose from his being educated at a public School.'

'It doth not become me,' answer'd Joseph, 'to dispute any thing, Sir, with you, especially a Matter of this Kind; for to be sure you must be allowed by all the World to be the best Teacher of a School in all our County.' 'Yes, that,' says Adams, 'I believe, is granted me; that I may without much Vanity pretend to—nay I believe I may go to the next County too—but *gloriari non est meum*—'[2] 'However, Sir, as you are pleased to bid me speak,' says Joseph, 'you know, my late Master, Sir Thomas Booby, was bred at a public School, and he was the finest Gentleman in all the Neigbourhood. And I have often heard him say, if he had a hundred Boys he would breed them all at

[1] On public schools, see above, Chapter 3 n. 1.

[2] "It is not like me to boast."

the same Place. It was his Opinion, and I have often heard him deliver it, that a Boy taken from a public School, and carried into the World, will learn more in one Year there, than one of a private Education will in five. He used to say, the School itself initiated him a great Way, (I remember that was his very Expression) for great Schools are little Societies, where a Boy of any Observation may see in Epitome what he will afterwards find in the World at large.' '*Hinc illae lachrymae;*[3] for that very Reason,' quoth Adams, 'I prefer a private School, where Boys may be kept in Innocence and Ignorance: for, according to that fine Passage in the Play of *Cato,* the only English Tragedy I ever read,

> If Knowledge of the World must make Men Villains,
> May Juba ever live in Ignorance.[4]

Who would not rather preserve the Purity of his Child, than wish him to attain the whole Circle of Arts and Sciences; which, by the bye, he may learn in the Classes of private School? For I would not be vain, but I esteem myself to be second to none, *nulli secundum,* in teaching these things; so that a Lad may have as much Learning in a private as in a public Education.' 'And with Submission,' answered Joseph, 'he may get as much Vice, witness several Country Gentlemen, who were educated within five Miles of their own Houses, and are as wicked as if they had known the World from their Infancy. I remember when I was in the Stable, if a young Horse was vicious in his Nature, no Correction would make him otherwise; I take it to be equally the same among Men: if a Boy be of a mischievous, wicked Inclination, no School, tho' ever so private, will ever make him good; on the contrary, if he be of a righteous Temper, you may trust him to London, or wherever else you please, he will be in no danger of being corrupted. Besides, I have often heard my Master say, that the Discipline practised in public Schools was much better than that in private.'—'You talk like a Jackanapes,' says Adams, 'and so did your Master. Discipline indeed! because one Man scourges twenty or thirty Boys more in a Morning than another, is he therefore a better Disciplinarian? I do presume to confer in this Point with all who have taught from Chiron's[5] Time to this Day; and, if I was Master of

---

[3] "From this cause those tears."

[4] From Joseph Addison's drama *Cato* (1713), 2.5.

[5] In Greek myth, the centaur Chiron tutored demi-gods and heroes including Ascelpius, Ajax, and Achilles.

six Boys only, I would preserve as good Discipline amongst them as the Master of the greatest School in the World. I say nothing, young Man; remember, I say nothing; but if Sir Thomas himself had been educated nearer home, and under the Tuition of somebody, remember I name nobody, it might have been better for him—but his Father must institute him in the Knowledge of the World. *Nemo mortalium omnibus horis sapit.*[6] Joseph, seeing him run on in this manner, asked pardon many times, assuring him he had no Intention to offend. 'I believe you had not, Child,' said he, 'and I am not angry with you: but for maintaining good Discipline in a School; for this'—And then he ran on as before, named all the Masters who are recorded in old Books, and preferred himself to them all. Indeed, if this good Man had an Enthusiasm, or what the Vulgar call a Blindside, it was this: He thought a Schoolmaster the greatest Character in the World, and himself the greatest of all Schoolmasters, neither of which Points he would have given up to Alexander the Great at the Head of his Army.

Adams continued his Subject till they came to one of the beautifullest Spots of Ground in the Universe. It was a kind of natural Amphitheatre, formed by the winding of a small Rivulet, which was planted with thick Woods, whose Trees rose gradually above each other by the natural Ascent of the Ground they stood on; which Ascent as they hid with their Boughs, they seemed to have been disposed by the Design of the most skillful Planter. The Soil was spread with a Verdure which no Paint could imitate, and the whole Place might have raised romantic Ideas in elder Minds than those of Joseph and Fanny, without the Assistance of Love.

Here they arrived about Noon, and Joseph proposed to Adams that they should rest a while in this delightful Place, and refresh themselves with some Provisions which the Good-nature of Mrs. Wilson had provided them with. Adams made no Objection to the Proposal; so down they sat, and pulling out a cold Fowl, and a Bottle of Wine, they made a Repast with a Cheerfulness which might have attracted the Envy of more splendid Tables. I should not omit, that they found among their Provision a little Paper, containing a piece of Gold, which Adams imagining it had been put there by Mistake would have returned back, to restore it; but he was at last convinced by Joseph, that Mr. Wilson had taken this handsome

---

[6] "No one among mortals is wise at all times," Pliny, *Natural History* 7.40.131.

way of furnishing them with a Supply for their Journey, on his having related the Distress which they had been in, when they were relieved by the Generosity of the Pedlar. Adams said, he was glad to see such an Instance of Goodness, not so much for the Conveniency which it brought to them, but for the sake of the Doer, whose Reward would be great in Heaven. He likewise comforted himself with a Reflection, that he should shortly have an Opportunity of returning it him; for the Gentleman was within a Week to make a Journey into Somersetshire, to pass through Adams's Parish, and had faithfully promised to call on him: A Circumstance which we thought too immaterial to mention before; but which those who have as great an Affection for that Gentleman as ourselves will rejoice at, as it may give them Hopes of seeing him again. Then Joseph made a Speech on Charity, which the Reader, if he is so disposed, may see in the next Chapter; for we scorn to betray him into any such Reading, without first giving him Warning.

CHAP. VI.

Moral Reflections by Joseph Andrews, *with the Hunting Adventure, and Parson* Adams's *miraculous Escape.*

I have often wondered, Sir, said Joseph, to observe so few Instances of Charity among Mankind; for tho' the Goodness of a Man's Heart did not incline him to relieve the Distresses of his Fellow-Creatures, methinks the Desire of Honour should move him to it. What inspires a Man to build fine Houses, to purchase fine Furniture, Pictures, Clothes, and other Things at a great Expence, but an Ambition to be respected more than other People? Now, would not one great Act of Charity, one Instance of redeeming a poor Family from all the Miseries of Poverty, restoring an unfortunate Tradesman by a Sum of Money to the means of procuring a Livelihood by his Industry, discharging an undone Debtor from his Debts or a Goal, or any such like Example of Goodness, create a Man more Honour and Respect than he could acquire by the finest House, Furniture, Pictures or Clothes, that were ever beheld? For not only the Object himself, who was thus relieved, but all who heard the Name of such a Person, must, I imagine, reverence him infinitely more than the Possessor of all those other things: which when we so admire, we rather praise the Builder, the Workman, the Painter, the Lacemaker, the Taylor, and the rest, by whose Ingenuity they are produced, than the Person who by his Money makes them his own. For my own part, when I have waited behind my Lady in a Room hung with fine Pictures, while I have been looking at them I have never once thought of their Owner, nor hath any one else, as I ever observed; for when it hath been asked whose Picture that was, it was never once answered, the Master's of the House; but *Ammyconni, Paul Varnish, Hannibal Scratchi,* or *Hogarthi,* which I suppose were the Names of the Painters:[1] but if it was asked, who redeemed such a one out of Prison? who lent such a ruined Tradesman Money to set up? who cloathed that Family of poor small Children? it is very plain what must be the Answer. And besides, these great Folks are mistaken, if they imagine they get any Honour at all by these means; for I do not remember I ever was with my Lady at any House where she commended the House or Furniture; but I have heard her at her return home make sport and jeer at whatever she had before commended: and I have been told by other Gentlemen in Livery, that it is the same in their Families: but I defy the wisest Man in the World to turn a true good Action into Ridicule.[2] I defy him to do it. He who should endeavour it, would be laughed at himself, instead of making others laugh. Nobody scarce doth any Good, yet they all agree in praising those who do. Indeed it is strange that all Men should consent in commending Goodness, and no Man endeavour to deserve that Commendation; whilst, on the contrary, all rail at Wickedness, and all are as eager to be what they abuse. This I know not the Reason of; but it is as plain as Daylight to those who converse in the World, as I have done these three Years. 'Are all the great Folks wicked then?' says Fanny. 'To be sure there are some Exceptions,' answered Joseph. 'Some Gentlemen of our Cloth report charitable Actions done by their Lords and Masters; and I have heard Squire Pope, the great Poet, at my Lady's Table, tell Stories of a Man that lived at a Place called Ross, and another at the Bath, one Al—Al—I forget his Name, but it is in the Book of Verses.[3] This Gentleman hath built up

---

[1] Joseph links Hogarth's name with garbled versions of the names of three celebrated Italian painters: Jacopo Amigoni (1675–1752), Paolo Veronese (1528–88), and Annibale Carraci (1560–1609).

[2] Joseph echoes Shaftesbury's *Sensus Communis* 4.1: "One may defy the World to turn real Bravery or Generosity into ridicule."

[3] Fielding's patron Ralph Allen, was eulogized in Alexander Pope's poem *Epilogue to the Satires* (1738), dialogue 1, ll.135–36. Earlier, in *Of the Use of Riches, an Epistle to . . . Bathurst* (1733), ll.249–90, Pope had praised the philanthropist John Kyrle (1637–1724), known as "the Man of Ross" after his Herefordshire town.

a stately House too, which the Squire likes very well; but his Charity is seen farther than his House, tho' it stands on a Hill, ay, and brings him more Honour. It was his Charity that put him in the Book, where the Squire says he puts all those who deserve it; and to be sure, as he lives among all the great People, if there were any such, he would know them.' —This was all of Mr. Joseph Andrews's Speech which I could get him to recollect, which I have delivered as near as was possible in his own Words, with a very small Embellishment. But I believe the Reader hath not been a little surprized at the long Silence of Parson Adams, especially as so many Occasions offered themselves to exert his Curiosity and Observation. The Truth is, he was fast asleep, and had so been from the Beginning of the preceding Narrative: and indeed if the Reader considers that so many Hours had past since he had closed his Eyes, he will not wonder at his Repose, tho' even Henley himself, or as great an Orator (if any such be) had been in his *Rostrum* or Tub before him.[4]

Joseph, who, whilst he was speaking, had continued in one Attitude, with his Head reclining on one Side, and his Eyes cast on the Ground, no sooner perceived, on looking up, the Position of Adams, who was stretched on his Back, and snored louder than the usual braying of the Animal with long Ears; than he turned towards Fanny, and, taking her by the Hand, began a Dalliance, which, tho' consistent with the purest Innocence and Decency, neither he would have attempted, nor she permited before any Witness. Whilst they amused themselves in this harmless and delightful manner, they heard a Pack of Hounds approaching in full Cry towards them, and presently afterwards saw a Hare pop forth from the Wood, and, crossing the Water, land within a few Yards of them in the Meadows. The Hare was no sooner on Shore, than it seated itself on its hinder Legs, and listened to the Sound of the Pursuers. Fanny was wonderfully pleased with the little Wretch, and eagerly longed to have it in her Arms, that she might preserve it from the Dangers which seemed to threaten it: but the rational Part of the Creation do not always aptly distinguish their Friends from their Foes; what

---

[4] John "Orator" Henley (1692–1756), an eccentric London figure who lectured on, among other things, the art of public speaking and how to return the Church to its primitive purity; Hogarth depicted him in a caricature-like manner, and Pope earlier satirized him in his *Dunciad Variorum* (1729), referring to Henley's fancy lectern as a "gilt Tub" (2.2). *Tub,* slang for the pulpit of any dissenting (that is, non-Church of England) preacher, is a falling off from the *Rostrum* or speaker's platform in the Roman forum, associated with Cicero and sublime eloquence.

wonder then if this silly Creature, the Moment it beheld, fled from the Friend, who would have protected it, and, traversing the Meadows again, past the little Rivulet on the opposite Side. It was however so spent and weak, that it fell down twice or thrice in its Way. This affected the tender Heart of Fanny, who exclaimed, with Tears in her Eyes, against the Barbarity of worrying a poor innocent defenceless Animal out of its Life, and putting it to the extremest Torture for Diversion. She had not much time to make Reflections of this kind; for on a sudden the Hounds rushed through the Wood, which resounded with their Throats, and the Throats of their *Retinue,* who *attended* on them on Horseback. The Dogs now past the Rivulet, and pursued the Footsteps of the Hare; five Horsemen attempted to leap over, three of whom succeeded, and two were in the Attempt thrown from their Saddles into the Water; their Companions, and their own Horses too, proceeded after their Sport, and left their Friends and Riders to invoke the Assistance of Fortune, or employ the more active Means of Strength and Agility for their Deliverance. Joseph however was not so unconcerned on this Occasion; he left Fanny for a Moment to herself, and ran to the Gentlemen, who were immediately on their Legs, shaking their Ears, and easily with the Help of his Hand attained the Bank; (for the Rivulet was not at all deep) and without staying to thank their kind Assister, ran dripping across the Meadow, calling to their Brother Sportsmen to stop their Horses: but they heard them not.

The Hounds were now very little behind their poor reeling, staggering Prey, which fainting almost at every Step, crawled through the Wood, and had almost got round to the Place where Fanny stood, when it was overtaken by its Enemies; and, being driven out of the Covert, was caught, and instantly tore to pieces before Fanny's Face, who was unable to assist it with any Aid more powerful than Pity; nor could she prevail on Joseph, who had been himself a Sportsman in his Youth, to attempt any thing contrary to the Laws of Hunting, in favour of the Hare, which he said was killed fairly.

The Hare was caught within a Yard or two of Adams, who lay asleep at some Distance from the Lovers; and the Hounds in devouring it, and pulling it backwards and forwards, had drawn it so close to him, that some of them (by Mistake perhaps for the Hare's Skin) laid hold of the Skirts of his Cassock; others at the same time applying their Teeth to his Wig, which he had with a Handkerchief fastened to his Head, began to pull him about; and had not the Motion of his Body had more Effect on him than seemed to be wrought by the Noise, they must certainly have tasted his Flesh, which delicious Flavour might have been fatal to him: But being roused by these Tuggings, he instantly awaked, and with a Jerk delivering his Head from his Wig, he with most admirable Dexterity recovered his Legs, which now seemed the only Members he could entrust his Safety to. Having therefore escaped likewise from at least a third Part of his Cassock, which he willingly left as his *Exuviae* or Spoils to the Enemy, he fled with the utmost speed he could summon to his Assistance. Nor let this be any Detraction from the Bravery of his Character; let the Number of the Enemies, and the Surprize in which he was taken, be considered; and if there be any Modern so outrageously brave, that he cannot admit of Flight in any Circumstance whatever, I say (but I whisper that softly, and I solemnly declare, without any Intention of giving Offence to any brave Man in the Nation) I say, or rather I whisper that he is an ignorant Fellow, and hath never read Homer, nor Virgil, nor knows he any thing of Hector or Turnus;[5] nay, he is unacquainted with the History of some great Men living, who, tho' as brave as Lions, ay, as Tigers, have run away, the Lord knows how far, and the Lord knows why, to the Surprize of their Friends, and the Entertainment of their Enemies. But if Persons of such heroick Disposition are a little offended at the Behaviour of Adams, we assure them they shall be as much pleased with what we shall immediately relate of Joseph Andrews. The Master of the Pack was just arrived, or, as the Sportsmen call it, *come in,* when Adams set out, as we have before mentioned. This Gentleman was generally said to be a great Lover of Humour; but not to mince the Matter, especially as we are upon this Subject, he was a great *Hunter of Men:*[6] Indeed he had hitherto followed the Sport only with Dogs of his own Species; for he kept two or three Couple of barking Curs for that Use only. However, as he thought he had now found a Man nimble enough, he was willing to indulge himself with other Sport,

---

[5] At the end of Virgil's *Aeneid* Turnus flees from the hero Aeneas, as in Homer's *Iliad* (Book 22) Hector fled from Achilles.

[6] Nimrod is called "a mighty hunter before the Lord" in Genesis 10:9, but according to later Jewish tradition (and thus Milton's *Paradise Lost* 12.24–37) he is a despotic "hunter of men." Jewish tradition also records that the patriarch Abraham defied Nimrod and avoided death in his fiery furnace; in *Joseph Andrews* 3.6–7, Abraham Adams escapes an updated Nimrod, and finally gives him a dunking in his own watery tub.

and accordingly crying out, *Stole away*, encouraged the Hounds to pursue Mr. Adams, swearing it was the largest Jack-Hare he ever saw; at the same time hallooing and hooping as if a conquered Foe was flying before him; in which he was imitated by these two or three Couple of Human, or rather two-leg'd Curs on Horseback which we have mentioned before.

Now thou, whoever thou art, whether a Muse, or by what other Name soever thou chusest to be called, who presidest over Biography, and hast inspired all the Writers of Lives in these our Times: Thou who didst infuse such wonderful Humour into the Pen of immortal Gulliver;[7] who hast carefully guided the Judgment, whilst thou hast exalted the nervous manly Style of thy Mallet: Thou who hadst no Hand in that Dedication and Preface, or the Translations which thou wouldst willingly have struck out of the Life of Cicero: Lastly, Thou who without the Assistance of the least Spice of Literature, and even against his Inclination, hast, in some Pages of his Book, forced Colley Cibber to write English; do thou assist me in what I find myself unequal to. Do thou introduce on the Plain, the young, the gay, the brave Joseph Andrews, whilst Men shall view him with Admiration and Envy; tender Virgins with Love and anxious Concern for his Safety.

No sooner did Joseph Andrews perceive the Distress of his Friend, when first the quick-scenting Dogs attacked him, than he grasped his Cudgel in his right Hand, a Cudgel which his Father had of his Grandfather, to whom a mighty strong Man of Kent had given it for a Present in that Day, when he broke three Heads on the Stage.[8] It was a Cudgel of mighty Strength and wonderful Art, made by one of Mr. Deard's best Workmen, whom no other Artificer can equal; and who hath made all those Sticks which the Beaus have lately walked with about the Park in a Morning: But this was far his Master-piece; on its Head was engraved a Nose and Chin, which might have been mistaken for a Pair of Nut-crackers. The

---

[7] Fielding invokes the muse who inspired Jonathan Swift's *Gulliver's Travels* (1726) and the "nervous"—that is, "strong; vigorous" (Johnson)—style of the Scottish dramatist and poet David Mallet (1705–65). Conyers Middleton (1683–1750) wrote a fulsome dedication to his *History of the Life of Marcus Tullius Cicero* (1741) that Fielding parodied in his prefatory material to *Shamela*. On Colley Cibber, see Book 1, Chapter 1, n. 4.

[8] Fielding here burlesques the genealogy of Agamemnon's scepter in *Iliad* 2.102–8; his subsequent depiction of the Andrews-family cudgel is a burlesque of Homer's description of the shield of Achilles, *Iliad* 18.478–607.

Learned have imagined it designed to represent the Gorgon: but it was in Fact copied from the Face of a certain English Baronet of infinite Wit, Humour, and Gravity. He did intend to have engraved here many Histories: As the first Night of Captain B—'s Play, where you would have seen Critics in Embroidery transplanted from the Boxes to the Pit, whose ancient Inhabitants were exalted to the Galleries, where they played on Catcalls.[9] He did intend to have painted an Auction-Room, where Mr. Cock would have appeared aloft in his Pulpit, trumpeting forth the Praises of a China Bason; and with Astonishment wondering that *Nobody bids more for that fine, that superb*—He did intend to have engraved many other Things, but was forced to leave all out for want of room.

No sooner had Joseph grasped this Cudgel in his Hands, than Lightning darted from his Eyes; and the heroick Youth, swift of Foot,[10] ran with the utmost speed to his Friend's Assistance. He overtook him just as *Rockwood*[11] had laid hold of the Skirt of his Cassock, which being torn, hung to the Ground. Reader, we would make a Simile on this Occasion, but for two Reasons: The first is, it would interrupt the Description, which should be *rapid* in this Part; but that doth not weigh much, many Precedents occurring for such an Interruption: The second, and much the greater Reason is, that we could find no Simile adequate to our Purpose: For indeed, what Instance could we bring to set before our Reader's Eyes at once the Idea of Friendship, Courage, Youth, Beauty, Strength, and Swiftness; all which blazed in the Person of Joseph Andrews. Let those therefore that describe Lions and Tigers, and Heroes fiercer than both, raise their Poems or Plays with the Simile of Joseph Andrews, who is himself above the Reach of any Simile.

Now *Rockwood* had laid fast hold on the Parson's Skirts, and stopt his Flight; which Joseph no sooner perceived, than he levelled his Cudgel at his Head, and laid him sprawling. *Jowler* and

---

[9] Grose defines "cat call": "A kind of whistle, chiefly used at theatres, to interrupt the actors, and damn a new piece. It derives its name from one of its sounds, which greatly resembles the modulations of an intriguing . . . cat." For an account of the noisy rejection of a 1732 comedy attributed to the guards officer Charles Bodens, with an epilogue by Fielding, see Charles B. Woods, "Captain B—'s Play," *Harvard Studies and Notes in Philology and Literature* 15 (1933): 243–55.

[10] Achilles' epithet in *Iliad.*

[11] The dogs' names—Rockwood, Jowler, Ringwood, *et al.*—were standard names for hunting hounds. See Arthur Sherbo, "Fielding's Dogs," *Notes & Queries* 17 (1970): 302–303.

"Parson Adams pursued by hunting dogs," illustration by James Hulett for
History of the Adventures of Joseph Andrews, 3rd edition (1743), opposite
volume 2, p. 71. (Special Collections, University of Virginia Library.)

Ringwood then fell on his Great-Coat, and had undoubtedly brought him to the Ground, had not Joseph, collecting all his Force, given *Jowler* such a Rap on the Back, that quitting his Hold he ran howling over the Plain: A harder Fate remained for thee, O *Ringwood, Ringwood* the best Hound that ever pursued a Hare, who never threw his Tongue but where the Scent was undoubtedly true; good at *trailing;* and *sure in a Highway,* no *Babler,* no *Over-runner,* respected by the whole Pack, who, whenever he opened, knew the Game was at hand. He fell by the Stroke of Joseph. *Thunder,* and *Plunder,* and *Wonder,* and *Blunder,* were the next Victims of his Wrath, and measured their Lengths on the Ground. Then *Fairmaid,* a Bitch which Mr. John Temple had bred up in his House, and fed at his own Table, and lately sent the Squire fifty Miles for a Present, ran fiercely at Joseph, and bit him by the Leg; no Dog was ever fiercer than she, being descended from an Amazonian Breed, and had worried Bulls in her own Country, but now waged an unequal Fight; and had shared the Fate of these we have mentioned before, had not *Diana*[12] (the Reader may believe it or not as he pleases) in that Instant interposed, and in the Shape of the Huntsman snatched her Favourite up in her Arms.

The Parson now faced about, and with his Crab-Stick felled many to the Earth, and scattered others, till he was attacked by *Caesar* and pulled to the Ground; then Joseph flew to his Rescue, and with such Might fell on the Victor, that, O eternal Blot to his Name! *Caesar* ran yelping away.

The Battle now raged with the most dreadful Violence, when lo the Huntsman, a Man of Years and Dignity, lifted his Voice, and called his Hounds from the Fight; telling them, in a Language they understood, that it was in vain to contend longer; for that Fate had decreed the Victory to their Enemies.

Thus far the Muse hath with her usual Dignity related this prodigious Battle, a Battle we apprehend never equalled by any Poet, Romance or Life-writer whatever, and having brought it to a Conclusion she ceased; we shall therefore proceed in our ordinary Style with the Continuation of this History. The Squire and his Companions, whom the Figure of Adams, and the Gallantry of Joseph, had at first thrown into a violent Fit of Laughter, and who had hitherto beheld the Engagement with more Delight than any

---

[12] The virgin goddess of the hunt.

Chace, Shooting-Match, Race, Cock-fighting, Bull or Bear-Baiting had ever given them, began now to apprehend the Danger of their Hounds, many of which lay sprawling in the Fields. The Squire therefore having first called his Friends about him, as Guards for Safety of his Person, rode manfully up to the Combatants, and summoning all the Terror he was Master of into his Countenance, demanded with an authoritative Voice of Joseph, what he meant by assaulting his Dogs in that Manner. Joseph answered with great Intrepidity, that they had first fallen on his Friend; and if they had belonged to the greatest Man in the Kingdom, he would have treated them in the same way; for whilst his Veins contained a single Drop of Blood, he would not stand idle by, and see that Gentleman, (*pointing to Adams*) abused either by Man or Beast; and having so said, both he and Adams brandished their wooden Weapons, and put themselves into such a Posture, that the Squire and his Company thought proper to preponderate, before they offered to revenge the Cause of their four-footed Allies.

At this Instant Fanny, whom the Apprehension of Joseph's Danger had alarmed so much, that, forgetting her own, she had made the utmost Expedition, came up. The Squire and all the Horsemen were so surprized with her Beauty, that they immediately fixed both their Eyes and Thoughts solely on her, every one declaring he had never seen so charming a Creature. Neither Mirth nor Anger engaged them a Moment longer; but all sat in silent Amaze. The Huntsman only was free from her Attraction, who was busy in cutting the Ears of the Dogs,[13] and endeavouring to recover them to Life; in which he succeeded so well, that only two of no great Note remained slaughtered on the Field of Action. Upon this the Huntsman declared, 'Twas well it was no worse; for his part he could not blame the Gentleman, and wondered his Master would encourage the Dogs to hunt Christians; that it was the surest way to spoil them, to make them follow *Vermin* instead of sticking to a Hare.'

The Squire being informed of the little Mischief that had been done; and perhaps having more Mischief of another kind in his Head, accosted Mr. Adams with a more favourable Aspect than before: he told him he was sorry for what had happened; that he had endeavoured all he could to prevent it the Moment he was acquainted with

---

[13] Bloodletting was prescribed medicinally for dogs as well as humans through the late nineteenth century.

his Cloth, and greatly commended the Courage of his Servant; for so he imagined Joseph to be. He then invited Mr. Adams to Dinner, and desired the young Woman might come with him. Adams refused a long while; but the Invitation was repeated with so much Earnestness and Courtesy, that at length he was forced to accept it. His Wig and Hat, and other Spoils of the Field, being gathered together by Joseph, (for otherwise probably they would have been forgotten) he put himself into the best Order he could; and then the Horse and Foot moved forward in the same Pace towards the Squire's House, which stood at a very little Distance.

Whilst they were on the Road, the lovely Fanny attracted the Eyes of all; they endeavoured to outvie one another in Encomiums on her Beauty; which the Reader will pardon my not relating, as they had not any thing new or uncommon in them: So must he likewise my not setting down the many curious Jests which were made on Adams; some of them declaring that Parson-hunting was the best Sport in the World; Others commending his standing at Bay, which they said he had done as well as any Badger; with such like Merriment, which, though it would ill become the Dignity of this History, afforded much Laughter and Diversion to the Squire and his facetious Companions.

CHAP. VII.

A Scene of Roasting[1] very nicely adapted to the present Taste and Times.

THEY arrived at the Squire's House just as his Dinner was ready. A little Dispute arose on the account of Fanny, whom the Squire, who was a Batchelor, was desirous to place at his own Table; but she would not consent, nor would Mr. Adams permit her to be parted from Joseph: so that she was at length with him consigned over to the Kitchin, where the Servants were ordered to make him drunk; a Favour which was likewise intended for Adams: which Design being executed, the Squire thought he should easily accomplish what he had, when he first saw her, intended to perpetrate with Fanny.

It may not be improper, before we proceed farther, to open a little the Character of this Gentleman, and that of his Friends.

---

[1] That is, rough jesting.

The Master of this House then was a Man of a very considerable Fortune; a Batchelor, as we have said, and about forty Years of Age: he had been educated (if we may use the Expression) in the Country, and at his own Home, under the Care of his Mother and a Tutor, who had Orders never to correct him, nor to compel him to learn more than he liked, which it seems was very little, and that only in his Childhood; for from the Age of fifteen he addicted himself entirely to Hunting and other rural Amusements, for which his Mother took care to equip him with Horses, Hounds, and all other Necessaries: and his Tutor, endeavouring to ingratiate himself with his young Pupil, who would, he knew, be able handsomely to provide for him, became his Companion, not only at these Exercises, but likewise over a Bottle, which the young Squire had a very early Relish for. At the Age of twenty, his Mother began to think she had not fulfilled the Duty of a Parent; she therefore resolved to persuade her Son, if possible, to that which she imagined would well supply all that he might have learned at a public School or University. This is what they commonly call *Travelling;* which, with the Help of the Tutor who was fixed on to attend him, she easily succeeded in. He made in three Years the Tour of Europe, as they term it,[2] and returned home well furnished with French Clothes, Phrases and Servants, with a hearty Contempt for his own Country; especially what had any Savour of the plain Spirit and Honesty of our Ancestors. His Mother greatly applauded herself at his Return; and now being Master of his own Fortune, he soon procured himself a Seat in Parliament, and was in the common Opinion one of the finest Gentlemen of his Age: But what distinguished him chiefly, was a strange Delight which he took in every thing which is ridiculous, odious, and absurd in his own Species; so that he never chose a Companion without one or more of these Ingredients, and those who were marked by Nature in the most eminent Degree with them, were most his Favourites: if he ever found a Man who either had not, or endeavoured to conceal these Imperfections, he took great Pleasure in inventing Methods of forcing him into Absurdities, which were not natural to him, or in drawing forth and exposing those that were; for

---

[2] The Grand Tour, a voyage of a year or more typically through France and Italy, was much in vogue among young English gentlemen as a supplement to or substitute for a university education. Fielding's low opinion of the education typically acquired on the Tour may be inferred from his characterization of this squire as well as Bellarmine (2.4–6) and the Italianate traveler (2.5).

which Purpose he was always provided with a Set of Fellows whom we have before called Curs; and who did indeed no great Honour to the Canine Kind: Their Business was to hunt out and display every thing that had any Savour of the above mentioned Qualities, and especially in the gravest and best Characters: But if they failed in their Search, they were to turn even Virtue and Wisdom themselves into Ridicule for the Diversion of their Master and Feeder. The Gentlemen of Curlike Disposition, who were now at his House, and whom he had brought with him from London, were an old Half-pay Officer, a Player, a dull Poet, a Quack-Doctor, a Scraping-Fidler, and a lame German Dancing-Master.

As soon as Dinner was served, while Mr. Adams was saying Grace, the Captain convey'd his Chair from behind him; so that when he endeavoured to seat himself, he fell down on the Ground; and thus compleated Joke the first, to the great Entertainment of the whole Company. The second Joke was performed by the Poet, who sat next him on the other side, and took an Opportunity, while poor Adams was respectfully drinking to the Master of the House, to overturn a Plate of Soup into his Breeches; which, with the many Apologies he made, and the Parson's gentle Answers, caused much Mirth in the Company. Joke the third was served up by one of the Waiting-men, who had been ordered to convey a Quantity of Gin into Mr. Adams's Ale, which he declaring to be the best Liquor he ever drank, but rather too rich of the Malt, contributed again to their Laughter. Mr. Adams, from whom we had most of this Relation, could not recollect all the Jests of this kind practised on him, which the inoffensive Disposition of his own Heart made him slow in discovering; and indeed, had it not been for the Information which we received from a Servant of the Family, this Part of our History, which we take to be none of the least curious, must have been deplorably imperfect; tho' we must own it probable, that some more Jokes were (as they call it) *cracked* during their Dinner; but we have by no means been able to come at the Knowledge of them. When Dinner was removed, the Poet began to repeat some Verses, which he said were made *extempore*. The following is a Copy of them, procured with the greatest difficulty.

An extempore Poem on Parson Adams

Did ever Mortal such a Parson view;
His Cassock old, his Wig not over-new?

Well might the Hounds have him for Fox mistaken,
In Smell more like to that than rusty[3] Bacon.*
But would it not make any Mortal stare,
To see this Parson taken for a Hare?
Could Phoebus err thus grossly, even he
For a good Player might have taken thee.

At which Words the Bard whip'd off the Player's Wig, and received the Approbation of the Company, rather perhaps for the Dexterity of his Hand than his Head. The Player, instead of retorting the Jest on the Poet, began to display his Talents on the same Subject. He repeated many Scraps of Wit out of Plays, reflecting on the whole Body of the Clergy, which were received with great Acclamations by all present. It was now the Dancing-Master's Turn to exhibit his Talents; he therefore addressing himself to Adams in broken English, told him, 'He was a Man ver well made for de Dance, and he suppose by his Walk, dat he had learn of some great Master. He said it was ver pretty Quality in Clergyman to dance;' and concluded with desiring him to dance a Minuet, telling him, 'his Cassock would serve for Petticoats; and that he would himself be his Partner.' At which Words, without waiting for an Answer, he pulled out his Gloves, and the Fiddler was preparing his Fiddle. The Company all offered the Dancing-Master Wagers that the Parson outdanced him, which he refused, saying, 'He believed so too; for he had never seen any Man in his Life who looked de Dance so well as de Gentleman:' He then stepped forwards to take Adams by the Hand, which the latter hastily withdrew, and at the same time clenching his Fist, advised him not to carry the Jest too far, for he would not endure being put upon. The Dancing-master no sooner saw the Fist than he prudently retired out of its Reach, and stood aloof mimicking Adams, whose Eyes were fixed on him, not guessing what he was at, but to avoid his laying hold on him, which he had once attempted. In the mean while, the Captain perceiving an Opportunity, pinned a Cracker[4] or Devil to the Cassock, and then lighted it with their little Smoking-Candle. Adams being a Stranger to this Sport, and believing he had been blown up in reality, started from his Chair, and jumped about the Room, to the infinite Joy of

---

[3] "Rancid" (Johnson).

Fielding's note: All Hounds that will hunt Fox or other Vermin, will hunt a Piece of rusty Bacon trailed on the Ground.

[4] That is, a firecracker.

the Beholders, who declared he was the best Dancer in the Universe. As soon as the Devil had done tormenting him, and he had a little recovered his Confusion, he returned to the Table, and standing up in the Posture of one who intended to make a Speech. They all cried out, *Hear him, Hear him*; and he then spoke in the following Manner: 'Sir, I am sorry to see one to whom Providence hath been so bountiful in bestowing his Favours, make so ill and ungrateful a Return for them; for tho' you have not insulted me yourself, it is visible you have delighted in those that do it, nor have once discouraged the many Rudenesses which have been shewn towards me; indeed towards yourself, if you rightly understood them; for I am your Guest, and by the Laws of Hospitality entitled to your Protection. One Gentleman hath thought proper to produce some Poetry upon me, of which I shall only say, that I had rather be the Subject than the Composer. He hath pleased to treat me with Disrespect as a Parson. I apprehend my Order is not the Object of Scorn, nor that I can become so, unless by being a Disgrace to it, which I hope Poverty will never be called. Another Gentleman indeed hath repeated some Sentences, where the Order itself is mentioned with Contempt. He says they are taken from Plays. I am sure such Plays are a Scandal to the Government which permits them, and cursed will be the Nation where they are represented. How others have treated me, I need not observe; they themselves, when they reflect, must allow the Behaviour to be as improper to my Years as to my Cloth. You found me, Sir, travelling with two of my Parishioners, (I omit your Hounds falling on me; for I have quite forgiven it, whether it proceeded from the Wantonness or Negligence of the Huntsman) my Appearance might very well persuade you that your Invitation was an Act of Charity, tho' in reality we were well provided; yes, Sir, if we had had an hundred Miles to travel, we had sufficient to bear our Expences in a noble manner.' (At which Words he produced the Half-Guinea which was found in the Basket.) 'I do not shew you this out of Ostentation of Riches, but to convince you I speak Truth. Your seating me at your Table was an Honour which I did not ambitiously affect. When I was here, I endeavoured to behave towards you with the utmost Respect; if I have failed, it was not with Design; nor could I, certainly, so far be guilty as to deserve the Insults I have suffered. If they were meant therefore either to my Order or my Poverty (and you see I am not very poor) the Shame doth not lie at my Door, and I heartily pray that the Sin may be averted from yours.' He thus finished, and received a general Clap from the whole Company. Then the Gentleman of the House told him, 'he was sorry for what had happened; that he could not accuse him of any Share in it: That the Verses were, as himself had well observed, so bad, that he might easily answer them; and for the Serpent,[5] it was undoubtedly a very great Affront done him by the Dancing-Master, for which, if he well threshed him, as he deserved, he should be very much pleased to see it;' (in which probably he spoke Truth.) Adams answered, 'Whoever had done it, it was not his Profession to punish him that Way; but for the Person whom he had accused, I am a Witness, says he, of his Innocence; for I had my Eye on him all the while. Whoever he was, God forgive him, and bestow on him a little more Sense as well as Humanity.' The Captain answer'd with a surly Look and Accent, 'That he hoped he did not mean to reflect on him; d—n him, he had as much *Imanity* as another, and if any Man said he had not, he would convince him of his Mistake by cutting his Throat.' Adams smiling, said, 'He believed he had spoke right by Accident.' To which the Captain returned, 'What do you mean by my speaking right? if you was not a Parson, I would not take these Words; but your Gown protects you. If any Man who wears a Sword had said so much, I had pulled him by the Nose before this.' Adams replied, 'If he attempted any Rudeness to his Person, he would not find any Protection for himself in his Gown;' and clenching his Fist, declared he had threshed many a stouter Man. The Gentleman did all he could to encourage the warlike Disposition in Adams, and was in Hopes to have produced a Battle: But he was disappointed; for the Captain made no other Answer than, 'It is very well you are a Parson,' and so drinking off a Bumper to old Mother Church, ended the Dispute.

Then the Doctor, who had hitherto been silent, and who was the gravest, but most mischievous Dog of all, in a very pompous Speech highly applauded what Adams had said; and as much discommended the Behaviour to him. He proceeded to Encomiums on the Church and Poverty; and lastly recommended Forgiveness of what had past to Adams, who immediately answered, 'That every thing was forgiven;' and in the Warmth of his Goodness he filled a Bumper of strong Beer, (a Liquor he preferred to Wine) and drank a Health to the whole Company, shaking the Captain and the Poet heartily by the Hand, and addressing himself with great Respect to the Doctor;

---

[5] Referring to the firecracker's shape.

who indeed had not laughed outwardly at any thing that past, as he had a perfect Command of his Muscles, and could laugh inwardly without betraying the least Symptoms in his Countenance. The Doctor now began a second formal Speech, in which he declaimed against all Levity of Conversation, and what is usually called Mirth. He said, 'There were Amusements fitted for Persons of all Ages and Degrees, from the Rattle to the discussing a Point of Philosophy, and that Men discovered themselves in nothing more than in the Choice of their Amusements; for,' says he, 'as it must greatly raise our Expectation of the future Conduct in Life of Boys, whom in their tender Years we perceive instead of Taw or Balls, or other childish Play-things, to chuse, at their Leisure-Hours, to exercise their Genius in Contentions of Wit, Learning, and such like; so must it inspire one with equal Contempt of a Man, if we should discover him playing at Taw or other childish Play.' Adams highly commended the Doctor's Opinion, and said, 'He had often wondered at some Passages in ancient Authors, where Scipio, Laelius, and other great Men, were represented to have passed many Hours in Amusements of the most trifling kind.' The Doctor replied, 'He had by him an old Greek Manuscript where a favourite Diversion of Socrates was recorded.' 'Ay,' says the Parson eagerly, 'I should be most infinitely obliged to you for the Favour of perusing it.' The Doctor promised to send it him, and farther said, 'that he believed he could describe it. I think,' says he, 'as near as I can remember, it was this. There was a Throne erected, on one Side of which sat a King, and on the other a Queen, with their Guards and Attendants ranged on both sides; to them was introduced an Ambassador, which Part Socrates always used to perform himself; and when he was led up to the Footsteps of the Throne, he addressed himself to the Monarchs in some grave Speech, full of Virtue and Goodness, and Morality, and such like. After which, he was seated between the King and Queen, and royally entertained. This I think was the chief part.—Perhaps I may have forgot some Particulars; for it is long since I read it.' Adams said, 'It was indeed a Diversion worthy the Relaxation of so great a Man; and thought something resembling it should be instituted among our great Men, instead of Cards and other idle Pastime, in which he was informed they trifled away too much of their Lives.' He added, 'The Christian Religion was a nobler Subject for these Speeches than any Socrates could have invented.' The Gentleman of the House approved what Mr. Adams said, and declared, 'he was resolved to perform the Ceremony this very Evening.' To which the

Doctor objected, as no one was prepared with a Speech, unless, said he, (turning to Adams with a Gravity of Countenance which would have deceived a more knowing Man) 'you have a Sermon about you, Doctor.'—'Sir,' says Adams, 'I never travel without one, for fear what may happen.' He was easily prevailed on by his worthy Friend, as he now called the Doctor, to undertake the Part of the Ambassador; so that the Gentleman sent immediate Orders to have the Throne erected; which was performed before they had drank two Bottles: And perhaps the Reader will hereafter have no great reason to admire the Nimbleness of the Servants. Indeed, to confess the Truth, the Throne was no more than this; there was a great Tub of Water provided, on each Side of which were placed two Stools raised higher than the Surface of the Tub, and over the whole was laid a Blanket; on these Stools were placed the King and Queen, namely, the Master of the House, and the Captain. And now the Ambassador was introduced, between the Poet and the Doctor, who, having read his Sermon to the great Entertainment of all present, was led up to his Place, and seated between their Majesties. They immediately rose up, when the Blanket wanting its Supports at either End, gave way, and soused Adams over Head and Ears in the Water; the Captain made his Escape, but unluckily the Gentleman himself not being as nimble as he ought, Adams caught hold of him before he descended from his Throne, and pulled him in with him, to the entire secret Satisfaction of all the Company. Adams, after ducking the Squire twice or thrice, leapt out of the Tub, and looked sharp for the Doctor, whom he would certainly have conveyed to the same Place of Honour; but he had wisely withdrawn: he then searched for his Crab-stick, and having found that, as well as his Fellow-Travellers, he declared he would not stay a Moment longer in such a House. He then departed, without taking leave of his Host, whom he had exacted a more severe Revenge on than he intended: For as he did not use sufficient care to dry himself in time, he caught a Cold by the Accident, which threw him into a Fever, that had like to have cost him his Life.

CHAP. VIII.

Which some Readers will think too short, and others too long.

ADAMS, and Joseph, who was no less enraged than his Friend at the Treatment he met with, went out with their Sticks in their Hands, and carried off Fanny, notwithstanding the Opposition of the Servants, who did all, without proceeding to Violence, in their Power to detain them. They walked as fast as they could, not so much from any Apprehension of being pursued, as that Mr. Adams might by Exercise prevent any harm from the Water. The Gentleman, who had given such Orders to his Servants concerning Fanny, that he did not in the least fear her getting away, no sooner heard that she was gone, than he began to rave, and immediately dispatched several with Orders, either to bring her back, or never return. The Poet, the Player, and all but the Dancing-Master and Doctor went on this Errand.

The Night was very dark, in which our Friends began their Journey; however they made such Expedition, that they soon arrived at an Inn, which was at seven Miles Distance. Here they unanimously consented to pass the Evening, Mr. Adams being now as dry as he was before he had set out on his Embassy.

This Inn, which indeed we might call an Ale-house, had not the Words, *The New Inn*, been writ on the Sign, afforded them no better Provision than Bread and Cheese, and Ale; on which, however, they made a very comfortable Meal; for Hunger is better than a French Cook.

They had no sooner supped, than Adams, returning Thanks to the Almighty for his Food, declared he had eat his homely Commons with much greater Satisfaction than his splendid Dinner, and exprest great Comtempt for the Folly of Mankind, who sacrificed their Hopes of Heaven to the Acquisition of vast Wealth, since so much Comfort was to be found in the humblest State and the lowest Provision. 'Very true, Sir,' says a grave Man, who sat smoking his Pipe by the Fire, and who was a Traveller as well as himself. 'I have often been as much surprized as you are, when I consider the Value which Mankind in general set on Riches; since every Day's Experience shews us how little is in their Power; for what indeed truly desirable can they bestow on us? Can they give Beauty to the Deformed, Strength to the Weak, or Health to the Infirm? Surely if they could, we should not see so many ill-favoured Faces haunting the Assemblies of the Great, nor would such Numbers of feeble Wretches languish in their Coaches and Palaces. No, not the Wealth of a Kingdom can purchase any Paint to dress pale Ugliness in the Bloom of that young Maiden, nor any Drugs to equip Disease with the Vigour of that young Man. Do not Riches bring us Sollicitude instead of Rest, Envy instead of Affection, and Danger instead of Safety? Can they prolong their own Possession, or lengthen his

Days who enjoys them? So far otherwise, that the Sloth, the Luxury, the Care which attend them, shorten the Lives of Millions, and bring them with Pain and Misery, to an untimely Grave. Where then is their Value, if they can neither embellish, or strengthen our Forms, sweeten or prolong our Lives? Again—Can they adorn the Mind more than the Body? Do they not rather swell the Heart with Vanity, puff up the Cheeks with Pride, shut our Ears to every Call of Virtue, and our Bowels to every Motive of Compassion!' 'Give me your Hand, Brother,' said Adams in a Rapture; 'for I suppose you are a Clergyman.' 'No truly,' answered the other, (indeed he was a Priest of the Church of Rome; but those who understand our Laws, will not wonder he was not over-ready to own it.[1]) 'Whatever you are,' cries Adams, 'you have spoken my Sentiments: I believe I have preached every Syllable of your Speech twenty times over: For it hath always appeared to me easier for a Cable Rope (which by the way is the true rendering of that Word we have translated *Camel*) to go through the Eye of a Needle, than for a rich Man to get into the Kingdom of Heaven.'[2] 'That, Sir,' said the other, 'will be easily granted you by Divines, and is deplorably true: But as the Prospect of our Good at a Distance doth not so forcibly affect us, it might be of some Service to Mankind to be made thoroughly sensible, which I think they might be with very little serious Attention, that even the Blessings of this World are not to be purchased with Riches. A Doctrine, in my Opinion, not only metaphysically, but, if I may so say, mathematically demonstrable; and which I have been always so perfectly convinced of, that I have a Contempt for nothing so much as for Gold.' Adams now began a long Discourse; but as most which he said occurs among many Authors, who have treated this Subject, I shall omit inserting it. During its Continuance Joseph and Fanny retired to Rest, and the Host likewise left the Room. When the English Parson had concluded, the Romish resumed the Discourse, which he continued with great Bitterness and Invective; and at last ended by desiring Adams to lend him eighteen Pence to pay his Reckoning; promising, if he never paid him, he might be assured of his Prayers. The good Man answered, that eighteen Pence would

---

[1] Roman Catholic priests could, at this time, be fined or charged with high treason for celebrating Mass in England.

[2] Referring to the original Greek of Matthew 19:24, Adams dubiously claims that *kamelos* (camel) should be read as *kamilos* or "rope," a rare word that does not appear in the New Testament.

be too little to carry him any very long Journey; that he had half a Guinea in his Pocket, which he would divide with him. He then fell to searching his Pockets, but could find no Money: For indeed the Company with whom he dined, had past one Jest upon him which we did not then enumerate, and had picked his Pocket of all that Treasure which he had so ostentatiously produced.

'Bless me,' cried Adams, 'I have certainly lost it; I can never have spent it. Sir, as I am a Christian, I had a whole half Guinea in my Pocket this Morning, and have not now a single Halfpenny of it left. Sure the Devil must have taken it from me.' 'Sir,' answered the Priest smiling, 'You need make no Excuses; if you are not willing to lend me the Money, I am contented.' 'Sir,' cries Adams, 'if I had the greatest Sum in the World; ay, if I had ten Pounds about me, I would bestow it all to rescue any Christian from Distress. I am more vexed at my Loss on your account than my own. Was ever any thing so unlucky? because I have no Money in my Pocket, I shall be suspected to be no Christian.' 'I am more unlucky,' quoth the other, 'if you are as generous as you say: For really a Crown would have made me happy, and conveyed me in plenty to the Place I am going, which is not above twenty Miles off, and where I can arrive by to-morrow Night. I assure you I am not accustomed to travel Penny-less. I am but just arrived in England; and we were forced by a Storm in our Passage to throw all we had overboard. I don't suspect but this Fellow will take my Word for the Trifle I owe him; but I hate to appear so mean as to confess myself without a Shilling to such People: For these, and indeed too many others, know little Difference in their Estimation between a Beggar and a Thief.' However, he thought he should deal better with the Host that Evening than the next Morning; he therefore resolved to set out immediately, notwithstanding the Darkness; and accordingly, as soon as the Host returned, he communicated to him the Situation of his Affairs; upon which the Host scratching his Head, answered, 'Why, I do not know, Master, if it be so, and you have no Money, I must trust I think, tho' I had rather always have ready Money if I could; but, marry, you look like so honest a Gentleman, that I don't fear your paying me, if it was twenty times as much.' The Priest made no Reply, but taking Leave of him and Adams, as fast as he could, not without Confusion, and perhaps with some Distrust of Adams's Sincerity, departed.

He was no sooner gone than the Host fell a shaking his Head, and declared, if he had suspected the Fellow had no Money, he would not have drawn him a single Drop of Drink; saying, he despaired of ever seeing his Face again; for that he looked like a confounded Rogue. 'Rabbit the Fellow,' cries he, 'I thought by his talking so much about Riches, that he had a hundred Pounds at least in his Pocket.' Adams chid him for his Suspicions, which he said were not becoming a Christian; and then, without reflecting on his Loss, or considering how he himself should depart in the Morning, he retired to a very homely Bed, as his Companions had before; however, Health and Fatigue gave them a sweeter Repose than is often in the power of Velvet and Down to bestow.

CHAP. IX.

Containing as surprizing and bloody Adventures as can be found in this,
or perhaps any other authentic History.

It was almost Morning, when Joseph Andrews, whose Eyes the Thoughts of his dear Fanny had opened, as he lay fondly meditating on that lovely Creature, heard a violent Knocking at the Door over which he lay. He presently jumped out of Bed, and opening the Window, was asked if there were no Travellers in the House; and presently by another Voice, If two Men and a young Woman had not taken up their Lodgings there that Night. Tho' he knew not the Voices, he began to entertain a Suspicion of the Truth; for indeed he had received some Information from one of the Servants of the Squire's House, of his Design; and answered in the Negative. One of the Servants who knew the Host well, called out to him by his Name, just as he had opened another Window, and asked him the same Question; to which he answered in the Affirmative. 'O ho!' said another; 'have we found you?' And ordered the Host to come down and open his Door. Fanny, who was as wakeful as Joseph, no sooner heard all this, than she leap'd from her Bed, and hastily putting on her Gown and Petticoats, ran as fast as possible to Joseph's Room, who then was almost drest; he immediately let her in, and embracing her with the most passionate Tenderness, bid her fear nothing: For he would die in her Defence. 'Is that a Reason why I should not fear,' says she, 'when I should lose what is dearer to me than the whole World?' Joseph then kissing her Hand, said he could almost thank the Occasion which had extorted from her a Tenderness she would never indulge him with before. He then ran and waked his Bedfellow Adams, who was yet fast asleep, notwithstanding many Calls from

Joseph: But was no sooner made sensible of their Danger than he leaped from his Bed, without considering the Presence of Fanny, who hastily turned her Face from him, and enjoyed a double Benefit from the dark, which as it would have prevented any Offence to an Innocence less pure, or a Modesty less delicate, so it concealed even those Blushes which were raised in her.

Adams had soon put on all his Clothes but his Breeches, which in the Hurry he forgot; however, they were pretty well supplied by the Length of his other Garments: And now the House-Door being opened, the Captain, the Poet, the Player, and three Servants came in. The Captain told the Host, that two Fellows who were in his House, had run away with a young Woman; and desired to know in which Room she lay. The Host, who presently believed the Story, directed them, and instantly the Captain and Poet, jostling one another, ran up. The Poet, who was the nimblest, entering the Chamber first, searched the Bed and every other Part, but to no Purpose; the Bird was flown, as the impatient Reader, who might otherwise have been in Pain for her, was before advertised.[1] They then enquired where the Men lay, and were approaching the Chamber, when Joseph roared out in a loud Voice, that he would shoot the first Man who offered to attack the Door. The Captain enquired what Fire-Arms they had; to which the Host answered, he believed they had none; nay, he was almost convinced of it: For he had heard one ask the other in the Evening, what they should have done, if they had been overtaken when they had no Arms; to which the other answered, they would have defended themselves with their Sticks as long as they were able, and God would assist a just Cause. This satisfied the Captain, but not the Poet, who prudently retreated down Stairs, saying, it was his Business to record great Actions, and not to do them. The Captain was no sooner well satisfied that there were no Fire-Arms, than bidding Defiance to Gunpowder, and swearing he loved the Smell of it, he ordered the Servants to follow him, and marching boldly up, immediately attempted to force the Door, which the Servants soon helped him to accomplish. When it was opened, they discovered the Enemy drawn up three deep; Adams in the Front, and Fanny in the Rear. The Captain told Adams, that if they would go all back to the House again, they should be civilly treated: but unless they consented, he had

---

[1] Informed.

Orders to carry the young Lady with him, whom there was great Reason to believe they had stolen from her Parents; for notwithstanding her Disguise, her Air, which she could not conceal, sufficiently discovered her Birth to be infinitely superior to theirs. Fanny bursting into Tears, solemnly assured him he was mistaken; that she was a poor helpless Foundling, and had no Relation in the World which she knew of; and throwing herself on her Knees, begged that he would not attempt to take her from her Friends, who she was convinced would die before they would lose her; which Adams confirmed with Words not far from amounting to an Oath. The Captain swore he had no Leisure to talk, and bidding them thank themselves for what happened, he ordered the Servants to fall on, at the same time endeavouring to pass by Adams, in order to lay hold on Fanny; but the Parson interrupting him, received a Blow from one of them, which, without considering whence it came, he returned to the Captain, and gave him so dextrous a Knock in that Part of the Stomach which is vulgarly called the Pit, that he staggered some Paces backwards. The Captain, who was not accustomed to this kind of Play, and who wisely apprehended the Consequence of such another Blow, two of them seeming to him equal to a Thrust through the Body, drew forth his Hanger,[2] as Adams approached him, and was levelling a Blow at his Head, which would probably have silenced the Preacher for ever, had not Joseph in that Instant lifted up a certain huge Stone Pot of the Chamber with one Hand, which six Beaus could not have lifted with both, and discharged it, together with the Contents, full in the Captain's Face. The uplifted Hanger dropped from his Hand, and he fell prostrate on the Floor *with a lumpish Noise, and his Halfpence rattled in his Pocket;*[3] the red Liquour which his Veins contained, and the white Liquor which the Pot contained, ran in one Stream down his Face and his Clothes. Nor had Adams quite escaped, some of the Water having in its Passage shed its Honours on his Head, and began to trickle down the Wrinkles or rather Furrows of his Cheeks, when one of the Servants snatching a Mop out of a Pail of Water which had already done its Duty in washing the House, pushed it in the Parson's Face; yet could not he bear him

---

[2] Short sword.

[3] A burlesque of a stock Homeric phrase for a fallen warrior; cf. Pope's translation of *Iliad* 5.73–74: "Down sinks the warriour with a thundering sound, / His brazen armour rings against the ground."

down; for the Parson wresting the Mop from the Fellow with one Hand, with the other brought his Enemy as low as the Earth, having given him a Stroke over that part of the Face, where, in some Men of Pleasure, the natural and artificial Noses are conjoined.[4]

Hitherto Fortune seemed to incline the Victory on the Travellers side, when, according to her Custom, she began to shew the Fickleness of her Disposition: For now the Host entering the Field, or rather Chamber of Battle, flew directly at Joseph, and darting his Head into his Stomach (for he was a stout Fellow, and an expert Boxer) almost staggered him; but Joseph stepping one Leg back, did with his left Hand so chuck him under the Chin that he reeled. The Youth was pursuing his Blow with his right Hand, when he received from one of the Servants such a Stroke with a Cudgel on his Temples, that it instantly deprived him of Sense, and he measured his Length on the Ground.

Fanny rent the Air with her Cries, and Adams was coming to the Assistance of Joseph: But the two Serving Men and the Host now fell on him, and soon subdued him, tho' he fought like a Madman, and looked so black with the Impressions he had received from the Mop, that Don Quixote would certainly have taken him for an inchanted Moor.[5] But now follows the most tragical Part; for the Captain was risen again; and seeing Joseph on the Floor, and Adams secured, he instantly laid hold on Fanny, and with the Assistance of the Poet and Player, who hearing the Battle was over, were now come up, dragged her, crying and tearing her Hair, from the Sight of her Joseph, and with a perfect Deafness to all her Entreaties, carried her down Stairs by Violence, and fastened her on the Player's Horse; and the Captain mounting his own, and leading that, on which this poor miserable Wretch was, departed without any more Consideration of her Cries than a Butcher hath of those of a Lamb; for indeed his Thoughts were entertained only with the Degree of Favour which he promised himself from the Squire on the Success of this Adventure.

The Servants, who were ordered to secure Adams and Joseph as safe as possible, that the Squire might receive no Interruption to his Design on poor Fanny, immediately, by the Poet's Advice, tied Adams to one of the Bed-posts, as they did Joseph on the other Side,

---

[4] Untreated venereal disease (syphilis) can cause the nose to decay, and sufferers sometimes resorted to wearing artificial noses. The blow to the place where natural and artificial noses meet is a burlesque of the Homeric convention of warriors being hit where two bones meet: cf. Pope's version of *Iliad* 5.175–76: "Where to the hip th'inserted thigh unites, / Full on the bone the pointed marble lights."

[5] *Don Quixote* 1.3.3.

as soon as they could bring him to himself; and then leaving them together, back to back, and desiring the Host not to set them at Liberty, nor go near them till he had farther Orders, they departed towards their Master; but happened to take a different Road from that which the Captain had fallen into.

CHAP. X.

A Discourse between the Poet and Player; of no other Use in this History, but to divert the Reader.

BEFORE we proceed any farther in this Tragedy, we shall leave Mr. Joseph and Mr. Adams to themselves, and imitate the wise Conductors of the Stage; who in the midst of a grave Action entertain you with some excellent Piece of Satire or Humour called a Dance. Which Piece is indeed therefore danced, and not spoke, as it is delivered to the Audience by Persons whose thinking Faculty is by most People held to lie in their Heels; and to whom, as well as Heroes, who think with their Hands, Nature hath only given Heads for the Sake of Conformity, and as they are of Use in Dancing, to hang their Hats on.

The Poet, addressing the Player, proceeded thus: 'As I was saying' (for they had been at this Discourse all the time of the Engagement above Stairs) 'the Reason you have no good new Plays is evident; it is from your Discouragement of Authors. Gentlemen will not write, Sir, they will not write without the Expectation of Fame or Profit, or perhaps both. Plays are like Trees which will not grow without Nourishment; but, like Mushrooms, they shoot up spontaneously, as it were, in a rich Soil. The Muses, like Vines, may be pruned, but not with a Hatchet. The Town, like a peevish Child, knows not what it desires, and is always best pleased with a Rattle. A Farce-Writer hath indeed some Chance for Success; but they have lost all Taste for the Sublime. Tho' I believe one Reason of their Depravity is the Badness of the Actors. If a Man writes like an Angel, Sir, those Fellows know not how to give a Sentiment Utterance.' 'Not so fast,' says the Player, 'the modern Actors are as good at least as their Authors, nay, they come nearer their illustrious Predecessors, and I expect a Booth[1] on the Stage again, sooner than

---

[1] Barton Booth (1681–1733), celebrated tragic actor; Thomas Betterton (d. 1710), mentioned below, was his mentor. Samuel Sanford was another popular actor of the later seventeenth century.

a Shakespear or an Otway; and indeed I may turn your Observation against you, and with Truth say, that the Reason no Authors are encouraged, is because we have no good new Plays.' 'I have not affirmed the contrary,' said the Poet; 'but I am surprized you grow so warm; you cannot imagine yourself interested in this Dispute; I hope you have a better Opinion of my Taste, than to apprehend I squinted at yourself. No, Sir, if we had six such Actors as you, we should soon rival the Bettertons and Sandfords of former Times; for, without a Compliment to you, I think it impossible for any one to have excelled you in most of your Parts. Nay, it is solemn Truth, and I have heard many, and all great Judges, express as much; and you will pardon me if I tell you, I think every time I have seen you lately, you have constantly acquired some new Excellence, like a Snowball. You have deceived me in my Estimation of Perfection, and have outdone what I thought inimitable.' 'You are as little interested,' answered the Player, 'in what I have said of other Poets; for d—n me if there are not manly Strokes, ay whole Scenes, in your last Tragedy, which at least equal Shakespear. There is a Delicacy of Sentiment, a Dignity of Expression in it, which I will own many of our Gentlemen did not do adequate Justice to. To confess the Truth, they are bad enough, and I pity an Author who is present at the Murder of his Works.'—'Nay, it is but seldom that it can happen,' returned the Poet, 'the Works of most modern Authors, like dead-born Children, cannot be murdered. It is such wretched half-begotten, half-writ, lifeless, spiritless, low, groveling Stuff, that I almost pity the Actor who is oblig'd to get it by heart, which must be almost as difficult to remember as Words in a Language you don't understand.' 'I am sure,' said the Player, 'if the Sentences have little Meaning when they are writ, when they are spoken they have less. I know scarce one who ever lays an Emphasis right, and much less adapts his Action to his Character. I have seen a tender Lover in an Attitude of fighting with his Mistress, and a brave Hero suing to his Enemy with his Sword in his Hand.—I don't care to abuse my Profession, but rot me if in my Heart I am not inclined to the Poet's Side.' 'It is rather generous in you than just,' said the Poet; 'and tho' I hate to speak ill of any Person's Production; nay, I never do it, nor will—but yet, to do Justice to the Actors, what could Booth or Betterton have made of such horrible Stuff as Fenton's *Marianne*, Frowd's *Philotas*, or Mallet's *Eurydice*, or those low, dirty, last dying Speeches, which a Fellow in the City or Wapping, your Dillo or Lillo, what was his Name, called

Tragedies?'[2]—'Very well,' says the Player, 'and pray what do you think of such Fellows as Quin and Delane, or that face-making Puppy young Cibber, that ill-looked Dog Macklin, or that saucy Slut Mrs. Clive?[3] What Work would they make with your Shake-spears, Otways and Lees? How would those harmonious Lines of the last come from their Tongues?

> —No more; for I disdain
> All Pomp when thou art by—far be the Noise
> Of Kings and Crowns from us, whose gentle Souls
> Our kinder Fates have steer'd another Way.
> Free as the Forest Birds we'll pair together,
> Without rememb'ring who our Fathers were:
> Fly to the Arbors, Grots, and flow'ry Meads,
> There in soft Murmurs interchange our Souls,
> Together drink the Crystal of the Stream,
> Or taste the yellow Fruit which Autumn yields.
> And when the golden Evening calls us home,
> Wing to our downy Nests, and sleep till Morn.[4]

'Or how would this Disdain of Otway,

> Who'd be that foolish, sordid thing, call'd Man?'[5]

'Hold, hold, hold,' said the Poet, 'Do repeat that tender Speech in the third Act of my Play which you made such a Figure in.'—'I would willingly,' said the Player, 'but I have forgot it.'—'Ay, you was not quite perfect enough in it when you play'd it,' cries the Poet, 'or you would have had such an Applause as was never given on the Stage; an Applause I was extremely concerned for your losing.'—'Sure,' says the Player, 'if I remember, that was hiss'd more than any Passage in the whole Play.'—'Ay, your speaking it was hiss'd,' said the Poet. 'My speaking it!' said the Player.—'I mean your not speaking it,' said the Poet. 'You was out, and then they hiss'd.'—'They hiss'd, and then I was out, if I remember,' answered the Player; 'and I must say this for

[2] The poet mentions several popular stage tragedies: Elijah Fenton's *Mariamne* (1732); David Mallet's *Eurydice* (1731); Philip Frowde's *Philotas* (1731); George Lillo's *The London Merchant* (1731). Wapping was a dockside area near the commercial center or "City" of London.

[3] Popular actors of the day. "Young Cibber" is Colley Cibber's son Theophilus (1703–58), a noted comedian.

[4] From Nathaniel Lee (1653–1692), *Theodosius; or The Force of Love* (1680), 2.1.

[5] From Thomas Otway (1652–1685), *The Orphan; or The Unhappy Marriage* (1680), 1.1.

myself, that the whole Audience allowed I did your Part Justice: so don't lay the Damnation of your Play to my Account.' 'I don't know what you mean by Damnation,' replied the Poet. 'Why, you know it was acted but one Night,' cried the Player. 'No,' said the Poet, 'you and the whole Town were Enemies; the Pit were all my Enemies, Fellows that would cut my Throat, if the Fear of hanging did not restrain them. All Taylors, Sir, all Taylors.' 'Why should the Taylors be so angry with you?' cries the Player. 'I suppose you don't employ so many in making your Clothes.' 'I admit your Jest,' answered the Poet; 'but you remember the Affair as well as myself; you know there was a Party in the Pit and Upper-Gallery would not suffer it to be given out again; tho' much, ay infinitely, the Majority, all the Boxes in particular, were desirous of it; nay, most of the Ladies swore they never would come to the House till it was acted again.—Indeed I must own their Policy was good, in not letting it be given out a second time; for the Rascals knew if it had gone a second Night, it would have run fifty: for if ever there was Distress in a Tragedy,—I am not fond of my own Performance; but if I should tell you what the best Judges said of it—Nor was it entirely owing to my Enemies neither, that it did not succeed on the Stage as well as it hath since among the polite Readers; for you can't say it had Justice done it by the Performers.'—'I think,' answered the Player, 'the Performers did the Distress of it Justice: for I am sure we were in Distress enough, who were pelted with Oranges all the last Act; we all imagined it would have been the last Act of our Lives.'

The Poet, whose Fury was now raised, had just attempted to answer, when they were interrupted, and an end put to their Discourse by an Accident; which, if the Reader is impatient to know, he must skip over the next Chapter, which is a sort of Counterpart to this, and contains some of the best and gravest Matters in the whole Book, being a Discourse between Parson Abraham Adams and Mr. Joseph Andrews.

CHAP. XI.

Containing the Exhortations of Parson Adams *to his Friend in Affliction; calculated for the Instruction and Improvement of the Reader.*

JOSEPH no sooner came perfectly to himself, than perceiving his Mistress gone, he bewailed her Loss with Groans, which would have pierced any Heart but those which are possessed by some

People, and are made of a certain Composition not unlike Flint in its Hardness and other Properties; for you may strike Fire from them which will dart through the Eyes, but they can never distil one Drop of Water the same way. His own, poor Youth, was of a softer Composition; and at those Words, O *my dear Fanny! O my Love! shall I never, never see thee more?* his Eyes overflowed with Tears, which would have become any thing but a Hero. In a word, his Despair was more easy to be conceived than related.—

Mr. Adams, after many Groans, sitting with his Back to Joseph, began thus in a sorrowful Tone: 'You cannot imagine, my good Child, that I entirely blame these first Agonies of your Grief; for, when Misfortunes attack us by Surprize, it must require infinitely more Learning than you are Master of to resist them: but it is the Business of a Man and a Christian, to summon Reason as quickly as he can to his Aid; and she will presently teach him Patience and Submission. Be comforted, therefore, Child, I say be comforted. It is true you have lost the prettiest, kindest, loveliest, sweetest young Woman, One with whom you might have expected to have lived in Happiness, Virtue and Innocence. By whom you might have promised yourself many little Darlings, who would have been the Delight of your Youth, and the Comfort of your Age. You have not only lost her, but have Reason to fear the utmost Violence which Lust and Power can inflict upon her. Now indeed you may easily raise Ideas of Horror, which might drive you to Despair.'—'O I shall run mad,' cries Joseph, 'O that I could but command my Hands to tear my Eyes out and my Flesh off.'—'If you would use them to such Purposes, I am glad you can't,' answer'd Adams. 'I have stated your Misfortune as strong as I possibly can; but on the other side, you are to consider you are a Christian, that no Accident happens to us without the Divine Permission, and that it is the Duty of a Man and a Christian to submit. We did not make ourselves; but the same Power which made us, rules over us, and we are absolutely at his Disposal; he may do with us what he pleases, nor have we any Right to complain. A second Reason against our Complaint is our Ignorance; for as we know not future Events, so neither can we tell to what Purpose any Accident tends; and that which at first threatens us with Evil, may in the End produce our Good. I should indeed have said our Ignorance is twofold (but I have not at present time to divide properly) for as we know not to what purpose any Event is ultimately directed; so neither can we affirm from what Cause it originally sprung. You are a Man, and consequently a Sinner; and this may be a Punishment to you for your Sins; indeed in this Sense it may be esteemed as a Good, yea, as the greatest Good, which satisfies the Anger of Heaven, and averts that Wrath which cannot continue without our Destruction. Thirdly, Our Impotency of relieving ourselves, demonstrates the Folly and Absurdity of our Complaints: For whom do we resist? or against whom do we complain, but a Power from whose Shafts no Armour can guard us, no Speed can fly? A Power which leaves us no Hope but in Submission.'—'O Sir,' cried Joseph, 'all this is very true, and very fine, and I could hear you all Day, if I was not so grieved at Heart as now I am.' 'Would you take Physic,' says Adams, 'when you are well, and refuse it when you are sick? Is not Comfort to be administred to the Afflicted, and not to those who rejoice, or those who are at ease?'—'O you have not spoken one Word of Comfort to me yet,' returned Joseph. 'No!' cries Adams, 'What am I then doing? what can I say to comfort you?'—'O tell me,' cries Joseph, 'that Fanny will escape back to my Arms, that they shall again inclose that lovely Creature, with all her Sweetness, all her untainted Innocence about her.'—'Why, perhaps you may,' cries Adams; 'but I can't promise you what's to come. You must with perfect Resignation wait the Event; if she be restored to you again, it is your Duty to be thankful, so it is if she be not: Joseph, if you are wise, and truly know your own Interest, you will peaceably and quietly submit to all the Dispensations of Providence, being thoroughly assured, that all the Misfortunes, how great soever, which happen to the Righteous, happen to them for their own Good.—Nay, it is not your Interest only, but your Duty to abstain from immoderate Grief; which if you indulge, you are not worthy the Name of a Christian.'—He spoke these last Words with an Accent a little severer than usual; upon which Joseph begged him not to be angry, saying, he mistook him, if he thought he denied it was his Duty; for he had known that long ago. 'What signifies knowing your Duty, if you do not perform it?' answer'd Adams. 'Your Knowledge increases your Guilt—O Joseph, I never thought you had this Stubbornness in your Mind.' Joseph replied, 'he fancied he misunderstood him, which I assure you,' says he, 'you do, if you imagine I endeavour to grieve; upon my Soul I don't.' Adams rebuked him for swearing, and then proceeded to enlarge on the Folly of Grief, telling him, all the wise Men and Philosophers, even among the Heathens, had written against it, quoting several Passages from Seneca, and the *Consolation*, which tho' it was not Cicero's, was, he said, as good almost as any of his Works,[1] and concluded all by hinting, that immoderate Grief in this Case might incense that Power which alone could restore him his Fanny. This Reason, or indeed rather the Idea which it raised of the Restoration of his Mistress, had more Effect than all which the Parson had said before, and for a Moment abated his Agonies: But when his Fears sufficiently set before his Eyes the Danger that poor Creature was in, his Grief returned again with repeated Violence, nor could Adams in the least asswage it; tho' it may be doubted in his Behalf, whether Socrates himself could have prevailed any better.

They remained some time in Silence; and Groans and Sighs issued from them both; at length Joseph burst out into the following Soliloquy:

> Yes, I will bear my Sorrows like a Man,
> But I must also feel them as a Man.
> I cannot but remember such Things were,
> And were most dear to me.—[2]

Adams asked him what Stuff that was he repeated?—To which he answer'd, they were some Lines he had gotten by heart out of a Play—'Ay, there is nothing but Heathenism to be learn'd from Plays,' reply'd he—'I never heard of any Plays fit for a Christian to read, but *Cato* and the *Conscious Lovers;* and I must own in the latter there are some Things almost solemn enough for a Sermon.'[3] But we shall now leave them a little, and enquire after the Subject of their Conversation.

---

[1] Battestin notes that the reference is probably not to Boethius's *Consolation of Philosophy* but rather to the sixteenth-century pseudo-Ciceronian *Consolation* with which Fielding was reportedly familiar. The Roman Stoic Seneca wrote several consolatory works, including *De Consolatione* and sections of his *Epistulae Morales* ("Moral Letters").

[2] Adapted from *Macbeth* 4.3.222–25.

[3] Adams earlier quoted from Addison's *Cato* in Chapter 5. Richard Steele sought in his sentimental comedy, *The Conscious Lovers* (1722), to exemplify virtue rather than ridicule vice; his Preface to the play describes his intention to introduce on the stage "a joy too exquisite for laughter."

CHAP. XII.

More Adventures, which we hope will as much please as surprize the
Reader.

NEITHER the facetious Dialogue which pass'd between the Poet and
Player, nor the grave and truly solemn Discourse of Mr. Adams,
will, we conceive, make the Reader sufficient Amends for the Anxiety which he must have felt on the Account of poor Fanny, whom
we left in so deplorable a Condition. We shall therefore now proceed to the Relation of what happened to that beautiful and innocent Virgin, after she fell into the wicked Hands of the Captain.

The Man of War having conveyed his charming Prize out of the
Inn a little before Day, made the utmost Expedition in his Power
towards the Squire's House, where this delicate Creature was to be
offered up a Sacrifice to the Lust of a Ravisher. He was not only deaf
to all her Bewailings and Entreaties on the Road, but accosted her
Ears with Impurities, which, having been never before accustomed
to them, she happily for herself very little understood. At last he
changed this Note, and attempted to sooth and mollify her, by setting forth the Splendor and Luxury which would be her Fortune
with a Man who would have the Inclination, and Power too, to give
her whatever her utmost Wishes could desire; and told her he
doubted not but she would soon look kinder on him, as the Instrument of her Happiness, and despise that pitiful Fellow, whom her
Ignorance only could make her fond of. She answered, She knew not
whom he meant; she never was fond of any pitiful fellow. 'Are you
affronted, Madam,' says he, 'at my calling him so? but what better
can be said of one in a Livery, notwithstanding your Fondness for
him?' She returned, That she did not understand him, that the Man
had been her Fellow-Servant, and she believed was as honest a Creature as any alive; but as for Fondness for Men—'I warrant ye,' cries
the Captain, 'we shall find Means to persuade you to be fond; and I
advise you to yield to gentle ones; for you may be assured that it is
not in your Power, by any Struggles whatever, to preserve your Vir-
ginity two Hours longer. It will be your Interest to consent; for the
Squire will be much kinder to you, if he enjoys you willingly than by
Force.'—At which Words she began to call aloud for Assistance (for
it was now open Day) but finding none, she lifted her Eyes to
Heaven, and supplicated the Divine Assistance to preserve her Innocence. The Captain told her, if she persisted in her Vociferation, he

would find a Means of stopping her Mouth. And now the poor Wretch perceiving no Hopes of Succour, abandoned herself to Despair, and sighing out the Name of *Joseph! Joseph!* a River of Tears ran down her lovely Cheeks, and wet the Handkerchief which covered her Bosom. A Horseman now appeared in the Road, upon which the Captain threatened her violently if she complained; however, the Moment they approached each other, she begged him with the utmost Earnestness to relieve a distressed Creature who was in the hands of a Ravisher. The Fellow stopt at those Words; but the Captain assured him it was his Wife, and that he was carrying her home from her Adulterer: Which so satisfied the Fellow, who was an old one, (and perhaps a married one too) that he wished him a good Journey, and rode on. He was no sooner past, than the Captain abused her violently for breaking his Commands, and threaten'd to gagg her, when two more Horsemen, armed with Pistols, came into the Road just before them. She again sollicited their Assistance, and the Captain told the same Story as before. Upon which one said to the other—'That's a charming Wench! Jack; I wish I had been the Fellow's Place whoever he is.' But the other, instead of answering him, cried out eagerly, 'Zounds, I know her:' and then turning to her said, 'Sure you are not Fanny Goodwill.'—'Indeed, indeed I am,' she cry'd—'O John, I know you now—Heaven hath sent you to my Assistance, to deliver me from this wicked Man, who is carrying me away for his vile Purposes—O for God's sake rescue me from him.' A fierce Dialogue immediately ensued between the Captain and these two Men, who being both armed with Pistols, and the Chariot which they attended being now arrived, the Captain saw both Force and Stratagem were vain, and endeavoured to make his Escape; in which however he could not succeed. The Gentleman who rode in the Chariot, ordered it to stop, and with an Air of Authority examined into the Merits of the Cause; of which being advertised by Fanny, whose Credit was confirmed by the Fellow who knew her, he ordered the Captain, who was all bloody from his Encounter at the Inn, to be conveyed as a Prisoner behind the Chariot, and very gallantly took Fanny into it; for, to say the Truth, this Gentleman (who was no other than Mr. Peter Pounce, and who preceded the Lady Booby only a few Miles, by setting out earlier in the Morning) was a very gallant Person, and loved a pretty Girl better than any Thing, besides his own Money, or the Money of other People.

The Chariot now proceeded towards the Inn, which, as Fanny was informed, lay in their Way, and where it arrived at that very time while the Poet and Player were disputing below Stairs, and Adams and Joseph were discoursing back to back above: just at that Period to which we brought them both in the two preceding Chapters, the Chariot stopt at the Door, and in an Instant Fanny leaping from it, ran up to her Joseph.—O Reader, conceive, if thou canst, the Joy which fired the Breasts of these Lovers on this Meeting; and if thy own Heart doth not sympathetically assist thee in this Conception, I pity thee sincerely from my own: for let the hardhearted Villain know this, that there is a Pleasure in a tender Sensation beyond any which he is capable of tasting.

Peter being informed by Fanny of the Presence of Adams, stopt to see him, and receive his Homage; for, as Peter was an Hypocrite, a sort of People whom Mr. Adams never saw through, the one paid that Respect to his seeming Goodness which the other believed to be paid to his Riches; hence Mr. Adams was so much his Favourite, that he once lent him four Pounds thirteen Shillings and Sixpence, to prevent his going to Goal, on no greater Security than a Bond and Judgment, which probably he would have made no use of, tho' the Money had not been (as it was) paid exactly at the time.

It is not perhaps easy to describe the Figure of Adams; he had risen in such a Hurry, that he had on neither Breeches, Garters, nor Stockings; nor had he taken from his Head a red spotted Handkerchief, which by Night bound his Wig, turned inside out, around his Head. He had on his torn Cassock, and his Great-Coat; but as the Remainder of his Cassock hung down below his Great-Coat; so did a small Stripe of white, or rather whitish Linen appear below that; to which we may add the several Colours which appeared on his Face, where a long Piss-burnt[1] Beard served to retain the Liquor of the Stone Pot, and that of a blacker Hue which distilled from the Mop.—This Figure, which Fanny had delivered from his Captivity, was no sooner spied by Peter, than it disordered the composed Gravity of his Muscles; however, he advised him immediately to make himself clean, nor would accept his Homage in that Pickle.

The Poet and Player no sooner saw the Captain in Captivity, than they began to consider of their own Safety, of which Flight presented itself as the only Means; they therefore both of them mounted the Poet's Horse, and made the most expeditious Retreat in their Power.

---

[1] "Discoloured" (Grose).

The Host, who well knew Mr. Pounce, and the Lady Booby's Livery, was not a little surprized at this Change of the Scene, nor was his Confusion much helped by his Wife, who was now just risen, and having heard from him the Account of what had past, comforted him with a decent Number of Fools and Blockheads; asked him why he did not consult her; and told him, he would never leave following the nonsensical Dictates of his own Numscull, till she and her Family were ruined.

Joseph being informed of the Captain's Arrival, and seeing his Fanny now in Safety, quitted her a Moment, and running down Stairs, went directly to him, and stripping off his Coat, challenged him to fight; but the Captain refused, saying he did not understand Boxing. He then grasped a Cudgel in one Hand, and catching the Captain by the Collar with the other, gave him a most severe Drubbing, and ended with telling him, he had now had some Revenge for what his dear Fanny had suffered.

When Mr. Pounce had a little regaled himself with some Provision which he had in his Chariot, and Mr. Adams had put on the best Appearance his Clothes would allow him, Pounce ordered the Captain into his Presence; for he said he was guilty of Felony, and the next Justice of Peace should commit him: but the Servants (whose Appetite for Revenge is soon satisfied) being sufficiently contented with the Drubbing which Joseph had inflicted on him, and which was indeed of no very moderate kind, had suffered him to go off, which he did, threatening a severe Revenge against Joseph, which I have never heard he thought proper to take.

The Mistress of the House made her voluntary Appearance before Mr. Pounce, and with a thousand Curt'sies told him, 'she hoped his Honour would pardon her Husband, who was a very *nonsense* Man, for the sake of his poor Family; that indeed if he could be ruined alone, she should be very willing of it; *for because as why*, his Worship very well knew he deserved it: but she had three poor small Children, who were not capable to get their own Living; and if her Husband was sent to Goal, they must all come to the Parish;[2] for she was a poor weak Woman, continually a breeding, and had no time to work for them. She therefore hoped his Honour would take it into his Worship's Consideration, and forgive her Husband this time; for she was sure he never intended any Harm to Man, Woman, or Child; and if it was not for that Blockhead of his

---

[2] That is, depend on charity administered by the local parish.

own, the Man in some Things was well enough; for she had had three Children by him in less than three Years, and was almost ready to cry out the fourth Time.' She would have proceeded in this manner much longer, had not Peter stopt her Tongue, by telling her he had nothing to say to her Husband, nor her neither. So, as Adams and the rest had assured her of Forgiveness, she cried and curt'sied out of the Room.

Mr. Pounce was desirous that Fanny should continue her Journey with him in the Chariot; and she absolutely refused, saying she would ride behind Joseph, on a Horse which one of Lady Booby's Servants had equipped him with. But alas! when the Horse appeared, it was found to be no other than that identical Beast which Mr. Adams had left behind him at the Inn, and which these honest Fellows, who knew him, had redeemed. Indeed whatever Horse they had provided for Joseph, they would have prevailed with him to mount none, no not even to ride before his beloved Fanny, till the Parson was supplied; much less would he deprive his Friend of the Beast which belonged to him, and which he knew the Moment he saw, tho' Adams did not: however, when he was reminded of the Affair, and told that they had brought the Horse with them which he left behind, he answered—*Bless me! and so I did.*

Adams was very desirous that Joseph and Fanny should mount this Horse, and declared he could very easily walk home. 'If I walked alone,' says he, 'I would wage a Shilling, that the *Pedestrian* out-stripped the *Equestrian* Travellers: but as I intend to take the company of a Pipe, peradventure I may be an Hour later.' One of the Servants whispered Joseph to take him at his Word, and suffer the old Put[3] to walk if he would: This Proposal was answered with an angry Look and a peremptory Refusal by Joseph, who catching Fanny up in his Arms, aver'd he would rather carry her home in that manner, than take away Mr. Adams's Horse, and permit him to walk on Foot.

Perhaps, Reader, thou hast seen a Contest between two Gentlemen, or two Ladies quickly decided, tho' they have both asserted they would not eat such a nice Morsel, and each insisted on the other's accepting it; but in reality both were very desirous to swallow it themselves. Do not therefore conclude hence, that this Dispute would

---

[3] "An ignorant awkward clown" (Grose).

have come to a speedy Decision: for here both Parties were heartily in earnest, and it is very probable, they would have remained in the Inn-yard to this Day, had not the good Peter Pounce put a Stop to it; for finding he had no longer Hopes of satisfying his old Appetite with Fanny, and being desirous of having some one to whom he might communicate his Grandeur, he told the Parson he would convey him home in his Chariot. This Favour was by Adams, with many Bows and Acknowledgements, accepted, tho' he afterwards said, 'he ascended the Chariot rather that he might not offend, than from any Desire of riding in it, for that in his Heart he preferred the *Pedestrian* even to the *Vehicular* Expedition.' All matters being now settled, the Chariot in which rode Adams and Pounce, moved forwards; and Joseph, having borrowed a Pillion from the Host, Fanny had just seated herself thereon, and had laid hold of the Girdle which her Lover wore for that Purpose, when the wise Beast, who concluded that one at a Time was sufficient, that two to one were Odds, *&c.*, discovered much Uneasiness at this double Load, and began to con-sider his hinder as his Fore-legs, moving the direct contrary Way to that which is called forwards. Nor could Joseph, with all his Horse-manship persuade him to advance: but without having any regard to the lovely Part of the lovely Girl which was on his Back, he used such Agitations, that had not one of the Men come immediately to her Assistance, she had, in plain English, tumbled backwards on the Ground. This Inconvenience was presently remedied by an Exchange of Horses; and then Fanny being again placed on her Pillion, on a bet-ter natured, and somewhat better fed Beast, the Parson's Horse find-ing he had no longer Odds to contend with, agreed to march; and the whole Procession set forwards for Booby-Hall, where they arrived in a few Hours without any thing remarkable happening on the Road, unless it was a curious Dialogue between the Parson and the Steward; which, to use the Language of a late Apologist, a Pattern to all Biog-raphers, *waits for the Reader in the next Chapter.*

CHAP. XIII.

A curious Dialogue which passed between Mr. Abraham Adams *and Mr.* Peter Pounce, *better worth reading than all the Works of* Colley Cibber *and many others.*

THE Chariot had not proceeded far, before Mr. Adams observed it was a very fine Day. 'Ay, and a very fine Country too,' answered

Pounce. 'I should think so more,' returned Adams, 'if I had not lately travelled over the Downs,[1] which I take to exceed this and all other Prospects in the Universe.' 'A Fig for Prospects,' answered Pounce, 'one Acre here is worth ten there; and, for my own part, I have no Delight in the Prospect of any Land but my own.' 'Sir,' said Adams, 'you can indulge yourself with many fine Prospects of that kind.' 'I thank God I have a little,' replied the other, 'with which I am content, and envy no Man: I have a little, Mr. Adams, with which I do as much good as I can.' Adams answered, 'that Riches without Charity were nothing worth; for that they were a Blessing only to him who made them a Blessing to others.' 'You and I,' said Peter, 'have different Notions of Charity. I own, as it is generally used, I do not like the Word, nor do I think it becomes one of us Gentlemen; it is a mean Parson-like Quality; tho' I would not infer many Parsons have it neither.' 'Sir,' said Adams, 'my Definition of Charity is a generous Disposition to relieve the Distressed.' 'There is something in that Definition,' answered Peter, 'which I like well enough; it is, as you say, a Disposition,—and does not so much consist in the Act as in the Disposition to do it; but alas, Mr. Adams, who are meant by the Distressed? Believe me, the Distresses of Mankind are mostly imaginary, and it would be rather Folly than Goodness to relieve them.' 'Sure, Sir,' replied Adams, 'Hunger and Thirst, Cold and Nakedness, and other Distresses which attend the Poor, can never be said to be imaginary Evils.' 'How can any Man complain of Hunger,' said Peter, 'in a Country where such excellent Sallads are to be gathered in almost every Field? or of Thirst, where every River and Stream produces such delicious Potations? And as for Cold and Nakedness, they are Evils introduced by Luxury and Custom. A Man naturally wants Clothes no more than a Horse or any other Animal; and there are whole Nations who go without them: but these are things perhaps which you, who do not know the World—' 'You will pardon me, Sir,' returned Adams; 'I have read of the *Gymnosophists*.'[2] 'A plague of your *Jehosaphats*,' cried Peter; 'the greatest Fault in our Constitution is the Provision made for the

---

[1] Low, grassy hills extending south of London to the English Channel.

[2] The Greek name ("naked philosophers") for an ancient Hindu ascetic sect. "Jehosaphat" is the name of a king of Judah (1 Kings 22:2–50); according to the *OED,* the name does not become a mild expletive (as in "jumpin' Jehosaphat") until the later nineteenth century.

Poor, except that perhaps made for some others.[3] Sir, I have not an Estate which doth not contribute almost as much again to the Poor as to the Land-Tax, and I do assure you I expect to come myself to the Parish in the end.' To which Adams giving a dissenting Smile, Peter thus proceeded: 'I fancy, Mr. Adams, you are one of those who imagine I am a Lump of Money; for there are many who, I fancy, believe that not only my Pockets, but my whole Clothes, are lined with Bank-Bills; but I assure you, you are all mistaken: I am not the Man the World esteems me. If I can hold my Head above Water, it is all I can. I have injured myself by purchasing. I have been too liberal of my Money. Indeed I fear my Heir will find my Affairs in a worse Situation than they are reputed to be. Ah! he will have reason to wish I had loved Money more, and Land less. Pray, my good Neighbour, where should I have that Quantity of Riches the World is so liberal to bestow on me? Where could I possibly, without I had stole it, acquire such a Treasure?' 'Why truly,' says Adams, 'I have been always of your Opinion; I have wondered as well as yourself with what Confidence they could report such things of you, which have to me appeared as mere Impossibilities; for you know, Sir, and I have often heard you say it, that your Wealth is your own Acquisition, and can it be credible that in your short time you should have amassed such a heap of Treasure as these People will have you worth? Indeed had you inherited an Estate like Sir Thomas Booby, which had descended in your Family for many Generations, they might have had a Colour for their Assertions.' 'Why, what do they say I am worth?' cries Peter with a malicious Sneer. 'Sir,' answered Adams, 'I have heard some aver you are not worth less than twenty thousand Pounds.' At which Peter frowned. 'Nay, Sir,' said Adams, 'you ask me only the Opinion of others, for my own part I have always denied it, nor did I ever believe you could possibly be worth half that Sum.' 'However, Mr. Adams,' said he, squeezing him by the Hand, 'I would not sell them all I am worth for double that Sum; and as to what you believe, or they believe, I care not a Fig, no not a Fart. I am not poor, because you think me so, nor because you attempt to undervalue me in the Country. I know the Envy of Mankind very well; but I thank Heaven I am

---

[3] That is, for clergymen, who were supported by the tithing of large landowners such as Pounce.

above them. It is true my Wealth is of my own Acquisition. I have not an Estate like Sir Thomas Booby, that has descended in my Family through many Generations; but I know Heirs of such Estates who are forced to travel about the Country like some People in torn Cassocks, and might be glad to accept of a pitiful Curacy for what I know. Yes, Sir, as shabby Fellows as yourself, whom no Man of my Figure, without that Vice of Good-nature about him, would suffer to ride in a Chariot with him.' 'Sir,' said Adams, 'I value not your Chariot of a Rush;[4] and if I had known you had intended to affront me, I would have walked to the World's End on foot, ere I would have accepted a place in it. However, Sir, I will soon rid you of that Inconvenience;' and so saying, he opened the Chariot-Door without calling to the Coachman, and leapt out into the High-way, forgetting to take his Hat along with him; which however Mr. Pounce threw after him with great Violence. Joseph and Fanny stopt to bear him Company the rest of the Way, which was not above a Mile.

---

[4] "Any thing proverbially worthless" (Johnson).

THE

HISTORY

OF THE

ADVENTURES

OF

Joseph Andrews, and his Friend
Mr. *Abraham Adams.*

BOOK IV.

CHAP. I.

The Arrival of Lady Booby *and the rest at Booby-Hall.*

THE Coach and Six, in which Lady Booby rode, overtook the other Travellers as they entered the Parish. She no sooner saw Joseph, than her Cheeks glowed with red, and immediately after became as totally pale. She had in her Surprize almost stopt her Coach; but recollected herself timely enough to prevent it. She entered the Parish amidst the ringing of Bells, and the Acclamations of the Poor, who were rejoiced to see their Patroness returned after so long an Absence, during which time all her Rents had been drafted to London, without a Shilling being spent among them, which tended not a little to their utter impoverishing; for if the Court would be severely missed in such a City as London, how much more must the Absence of a Person of great Fortune be felt in a little Country Village, for whose Inhabitants such a Family finds a constant Employment and Supply; and with the

Offals of whose Table the infirm, aged, and infant Poor are abundantly fed, with a Generosity which hath scarce a visible Effect on their Benefactor's Pockets?

But if their Interest inspired so public a Joy into every Countenance, how much more forcibly did the Affection which they bore Parson Adams operate upon all who beheld his Return? They flocked about him like dutiful Children round an indulgent Parent, and vyed with each other in Demonstrations of Duty and Love. The Parson on his side shook every one by the Hand, enquired heartily after the Healths of all that were absent, of their Children and Relations, and exprest a Satisfaction in his Face, which nothing but Benevolence made happy by its Objects could infuse.

Nor did Joseph and Fanny want a hearty Welcome from all who saw them. In short, no three Persons could be more kindly received, as indeed none ever more deserved to be universally beloved.

Adams carried his Fellow-Travellers home to his House, where he insisted on their partaking whatever his Wife, whom, with his Children he found in Health and Joy, could provide. Where we shall leave them enjoying perfect Happiness over a homely Meal, to view Scenes of greater Splendor, but infinitely less Bliss.

Our more intelligent Readers will doubtless suspect by this second Appearance of Lady Booby on the Stage, that all was not ended by the Dismission of Joseph; and, to be honest with them, they are in the right; the Arrow had pierced deeper than she imagined; nor was the Wound so easily to be cured. The Removal of the Object soon cooled her Rage, but it had a different Effect on her Love; that departed with his Person; but this remained lurking in her Mind with his Image. Restless, interrupted Slumbers, and confused horrible Dreams were her Portion the first Night. In the Morning, Fancy painted her a more delicious Scene; but to delude, not delight her: for before she could reach the promised Happiness, it vanished, and left her to curse, not bless the Vision.

She started from her Sleep, her Imagination being all on fire with the Phantom, when her Eyes accidentally glancing towards the Spot where yesterday the real Joseph had stood, that little Circumstance raised his Idea in the liveliest Colours in her Memory. Each Look, each Word, each Gesture rushed back on her Mind with Charms which all his Coldness could not abate. Nay, she imputed that to his Youth, his Folly, his Awe, his Religion, to every thing, but what would instantly have produced Contempt, want of Passion for the Sex; or, that which would have roused her Hatred, want of Liking to her.

Reflection then hurried her farther, and told her, she must see this beautiful Youth no more; nay, suggested to her, that she herself had dismissed him for no other Fault than probably that of too violent an Awe and Respect for herself; and which she ought rather to have esteemed a Merit, the Effects of which were besides so easily and surely to have been removed; she then blamed, she cursed the hasty Rashness of her Temper; her Fury was vented all on herself, and Joseph appeared innocent in her Eyes. Her Passion at length grew so violent, that it forced her on seeking Relief, and now she thought of recalling him: But Pride forbad that, Pride which soon drove all softer Passions from her Soul, and represented to her the Meanness of him she was fond of. That Thought soon began to obscure his Beauties; Contempt succeeded next, and then Disdain, which presently introduced her Hatred of the Creature who had given her so much Uneasiness. These Enemies of Joseph had no sooner taken Possession of her Mind, than they insinuated to her a thousand things in his Disfavour; every thing but Dislike of her Person; a Thought, which as it would have been intolerable to bear, she checked the Moment it endeavoured to arise. Revenge came now to her Assistance; and she considered her Dismission of him stript, and without a Character,[1] with the utmost Pleasure. She rioted in the several kinds of Misery, which her Imagination suggested to her, might be his Fate; and with a Smile composed of Anger, Mirth, and Scorn, viewed him in the Rags in which her Fancy had drest him.

Mrs. Slipslop being summoned, attended her Mistress, who had now in her own Opinion totally subdued this Passion. Whilst she was dressing, she asked if that Fellow had been turned away according to her Orders. Slipslop answered, she had told her Ladyship so, (as indeed she had) —'And how did he behave?' replied the Lady. 'Truly Madam,' cries Slipslop, 'in such a manner that *infected* every body who saw him. The poor Lad had but little Wages to receive: for he constantly allowed his Father and Mother half his Income; so that when your Ladyship's Livery was stript off, he had not wherewithal to buy a Coat, and must have gone naked, if one of the Footmen had not *incommodated* him with one, and whilst he was standing in his Shirt, (and, to say truth, he was an *amorous* Figure) being told your Ladyship would not give him a Character, he sighed, and said, he had done nothing willingly to offend; that for his part he should always give your Ladyship a good Character

---

[1] That is, a character reference or letter of recommendation.

wherever he went; and he prayed God to bless you; for you was the best of Ladies, tho' his Enemies had set you against him: I wish you had not turned him away; for I believe you have not a faithfuller Servant in the House.'—'How came you then,' replied the Lady, 'to advise me to turn him away?' 'I, Madam!' said Slipslop, 'I am sure you will do me the Justice to say, I did all in my power to prevent it; but I saw your Ladyship was angry; and it is not the Business of us upper Servants to *hinterfear* on those Occasions.'—'And was it not you, audacious Wretch,' cried the Lady, 'who made me angry? Was it not your Tittle-tattle, in which I believe you belyed the poor Fellow, which incensed me against him? He may thank you for all that hath happened; and so may I for the Loss of a good Servant, and one who probably had more Merit than all of you. Poor Fellow! I am charmed with his Goodness to his Parents. Why did not you tell me of that, but suffer me to dismiss so good a Creature without a Character? I see the Reason of your whole Behaviour now as well as your Complaint; you was jealous of the Wenches.' 'I jealous!' said Slipslop, 'I assure you I look upon myself as his Betters; I am not Meat for a Footman I hope.' These Words threw the Lady into a violent Passion, and she sent Slipslop from her Presence, who departed tossing her Nose, and crying, 'Marry come up! there are some People more jealous than I, I believe.' Her Lady affected not to hear the Words, tho' in reality she did, and understood them too. Now ensued a second Conflict, so like the former, that it might savour of Repetition to relate it minutely. It may suffice to say, that Lady Booby found good Reason to doubt whether she had so absolutely conquered her Passion, as she had flattered herself; and, in order to accomplish it quite, took a Resolution more common than wise, to retire immediately into the Country. The Reader hath long ago seen the Arrival of Mrs. Slipslop, whom no Pertness could make her Mistress resolve to part with; lately, that of Mr. Pounce, her Fore-runners; and lastly, that of the Lady herself.

The Morning after her Arrival, being Sunday, she went to Church, to the great Surprize of every Body, who wondered to see her Ladyship, being no very constant Church-woman, there so suddenly upon her Journey. Joseph was likewise there; and I have heard it was remarked, that she fixed her Eyes on him much more than on the Parson; but this I believe to be only a malicious Rumour. When the Prayers were ended, Mr. Adams stood up, and with a loud Voice pronounced: *I publish the Banns of Marriage between Joseph Andrews and Frances Goodwill, both of this Parish, &c.* Whether this had any Effect on Lady Booby or no, who was then in her Pew, which the Congregation could not see into, I could never discover: But certain it is, that in about a quarter of an Hour she stood up, and directed her Eyes to that part of the Church where the Women sat, and persisted in looking that Way during the Remainder of the Sermon, in so scrutinizing a manner, and with so angry a Countenance, that most of the Women were afraid she was offended at them.

The Moment she returned home, she sent for Slipslop into her Chamber, and told her, she wondered what that impudent Fellow Joseph did in that Parish? Upon which Slipslop gave her an Account of her meeting Adams with him on the Road, and likewise the Adventure with Fanny. At the Relation of which, the Lady often changed her Countenance; and when she had heard all, she ordered Mr. Adams into her Presence, to whom she behaved as the Reader will see in the next Chapter.

CHAP. II.

A Dialogue between Mr. Abraham Adams *and the Lady* Booby.

Mr. Adams was not far off; for he was drinking her Ladyship's Health below in a Cup of her Ale. He no sooner came before her, than she began in the following manner: 'I wonder, Sir, after the many great Obligations you have had to this Family,' (with all which the Reader hath, in the Course of this History, been minutely acquainted) 'that you will ungratefully show any Respect to a Fellow who hath been turned out of it for his Misdeeds. Nor doth it, I can tell you, Sir, become a Man of your Character, to run about the Country with an idle Fellow and Wench. Indeed, as for the Girl, I know no Harm of her. Slipslop tells me she was formerly bred up in my House, and behaved as she ought, till she hankered after this Fellow, and he spoiled her. Nay, she may still, perhaps, do very well, if he will let her alone. You are therefore doing a monstrous Thing, in endeavouring to procure a Match between these two People, which will be to the Ruin of them both.'—'Madam,' says Adams, 'if your Ladyship will but hear me speak, I protest I never heard any harm of Mr. Joseph Andrews; if I had, I should have corrected him for it: For I never have, nor will encourage the Faults of those under my Cure. As for the young Woman, I assure your Ladyship I have as good an Opinion of her as your Ladyship yourself, or any other can have. She is the sweetest-tempered, honestest, worthiest, young

Creature; indeed as to her Beauty, I do not commend her on that Account, tho' all Men allow she is the handsomest Woman, Gentle or Simple, that ever appeared in the Parish.' 'You are very impertinent,' says she, 'to talk such fulsome Stuff to me. It is mighty becoming truly in a Clergyman to trouble himself about handsome Women, and you are a delicate Judge of Beauty, no doubt. A Man who hath lived all his Life in such a Parish as this, is a rare Judge of Beauty. Ridiculous! Beauty indeed,—a Country Wench a Beauty.—I shall be sick whenever I hear Beauty mentioned again—And so this Wench is to stock the Parish with Beauties, I hope.—But, Sir, our Poor is numerous enough already; I will have no more Vagabonds settled here.' 'Madam,' says Adams, 'your Ladyship is offended with me, I protest, without any Reason. This Couple were desirous to consummate long ago, and I dissuaded them from it; nay, I may venture to say, I believe, I was the sole Cause of their delaying it.' 'Well,' says she, 'and you did very wisely and honestly too, notwithstanding she is the greatest Beauty in the Parish.'—'And now, Madam,' continued he, 'I only perform my Office to Mr. Joseph.'— 'Pray, don't Mister such Fellows to me,' cries the Lady. 'He,' said the Parson, 'with the Consent of Fanny, before my Face, put in the Banns.'—'Yes,' answered the Lady, 'I suppose the Slut is forward enough; Slipslop tells me how her Head runs on Fellows; that is one of her Beauties, I suppose. But if they have put in the Banns, I desire you will publish them no more without my Orders.' 'Madam,' cries Adams, 'if any one puts in sufficient Caution, and assigns a proper Reason against them, I am willing to surcease.'—'I tell you a Reason,' says she, 'he is a Vagabond, and he shall not settle here, and bring a Nest of Beggars into the Parish; it will make us but little Amends that they will be Beauties.' 'Madam,' answered Adams, 'with the utmost Submission to your Ladyship, I have been informed by Lawyer Scout, that any Person who serves a Year, gains a Settlement in the Parish where he serves.'[1] 'Lawyer Scout,' replied the Lady, 'is an impudent Coxcomb; I will have no Lawyer Scout interfere with me. I repeat to you again, I will have no more Incumbrances brought on us; so I desire you will proceed no further.' 'Madam,' returned Adams, 'I would obey your Ladyship in every Thing that is lawful; but surely the Parties being poor is no Reason

---

[1] According to the Act of Settlements (1662), a settlement or legal residence could be established by one year of service in a place. Settled persons were entitled to charitable assistance from the parish under the Poor Law.

against their marrying. God forbid there should be any such Law. The Poor have little Share enough of this World already; it would be barbarous indeed to deny them the common Privileges, and innocent Enjoyments which Nature indulges to the animal Creation.' 'Since you understand yourself no better,' cries the Lady, 'nor the Respect due from such as you to a Woman of my Distinction, than to affront my Ears by such loose Discourse, I shall mention but one short Word; it is my Orders to you, that you publish these Banns no more; and if you dare, I will recommend it to your Master, the Doctor,[2] to discard you from his Service. I will, Sir, notwithstanding your poor Family; and then you and the greatest Beauty in the Parish may go and beg together.' 'Madam,' answered Adams, 'I know not what your Ladyship means by the Terms *Master* and *Service*. I am in the Service of a Master who will never discard me for doing my Duty: And if the Doctor (for indeed I have never been able to pay for a Licence) thinks proper to turn me from my Cure, God will provide me, I hope, another. At least, my Family, as well as myself, have Hands; and he will prosper, I doubt not, our Endeavours to get our Bread honestly with them. Whilst my Conscience is pure, I shall never fear what Man can do unto me.'—'I condemn my Humility,' said the Lady, 'for demeaning myself to converse with you so long. I shall take other Measures; for I see you are a Confederate with them. But the sooner you leave me, the better; and I shall give Orders that my Doors may no longer be open to you. I will suffer no Parsons who run about the Country with Beauties, to be entertained here.' 'Madam,' said Adams, 'I shall enter into no Person's Doors against their Will: But I am assured, when you have enquired farther into this Matter, you will applaud, not blame my Proceeding; and so I humbly take my Leave:' Which he did with many Bows, or at least many Attempts at a Bow.

CHAP. III.

What past between the Lady and Lawyer Scout.

IN the Afternoon the Lady sent for Mr. Scout, whom she attacked most violently for intermeddling with her Servants; which he denied, and indeed with Truth; for he had only asserted accidentally, and

---

[2] That is, the rector of the parish under whom Adams serves as curate: see Book 1, Chapter 2, n. 7.

perhaps rightly, that a Year's Service gained a Settlement; and so far
he owned he might have formerly informed the Parson, and believed
it was Law. 'I am resolved,' said the Lady, 'to have no discarded Servants of mine settled here; and so, if this be your Law, I shall send to
another Lawyer.' Scout said, 'If she sent to a hundred Lawyers, not
one or all of them could alter the Law. The utmost that was in the
Power of a Lawyer, was to prevent the Law's taking effect; and that
he himself could do for her Ladyship as well as any other: And I
believe,' says he, 'Madam, your Ladyship not being conversant in
these Matters, hath mistaken a Difference: For I asserted only, that a
Man who served a Year was settled. Now there is a material Difference between being settled in Law and settled in Fact; and as I
affirmed generally he was settled, and Law is preferable to Fact, my
Settlement must be understood in Law, and not in Fact. And suppose, Madam, we admit he was settled in Law, what Use will they
make of it, how doth that relate to Fact? He is not settled in Fact;
and if he be not settled in Fact, he is not an Inhabitant; and if he is
not an Inhabitant, he is not of this Parish; and then undoubtedly he
ought not to be published here; for Mr. Adams hath told me your
Ladyship's Pleasure, and the Reason, which is a very good one, to
prevent burdening us with the Poor; we have too many already; and
I think we ought to have an Act to hang or transport half of them. If
we can prove in Evidence, that he is not settled in Fact, it is another
matter. What I said to Mr. Adams, was on a Supposition that he was
settled in Fact; and indeed if that was the Case, I should doubt.—'
'Don't tell me your *Facts* and your *ifs*,' said the Lady, 'I don't understand your Gibberish: You take too much upon you, and are very
impertinent in pretending to direct in this Parish, and you shall be
taught better, I assure you, you shall. But as to the Wench, I am
resolved she shall not settle here; I will not suffer such Beauties
as these to produce Children for us to keep.'—'Beauties indeed! your
Ladyship is pleased to be merry,'—answered Scout.—'Mr. Adams
described her so to me,' said the Lady.—'Pray what sort of Dowdy is
it, Mr. Scout?'—'The ugliest Creature almost I ever beheld, a poor
dirty Drab,[1] your Ladyship never saw such a Wretch.'—'Well but,
dear Mr. Scout, let her be what she will,—these ugly Women will bring
Children, you know; so that we must prevent the Marriage.'—'True,
Madam,' replied Scout, 'for the subsequent Marriage co-operating

---

[1] "A nasty, sluttish whore" (Grose).

with the Law, will carry Law into Fact. When a Man is married, he is settled in Fact; and then he is not removeable. I will see Mr. Adams, and I make no doubt of prevailing with him. His only Objection is, doubtless, that he shall lose his Fee: But that being once made easy, as it shall be, I am confident no farther Objection will remain. No, no, it is impossible: But your Ladyship can't discommend his Unwillingness to depart with his Fee. Every Man ought to have a proper Value for his Fee. As to the Matter in question, if your Ladyship pleases to employ me in it, I will venture to promise you Success. The Laws of this Land are not so vulgar, to permit a mean Fellow to contend with one of your Ladyship's Fortune. We have one sure Card, which is to carry him before Justice Frolick, who, upon hearing your Ladyship's Name, will commit him without any farther Questions. As for the dirty Slut, we shall have nothing to do with her: for if we get rid of the Fellow, the ugly Jade will—' 'Take what Measures you please, good Mr. Scout,' answered the Lady, 'but I wish you could rid the Parish of both; for Slipslop tells me such Stories of this Wench, that I abhor the Thoughts of her; and tho' you say she is such an ugly Slut, yet you know, dear Mr. Scout, these forward Creatures who run after Men, will always find some as forward as themselves: So that, to prevent the Increase of Beggars, we must get rid of her.'—'Your Ladyship is very much in the right,' answered Scout, 'but I am afraid the Law is a little deficient in giving us any such Power of Prevention; however the Justice will stretch it as far as he is able, to oblige your Ladyship. To say Truth, it is a great Blessing to the Country that he is in the Commission; for he hath taken several Poor off our Hands that the Law would never lay hold on. I know some Justices who make as much of committing a Man to Bridewell,[2] as his Lordship at *Size* would of hanging him: But it would do a Man good to see his Worship, our Justice, commit a Fellow to Bridewell; he takes so much pleasure in it: And when once we ha' um there, we seldom hear any more o' um. He's either starved or eat up by Vermin in a Month's Time.'—Here the Arrival of a Visitor put an End to the Conversation, and Mr. Scout, having undertaken the Cause, and promised it Success, departed.

This Scout was one of those Fellows who, without any Knowledge of the Law, or being bred to it, take upon them, in Defiance of

---

[2] The London Bridewell, established 1555, was the first "house of correction," a workhouse designed to punish and reform petty offenders or simply those regarded as anti-social or idle (gypsies, vagabonds).

an Act of Parliament,[3] to act as Lawyers in the Country, and are called so. They are the Pests of Society, and a Scandal to a Profession to which indeed they do not belong; and which owes to such kind of Rascallions the Ill-will which weak Persons bear towards it. With this Fellow, to whom a little before she would not have condescended to have spoken, did a certain Passion for Joseph, and the Jealousy and Disdain of poor innocent Fanny, betray the Lady Booby into a familiar Discourse, in which she inadvertently confirmed many Hints, with which Slipslop, whose Gallant he was, had pre-acquainted him; and whence he had taken an Opportunity to assert those severe Falshoods of little Fanny, which possibly the Reader might not have been well able to account for, if we had not thought proper to give him this Information.

CHAP. IV.

A short Chapter, but very full of Matter; particularly the Arrival of Mr. Booby and his Lady.

ALL that Night, and the next Day, the Lady Booby past with the utmost Anxiety; her Mind was distracted, and her Soul tossed up and down by many turbulent and opposite Passions. She loved, hated, pitied, scorned, admired, despised the same Person by Fits, which changed in a very short Interval. On Tuesday Morning, which happened to be a Holiday, she went to Church, where, to her Surprize, Mr. Adams published the Banns again with as audible a Voice as before. It was lucky for her, that as there was no Sermon, she had an immediate Opportunity of returning home to vent her Rage, which she could not have concealed from the Congregation five Minutes; indeed it was not then very numerous, the Assembly consisting of no more than Adams, his Clerk, his Wife, the Lady, and one of her Servants. At her Return she met Slipslop, who accosted her in these Words:—'O Meam, what doth your Ladyship think? To be sure Lawyer Scout hath carried Joseph and Fanny both before the Justice. All the Parish are in Tears, and say they will certainly be hanged: For no body knows what it is for.'—'I suppose they deserve it,' says the Lady. 'What dost thou mention such Wretches to me?'—'O dear Madam,' answered Slipslop, 'is it not a

---

[3] Battestin identifies the 1729 "Act for the better Regulation of Attorneys and Solicitors," according to which unqualified "lawyers" such as Scout were liable to fines.

pity such a *graceless* young Man should die a *virulent* Death? I hope the Judge will take *Commensuration* on his Youth. As for Fanny, I don't think it signifies much what becomes of her; and if poor Joseph hath done any thing, I could venture to swear she *traduced* him to it: Few Men ever come to *fragrant* Punishment, but by those nasty Creatures, who are a Scandal to our *Sect*.' The Lady was no more pleased at this News, after a Moment's Reflection, than Slipslop herself: For tho' she wished Fanny far enough, she did not desire the Removal of Joseph, especially with her. She was puzzled how to act, or what to say on this Occasion, when a Coach and six drove into the Court, and a Servant acquainted her with the Arrival of her Nephew Booby and his Lady. She ordered them to be conducted into a Drawing-Room, whither she presently repaired, having composed her Countenance as well as she could; and being a little satisfied that the Wedding would by these Means be at least interrupted; and that she should have an Opportunity to execute any Resolution she might take, for which she saw herself provided with an excellent Instrument in Scout.

The Lady Booby apprehended her Servant had made a Mistake, when he had mentioned Mr. Booby's Lady; for she had never heard of his Marriage; but how great was her Surprize, when, at her entering the Room, her Nephew presented his Wife to her! saying, 'Madam, this is that charming Pamela, of whom I am convinced you have heard so much.' The Lady received her with more Civility than he expected; indeed with the utmost: For she was perfectly polite, nor had any Vice inconsistent with Good-breeding. They past some little time in ordinary Discourse, when a Servant came and whispered Mr. Booby, who presently told the Ladies he must desert them a little on some Business of Consequence; and as their Discourse during his Absence would afford little Improvement or Entertainment to the Reader, we will leave them for a while to attend Mr. Booby.

CHAP. V.

Containing Justice Business; Curious Precedents of Depositions, and other Matters necessary to be perused by all Justices of the Peace and their Clerks.

THE young Squire and his Lady were no sooner alighted from their Coach, than the Servants began to enquire after Mr. Joseph, from whom they said their Lady had not heard a Word, to her great

Surprize, since he had left Lady Booby's. Upon this they were instantly informed of what had lately happened, with which they hastily acquainted their Master, who took an immediate Resolution to go himself, and endeavour to restore his Pamela her Brother, before she even knew she had lost him.

The Justice, before whom the Criminals were carried, and who lived within a short Mile of the Lady's House, was luckily Mr. Booby's Acquaintance, by his having an Estate in his Neighbourhood. Ordering therefore his Horses to his Coach, he set out for the Judgment-Seat, and arrived when the Justice had almost finished his Business. He was conducted into a Hall, where he was acquainted that his Worship would wait on him in a Moment; for he had only a Man and a Woman to commit to Bridewell first. As he was now convinced he had not a Minute to lose, he insisted on the Servants introducing him directly to the Room where the Justice then was executing his Office, as he called it. Being brought thither, and the first Compliments being past between the Squire and his Worship, the former asked the latter what Crime those two young People had been guilty of. 'No great Crime,' answered the Justice, 'I have only ordered them to Bridewell for a Month.' 'But what is their Crime?' repeated the Squire. 'Larceny, an't please your Honour,' said Scout. 'Ay,' says the Justice, 'a kind of felonious larcenous Thing. I believe I must order them a little Correction too, a little Stripping and Whipping.' (Poor Fanny, who had hitherto supported all with the Thoughts of her Joseph's Company, trembled at that Sound; but indeed without Reason, for none but the Devil himself would have executed such a Sentence on her.) 'Still,' said the Squire, 'I am ignorant of the Crime, the Fact I mean.' 'Why, there it is in Peaper,' answered the Justice, shewing him a Deposition, which in the Absence of his Clerk, he had writ himself, of which we have with great Difficulty procured an authentic Copy; and here it follows *verbatim & literatim.*

The Depusition of James Scout, *Layer, and* Thomas Trotter, *Yeoman, taken befor mee, on of his Magesty's Justasses of the Piece for* Zumersetshire.

'These Deponants saith, and first Thomas Trotter for himself saith, that on the—of this Instant October, being Sabbath-Day, betwin the Ours of 2 and 4 in the Afternoon, he zeed Joseph Andrews and Francis Goodwill walk akross a certane Felde belunging to Layer Scout, and out of the Path which ledes thru the said Felde, and there he zede Joseph Andrews with a Nife cut one

Hassel-Twig,[1] of the value, as he believes, of 3 half pence, or thereabouts; and he saith, that the said Francis Goodwill was likewise walking on the Grass out of the said Path in the said Felde, and did receive and karry in her Hand the said Twig, and so was cumfarting eading and abatting to the said Joseph therein. And the said James Scout for himself says, that he verily believes the said Twig to be his own proper Twig, &c.'

'*Jesu!*' said the Squire, 'would you commit two Persons to Bridewell for a Twig?' 'Yes,' said the Lawyer, 'and with great Lenity too; for if we had called it a young Tree they would have been both hanged.'—'Harkee,' (says the Justice, taking aside the Squire) 'I should not have been so severe on this Occasion, but Lady Booby desires to get them out of the Parish; so Lawyer Scout will give the Constable Orders to let them run away, if they please; but it seems they intend to marry together, and the Lady hath no other Means, as they are legally settled there, to prevent their bringing an Incumbrance on her own Parish.' 'Well,' said the Squire, 'I will take care my Aunt shall be satisfied in this Point; and likewise I promise you, Joseph here shall never be any Incumbrance on her. I shall be obliged to you therefore, if, instead of Bridewell, you will commit them to my Custody.'—'O to be sure, Sir, if you desire it,' answered the Justice; and without more ado, Joseph and Fanny were delivered over to Squire Booby, whom Joseph very well knew; but little guess'd how nearly he was related to him. The Justice burnt his Mittimus: The Constable was sent about his Business: The Lawyer made no Complaint for want of Justice; and the Prisoners, with exulting Hearts, gave a thousand Thanks to his Honour Mr. Booby, who did not intend their Obligations to him should cease here; for ordering his Man to produce a Cloak-bag which he had caused to be brought from Lady Booby's on purpose, he desired the Justice that he might have Joseph with him into a Room; where ordering his Servant to take out a Suit of his own Clothes, with Linnen and other Necessaries, he left Joseph to dress himself, who not yet knowing the Cause of all this Civility, excused his accepting such a Favour, as long as decently he could. Whilst Joseph was dressing, the Squire repaired to the Justice, whom he found talking with Fanny; for during the Examination, she had lopped her Hat over her Eyes, which were also bathed in Tears, and had by that Means

---

[1] A twig of the hazel tree, bearing hazel nuts.

concealed from his Worship what might perhaps have rendered the Arrival of Mr. Booby unnecessary, at least for herself. The Justice no sooner saw her Countenance cleared up, and her bright Eyes shining through her Tears, than he secretly cursed himself for having once thought of Bridewell for her. He would willingly have sent his own Wife thither, to have had Fanny in her Place. And conceiving almost at the same instant Desires and Schemes to accomplish them, he employed the Minutes whilst the Squire was absent with Joseph, in assuring her how sorry he was for having treated her so roughly before he knew her Merit; and told her, that since Lady Booby was unwilling that she should settle in her Parish, she was heartily welcome to his, where he promised her his Protection, adding, that he would take Joseph and her into his own Family, if she liked it; which Assurance he confirmed with a Squeeze by the Hand. She thanked him very kindly, and said, 'She would acquaint Joseph with the Offer, which he would certainly be glad to accept; for that Lady Booby was angry with them both; tho' she did not know either had done any Thing to offend her: but imputed it to Madam Slipslop, who had always been her Enemy.'

The Squire now returned, and prevented any farther Continuance of this Conversation; and the Justice, out of a pretended Respect to his Guest, but in reality from an Apprehension of a Rival, (for he knew nothing of his Marriage) ordered Fanny into the Kitchin, whither she gladly retired; nor did the Squire, who declined the Trouble of explaining the whole Matter, oppose it.

It would be unnecessary, if I was able, which indeed I am not, to relate the Conversation between these two Gentlemen, which rolled, as I have been informed, entirely on the Subject of Horse-racing. Joseph was soon drest in the plainest Dress he could find, which was a blue Coat and Breeches, with a Gold Edging, and a red Waistcoat with the same; and as this Suit, which was rather too large for the Squire, exactly fitted him; so he became it so well, and looked so genteel, that no Person would have doubted its being as well adapted to his Quality as his Shape; nor have suspected, as one might, when my Lord——, or Sir——, or Mr.—— appear in Lace or Embroidery, that the Taylor's Man wore those Clothes home on his Back, which he should have carried under his Arm.

The Squire now took leave of the Justice, and calling for Fanny, made her and Joseph, against their Wills, get into the Coach with him, which he then ordered to drive to Lady Booby's.—It had moved a few Yards only, when the Squire asked Joseph, if he knew who that Man was crossing the Field; for, added he, I never saw one take such Strides before. Joseph answered eagerly, 'O Sir, it is Parson Adams.'—'O la, indeed, and so it is,' said Fanny; 'poor Man, he is coming to do what he could for us. Well, he is the worthiest best natur'd Creature.'—'Ay,' said Joseph, 'God bless him; for there is not such another in the Universe.'—'The best Creature living sure,' cries Fanny. 'Is he?' says the Squire, 'then I am resolved to have the best Creature living in my Coach;' and so saying he ordered it to stop, whilst Joseph, at his Request, hallowed to the Parson, who well knowing his Voice, made all the haste imaginable, and soon came up with them. He was desired by the Master, who could scarce refrain from Laughter at his Figure, to mount into the Coach, which he with many Thanks refused, saying he could walk by its Side, and he'd warrant he kept up with it; but he was at length over-prevailed on. The Squire now acquainted Joseph with his Marriage; but he might have spared himself that Labour; for his Servant, whilst Joseph was dressing, had performed that Office before. He continued to express the vast Happiness he enjoyed in his Sister, and the Value he had for all who belonged to her. Joseph made many Bows, and exprest as many Acknowledgments; and Parson Adams, who now first perceived Joseph's new Apparel, burst into Tears with Joy, and fell to rubbing his Hands and snapping his Fingers, as if he had been mad.

They were now arrived at the Lady Booby's, and the Squire desiring them to wait a Moment in the Court, walked in to his Aunt, and calling her out from his Wife, acquainted her with Joseph's Arrival; saying, 'Madam, as I have married a virtuous and worthy Woman, I am resolved to own her Relations, and to shew them all proper Respect; I shall think myself therefore infinitely obliged to all mine, who will do the same. It is true her Brother hath been your Servant, but he is now become my Brother; and I have one Happiness, that neither his Character, his Behaviour or Appearance, give me any Reason to be ashamed of calling him so. In short, he is now below, dress'd like a Gentleman, in which Light I intend he shall hereafter be seen; and you will oblige me beyond Expression, if you will admit him to be of our Party; for I know it will give great Pleasure to my Wife, tho' she will not mention it.'

This was a Stroke of Fortune beyond the Lady Booby's Hopes or Expectation; she answered him eagerly, 'Nephew, you know how easily I am prevailed on to do any thing which Joseph Andrews desires—Phoo', I mean which you desire me; and as he is now your

Relation, I cannot refuse to entertain him as such.' The Squire told her, he knew his Obligation to her for her Compliance; and going three Steps, returned and told her—he had one more Favour, which he believed she would easily grant, as she had accorded him the former. 'There is a young Woman—' 'Nephew,' says she, 'don't let my Good-nature make you desire, as is too commonly the Case, to impose on me. Nor think, because I have with so much Condescension agreed to suffer your Brother-in-law to come to my Table, that I will submit to the Company of all my own Servants, and all the dirty Trollops in the Country.' 'Madam,' answer'd the Squire, 'I believe you never saw this young Creature. I never beheld such Sweetness and Innocence, joined with such Beauty, and withal so genteel.' 'Upon my Soul, I won't admit her,' reply'd the Lady in a Passion; 'the whole World shan't prevail on me, I resent even the Desire as an Affront, and—' The Squire, who knew her Inflexibility, interrupted her, by asking Pardon, and promising not to mention it more. He then returned to Joseph, and she to Pamela. He took Joseph aside and told him, he would carry him to his Sister; but could not prevail as yet for Fanny. Joseph begged that he might see his Sister alone, and then be with his Fanny; but the Squire knowing the Pleasure his Wife would have in her Brother's Company, would not admit it, telling Joseph there would be nothing in so short an Absence from Fanny, whilst he was assured of her Safety; adding, he hoped he could not so easily quit a Sister whom he had not seen so long, and who so tenderly loved him—Joseph immediately complied; for indeed no Brother could love a Sister more; and recommending Fanny, who rejoiced that she was not to go before Lady Booby, to the Care of Mr. Adams, he attended the Squire up Stairs, whilst Fanny repaired with the Parson to his House, where she thought herself secure of a kind Reception.

CHAP. VI.

Of which you are desired to read no more than you like.

THE Meeting between Joseph and Pamela was not without Tears of Joy on both Sides; and their Embraces were full of Tenderness and Affection. They were however regarded with much more Pleasure by the Nephew than by the Aunt, to whose Flame they were Fuel only; and being assisted by the Addition of Dress, which was indeed not wanted to set off the lively Colours in which Nature had drawn

Health, Strength, Comeliness, and Youth. In the Afternoon Joseph, at their Request, entertained them with an Account of his Adventures; nor could Lady Booby conceal her Dissatisfaction at those Parts in which Fanny was concerned, especially when Mr. Booby launched forth into such rapturous Praises of her Beauty. She said, applying to her Niece, that she wondered her Nephew, who had pretended to marry for Love, should think such a Subject proper to amuse his Wife with; adding, that for her Part, she should be jealous of a Husband who spoke so warmly in praise of another Woman. Pamela answer'd, indeed she thought she had Cause; but it was an Instance of Mr. Booby's aptness to see more Beauty in Women than they were Mistresses of. At which Words both the Women fixed their Eyes on two Looking-Glasses; and Lady Booby replied, that Men were, in the general, very ill Judges of Beauty; and then, whilst both contemplated only their own Faces, they paid a cross Compliment to each other's Charms. When the Hour of Rest approached, which the Lady of the House deferred as long as decently she could, she informed Joseph (whom for the future we shall call Mr. Joseph, he having as good a Title to that Appellation as many others, I mean that incontested one of good Clothes) that she had ordered a Bed to be provided for him. He declined this Favour to his utmost; for his Heart had long been with his Fanny; but she insisted on his accepting it, alledging that the Parish had no proper Accommodation for such a Person as he was now to esteem himself. The Squire and his Lady both joining with her, Mr. Joseph was at last forced to give over his Design of visiting Fanny that Evening, who, on her Side, as impatiently expected him till Midnight, when in complacence to Mr. Adams's Family, who had sat up two Hours out of Respect to her, she retired to Bed, but not to sleep; the Thoughts of her Love kept her waking, and his not returning according to his Promise filled her with Uneasiness; of which, however, she could not assign any other Cause than merely that of being absent from him.

Mr. Joseph rose early in the Morning, and visited her in whom his Soul delighted. She no sooner heard his Voice in the Parson's Parlour, than she leapt from her Bed, and dressing herself in a few Minutes, went down to him. They past two Hours with inexpressible Happiness together; and then having appointed Monday, by Mr. Adams's Permission, for their Marriage, Mr. Joseph returned, according to his Promise, to Breakfast at the Lady Booby's, with whose Behaviour since the Evening we shall now acquaint the Reader.

She was no sooner retired to her Chamber than she asked Slipslop what she thought of this wonderful Creature her Nephew had married. 'Madam!' said Slipslop, not yet sufficiently understanding what Answer she was to make. 'I ask you,' answered the Lady, 'what you think of the Dowdy, my Niece I think I am to call her?' Slipslop, wanting no further Hint, began to pull her to Pieces, and so miserably defaced her, that it would have been impossible for any one to have known the Person. The Lady gave her all the Assistance she could, and ended with saying,—'I think, Slipslop, you have done her Justice; but yet, bad as she is, she is an Angel compared to this Fanny.' Slipslop then fell on Fanny, whom she hacked and hewed in the like barbarous Manner, concluding with an Observation, that there was always something in those low-life Creatures which must eternally distinguish them from their Betters. 'Really,' said the Lady, 'I think there is one Exception to your Rule; I am certain you may guess who I mean.'—'Not I, upon my word, Madam,' said Slipslop.—'I mean a young Fellow; sure you are the dullest Wretch,' said the Lady.—'O la, I am indeed.—Yes truly, Madam, he is an *Accession*,' answered Slipslop.—'Ay, is he not, Slipslop?' returned the Lady. 'Is he not so genteel that a Prince might without a Blush acknowledge him for his Son. His Behaviour is such that would not shame the best Education. He borrows from his Station a Condescension in every thing to his Superiours, yet unattended by that mean Servility which is called Good-Behaviour in such Persons. Every thing he doth, hath no Mark of the base Motive of Fear, but visibly shews some Respect and Gratitude, and carries with it the Persuasion of Love.—And then for his Virtues; such Piety to his Parents, such tender Affection to his Sister, such Integrity in his Friendship, such Bravery, such Goodness, that if he had been born a Gentleman, his Wife would have possessed the most invaluable Blessing.'—'To be sure, Ma'am,' says Slipslop.—'But as he is,' answered the Lady, 'if he had a thousand more good Qualities, it must render a Woman of Fashion contemptible even to be suspected of thinking of him, yes I should despise myself for such a Thought.' 'To be sure, Ma'am,' said Slipslop. 'And why to be sure?' replied the Lady; 'thou art always one's Echo. Is he not more worthy of Affection than a dirty Country Clown, tho' born of a Family as old as the Flood, or an idle worthless Rake, or little puisny[1] Beau of Quality? And yet these we must condemn ourselves to, in order to

---

[1] Puny.

avoid the Censure of the World; to shun the Contempt of others, we must ally ourselves to those we despise; we must prefer Birth, Title and Fortune, to real Merit. It is a Tyranny of Custom, a Tyranny we must comply with: For we People of Fashion are the Slaves of Custom.'—'Marry come up!' said Slipslop, who now well knew which Party to take, 'if I was a Woman of your Ladyship's Fortune and Quality, I would be a Slave to no body.'—'Me,' said the Lady, 'I am speaking, if a young Woman of Fashion who had seen nothing in the World, should happen to like such a Fellow.—Me indeed; I hope thou dost not imagine'—'No, Ma'am, to be sure,' cried Slipslop.—'No! what no?' cried the Lady. 'Thou art always ready to answer, before thou hast heard one. So far I must allow he is a charming Fellow. Me indeed! No, Slipslop, all Thoughts of Men are over with me.—I have lost a Husband, who—but if I should reflect, I should run mad.—My future Ease must depend upon Forgetfulness. Slipslop, let me hear some of thy Nonsense to turn my Thoughts another way. What dost thou think of Mr. Andrews?' 'Why I think,' says Slipslop, 'he is the handsomest, most properest Man I ever saw; and if I was a Lady of the greatest Degree, it would be well for some Folks. Your Ladyship may talk of Custom if you please; but I am *confidous* there is no more Comparison between young Mr. Andrews, and most of the young Gentlemen who come to your Ladyship's House in London; a Parcel of *Whipper-snapper* Sparks: I would sooner marry our old Parson Adams: Never tell me what People say, whilst I am happy in the Arms of him I love. Some Folks rail against other Folks, because other Folks have what some Folks would be glad of.'—'And so,' answered the Lady, 'if you was a Woman of Condition, you would really marry Mr. Andrews?'—'Yes, I assure your Ladyship,' replied Slipslop, 'if he would have me.'—'Fool, Idiot,' cries the Lady, 'if he would have a Woman of Fashion! Is that a Question?' 'No truly, Madam,' said Slipslop, 'I believe it would be none if Fanny was out of the way; and I am *confidous* if I was in your Ladyship's Place, and liked Mr. Joseph Andrews, she should not stay in the Parish a Moment. I am sure Lawyer Scout would send her packing, if your Ladyship would but say the Word.' This last Speech of Slipslop raised a Tempest in the Mind of her Mistress. She feared Scout had betrayed her, or rather that she had betrayed herself. After some Silence and a double Change of her Complexion; first to pale, and then to red, she thus spoke: 'I am astonished at the Liberty you give your Tongue. Would you insinuate, that I employed Scout against this Wench, on the account of the Fellow?' 'La Ma'am,' said Slipslop, frighted out of her

Wits, 'I *assassinate* such a Thing!' 'I think you dare not,' answered the Lady, 'I believe my Conduct may defy Malice itself to assert so cursed a Slander. If I had ever discovered any Wantonness, any Lightness in my Behaviour: if I had followed the Example of some whom thou hast, I believe, seen, in allowing myself indecent Liberties, even with a Husband: But the dear Man who is gone,' (*here she began to sob*) 'was he alive again,' (*then she produced Tears*) 'could not upbraid me with any one Act of Tenderness or Passion. No, Slipslop, all the time I cohabited with him, he never obtained even a Kiss from me, without my expressing Reluctance in the granting it. I am sure he himself never suspected how much I loved him.—Since his Death, thou knowest, tho' it is almost six Weeks (it wants but a Day) ago, I have not admitted one Visitor, till this Fool my Nephew arrived. I have confined myself quite to one Party of Friends.—And can such a Conduct as this fear to be arraigned? To be accused not only of a Passion which I have always despised, but of fixing it on such an Object, a Creature so much beneath my Notice.'—'Upon my word, Ma'am,' says Slipslop, 'I do not understand your Ladyship, nor know I any thing of the Matter.'—'I believe indeed thou dost not understand me.—Those are Delicacies which exist only in superior Minds; thy coarse Ideas cannot comprehend them. Thou art a low Creature, of the Andrews Breed, a Reptile of a lower Order, a Weed that grows in the common Garden of the Creation.'—'I assure your Ladyship,' says Slipslop, whose Passions were almost of as high an Order as her Lady's, 'I have no more to do with *Common Garden*[2] than other Folks. Really, your Ladyship talks of Servants as if they were not born of the Christian Specious. Servants have Flesh and Blood as well as Quality; and Mr. Andrews himself is a Proof that they have as good, if not better. And for my own Part, I can't perceive my *Dears** are coarser than other People's; and I am sure, if Mr. Andrews was a *Dear* of mine, I should not be ashamed of him in company with Gentlemen; for whoever hath seen him in his new Clothes, must confess he looks as much like a Gentleman as any body. Coarse, quotha! I can't bear to hear the poor young Fellow run down neither; for I will say this, I never heard him say an ill Word of any body in his Life. I am sure his Coarseness doth not lie in his Heart; for he is the best-natured Man in the World; and as for his Skin, it is no coarser than

---

[2] That is, Covent Garden, the theater district, "vulgarly called Common Garden" (Grose) because of the "common women" or prostitutes who plied their trade there.

* *Fielding's Note:* Meaning perhaps Ideas.

other People's, I am sure. His Bosom, when a Boy, was as white as driven Snow; and where it is not covered with Hairs, is so still. Ifaukins! if I was Mrs. Andrews, with a hundred a Year, I should not envy the best She who wears a Head. A Woman that could not be happy with such a Man, ought never to be so: For if he can't make a Woman happy, I never yet beheld the Man who could. I say again I wish I was a great Lady for his sake, I believe when I had made a Gentleman of him, he'd behave so, that no body should *deprecate* what I had done; and I fancy few would venture to tell him he was no Gentleman to his Face, nor to mine neither.' At which Words, taking up the Candles, she asked her Mistress, who had been some time in her Bed, if she had any farther Commands; who mildly answered she had none; and telling her, she was a comical Creature, bid her Good-night.

CHAP. VII.

Philosophical Reflections, the like not to be found in any light French *Romance. Mr.* Booby's *grave Advice to* Joseph, *and* Fanny's *Encounter with a Beau.*

HABIT, my good Reader, hath so vast a Prevalence over the human Mind, that there is scarce any thing too strange or too strong to be asserted of it. The Story of the Miser, who, from long accustoming to cheat others, came at last to cheat himself, and with great Delight and Triumph picked his own Pocket of a Guinea, to convey to his Hoard, is not impossible or improbable. In like manner, it fares with the Practisers of Deceit, who, from having long deceived their Acquaintance, gain at last a Power of deceiving themselves, and acquire that very Opinion (however false) of their own Abilities, Excellencies and Virtues, into which they have for Years perhaps endeavoured to betray their Neighbours. Now, Reader, to apply this Observation to my present Purpose, thou must know, that as the Passion, generally called Love, exercises most of the Talents of the Female or fair World; so in this they now and then discover a small Inclination to Deceit; for which thou wilt not be angry with the beautiful Creatures, when thou hast considered, that at the Age of seven, or something earlier, Miss is instructed by her Mother, that Master is a very monstrous kind of Animal, who will, if she suffers him to come too near her, infallibly eat her up, and grind her to Pieces. That so far from kissing or toying with him of her own accord, she must not admit him to kiss or toy with her. And lastly, that she must never have any Affection towards him; for if she should, all her Friends in Petticoats would esteem her a Traitress, point at her, and hunt her out of their Society. These Impressions being first received, are farther and deeper inculcated by their School-mistresses and Companions; so that by the Age of Ten they have contracted such a Dread and Abhorrence of the above named Monster, that, whenever they see him, they fly from him as the innocent Hare doth from the Greyhound. Hence to the Age of fourteen or fifteen, they entertain a mighty Antipathy to Master; they resolve and frequently profess, that they will never have any Commerce with him, and entertain fond Hopes of passing their Lives out of his Reach, of the Possibility of which they have so visible an Example in their good Maiden Aunt. But when they arrive at this Period, and have now past their second Climacteric,[1] when their Wisdom, grown riper, begins to see a little farther, and from almost daily falling in Master's Way, to apprehend the great Difficulty of keeping out of it; and when they observe him look often at them, and sometimes very eagerly and earnestly too, (for the Monster seldom takes any notice of them till at this Age) they then begin to think of their Danger; and as they perceive they cannot easily avoid him, the wiser Part bethink themselves of providing by other Means for their Security. They endeavour by all the Methods they can invent to render themselves so amiable in his Eyes, that he may have no Inclination to hurt them; in which they generally succeed so well, that his Eyes, by frequent languishing, soon lessen their Idea of his Fierceness, and so far abate their Fears, that they venture to parley with him; and when they perceive him so different from what he hath been described, all Gentleness, Softness, Kindness, Tenderness, Fondness, their dreadful Apprehensions vanish in a Moment; and now, (it being usual with the human Mind to skip from one Extreme to its Opposite, as easily, and almost as suddenly, as a Bird from one Bough to another;) Love instantly succeeds to Fear: But as it happens to Persons, who have in their Infancy been thoroughly frightened with certain No-Persons called Ghosts, that they retain their Dread of those Beings, after they are convinced that there are no such things; so these young Ladies, tho' they no

---

[1] That is, over 14 years old. A "climacteric" is "a certain number of years (typically seven), at the end of which some great change is supposed to befall the body" (Johnson); the second climacteric marks the onset of puberty.

longer apprehend devouring, cannot so entirely shake off all that
hath been instilled into them; they still entertain the Idea of that
Censure which was so strongly imprinted on their tender Minds, to
which the Declarations of Abhorrence they every Day hear from
their Companions greatly contribute. To avoid this Censure therefore, is now their only Care; for which Purpose they still pretend the
same Aversion to the Monster: And the more they love him, the
more ardently they counterfeit the Antipathy. By the continual and
constant Practice of which Deceit on others, they at length impose
on themselves, and really believe they hate what they love. Thus
indeed it happened to Lady Booby, who loved Joseph long before
she knew it; and now loved him much more than she suspected. She
had indeed, from the time of his Sister's Arrival in the Quality of her
Niece, and from the Instant she viewed him in the Dress and Character of a Gentleman, began to conceive secretly a Design which
Love had concealed from herself, till a Dream betrayed it to her.

She had no sooner risen than she sent for her Nephew; when he
came to her, after many Compliments on his Choice, she told him,
'He might perceive in her Condescension to admit her own Servant
to her Table, that she looked on the Family of Andrews as his Relations, and indeed hers; that as he had married into such a Family, it
became him to endeavour by all Methods to raise it as much as possible.' At length she advised him to use all his Art to dissuade
Joseph from his intended Match, which would still enlarge their
Relation to Meanness and Poverty; concluding, that by a Commission in the Army, or some other genteel Employment, he might soon
put young Mr. Andrews on the foot of a Gentleman; and that being
once done, his Accomplishments might quickly gain him an
Alliance, which would not be to their Discredit.'

Her Nephew heartily embraced this Proposal; and finding Mr.
Joseph with his Wife, at his Return to her Chamber, he immediately
began thus: 'My Love to my dear Pamela, Brother, will extend to all
her Relations; nor shall I shew them less Respect than if I had married into the Family of a Duke. I hope I have given you some early
Testimonies of this, and shall continue to give you daily more. You
will excuse me therefore, Brother, if my Concern for your Interest
makes me mention what may be, perhaps, disagreeable to you to
hear: But I must insist upon it, that if you have any Value for my
Alliance or my Friendship, you will decline any Thoughts of engaging farther with a Girl, who is, as you are a Relation of mine, so
much beneath you. I know there may be at first some Difficulty in

your Compliance, but that will daily diminish; and you will in the End sincerely thank me for my Advice. I own, indeed, the Girl is handsome: But Beauty alone is a poor Ingredient, and will make but an uncomfortable Marriage.' 'Sir,' said Joseph, 'I assure you her Beauty is her least Perfection; nor do I know a Virtue which that young Creature is not possest of.' 'As to her Virtues,' answered Mr. Booby, 'you can be yet but a slender Judge of them: But if she had never so many, you will find her Equal in these among her Superiors in Birth and Fortune, which now you are to esteem on a Footing with yourself; at least I will take care they shall shortly be so, unless you prevent me by degrading yourself with such a Match, a Match I have hardly Patience to think of; and which would break the Hearts of your Parents, who now rejoice in the Expectation of seeing you make a Figure in the World.' 'I know not,' replied Joseph, 'that my Parents have any Power over my Inclinations; nor am I obliged to sacrifice my Happiness to their Whim or Ambition: Besides, I shall be very sorry to see, that the unexpected Advancement of my Sister, should so suddenly inspire them with this wicked Pride, and make them despise their Equals, I am resolved on no Account to quit my dear Fanny, no, tho' I could raise her as high above her present Station as you have raised my Sister.' 'Your Sister, as well as myself,' said Booby, 'are greatly obliged to you for the Comparison: But, Sir, she is not worthy to be compared in Beauty to my Pamela; nor hath she half her Merit. And besides, Sir, as you civilly throw my Marriage with your Sister in my Teeth, I must teach you the wide Difference between us; my Fortune enabled me to please myself; and it would have been as overgrown a Folly in me to have omitted it, as in you to do it.' 'My Fortune enables me to please myself likewise,' said Joseph; 'for all my Pleasure is centred in Fanny; and whilst I have Health, I shall be able to support her with my Labour in that Station to which she was born, and with which she is content.' 'Brother,' said Pamela, 'Mr. Booby advises you as a Friend; and, no doubt, my Papa and Mamma will be of his Opinion, and will have great Reason to be angry with you for destroying what his Goodness hath done, and throwing down our Family again, after he hath raised it. It would become you better, Brother, to pray for the Assistance of Grace against such a Passion, than to indulge it.'— 'Sure, Sister, you are not in earnest; I am sure she is your Equal at least.'—'She was my Equal,' answered Pamela, 'but I am no longer Pamela Andrews, I am now this Gentleman's Lady, and as such am above her—I hope I shall never behave with an unbecoming Pride;

but at the same time, I shall always endeavour to know myself, and question not the Assistance of Grace to that Purpose.' They were now summoned to Breakfast, and thus ended their Discourse for the present, very little to the Satisfaction of any of the Parties.

Fanny was now walking in an Avenue at some Distance from the House, where Joseph had promised to take the first Opportunity of coming to her. She had not a Shilling in the World, and had subsisted ever since her Return, entirely on the Charity of Parson Adams. A young Gentleman, attended by many Servants, came up to her, and asked her if that was not the Lady Booby's House before him? This indeed he well knew, but had framed the Question for no other Reason than to make her look up, and discover if her Face was equal to the Delicacy of her Shape. He no sooner saw it, than he was struck with Amazement. He stopt his Horse, and swore she was the most beautiful Creature he ever beheld. Then instantly alighting, and delivering his Horse to his Servant, he rapt out half a dozen Oaths that he would kiss her; to which she at first submitted, begging he would not be rude: but he was not satisfied with the Civility of a Salute, nor even with the rudest Attack he could make on her Lips, but caught her in his Arms, and endeavoured to kiss her Breasts, which with all her Strength she resisted; and, as our Spark was not of the Herculean Race, with some Difficulty prevented. The young Gentleman being soon out of Breath in the Struggle, quitted her, and remounting his Horse called one of his Servants to him, whom he ordered to stay behind with her, and make her any Offers whatever, to prevail on her to return home with him in the Evening; and to assure her he would take her into Keeping. He then rode on with his other Servants, and arrived at the Lady's House, to whom he was a distant Relation, and was come to pay a Visit.

The trusty Fellow, who was employed in an Office he had been long accustomed to, discharged his Part with all the Fidelity and Dexterity imaginable; but to no Purpose. She was entirely deaf to his Offers, and rejected them with the utmost Disdain. At last the Pimp, who had perhaps more warm Blood about him than his Master, began to sollicit for himself; he told her, tho' he was a Servant, he was a Man of some Fortune, which he would make her Mistress of—and this without any Insult to her Virtue, for that he would marry her. She answer'd, if his Master himself, or the greatest Lord in the Land would marry her, she would refuse him. At last being weary with Persuasions, and on Fire with Charms, which would have almost kindled a Flame in the Bosom of an antient Philosopher, or modern Divine, he fastened his Horse to the Ground, and attacked her with much more Force than the Gentleman had exerted. Poor Fanny would not have been able to resist his Rudeness a very short time, but the Deity, who presides over chaste Love, sent her Joseph to her Assistance. He no sooner came within Sight, and perceived her struggling with a Man, than like a Cannon-Ball, or like Lightning, or any thing that is swifter, if any thing be, he ran towards her, and coming up just as the Ravisher had torn her Handkerchief from her Breast, before his Lips had touched that Seat of Innocence and Bliss, he dealt him so lusty a Blow in that Part of his Neck which a Rope would have become with the utmost Propriety, that the Fellow staggered backwards, and perceiving he had to do with something rougher than the little, tender, trembling Hand of Fanny, he quitted her, and turning about saw his Rival, with Fire flashing from his Eyes, again ready to assail him; and indeed before he could well defend himself, or return the first Blow, he received a second, which, had it fallen on that Part of the Stomach to which it was directed, would have been probably the last he would have had any Occasion for; but the Ravisher lifting up his Hand, drove the Blow upwards to his Mouth, whence it dislodged three of his Teeth; and now not conceiving any extraordinary Affection for the Beauty of Joseph's Person, nor being extremely pleased with this Method of Salutation, he collected all his Force, and aimed a Blow at Joseph's Breast, which he artfully parry'd with one Fist, so that it lost its Force entirely in Air; and stepping one Foot backward, he darted his Fist so fiercely at his Enemy, that had he not caught it in his Hand (for he was a Boxer of no inferiour Fame) it must have tumbled him on the Ground. And now the Ravisher meditated another Blow, which he aimed at that Part of the Breast where the Heart is lodged; Joseph did not catch it as before, yet so prevented its Aim, that it fell directly on his Nose, but with abated Force. Joseph then moving both Fist and Foot forwards at the same time, threw his Head so dextrously into the Stomach of the Ravisher, that he fell a lifeless Lump on the Field, where he lay many Minutes breathless and motionless.

When Fanny saw her Joseph receive a Blow in his Face, and Blood running in a Stream from him, she began to tear her Hair, and invoke all human and divine Power to his Assistance. She was not, however, long under this Affliction, before Joseph having conquered his Enemy, ran to her, and assured her he was not hurt;

she then instantly fell on her Knees, and thanked God that he had made Joseph the Means of her Rescue, and at the same time preserved him from being injured in attempting it. She offered with her Handkerchief to wipe his Blood from his Face; but he seeing his Rival attempting to recover his Legs, turned to him and asked him if he had enough; to which the other answered he had; for he believed he had fought with the Devil, instead of a Man; and loosening his Horse, said he should not have attempted the Wench if he had known she had been so well provided for.

Fanny now begged Joseph to return with her to Parson Adams, and to promise that he would leave her no more; these were Propositions so agreeable to Joseph, that had he heard them he would have given an immediate Assent: but indeed his Eyes were now his only Sense; for you may remember, Reader, that the Ravisher had tore her Handkerchief from Fanny's Neck, by which he had discovered such a Sight, that Joseph hath declared all the Statues he ever beheld, were so much inferiour to it in Beauty, that it was more capable of converting a Man into a Statue, than of being imitated by the greatest Master of that Art. This modest Creature, whom no Warmth in Summer could ever induce to expose her Charms to the wanton Sun, a Modesty to which perhaps they owed their inconceivable Whiteness, had stood many Minutes bare-necked in the Presence of Joseph, before her Apprehension of his Danger, and the Horror of seeing his Blood would suffer her once to reflect on what concerned herself; till at last, when the Cause of her Concern had vanished, an Admiration at his Silence, together with observing the fixed Position of his Eyes, produced an Idea in the lovely Maid, which brought more Blood into her Face than had flowed from Joseph's Nostrils. The snowy Hue of her Bosom was likewise exchanged to Vermillion at the Instant when she clapped her Handkerchief round her Neck. Joseph saw the Uneasiness she suffered, and immediately removed his Eyes from an Object, in surveying which he had felt the greatest Delight which the Organs of Sight were capable of conveying to his Soul. So great was his Fear of offending her, and so truly did his Passion for her deserve the noble Name of Love.

Fanny, being recovered from her Confusion, which was almost equalled by what Joseph had felt from observing it, again mentioned her Request; this was instantly and gladly complied with, and together they crossed two or three Fields, which brought them to the Habitation of Mr. Adams.

CHAP. VIII.

A Discourse which happened between Mr. Adams, Mrs. Adams, Joseph and Fanny; with some Behaviour of Mr. Adams, which will be called by some few Readers very low, absurd, and unnatural.

THE Parson and his Wife had just ended a long Dispute when the Lovers came to the Door. Indeed this young Couple had been the Subject of the Dispute; for Mrs. Adams was one of those prudent People who never do any thing to injure their Families, or perhaps one of those good Mothers who would even stretch their Conscience to serve their Children. She had long entertained Hopes of seeing her eldest Daughter succeed Mrs. Slipslop, and of making her second Son an Exciseman by Lady Booby's Interest. These were Expectations she could not endure the Thoughts of quitting, and was therefore very uneasy to see her Husband so resolute to oppose the Lady's Intention in Fanny's Affair. She told him, 'it behoved every Man to take the first Care of his Family; that he had a Wife and six Children, the maintaining and providing for whom would be Business enough for him without intermeddling in other Folks' Affairs; that he had always preached up Submission to Superiors, and would do ill to give an Example of the contrary Behaviour in his own Conduct; that if Lady Booby did wrong, she must answer for it herself, and the Sin would not lie at their Door;[1] that Fanny had been a Servant, and bred up in the Lady's own Family, and consequently she must have known more of her than they did, and it was very improbable, if she had behaved herself well, that the Lady would have been so bitterly her Enemy; that perhaps he was too much inclined to think well of her because she was handsome; but handsome Women were often no better than they should be; that G— made ugly Women as well as handsome ones, and that if a Woman had Virtue, it signified nothing whether she had Beauty or no.' For all which Reasons she concluded he should oblige the Lady, and stop the future Publication of the Banns. But all these excellent Arguments had no Effect on the Parson, who persisted in doing his Duty without regarding the Consequence it might have on his worldly Interest; he endeavoured to answer her as well as he could, to which she had just finished her Reply, (for she had always

---

[1] That is, "the fault would not be theirs"; Adams's locution is from Genesis 4:7.

the last Word every where but at Church) when Joseph and Fanny
entered their Kitchin, where the Parson and his Wife then sat at
Breakfast over some Bacon and Cabbage. There was a Coldness in
the Civility of Mrs. Adams, which Persons of accurate Speculation
might have observed, but escaped her present Guests; indeed it was
a good deal covered by the Heartiness of Adams, who no sooner
heard that Fanny had neither eat nor drank that Morning, than he
presented her a Bone of Bacon he had just been gnawing, being the
only Remains of his Provision, and then ran nimbly to the Tap, and
produced a Mug of small Beer, which he called Ale; however it was
the best in his House. Joseph addressing himself to the Parson, told
him the Discourse which had past between Squire Booby, his Sister
and himself, concerning Fanny: he then acquainted him with the
Dangers whence he had rescued her, and communicated some
Apprehensions on her account. He concluded, that he should never
have an easy Moment till Fanny was absolutely his, and begged that
he might be suffered to fetch a Licence, saying, he could easily borrow the Money. The Parson answered, that he had already given his
Sentiments concerning a Licence, and that a very few Days would
make it unnecessary. 'Joseph,' says he, 'I wish this Haste doth not
arise rather from your Impatience than your Fear; but as it certainly
springs from one of these Causes, I will examine both. Of each of
these therefore in their Turn; and first, for the first of these, namely,
Impatience. Now, Child, I must inform you, that if in your pur-
posed Marriage with this young Woman, you have no Intention but
the Indulgence of carnal Appetites, you are guilty of a very heinous
Sin. Marriage was ordained for nobler Purposes, as you will learn
when you hear the Service provided on that Occasion read to you.
Nay perhaps, if you are a good Lad, I shall give you a Sermon
gratis, where in I shall demonstrate how little Regard ought to be
had to the Flesh on such Occasions. The Text will be, Child,
Matthew the 5th, and Part of the 28th Verse, *whosoever looketh on
a Woman so as to lust after her.* The latter part I shall omit, as foreign to my Purpose. Indeed all such brutal Lusts and Affections are
to be greatly subdued, if not totally eradicated, before the Vessel
can be said to be consecrated to Honour. To marry with a View of
gratifying those Inclinations is a Prostitution of that holy Ceremony, and must entail a Curse on all who so lightly undertake it. If,
therefore, this Haste arises from Impatience, you are to correct, and
not give way to it. Now as to the second Head which I proposed to
speak to, namely, Fear: It argues a Diffidence highly criminal of that

Power in which alone we should put our Trust, seeing we may be well assured that he is able not only to defeat the Designs of our Enemies, but even to turn their Hearts. Instead of taking therefore any unjustifiable or desperate Means to rid ourselves of Fear, we should resort to Prayer only on these Occasions; and we may be then certain of obtaining what is best for us. When any Accident threatens us, we are not to despair, nor, when it overtakes us, to grieve; we must submit in all things to the Will of Providence, and set our Affections so much on nothing here, that we cannot quit it without Reluctance. You are a young Man, and can know but little of this World; I am older, and have seen a great deal. All Passions are criminal in their Excess; and even Love itself, if it is not subservient to our Duty, may render us blind to it. Had Abraham so loved his Son Isaac, as to refuse the Sacrifice required,[2] is there any of us who would not condemn him? Joseph, I know your many good Qualities, and value you for them: but as I am to render an Account of your Soul, which is committed to my Cure, I cannot see any Fault without reminding you of it. You are too much inclined to Passion, Child, and have set your Affections so absolutely on this young Woman, that if G— required her at your Hands, I fear you would reluctantly part with her. Now, believe me, no Christian ought so to set his Heart on any Person or Thing in this World, but that whenever it shall be required or taken from him in any manner by Divine Providence, he may be able, peaceably, quietly, and contentedly to resign it.' At which Words one came hastily in and acquainted Mr. Adams that his youngest Son was drowned. He stood silent a Moment, and soon began to stamp about the Room and deplore his Loss with the bitterest Agony. Joseph, who was overwhelmed with Concern likewise, recovered himself sufficiently to endeavour to comfort the Parson; in which Attempt he used many Arguments that he had at several times remembered out of his own Discourses both in private and public, (for he was a great Enemy to the Passions, and preached nothing more than the Conquest of them by Reason and Grace) but he was not at leisure now to hearken to his Advice. 'Child, Child,' said he, 'do not go about Impossibilities. Had it been any other of my Children, I could have born it with Patience; but my little Prattler, the Darling and Comfort of my Old-Age,—the little Wretch to be snatched out of Life

---

[2] Genesis 22:1–18.

just at his Entrance into it; the sweetest, best-tempered Boy, who never did a thing to offend me. It was but this Morning I gave him his first Lesson in *Quae Genus*.[3] This was the very Book he learnt; poor Child! it is of no further use to thee now. He would have made the best Scholar, and have been an Ornament to the Church;—such Parts, and such Goodness, never met in one so young.' 'And the handsomest Lad too,' says Mrs. Adams, recovering from a Swoon in Fanny's Arms.—'My poor Jacky,[4] shall I never see thee more?' cries the Parson.—'Yes, surely,' says Joseph, 'and in a better Place, you will meet again never to part more.'—I believe the Parson did not hear these Words, for he paid little regard to them, but went on lamenting whilst the Tears trickled down into his Bosom. At last he cry'd out, 'Where is my little Darling?' and was sallying out, when, to his great Surprize and Joy, in which I hope the Reader will sympathize, he met his Son in a wet Condition indeed, but alive, and running towards him. The Person who brought the News of his Misfortune, had been a little too eager, as People sometimes are, from, I believe, no very good Principle, to relate ill News; and seeing him fall into the River, instead of running to his Assistance, directly ran to acquaint his Father of a Fate which he had concluded to be inevitable, but whence the Child was relieved by the same poor Pedlar who had relieved his Father before from a less Distress. The Parson's Joy was now as extravagant as his Grief had been before; he kissed and embraced his Son a thousand times, and danced about the Room like one frantic; but as soon as he discovered the Face of his old Friend the Pedlar, and heard the fresh Obligation he had to him, what were his Sensations? not those which two Courtiers feel in one another's Embraces; not those with which a great Man receives the vile, treacherous Engines of his wicked Purposes; not those with which a worthless younger Brother wishes his elder Joy of a Son, or a Man congratulates his Rival on his obtaining a Mistress, a Place, or an Honour.—No, Reader, he felt the Ebullition, the Overflowings of a full, honest, open Heart towards the Person who had conferred a real Obligation, and of which if thou canst not conceive an Idea within, I will not vainly endeavour to assist thee.

---

[3] A section on irregular nouns in Lily's Latin Grammar (see Book 2, Chapter 11, n. 5).

[4] In Chapter 9, Adams's youngest son is called "Dick"; one of Fielding's few narrative inconsistencies.

When these Tumults were over, the Parson, taking Joseph aside, proceeded thus—'No, Joseph, do not give too much way to thy Passions, if thou dost expect Happiness.'—The Patience of Joseph, nor perhaps of Job, could bear no longer; he interrupted the Parson, saying, 'it was easier to give Advice than take it; nor did he perceive he could so entirely conquer himself, when he apprehended he had lost his Son, or when he found him recover'd.' —'Boy,' replied Adams, raising his Voice, 'it doth not become green Heads to advise grey Hairs.—Thou art ignorant of the Tenderness of fatherly Affection; when thou art a Father, thou wilt be capable then only of knowing what a Father can feel. No Man is obliged to Impossibilities; and the Loss of a Child is one of those great Trials, where our Grief may be allowed to become immoderate.' 'Well, Sir,' cries Joseph, 'and if I love a Mistress as well as you your Child, surely her Loss would grieve me equally.' 'Yes, but such Love is Foolishness, and wrong in itself, and ought to be conquered,' answered Adams, 'it savours too much of the Flesh.' 'Sure, Sir,' says Joseph, 'it is not sinful to love my Wife, no not even to doat on her to Distraction!' 'Indeed but it is,' says Adams. 'Every Man ought to love his Wife, no doubt; we are commanded so to do; but we ought to love with Moderation and Discretion.'—'I am afraid I shall be guilty of some Sin, in spite of all my Endeavours,' says Joseph; 'for I shall love without any Moderation, I am sure.'—'You talk foolishly and childishly,' cries Adams. 'Indeed,' says Mrs. Adams, who had listened to the latter Part of their Conversation, 'you talk more foolishly yourself. I hope, my Dear, you will never preach any such Doctrine as that Husbands can love their Wives too well. If I knew you had such a Sermon in the House, I am sure I would burn it; and I declare, if I had not been convinced you had loved me as well as you could, I can answer for myself I should have hated and despised you. Marry come up! Fine Doctrine indeed! A Wife hath a Right to insist on her Husband's loving her as much as ever he can; and he is a sinful Villain who doth not. Doth he not promise to love her, and to comfort her, and to cherish her, and all that? I am sure I remember it all, as well as if I had repeated it over but yesterday, and shall never forget it. Besides, I am certain you do not preach as you practise; for you have been a loving and a cherishing Husband to me, that's the truth on't; and why you should endeavour to put such wicked Nonsense into this young Man's Head, I cannot devise. Don't hearken to him, Mr. Joseph, be as good a Husband as you are able, and love your Wife with all your Body and Soul too.' Here a violent Rap at the Door put

an end to their Discourse, and produced a Scene which the Reader
will find in the next Chapter.

CHAP. IX.

A Visit which the good Lady Booby *and her polite Friend paid to the
Parson.*

THE Lady Booby had no sooner had an Account from the Gentleman of his meeting a wonderful Beauty near her House, and perceived the Raptures with which he spoke of her, than immediately
concluding it must be Fanny, she began to meditate a Design of
bringing them better acquainted; and to entertain Hopes that the
fine Clothes, Presents and Promises of this Youth, would prevail on
her to abandon Joseph: She therefore proposed to her Company a
Walk in the Fields before Dinner, when she led them towards Mr.
Adams's House; and, as she approached it, told them, if they
pleased she would divert them with one of the most ridiculous
Sights they had ever seen, which was an old foolish Parson, who,
she said laughing, kept a Wife and six Brats on a Salary of about
20 Pounds a Year; adding, that there was not such another ragged
Family in the Parish. They all readily agreed to this Visit, and
arrived whilst Mrs. Adams was declaiming, as in the last Chapter.
Beau Didapper,[1] which was the Name of the young Gentleman we
have seen riding towards Lady Booby's, with his Cane mimicked
the Rap of a London Footman at the Door. The People within,
namely, Adams, his Wife, and three Children, Joseph, Fanny, and
the Pedlar, were all thrown into Confusion by this Knock; but
Adams went directly to the Door, which being opened, the Lady
Booby and her Company walked in, and were received by the Parson with about two hundred Bows; and by his Wife with as many
Curt'sies; the latter telling the Lady, 'She was ashamed to be seen in
such a Pickle, and that her House was in such a Litter: But that if
she had expected such an Honour from her Ladyship, she should
have found her in a better Manner.' The Parson made no Apologies,

---

[1] "Beau," French for "beautiful," refers in English to a handsome young man and
particularly a lover or suitor; "Didapper" incorporates "dapper" into the name of a
small water bird, "a bird that dives into the water" (Johnson). Battestin identifies the
original of Fielding's character as John, Lord Hervey (1696–1743), a loyal supporter
of Sir Robert Walpole, England's Whig "prime minister" (the term was not yet an
official one), or simply "the Great Man," till 1742.

tho' he was in his Half-Cassock, and a Flannel Night-Cap. He said, 'they were heartily welcome to his poor Cottage,' and, turning to Mr. Didapper, cried out, *Non mea renidet in Domo Lacunar.*[2] The Beau answered, 'He did not understand *Welch;*' at which the Parson stared, and made no Reply.

Mr. Didapper, or Beau Didapper, was a young Gentleman of about four Foot five Inches in Height. He wore his own Hair, tho' the Scarcity of it might have given him sufficient Excuse for a Periwig. His Face was thin and pale: The Shape of his Body and Legs none of the best; for he had very narrow Shoulders, and no Calf; and his Gait might more properly be called hopping than walking. The Qualifications of his Mind were well adapted to his Person. We shall handle them first negatively. He was not entirely ignorant: For he could talk a little French, and sing two or three Italian Songs: He had lived too much in the World to be bashful, and too much at Court to be proud: He seemed not much inclined to Avarice; for he was profuse in his Expences: Nor had he all the Features of Prodigality; for he never gave a Shilling:—No Hater of Women; for he always dangled after them; yet so little subject to Lust, that he had, among those who knew him best, the Character of great Moderation in his Pleasures. No Drinker of Wine; nor so addicted to Passion, but that a hot Word or two from an Adversary made him immediately cool.

Now, to give him only a Dash or two on the affirmative Side: 'Tho' he was born to an immense Fortune, he chose, for the pitiful and dirty Consideration of a Place[3] of little Consequence, to depend entirely on the Will of a Fellow, whom they call a great-Man; who treated him with the utmost Disrespect, and exacted of him a plenary Obedience to his Commands; which he implicitly submitted to, at the Expence of his Conscience, his Honour, and his Country; in which he had himself so very large a Share. And to finish his Character; as he was entirely well satisfied with his own Person and Parts, so he was very apt to ridicule and laugh at any Imperfection in another.' Such was the little Person or rather Thing that hopped after Lady Booby into Mr. Adams's Kitchin.

The Parson and his Company retreated from the Chimney-side, where they had been seated, to give Room to the Lady and hers. Instead of returning any of the Curt'sies or extraordinary Civility of

---

[2] "No paneled ceiling glistens in my home" (a contraction of Horace, *Odes* 2.18.1–2). The quotation is, of course, Latin, not Welsh.

[3] "A government appointment, an office in the service of the crown or state" (*OED*).

Mrs. Adams, the Lady turning to Mr. Booby, cried out, *'Quelle Bête! Quel Animal!'*[4] And presently after discovering Fanny (for she did not need the Circumstance of her standing by Joseph to assure the Identity of her Person) she asked the Beau, 'Whether he did not think her a pretty Girl?'—'Begad, Madam,' answered he, ''tis the very same I met.' 'I did not imagine,' replied the Lady, 'you had so good a Taste.' 'Because I never liked you, I warrant,' cries the Beau. 'Ridiculous!' said she, 'you know you was always my Aversion.' 'I would never mention Aversion,' answered the Beau, 'with that Face;* dear Lady Booby, wash your Face before you mention Aversion, I beseech you.' He then laughed, and turned about to coquette it with Fanny.

Mrs. Adams had been all this time begging and praying the Ladies to sit down, a Favour which she had at last obtained. The little Boy to whom the Accident had happened, still keeping his Place by the Fire, was chid by his Mother for not being more man-nerly: But Lady Booby took his Part, and commending his Beauty, told the Parson he was his very Picture. She then seeing a Book in his Hand, asked, 'if he could read?' 'Yes,' cried Adams, 'a little Latin, Madam, he is just got into *Quae Genus*.'—'A Fig for *quere genius*,' answered she, 'let me hear him read a little English.'—'*Lege*,[5] Dick, *Lege*,' said Adams: But the Boy made no Answer, till he saw the Parson knit his Brows; and then cried, 'I don't understand you, Father.' 'How, Boy!' says Adams, 'What doth *Lego* make in the imperative Mood? *Legito*, doth it not?' 'Yes,' answered Dick,—'And what besides?' says the Father. '*Lege*,' quoth the Son, after some Hesitation. 'A good Boy,' says the Father: 'And now, Child, What is the English of *Lego*?'—To which the Boy, after long puzzling, answered, he could not tell. 'How,' cries Adams, in a Passion,—"What, hath the Water washed away your Learning? Why, what is Latin for the English Verb *read*? Consider before you speak.'—The Child considered some time, and then the Parson cried twice or thrice, '*Le—, Le—*.'—Dick answered, '*Lego*.'—'Very well;—and then, what is the English,' says the Parson, 'of the Verb *Lego*.'—'To read,' cried Dick.—'Very well,' said the Parson, 'a good Boy, you

---

[4] "What a beast! What an animal!" (French).

* *Fielding's Note*: Lest this should appear unnatural to some Readers, we think proper to acquaint them, that it is taken *verbatim* from very polite Conversation.

[5] "Read." This is the singular imperative form of the Latin verb *lego*, "I read."

can do well, if you will take Pains.—I assure your Ladyship he is not much above eight Years old, and is out of his *Propria quae Maribus* already.—Come, Dick, read to her Ladyship;'—which she again desiring, in order to give the Beau Time and Opportunity with Fanny, Dick began as in the following Chapter.

CHAP. X.

The History of two Friends, which may afford an useful Lesson to all those Persons, who happen to take up their Residence in married Families.

'LEONARD and Paul were two Friends.'—'Pronounce it *Lennard*, Child,' cried the Parson.—'Pray, Mr. Adams,' says Lady Booby, 'let your Son read without Interruption.' Dick then proceeded. 'Lennard and Paul were two Friends, who, having been educated together at the same School, commenced a Friendship which they preserved a long time for each other. It was so deeply fixed in both their Minds, that a long Absence, during which they had maintained no Correspondence, did not eradicate nor lessen it: But it revived in all its Force at their first Meeting, which was not till after fifteen Years Absence, most of which Time Lennard had spent in the *East-Indi-es*.'—'Pronounce it short *Indies*,' says Adams.—'Pray, Sir, be quiet,' says the Lady.—The Boy repeated—'in the East-Indies, whilst Paul had served his King and Country in the Army. In which different Services, they had found such different Success, that Lennard was now married, and retired with a Fortune of thirty thousand Pound; and Paul was arrived to the Degree of a Lieutenant of Foot; and was not worth a single Shilling.'

'The Regiment in which Paul was stationed, happened to be ordered into Quarters, within a small Distance from the Estate which Lennard had purchased; and where he was settled. This latter, who was now become a Country Gentleman, and a Justice of Peace, came to attend the Quarter-Sessions, in the Town where his old Friend was quartered, soon after his Arrival. Some Affair in which a Soldier was concerned, occasioned Paul to attend the Justices. Manhood, and Time, and the Change of Climate, had so much altered Lennard, that Paul did not immediately recollect the Features of his old Acquaintance: But it was otherwise with Lennard. He knew Paul the moment he saw him; nor could he contain himself from quitting the Bench, and running hastily to embrace him. Paul stood at first a little surprized; but had soon sufficient Information from his Friend, whom he no sooner remembred, than he returned his Embrace with a Passion which made many of the Spectators laugh, and gave to some few a much higher and more agreeable Sensation.

'Not to detain the Reader with minute Circumstances, Lennard insisted on his Friend's returning with him to his House that Evening; which Request was complied with, and Leave for a Month's Absence for Paul obtained of the commanding Officer.

'If it was possible for any Circumstance to give any Addition to the Happiness which Paul proposed in this Visit, he received that additional Pleasure, by finding on his Arrival at his Friend's House, that his Lady was an old Acquaintance which he had formerly contracted at his Quarters; and who had always appeared to be of a most agreeable Temper. A Character she had ever maintained among her Intimates, being of that Number, every Individual of which is called quite the best sort of Woman in the World.

'But good as this Lady was, she was still a Woman; that is to say, an Angel, and not an Angel.'—'You must mistake, Child,' cries the Parson, 'for you read Nonsense.' 'It is so in the Book,' answered the Son. Mr. Adams was then silenced by Authority, and Dick proceeded.—'For tho' her Person was of that kind to which Men attribute the Name of Angel, yet in her Mind she was perfectly Woman. Of which a great Degree of Obstinacy gave the most remarkable, and perhaps most pernicious Instance.

'A Day or two past after Paul's Arrival, before any Instances of this appear'd; but it was impossible to conceal it long. Both she and her Husband soon lost all Apprehension from their Friend's Presence, and fell to their Disputes with as much Vigour as ever. These were still pursued with the utmost Ardour and Eagerness, however trifling the Causes were whence they first arose. Nay, however incredible it may seem, the little Consequence of the Matter in Debate was frequently given as a Reason for the Fierceness of the Contention, as thus: *If you loved me, sure you would never dispute with me such a Trifle as this.* The Answer to which is very obvious; for the Argument would hold equally on both Sides, and was constantly retorted with some Addition, as—*I am sure I have much more Reason to say so, who am in the right.* During all these Disputes, Paul always kept strict Silence, and preserved an even Countenance without shewing the least visible Inclination to either Party. One Day, however, when Madam had left the Room in a violent Fury, Lennard could not refrain from referring his Cause to his

Friend. Was ever any thing so unreasonable, says he, as this Woman? What shall I do with her? I doat on her to Distraction; nor have I any Cause to complain of more than this Obstinacy in her Temper; whatever she asserts she will maintain against all the Reason and Conviction in the World. Pray give me your Advice.—First, says Paul, I will give my Opinion, which is flatly that you are in the wrong; for supposing she is in the wrong, was the Subject of your Contention anyways material? What signified it whether you was married in a red or yellow Waistcoat? for that was your Dispute. Now suppose she was mistaken, as you love her you say so tenderly, and I believe she deserves it, would it not have been wiser to have yielded, tho' you certainly knew yourself in the right, than to give either her or yourself any Uneasiness? For my own Part, if ever I marry, I am resolved to enter into an Agreement with my Wife, that in all Disputes (especially about Trifles) that Party who is most convinced they are right, shall always surrender the Victory: by which Means we shall both be forward to give up the Cause. I own, said Lennard, my dear Friend, shaking him by the Hand, there is great Truth and Reason in what you say; and I will for the future endeavour to follow your Advice. They soon after broke up the Conversation, and Lennard going to his Wife asked her pardon, and told her his Friend had convinced him he had been in the wrong. She immediately began a vast Encomium on Paul, in which he seconded her, and both agreed he was the worthiest and wisest Man upon Earth. When next they met, which was at Supper, tho' she had promised not to mention what her Husband told her, she could not forbear casting the kindest and most affectionate Looks on Paul, and asked him with the sweetest Voice, whether she should help him to some Potted Woodcock?—Potted Partridge, my Dear, you mean, says the Husband. My Dear, says she, I ask your Friend if he will eat any potted Woodcock; and I am sure I must know, who potted it. I think I should know too who shot them, reply'd the Husband, and I am convinced I have not seen a Woodcock this Year; however, tho' I know I am in the right I submit, and the potted Partridge is potted Woodcock, if you desire to have it so. It is equal to me, says she, whether it is one or the other; but you would persuade one out of one's Senses; to be sure you are always in the right in your own Opinion; but your Friend, I believe, knows which he is eating. Paul answered nothing, and the Dispute continued, as usual, the greatest Part of the Evening. The next Morning the Lady accidentally meeting Paul, and being convinced he was her Friend, and of her Side, accosted him thus:—I am certain, Sir, you have long since wondered at the Unreasonableness of my Husband. He is indeed, in other respects a good sort of Man; but so positive, that no Woman but one of my complying Temper could possibly live with him. Why, last Night now, was ever any Creature so unreasonable?—I am certain you must condemn him.—Pray, answer me, was he not in the wrong? Paul, after a short Silence, spoke as follows: I am sorry, Madam, that as Good-manners obliges me to answer against my Will, so an Adherence to Truth forces me to declare myself of a different Opinion. To be plain and honest, you was entirely in the Wrong; the Cause I own not worth disputing, but the Bird was undoubtedly a Partridge. O Sir, reply'd the Lady, I cannot possibly help your Taste—Madam, returned Paul, that is very little material; for had it been otherwise, a Husband might have expected Submission—Indeed! Sir, says she, I assure you!—Yes, Madam, cry'd he, he might, from a Person of your excellent Understanding; and pardon me for saying such a Condescension would have shewn a Superiority of Sense even to your Husband himself—But, dear Sir, said she, why should I submit when I am in the right?—For that very Reason, answer'd he; it would be the greatest Instance of Affection imaginable: for can any thing be a greater Object of our Compassion than a Person we love, in the wrong? Ay, but I should endeavour, said she, to set him right. Pardon me, Madam, answer'd Paul, I will apply to your own Experience, if you ever found your Arguments had that effect. The more our Judgments err, the less we are willing to own it: for my own Part, I have always observed the Persons who maintain the worst side in any Contest, are the warmest. Why, says she, I must confess there is Truth in what you say, and I will endeavour to practice it. The Husband then coming in, Paul departed. And Lennard approaching his Wife with an Air of Good-humour, told her he was sorry for their foolish Dispute the last Night: but he was now convinced of his Error. She answer'd smiling, she believed she owed his Condescension to his Complacence; that she was ashamed to think a Word had past on so silly an Occasion, especially as she was satisfy'd she had been mistaken. A little Contention followed, but with the utmost Good-will to each other, and was concluded by her asserting that Paul had thoroughly convinced her she had been in the wrong. Upon which they both united in the Praises of their common Friend.

'Paul now past his time with great Satisfaction; these Disputes being much less frequent, as well as shorter than usual: but the

Devil, or some unlucky Accident, in which perhaps the Devil had no Hand, shortly put an end to his Happiness. He was now eternally the private Referee of every Difference; in which, after having perfectly, as he thought, established the Doctrine of Submission, he never scrupled to assure both privately that they were in the right in every Argument, as before he had followed the contrary Method. One day a violent Litigation happened in his Absence, and both Parties agreed to refer it to his Decision. The Husband professing himself sure the Decision would be in his Favour; the Wife answer'd, he might be mistaken; for she believed his Friend was convinced how seldom she was to blame—and that if he knew all—The Husband reply'd—My Dear, I have no Desire of any Retrospect; but I believe, if you knew all too, you would not imagine my Friend so entirely on your Side. Nay, says she, since you provoke me, I will mention one Instance. You may remember our Dispute about sending Jacky to School in cold Weather, which Point I gave up to you from mere Compassion, knowing myself to be in the right; and Paul himself told me afterwards, he thought me so. My Dear, replied the Husband, I will not scruple your Veracity; but I assure you solemnly, on my applying to him, he gave it absolutely on my Side, and said he would have acted in the same Manner. They then proceeded to produce numberless other Instances, in all which Paul had, on Vows of Secrecy, given his Opinion on both Sides. In the Conclusion, both believing each other, they fell severely on the Treachery of Paul, and agreed that he had been the Occasion of almost every Dispute which had fallen out between them. They then became extremely loving, and so full of Condescension on both Sides, that they vyed with each other in censuring their own Conduct, and jointly vented their Indignation on Paul, whom the Wife, fearing a bloody Consequence, earnestly entreated her Husband to suffer quietly to depart the next Day, which was the Time fixed for his Return to Quarters, and then drop his Acquaintance.

'However ungenerous this Behaviour in Lennard may be esteemed, his Wife obtain'd a Promise from him (tho' with difficulty) to follow her Advice; but they both express'd such unusual Coldness that Day to Paul, that he, who was quick of Apprehension, taking Lennard aside, press'd him so home, that he at last discovered the Secret. Paul acknowledged the Truth, but told him the Design with which he had done it—To which the other answered, he would have acted more friendly to have let him into the whole Design; for that he might have assured himself of his Secrecy. Paul reply'd, with some Indignation, he had given him a sufficient Proof how capable he was of concealing a Secret from his Wife. Lennard returned with some Warmth—He had more reason to upbraid him, for that he had caused most of the Quarrels between them by his strange Conduct, and might (if they had not discover'd the Affair to each other) have been the Occasion of their Separation. Paul then said'—But something now happened which put a stop to Dick's Reading, and of which we shall treat in the next Chapter.

CHAP. XI.

In which the History is continued.

JOSEPH Andrews had borne with great Uneasiness the Impertinence of Beau Didapper to Fanny, who had been talking pretty freely to her, and offering her Settlements;[1] but the Respect to the Company had restrained him from interfering, whilst the Beau confined himself to the Use of his Tongue only; but the said Beau, watching an Opportunity whilst the Ladies Eyes were disposed another Way, offered a Rudeness to her with his Hands; which Joseph no sooner perceived, than he presented him with so sound a Box on the Ear, that it conveyed him several Paces from where he stood. The Ladies immediately screamed out, rose from their Chairs, and the Beau, as soon as he recovered himself, drew his Hanger, which Adams observing, snatched up the Lid of a Pot in his left Hand, and covering himself with it as with a Shield, without any Weapon of Offence in his other Hand, stept in before Joseph, and exposed himself to the enraged Beau, who threatened such Perdition and Destruction, that it frighted the Women, who were all got in a Huddle together, out of their Wits, even to hear his Denunciations of Vengeance. Joseph was of a different Complexion, and begged Adams to let his Rival come on; for he had a good Cudgel in his Hand, and did not fear him. Fanny now fainted into Mrs. Adams's Arms, and the whole Room was in Confusion, when Mr. Booby passing by Adams, who lay snug under the Pot-Lid, came up to Didapper, and insisted on his sheathing the Hanger, promising he should have Satisfaction; which Joseph declared he would give him, and fight him at any Weapon whatever.

---

[1] "The act of settling property upon a person or persons; the particular terms of such an arrangement" (*OED*)—here, presumably, in exchange for Fanny's becoming his mistress.

The Beau now sheathed his Hanger, and taking out a Pocket-Glass, and vowing Vengeance all the Time, he re-adjusted his Hair; the Parson deposited his Shield, and Joseph running to Fanny, soon brought her back to Life. Lady Booby chid Joseph for his Insult on Didapper; but he answered he would have attacked an Army in the same Cause. 'What Cause?' said the Lady. 'Madam,' answered Joseph, 'he was rude to that young Woman.'—'What,' says the Lady, 'I suppose he would have kissed the Wench; and is a Gentleman to be struck for such an Offer? I must tell you, Joseph, these Airs do not become you.'—'Madam,' said Mr. Booby, 'I saw the whole Affair, and I do not commend my Brother; for I cannot perceive why he should take upon him to be this Girl's Champion.'—'I can commend him,' says Adams, 'he is a brave Lad; and it becomes any Man to be the Champion of the Innocent; and he must be the basest Coward, who would not vindicate a Woman with whom he is on the Brink of Marriage.'—'Sir,' says Mr. Booby, 'my Brother is not a proper Match for such a young Woman as this.'—'No,' says Lady Booby, 'nor do you, Mr. Adams, act in your proper Character, by encouraging any such Doings; and I am very much surprized you should concern yourself in it. I think your Wife and Family your properer Care.'—'Indeed, Madam, your Ladyship says very true,' answered Mrs. Adams, 'he talks a Pack of Nonsense, that the whole Parish are his Children. I am sure I don't understand what he means by it; it would make some Women suspect he had gone astray: but I acquit him of that; I can read Scripture as well as he; and I never found that the Parson was obliged to provide for other Folks Children; and besides, he is but a poor Curate, and hath little enough, as your Ladyship knows, for me and mine.'— 'You say very well, Mrs. Adams,' quoth the Lady Booby, who had not spoke a Word to her before, 'you seem to be a very sensible Woman; and I assure you, your Husband is acting a very foolish Part, and opposing his own Interest; seeing my Nephew is violently set against this Match: and indeed I can't blame him; it is by no means one suitable to our Family.' In this manner the Lady proceeded with Mrs. Adams, whilst the Beau hopped about the Room, shaking his Head, partly from Pain, and partly from Anger; and Pamela was chiding Fanny for her Assurance, in aiming at such a Match as her Brother.—Poor Fanny answered only with her Tears, which had long since begun to wet her Handkerchief; which Joseph perceiving, took her by the Arm, and, wrapping it in his, carried her off, swearing he would own no Relation to any one who was an Enemy to her he loved more than all the World. He went out with Fanny under his left

Arm, brandishing a Cudgel in his right, and neither Mr. Booby nor the Beau thought proper to oppose him. Lady Booby and her Company made a very short stay behind him; for the Lady's Bell now summoned them to dress; for which they had just time before Dinner.

Adams seemed now very much dejected, which his Wife perceiving, began to apply some matrimonial Balsam. She told him he had Reason to be concerned; for that he had most probably ruined his Family with his Tricks almost: But perhaps he was grieved for the Loss of his two Children, Joseph and Fanny. His eldest Daughter went on:—'Indeed, Father, it is very hard to bring Strangers here to eat your Childrens Bread out of their Mouths.—You have kept them ever since they came home; and for any thing I see to the contrary may keep them a Month longer: Are you obliged to give her Meat, tho'f she was never so handsome? But I don't see she is so much handsomer than other People. If People were to be kept for their Beauty, she would scarce fare better than her Neighbours, I believe.—As for Mr. Joseph, I have nothing to say, he is a young Man of honest Principles, and will pay some time or other for what he hath: But for the Girl,—Why doth she not return to her Place she ran away from? I would not give such a Vagabond Slut a Halfpenny, tho' I had a Million of Money; no, tho' she was starving.' 'Indeed but I would,' cries little Dick; 'and Father, rather than poor Fanny shall be starved, I will give her all this Bread and Cheese.'— (*Offering what he held in his Hand.*) Adams smiled on the Boy, and told him, he rejoiced to see he was a Christian; and that if he had a Halfpenny in his Pocket, he would have given it him; telling him, it was his Duty to look upon all his Neighbours as his Brothers and Sisters, and love them accordingly. 'Yes, Papa,' says he, 'I love her better than my Sisters; for she is handsomer than any of them.' 'Is she so, Saucebox?' says the Sister, giving him a Box on the Ear, which the Father would probably have resented, had not Joseph, Fanny, and the Pedlar, at that Instant returned together.—Adams bid his Wife prepare some Food for their Dinner; she said, 'truly she could not, she had something else to do.' Adams rebuked her for disputing his Commands, and quoted many Texts of Scripture to prove, *that the Husband is the Head of the Wife, and she is to submit and obey.*[2] The Wife answered, 'it was Blasphemy to talk Scripture out of Church; that such things were very proper to be said in the Pulpit: but that it was profane to talk them in common

[2] Ephesians 5:22–23.

Discourse.' Joseph told Mr. Adams 'he was not come with any Design to give him or Mrs. Adams any trouble; but to desire the Favour of all their Company to the *George* (an Alehouse in the Parish,) where he had bespoke a Piece of Bacon and Greens for their Dinner.' Mrs. Adams, who was a very good sort of Woman, only rather too strict in Œconomics,[3] readily accepted this Invitation, as did the Parson himself by her Example; and away they all walked together, not omitting little Dick, to whom Joseph gave a Shilling, when he heard of his intended Liberality to Fanny.

CHAP. XII.

Where the good-natured Reader will see something which will give him no great Pleasure.

THE Pedlar had been very inquisitive from the time he had first heard that the great House in this Parish belonged to the Lady Booby; and had learnt that she was the Widow of Sir Thomas, and that Sir Thomas had bought Fanny, at about the Age of three or four Years, of a travelling Woman; and now their homely but hearty Meal was ended, he told Fanny, he believed he could acquaint her with her Parents. The whole Company, especially she herself, started at this Offer of the Pedlar's.—He then proceeded thus, while they all lent their strictest Attention: 'Tho' I am now contented with this humble way of getting my Livelihood, I was formerly a Gentleman; for so all those of my Profession are called. In a word, I was a Drummer in an Irish Regiment of Foot. Whilst I was in this honourable Station, I attended an Officer of our Regiment into England a recruiting. In our March from Bristol to Froome (for since the Decay of the Woollen Trade, the clothing Towns have furnished the Army with a great Number of Recruits[1]) we overtook on the Road a Woman who seemed to be about thirty Years old, or thereabouts, not very handsome; but well enough for a Soldier. As we came up to her, she mended her Pace, and falling into Discourse with our Ladies, (for every Man of the Party, namely, a Serjeant, two private Men, and a Drum, were provided with their Woman, except myself) she continued to travel on with us.

---

[3] Or "economics," a word that retained its original Greek sense of "household management" through the eighteenth century.

[1] The decay of the West Country woolen trade—centered in the Somersetshire town of Frome, near Bath—led to a rise of army recruits from this area after 1739.

I, perceiving she must fall to my Lot, advanced presently to her, made Love to her in our military way, and quickly succeeded to my Wishes. We struck a Bargain within a Mile, and lived together as Man and Wife to her dying Day.'—'I suppose,' says Adams, interrupting him, 'you were married with a Licence: For I don't see how you could contrive to have the Banns published while you were marching from Place to Place.'—'No, Sir,' said the Pedlar, 'we took a Licence to go to Bed together, without any Banns.'—'Ay, ay,' said the Parson, '*ex Necessitate*, a Licence may be allowable enough; but surely, surely, the other is the more regular and eligible Way.'—The Pedlar proceeded thus; 'She returned with me to our Regiment, and removed with us from Quarters to Quarters, till at last, whilst we lay at Galloway, she fell ill of a Fever, and died. When she was on her Deathbed she called me to her, and, crying bitterly, declared she could not depart this World without discovering a Secret to me, which she said was the only Sin which sat heavy on her Heart. She said she had formerly travelled in a Company of Gypsies, who had made a Practice of stealing away Children; that for her own part, she had been only once guilty of the Crime; which she said she lamented more than all the rest of her Sins, since probably it might have occasioned the Death of the Parents: For, added she, it is almost impossible to describe the Beauty of the young Creature, which was about a Year and half old when I kidnapped it. We kept her (for she was a Girl) above two Years in our Company, when I sold her myself for three Guineas to Sir Thomas Booby in Somersetshire. Now, you know whether there are any more of that Name in this County.'—'Yes,' says Adams, 'there are several Boobys who are Squires, but I believe no Baronet now alive, besides it answers so exactly in every Point there is no room for Doubt; but you have forgot to tell us the Parents from whom the Child was stolen.'—'Their Name,' answered the Pedlar, 'was *Andrews*. They lived about thirty Miles from the Squire; and she told me, that I might be sure to find them out by one Circumstance; for that they had a Daughter of a very strange Name *Paměla*, or *Paméla*; some pronounced it one way, and some the other.'[2] Fanny, who had changed Colour at the first mention of the Name, now fainted away;

---

[2] Richardson named his novel's heroine after a character in Sir Philip Sidney's *Arcadia* (1590), and popularized the pronunciation we now give it, with a stress on "Pam" followed by a short "e" in "ela." Yet a more classical pronunciation of the name, which is derived from the Greek for "all sweetness," would be with a final long "e" and stress on "mela."

Joseph turned pale, and poor Dicky began to roar; the Parson fell on his Knees, and ejaculated many Thanksgivings that this Discovery had been made before the dreadful Sin of Incest was committed; and the Pedlar was struck with Amazement, not being able to account for all this Confusion, the Cause of which was presently opened by the Parson's Daughter, who was the only unconcerned Person; (for the Mother was chaffing Fanny's Temples, and taking the utmost care of her) and indeed Fanny was the only Creature whom the Daughter would not have pitied in her Situation; wherein, tho' we compassionate her ourselves, we shall leave her for a little while, and pay a short Visit to Lady Booby.

CHAP. XIII.

The History returning to the Lady Booby, *gives some Account of the terrible Conflict in her Breast between Love and Pride; with what happened on the present Discovery.*

THE Lady sat down with her Company to Dinner; but eat nothing. As soon as her Cloth was removed, she whispered Pamela, that she was taken a little ill, and desired her to entertain her Husband and Beau Didapper. She then went up into her Chamber, sent for Slip-slop, threw herself on the Bed, in the Agonies of Love, Rage, and Despair; nor could she conceal these boiling Passions longer, without bursting. Slipslop now approached her Bed, and asked how her Ladyship did; but instead of revealing her Disorder, as she intended, she entered into a long Encomium on the Beauty and Virtues of Joseph Andrews; ending at last with expressing her Concern, that so much Tenderness should be thrown away on so despicable an Object as Fanny. Slipslop well knowing how to humour her Mistress's Frenzy, proceeded to repeat, with Exaggeration, if possible, all her Mistress had said, and concluded with a Wish, that Joseph had been a Gentleman, and that she could see her Lady in the Arms of such a Husband. The Lady then started from the Bed, and taking a Turn or two cross the Room, cry'd out with a deep Sigh,—*Sure he would make any Woman happy.* —'Your Ladyship,' says she, 'would be the happiest Woman in the World with him.—A fig for Custom and Nonsense. What *vails* what People say? Shall I be afraid of eating Sweetmeats, because People may say I have a sweet Tooth? If I had a Mind to Marry a Man, all the World should not hinder me. Your Ladyship hath no Parents to *tutelar* your *Infections;* besides, he is of your Ladyship's Family now, and as good a Gentleman as any in the Country; and why should not a Woman follow her Mind as well as a Man? Why should not your Ladyship marry the Brother, as well as your Nephew the Sister? I am sure, if it was a *fragrant* Crime I would not persuade your Ladyship to it.'—'But, dear Slipslop,' answered the Lady, 'if I could prevail on myself to commit such a Weakness, there is that cursed Fanny in the way, whom the Idiot,—O how I hate and despise him!'—'She, a little ugly Mynx,' cries Slipslop, 'leave her to me.—I suppose your Ladyship hath heard of Joseph's *fitting* with one of Mr. Didapper's Servants about her; and his Master hath ordered them to carry her away by force this Evening. I'll take Care they shall not want Assistance. I was talking with his Gentleman, who was below just when your Ladyship sent for me.'—'Go back,' says the Lady Booby, 'this Instant; for I expect Mr. Didapper will soon be going. Do all you can; for I am resolved this Wench shall not be in our Family; I will endeavour to return to the Company; but let me know as soon as she is carried off.' Slipslop went away; and her Mistress began to arraign her own Conduct in the following Manner:

'What am I doing? How do I suffer this Passion to creep imperceptibly upon me! How many Days are past since I could have submitted to ask myself the Question?—Marry a Footman! Distraction! Can I afterwards bear the Eyes of my Acquaintance? But I can retire from them; retire with one in whom I propose more Happiness than the World without him can give me! Retire—to feed continually on Beauties, which my inflamed Imagination sickens with eagerly gazing on; to satisfy every Appetite, every Desire, with their utmost Wish.—Ha! and do I doat thus on a Footman! I despise, I detest my Passion.—Yet why? Is he not generous, gentle, kind?—Kind to whom? to the meanest Wretch, a Creature below my Consideration. Doth he not?—Yes, he doth prefer her; curse his Beauties, and the little low Heart that possesses them; which can basely descend to this despicable Wench, and be ungratefully deaf to all the Honours I do him.—And can I then love this Monster? No, I will tear his Image from my Bosom, tread on him, spurn him. I will have those pitiful Charms, which now I despise, mangled in my Sight; for I will not suffer the little Jade I hate to riot in the Beauties I contemn. No, tho' I despise him myself; tho' I would spurn him from my Feet, was he to languish at them, no other should taste the Happiness I scorn. Why do I say Happiness? To me it would be Misery.—To sacrifice my Reputation, my Character,

my Rank in Life, to the Indulgence of a mean and a vile Appetite.—
How I detest the Thought! How much more exquisite is the Pleasure resulting from the Reflection of Virtue and Prudence, than the
faint Relish of what flows from Vice and Folly! Whither did I suffer
this improper, this mad Passion to hurry me, only by neglecting to
summon the Aids of Reason to my Assistance? Reason, which hath
now set before me my Desires in their proper Colours, and immediately helped me to expel them. Yes, I thank Heaven and my Pride,
I have now perfectly conquered this unworthy Passion; and if there
was no Obstacle in its Way, my Pride would disdain any Pleasures
which could be the Consequence of so base, so mean, so vulgar'—
Slipslop returned at this Instant in a violent Hurry, and with the
utmost Eagerness, cry'd out,—'O, Madam, I have strange News.
Tom the Footman is just come from the George; where it seems
Joseph and the rest of them are a *jinketting*;[1] and he says, there is a
strange Man who hath discovered that Fanny and Joseph are
Brother and Sister.'—'How, Slipslop,' cries the Lady in a Surprize.—'I
had not time, Madam,' cries Slipslop, 'to enquire about *Particles*,
but Tom says, it is most certainly true.'

This unexpected Account entirely obliterated all those admirable
Reflections which the supreme Power of Reason had so wisely
made just before. In short, when Despair, which had more Share in
producing the Resolutions of Hatred we have seen taken, began to
retreat, the Lady hesitated a Moment, and then forgetting all the
Purport of her Soliloquy, dismissed her Woman again, with Orders
to bid Tom attend her in the Parlour, whither she now hastened to
acquaint Pamela with the News. Pamela said, she could not believe
it: For she had never heard that her Mother had lost any Child, or
that she had ever had more than Joseph and herself. The Lady flew
into a violent Rage with her, and talked of Upstarts and disowning
Relations, who had so lately been on a Level with her. Pamela made
no Answer: But her Husband, taking up her Cause, severely repri-
manded his Aunt for her Behaviour to his Wife; he told her, if it had
been earlier in the Evening she should not have staid a Moment
longer in her House; that he was convinced, if this young Woman
could be proved her Sister, she would readily embrace her as such;
and he himself would do the same: He then desired the Fellow

---

[1] For "junketing," meaning "to feast" or "to feast secretly: to make entertainment
by stealth" (Johnson).

might be sent for, and the young Woman with him; which Lady Booby immediately ordered, and thinking proper to make some Apology to Pamela for what she had said, it was readily accepted, and all Things reconciled.

The Pedlar now attended, as did Fanny and Joseph, who would not quit her; the Parson likewise was induced, not only by Curiosity, of which he had no small Portion, but his Duty, as he apprehended it, to follow them: for he continued all the way to exhort them, who were now breaking their Hearts, to offer up Thanksgivings, and be joyful for so miraculous an Escape.

When they arrived at Booby-Hall, they were presently called into the Parlour, where the Pedlar repeated the same Story he had told before, and insisted on the Truth of every Circumstance; so that all who heard him were extremely well satisfied of the Truth, except Pamela, who imagined, as she had never heard either of her Parents mention such an Accident, that it must be certainly false; and except the Lady Booby, who suspected the Falshood of the Story, from her ardent Desire that it should be true; and Joseph, who feared its Truth, from his earnest Wishes that it might prove false.

Mr. Booby now desired them all to suspend their Curiosity and absolute Belief or Disbelief, till the next Morning, when he expected old Mr. Andrews and his Wife to fetch himself and Pamela home in his Coach, and then they might be certain of certainly knowing the Truth or Falshood of this Relation; in which he said, as there were many strong Circumstances to induce their Credit, so he could not perceive any Interest the Pedlar could have in inventing it, or in endeavouring to impose such a Falshood on them.

The Lady Booby, who was very little used to such Company, entertained them all, *viz.* Her Nephew, his Wife, her Brother and Sister, the Beau and the Parson, with great Good-humour at her own Table. As to the Pedlar, she ordered him to be made as welcome as possible by her Servants. All the Company in the Parlour, except the disappointed Lovers, who sat sullen and silent, were full of Mirth: For Mr. Booby had prevailed on Joseph to ask Mr. Didapper's Pardon; with which he was perfectly satisfied. Many Jokes past between the Beau and the Parson, chiefly on each other's Dress; these afforded much Diversion to the Company. Pamela chid her Brother Joseph for the Concern which he exprest at discovering a new Sister. She said, if he loved Fanny as he ought, with a pure Affection, he had no Reason to lament being related to her.—Upon which Adams began to discourse on *Platonic* Love; whence he made a quick Transition to the Joys in the next World, and concluded with strongly asserting that there was no such thing as Pleasure in this. At which Pamela and her Husband smiled on one another.

This happy Pair proposing to retire (for no other Person gave the least Symptom of desiring Rest) they all repaired to several Beds provided for them in the same House; nor was Adams himself suffered to go home, it being a stormy Night. Fanny indeed often begged she might go home with the Parson; but her Stay was so strongly insisted on, that she at last, by Joseph's Advice, consented.

CHAP. XIV.

Containing several curious Night-Adventures, in which Mr. Adams fell into many Hair-breadth 'Scapes, partly owing to his Goodness, and partly to his Inadvertency.

ABOUT an Hour after they had all separated (it being now past three in the Morning) Beau Didapper, whose Passion for Fanny permitted him not to close his Eyes, but had employed his Imagination in Contrivances how to satisfy his Desires, at last hit on a Method by which he hoped to effect it. He had ordered his Servant to bring him word where Fanny lay, and had received his Information; he therefore arose, put on his Breeches and Night-gown, and stole softly along the Gallery which led to her Apartment; and being come to the Door, as he imagined it, he opened it with the least Noise possible, and entered the Chamber. A Savour now invaded his Nostrils which he did not expect in the Room of so sweet a young Creature, and which might have probably had no good Effect on a cooler Lover. However, he groped out the Bed with Difficulty; for there was not a Glimpse of Light, and opening the Curtains,[1] he whispered in Joseph's Voice (for he was an excellent Mimic) 'Fanny, my Angel, I am come to inform thee that I have discovered the Falshood of the Story we last Night heard. I am no longer thy Brother, but thy Lover; nor will I be delayed the Enjoyment of thee one Moment longer. You have sufficient Assurances of my Constancy not to doubt my marrying you, and it would be want of Love to deny me the Possession of thy Charms.'—So saying, he disencumbered

---

[1] Beds were canopied and curtained for warmth.

himself from the little Clothes he had on, and, leaping into Bed, embraced his Angel, as he conceived her, with great Rapture. If he was surprized at receiving no Answer, he was no less pleased to find his Hug returned with equal Ardour. He remained not long in this sweet Confusion; for both he and his Paramour presently discovered their error. Indeed it was no other than the accomplished Slipslop whom he had engaged; but tho' she immediately knew the Person whom she had mistaken for Joseph, he was at a loss to guess at the Representative of Fanny. He had so little seen or taken notice of this Gentlewoman, that Light itself would have afforded him no Assistance in his Conjecture. Beau Didapper no sooner had perceived his Mistake, than he attempted to escape from the Bed with much greater Haste than he had made to it; but the watchful Slipslop prevented him. For that prudent Woman being disappointed of those delicious Offerings which her Fancy had promised her Pleasure, resolved to make an immediate Sacrifice to her Virtue. Indeed she wanted an Opportunity to heal some Wounds which her late Conduct had, she feared, given her Reputation; and as she had a wonderful Presence of Mind, she conceived the Person of the unfortunate Beau to be luckily thrown in her way to restore her Lady's Opinion of her impregnable Chastity. At that Instant therefore, when he offered to leap from the Bed, she caught fast hold of his Shirt, at the same time roaring out, 'O thou Villain! who hast attacked my Chastity, and, I believe, ruined me in my Sleep; I will swear a Rape against thee, I will prosecute thee with the utmost Vengeance.' The Beau attempted to get loose, but she held him fast, and when he struggled, she cried out, 'Murther! Murther! Rape! Robbery! Ruin!' At which Words Parson Adams, who lay in the next Chamber, wakeful and meditating on the Pedlar's Discovery, jumped out of Bed, and without staying to put a rag of Clothes on, hastened into the Apartment whence the Cries proceeded. He made directly to the Bed in the dark, where laying hold of the Beau's Skin (for Slipslop had torn his Shirt almost off) and finding his Skin extremely soft, and hearing him in a low Voice begging Slipslop to let him go, he no longer doubted but this was the young Woman in danger of ravishing, and immediately falling on the Bed, and laying hold on Slipslop's Chin, where he found a rough Beard, his Belief was confirmed; he therefore rescued the Beau, who presently made his Escape, and then turning towards Slipslop, received such a Cuff on his Chops, that his Wrath kindling instantly, he offered to return the Favour so stoutly, that had poor Slipslop received the Fist, which in the dark past by her, and fell on the Pillow, she would most probably have given up the Ghost.—Adams, missing his Blow, fell directly on Slipslop, who cuffed and scratched as well as she could; nor was he behind hand with her in his Endeavours, but happily the Darkness of the Night befriended her.—She then cried she was a Woman; but Adams answered she was rather the Devil, and if she was, he would grapple with him; and being again irritated by another Stroke on his Chops, he gave her such a Remembrance in the Guts, that she began to roar loud enough to be heard all over the House. Adams then seizing her by the Hair (for her Double-clout had fallen off in the Scuffle) pinned her Head down to the Bolster, and then both called for Lights together. The Lady Booby, who was as wakeful as any of her Guests, had been alarmed from the beginning; and, being a Woman of a bold Spirit, she slipt on a Night-gown, Petticoat and Slippers, and taking a Candle, which always burnt in her Chamber, in her Hand, she walked undauntedly to Slipslop's Room; where she entered just at the instant as Adams had discovered, by the two Mountains which Slipslop carried before her, that he was concerned with a Female. He then concluded her to be a Witch, and said, he fancied those Breasts gave suck to a Legion of Devils. Slipslop seeing Lady Booby enter the Room, cried, *Help! or I am ravished,* with a most audible Voice, and Adams, perceiving the Light, turned hastily, and saw the Lady (as she did him) just as she came to the Feet of the Bed; nor did her Modesty, when she found the naked Condition of Adams,[2] suffer her to approach farther.—She then began to revile the Parson as the wickedest of all Men, and particularly railed at his Impudence in chusing her House for the Scene of his Debaucheries, and her own Woman for the Object of his Bestiality. Poor Adams had before discovered the Countenance of his Bedfellow, and now first recollecting he was naked, he was no less confounded than Lady Booby herself, and immediately whipt under the Bed-clothes, whence the chaste Slipslop endeavoured in vain to shut him out. Then putting forth his Head, on which, by way of Ornament, he wore a Flannel Nightcap, he protested his Innocence, and asked ten thousand Pardons of Mrs. Slipslop for the Blows he had struck her, vowing he had mistaken her for a Witch. Lady Booby then, casting her Eyes on the Ground, observed something sparkle with great Lustre, which,

---

[2] We discover later in the chapter that Adams has on a night-shirt, and so is "naked" only in the sense of being undressed.

when she had taken it up, appeared to be a very fine pair of Diamond Buttons for the Sleeves. A little farther she saw lie the Sleeve itself of a Shirt with laced Ruffles. 'Hey day!' says she, 'what is the meaning of this?'—'O, Madam,' says Slipslop, 'I don't know what hath happened, I have been so terrified. Here may have been a dozen Men in the Room.' 'To whom belongs this laced Shirt and Jewels?' says the Lady.———'Undoubtedly,' cries the Parson, 'to the young Gentleman whom I mistook for a Woman on coming into the Room, whence proceeded all the subsequent Mistakes; for if I had suspected him for a Man, I would have seized him had he been another Hercules, tho' indeed he seems rather to resemble Hylas.'[3] He then gave an account of the Reason of his rising from Bed, and the rest, till the Lady came into the Room; at which, and the Figures of Slipslop and her Gallant, whose Heads only were visible at the opposite Corners of the Bed, she could not refrain from Laughter, nor did Slipslop persist in accusing the Parson of any Motions towards a Rape. The Lady therefore desired him to return to his Bed as soon as she was departed, and then ordering Slipslop to rise and attend her in her own Room, she returned herself thither. When she was gone, Adams renewed his Petitions for Pardon to Mrs. Slipslop, who, with a most Christian Temper, not only forgave, but began to move with much Courtesy towards him, which he taking as a Hint to be gone, immediately quitted the Bed, and made the best of his way towards his own; but unluckily, instead of turning to the right, he turned to the left, and went to the Apartment where Fanny lay, who (as the Reader may remember) had not slept a Wink the preceding Night, and who was so hagged out with what had happened to her in the Day, that notwithstanding all Thoughts of her Joseph, she was fallen into so profound a Sleep, that all the Noise in the adjoining Room had not been able to disturb her. Adams groped out the Bed, and turning the Clothes down softly, a Custom Mrs. Adams had long accustomed him to, crept in, and deposited his Carcase on the Bedpost, a Place which that good Woman had always assigned him.

As the Cat or Lapdog of some lovely Nymph for whom ten thousand Lovers languish, lies quietly by the Side of the charming Maid, and, ignorant of the Scene of Delight on which they repose, meditates the future Capture of a Mouse, or Surprizal of a Plate of

---

[3] A beautiful young man, friend of Hercules, represented in European art as compact and slender.

Bread and Butter: so Adams lay by the Side of Fanny, ignorant of the Paradise to which he was so near; nor could the Emanation of Sweets which flowed from her Breath, overpower the Fumes of Tobacco which played in the Parson's Nostrils. And now Sleep had not overtaken the good Man, when Joseph, who had secretly appointed Fanny to come to her at the break of Day, rapped softly at the Chamber-Door, which when he had repeated twice, Adams cry'd, *Come in, whoever you are.* Joseph thought he had mistaken the Door, tho' she had given him the most exact Directions; however, knowing his Friend's Voice, he opened it, and saw some female Vestments lying on a Chair. Fanny waking at the same instant, and stretching out her Hand on Adams's Beard, she cry'd out,—'O Heavens! where am I?' 'Bless me! where am I?' said the Parson. Then Fanny screamed, Adams leapt out of Bed, and Joseph stood, as the Tragedian calls it, like the *Statue of Surprize*.[4] '*How came she into my Room?*' cry'd Adams. '*How came you into hers?*' cry'd Joseph, in an Astonishment. 'I know nothing of the Matter,' answered Adams, 'but that she is a Vestal for me. As I am a Christian, I know not whether she is a Man or Woman. He is an Infidel who doth not believe in Witchcraft. They as surely exist now as in the Days of Saul.[5] My Clothes are bewitched away too, and Fanny's brought into their place.' For he still insisted he was in his own Apartment; but Fanny denied it vehemently, and said, his attempting to persuade Joseph of such a Falshood, convinced her of his wicked Designs. 'How!' said Joseph, in a Rage, 'Hath he offered any Rudeness to you?'—She answered, she could not accuse him of more than villainously stealing to Bed to her, which she thought Rudeness sufficient, and what no Man would do without a wicked Intention. Joseph's great Opinion of Adams was not easily to be staggered, and when he heard from Fanny that no Harm had happened, he grew a little cooler; yet still he was confounded, and as he knew the House, and that the Womens Apartments were on this side Mrs. Slipslop's Room, and the Mens on the other, he was convinced that he was in Fanny's Chamber. Assuring Adams therefore of this Truth, he begged him to give some Account how he came there. Adams then, standing in his Shirt, which did not offend Fanny as the Curtains of the Bed were drawn, related all that had

---

[4] See Book 1, Chapter 8, n. 2.
[5] On Saul and the Witch of Endor, see 1 Samuel 28:7–25.

happened, and when he had ended, Joseph told him, it was plain he
had mistaken, by turning to the right instead of the left. 'Odso!'
cries Adams, 'that's true, as sure as Sixpence, you have hit on the
very thing.' He then traversed the Room, rubbing his Hands, and
begged Fanny's Pardon, assuring her he did not know whether she
was Man or Woman. That innocent Creature firmly believing all
he said, told him, she was no longer angry, and begged Joseph to
conduct him into his own Apartment, where he should stay himself,
till she had put her Clothes on. Joseph and Adams accordingly
departed, and the latter soon was convinced of the Mistake he had
committed; however, whilst he was dressing himself, he often
asserted he believed in the Power of Witchcraft notwithstanding,
and did not see how a Christian could deny it.

CHAP. XV.

The Arrival of Gaffar and Gammar Andrews, *with another Person not*
much expected; and a perfect Solution of the Difficulties raised by the
Pedlar.

As soon as Fanny was drest, Joseph returned to her, and they had a
long Conversation together, the Conclusion of which was, that if
they found themselves to be really Brother and Sister, they vowed a
perpetual Celibacy, and to live together all their Days, and indulge a
Platonic Friendship for each other.

The Company were all very merry at Breakfast, and Joseph and
Fanny rather more cheerful than the preceding Night. The Lady
Booby produced the Diamond Button, which the Beau most readily
owned, and alledged that he was very subject to walk in his Sleep.
Indeed he was far from being ashamed of his Amour, and rather
endeavoured to insinuate that more than was really true had past
between him and the fair Slipslop.

Their Tea was scarce over, when News came of the Arrival of
old Mr. Andrews and his Wife. They were immediately introduced,
and kindly received by the Lady Booby, whose Heart went now pit-
a-pat, as did those of Joseph and Fanny. They felt perhaps little less
Anxiety in this Interval than Oedipus himself, whilst his Fate was
revealing.[1]

---

[1] In Sophocles' *Oedipus Rex*, King Oedipus, discovering his true parentage, finds
that he has married his mother and murdered his father.

Mr. Booby first open'd the Cause, by informing the old Gentleman that he had a Child in the Company more than he knew of, and taking Fanny by the Hand, told him, this was that Daughter of his who had been stolen away by Gypsies in her Infancy. Mr. Andrews, after expressing some Astonishment, assured his Honour that he had never lost a Daughter by Gypsies, nor ever had any other Children than Joseph and Pamela. These Words were a Cordial to the two Lovers; but had a different Effect on Lady Booby. She ordered the Pedlar to be called, who recounted his Story as he had done before.—At the End of which old Mrs. Andrews running to Fanny, embraced her, crying out, *She is, she is my Child.* The Company were all amazed at this Disagreement between the Man and his Wife; and the Blood had now forsaken the Cheeks of the Lovers, when the old Woman turning to her Husband, who was more surprized than all the rest, and having a little recovered her own Spirits, delivered herself as follows. 'You may remember, my Dear, when you went a Serjeant to Gibraltar, you left me big with Child, you staid abroad, you know upwards of three Years. In your Absence I was brought to bed, I verily believe, of this Daughter, whom I am sure I have reason to remember, for I suckled her at this very Breast till the Day she was stolen from me. One Afternoon, when the Child was about a Year, or a Year and half old, or thereabouts, two Gypsy Women came to the Door, and offered to tell my Fortune. One of them had a Child in her Lap; I shewed them my Hand, and desired to know if you was ever to come home again, which I remember as well as if it was but Yesterday, they faithfully promised me you should—I left the Girl in the Cradle, and went to draw them a Cup of Liquor, the best I had; when I return'd with the Pot (I am sure I was not absent longer than whilst I am telling it to you) the Women were gone. I was afraid they had stolen something, and looked and looked, but to no Purpose, and Heaven knows I had very little for them to steal. At last hearing the Child cry in the Cradle, I went to take it up—but O *the living!* how was I surprized to find, instead of my own Girl that I had put into the Cradle, who was as fine a fat thriving Child as you shall see in a Summer's Day, a poor sickly Boy, that did not seem to have an Hour to live. I ran out, pulling my Hair off, and crying like any mad after the Women, but never could hear a Word of them from that Day to this. When I came back, the poor Infant (which is our Joseph there, as stout as he now stands) lifted up its Eyes upon me so piteously, that to be sure, notwithstanding my Passion, I could not find in my Heart to do it any mischief. A Neighbour of mine happening to come in at the same time, and hearing the Case, advised me to take care of this poor Child, and God would perhaps one Day restore me my own. Upon which I took the Child up, and suckled it, to be sure, all the World as if it had been born of my own natural Body. And as true as I am alive, in a little time I loved the Boy all to nothing as if it had been my own Girl.—Well, as I was saying, Times growing very hard, I having two Children, and nothing but my own Work, which was little enough, God knows, to maintain them, was obliged to ask Relief of the Parish; but instead of giving it me, they removed me, by Justices Warrants,[2] fifteen Miles to the Place where I now live, where I had not been long settled before you came home. Joseph (for that was the Name I gave him myself—the Lord knows whether he was baptized or no, or by what Name) Joseph, I say, seemed to me to be about five Years old when you returned; for I believe he is two or three Years older than our Daughter here; (for I am thoroughly convinced she is the same) and when you saw him you said he was a chopping Boy, without ever minding his Age; and so I seeing you did not suspect any thing of the Matter, thought I might e'en as well keep it to myself, for fear you should not love him as well as I did. And all this is veritably true, and I will take my Oath of it before any Justice in the Kingdom.'

The Pedlar, who had been summoned by the Order of Lady Booby, listened with the utmost Attention to Gammar Andrews's Story, and when she had finished, asked her if the supposititious Child had no Mark on its Breast? To which she answered, 'Yes, he had as fine a Strawberry as ever grew in a Garden.' This Joseph acknowledged, and unbuttoning his Coat, at the Intercession of the Company, shewed to them. 'Well,' says Gaffar Andrews, who was a comical sly old Fellow, and very likely desired to have no more Children than he could keep, 'you have proved, I think, very plainly, that this Boy doth not belong to us; but how are you certain that the Girl is ours?' The Parson then brought the Pedlar forward, and desired him to repeat the Story which he had communicated to him the preceding Day at the Alehouse; which he complied with, and related what the Reader, as well as Mr. Adams, hath seen before. He then confirmed, from his Wife's Report, all the Circumstances of the Exchange, and of the Strawberry on Joseph's Breast. At the

---

[2] The Andrews had apparently not gained a settlement in their parish, and so could be removed on the order of two justices to their last place of legal settlement.

Repetition of the Word *Strawberry*, Adams, who had seen it without any Emotion, started and cry'd, *Bless me! something comes into my Head*. But before he had time to bring any thing out, a Servant called him forth. When he was gone, the Pedlar assured Joseph, that his Parents were Persons of much greater Circumstances than those he had hitherto mistaken for such; for that he had been stolen from a Gentleman's House, by those whom they call Gypsies, and had been kept by them during a whole Year, when looking on him as in a dying Condition, they had exchanged him for the other healthier Child, in the manner before related. He said, as to the Name of his Father, his Wife had either never known or forgot it; but that she had acquainted him he lived about forty Miles from the Place where the Exchange had been made, and which way, promising to spare no Pains in endeavouring with him to discover the Place.

But Fortune, which seldom doth good or ill, or makes Men happy or miserable by Halves, resolved to spare him this Labour. The Reader may please to recollect, that Mr. Wilson had intended a Journey to the West, in which he was to pass through Mr. Adams's Parish, and had promised to call on him. He was now arrived at the Lady Booby's Gates for that Purpose, being directed thither from the Parson's House, and had sent in the Servant whom we have above seen call Mr. Adams forth. This had no sooner mentioned the Discovery of a stolen Child, and had uttered the Word *Strawberry*, than Mr. Wilson, with Wildness in his Looks, and the utmost Eagerness in his Words, begged to be shewed into the Room, where he entered without the least Regard to any of the Company but Joseph, and embracing him with a Complexion all pale and trembling, desired to see the Mark on his Breast; the Parson followed him capering, rubbing his Hands, and crying out, *Hic est quem quaeris, inventus est,*[3] *&c.* Joseph complied with the Request of Mr. Wilson, who no sooner saw the Mark, than abandoning himself to the most extravagant Rapture of Passion, he embraced Joseph, with inexpressible Ecstasy, and cried out in Tears of Joy, *I have discovered my Son, I have him again in my Arms!* Joseph was not sufficiently apprized yet, to taste the same Delight with his Father, (for so in reality he was;) however, he returned some Warmth to his Embraces: But he no sooner perceived from his Father's Account, the Agreement of every Circumstance, of Person, Time, and Place, than he threw himself at his Feet, and embracing his Knees, with Tears begged his Blessing,

---

[3] "This is him who you seek; he is found."

which was given with much Affection, and received with such Respect, mixed with such Tenderness on both Sides, that it affected all present: But none so much as Lady Booby, who left the Room in an Agony, which was but too much perceived, and not very charitably accounted for by some of the Company.

CHAP. XVI.

Being the last. In which this true History is brought to a happy Conclusion.

FANNY was very little behind her Joseph, in the Duty she exprest towards her Parents; and the Joy she evidenced in discovering them. Gammar Andrews kiss'd her, and said she was heartily glad to see her: But for her Part she could never love any one better than Joseph. Gaffar Andrews testified no remarkable Emotion, he blessed and kissed her, but complained bitterly, that he wanted his Pipe, not having had a Whiff that Morning.

Mr. Booby, who knew nothing of his Aunt's Fondness, imputed her abrupt Departure to her Pride, and Disdain of the Family into which he was married; he was therefore desirous to be gone with the utmost Celerity: And now, having congratulated Mr. Wilson and Joseph on the Discovery, he saluted Fanny, called her Sister, and introduced her as such to Pamela, who behaved with great Decency on the Occasion.

He now sent a Message to his Aunt, who returned, that she wished him a good Journey; but was too disordered to see any Company: He therefore prepared to set out, having invited Mr. Wilson to his House; and Pamela and Joseph both so insisted on his complying, that he at last consented, having first obtained a Messenger from Mr. Booby, to acquaint his Wife with the News; which, as he knew it would render her completely happy, he could not prevail on himself to delay a Moment in acquainting her with.

The Company were ranged in this manner. The two old People, with their two Daughters rode in the Coach; the Squire, Mr. Wilson, Joseph, Parson Adams, and the Pedlar proceeded on Horseback.

In their Way Joseph informed his Father of his intended Match with Fanny; to which, tho' he expressed some Reluctance at first, on the Eagerness of his Son's Instances he consented, saying, if she was so good a Creature as she appeared, and he described her, he thought the Disadvantages of Birth and Fortune might be compensated.

He however insisted on the Match being deferred till he had seen his Mother; in which Joseph perceiving him positive, with great Duty obeyed him, to the great Delight of Parson Adams, who by these means saw an Opportunity of fulfilling the Church Forms, and marrying his Parishioners without a Licence.

Mr. Adams greatly exulting on this Occasion, (for such Ceremonies were Matters of no small Moment with him) accidentally gave Spurs to his Horse, which the generous Beast disdaining, for he was high of Mettle, and had been used to more expert Riders than the Gentleman who at present bestrode him, for whose Horsemanship he had perhaps some Contempt, immediately ran away full speed, and played so many antic Tricks, that he tumbled the Parson from his Back; which Joseph perceiving, came to his Relief. This Accident afforded infinite Merriment to the Servants, and no less frighted poor Fanny, who beheld him as he past by the Coach; but the Mirth of the one, and Terror of the other were soon determined,[1] when the Parson declared he had received no Damage.

The Horse having freed himself from his unworthy Rider, as he probably thought him, proceeded to make the best of his Way; but was stopped by a Gentleman and his Servants, who were travelling the opposite Way; and were now at a little Distance from the Coach. They soon met; and as one of the Servants delivered Adams his Horse, his Master hail'd him, and Adams looking up, presently recollected he was the Justice of Peace before whom he and Fanny had made their Appearance. The Parson presently saluted him very kindly; and the Justice informed him, that he had found the Fellow who attempted to swear against him and the young Woman the very next Day, and had committed him to Salisbury Goal, where he was charged with many Robberies.

Many Compliments having past between the Parson and Justice, the latter proceeded on his Journey, and the former having with some Disdain refused Joseph's Offer of changing Horses, and declared he was as able a Horseman as any in the Kingdom, remounted his Beast; and now the Company again proceeded, and happily arrived at their Journey's End, Mr. Adams by good Luck, rather than by good Riding, escaping a second Fall.

The Company arriving at Mr. Booby's House, were all received by him in the most courteous, and entertained in the most splendid manner, after the Custom of the old English Hospitality, which is still

[1] "Bounded" or "concluded" (Johnson).

preserved in some very few Families in the remote Parts of England. They all past that Day with the utmost Satisfaction; it being perhaps impossible to find any Set of People more solidly and sincerely happy. Joseph and Fanny found means to be alone upwards of two Hours, which were the shortest, but the sweetest imaginable.

In the Morning, Mr. Wilson proposed to his Son to make a Visit with him to his Mother; which, notwithstanding his dutiful Inclinations, and a longing Desire he had to see her, a little concerned him; as he must be obliged to leave his Fanny: But the Goodness of Mr. Booby relieved him; for he proposed to send his own Coach and Six for Mrs. Wilson, whom Pamela so very earnestly invited, that Mr. Wilson at length agreed with the Entreaties of Mr. Booby and Joseph, and suffered the Coach to go empty for his Wife.

On Saturday Night the Coach returned with Mrs. Wilson, who added one more to this happy Assembly. The Reader may imagine much better and quicker too than I can describe, the many Embraces and Tears of Joy which succeeded her Arrival. It is sufficient to say, she was easily prevailed with to follow her Husband's Example, in consenting to the Match.

On Sunday Mr. Adams performed the Service at the Squire's Parish Church, the Curate of which very kindly exchanged Duty, and rode twenty Miles to the Lady Booby's Parish so to do; being particularly charged not to omit publishing the Banns, being the third and last Time.

At length the happy Day arrived, which was to put Joseph in the Possession of all his Wishes. He arose and drest himself in a neat, but plain Suit of Mr. Booby's, which exactly fitted him; for he refused all Finery; as did Fanny likewise, who could be prevailed on by Pamela to attire herself in nothing richer than a white Dimity Night-Gown.[2] Her Shift indeed, which Pamela presented her, was of the finest Kind, and had an Edging of Lace round the Bosom; she likewise equipped her with a Pair of fine white Thread Stockings, which were all she would accept; for she wore one of her own short round-eared Caps, and over it a little Straw Hat, lined with Cherry-coloured Silk, and tied with a Cherry-coloured Ribbon. In this Dress she came forth from her Chamber, blushing and breathing Sweets; and was by Joseph, whose Eyes sparkled Fire, led to Church, the whole Family attending, where Mr. Adams performed the Ceremony; at which nothing was so remarkable, as the extraordinary and unaffected

[2] Evening dress.

Modesty of Fanny, unless the true Christian Piety of Adams, who publicly rebuked Mr. Booby and Pamela for laughing in so sacred a Place, and so solemn an Occasion. Our Parson would have done no less to the highest Prince on Earth: For tho' he paid all Submission and Deference to his Superiors in other Matters, where the least Spice of Religion intervened, he immediately lost all Respect of Persons. It was his Maxim, That he was a Servant of the Highest, and could not, without departing from his Duty, give up the least Article of his Honour, or of his Cause, to the greatest earthly Potentate. Indeed he always asserted, that Mr. Adams at Church with his Surplice on, and Mr. Adams without that Ornament, in any other Place, were two very different Persons.

When the Church Rites were over, Joseph led his blooming Bride back to Mr. Booby's (for the Distance was so very little, they did not think proper to use a Coach;) the whole Company attended them likewise on foot; and now a most magnificent Entertainment was provided, at which Parson Adams demonstrated an Appetite surprizing, as well as surpassing every one present. Indeed the only Persons who betrayed any Deficiency on this Occasion, were those on whose account the Feast was provided. They pampered their Imaginations with the much more exquisite Repast which the Approach of Night promised them; the Thoughts of which filled both their Minds, tho' with different Sensations; the one all Desire, while the other had her Wishes tempered with Fears.

At length, after a Day past with the utmost Merriment, corrected by the strictest Decency; in which, however, Parson Adams, being well filled with Ale and Pudding, had given a Loose to more Facetiousness than was usual to him: The happy, the blest Moment arrived, when Fanny retired with her Mother, her Mother-in-law, and her Sister. She was soon undrest; for she had no Jewels to deposite in their Caskets, nor fine Laces to fold with the nicest Exactness. Undressing to her was properly discovering, not putting off Ornaments: For as all her Charms were the Gifts of Nature, she could divest herself of none. How, Reader, shall I give thee an adequate Idea of this lovely young Creature! the Bloom of Roses and Lillies might a little illustrate her Complexion, or their Smell her Sweetness: but to comprehend her entirely, conceive Youth, Health, Bloom, Beauty, Neatness, and Innocence, in her Bridal-Bed; conceive all these in their utmost Perfection, and you may place the charming Fanny's Picture before your Eyes.

Joseph no sooner heard she was in Bed, than he fled with the utmost Eagerness to her. A Minute carried him into her Arms, where we shall leave this happy Couple to enjoy the private Rewards of their Constancy; Rewards so great and sweet, that I apprehend Joseph neither envied the noblest Duke, nor Fanny the finest Duchess that Night.

The third Day, Mr. Wilson and his Wife, with their Son and Daughter returned home; where they now live together in a State of Bliss scarce ever equalled. Mr. Booby hath with unprecedented Generosity given Fanny a Fortune of two thousand Pound, which Joseph hath laid out in a little Estate in the same Parish with his Father, which he now occupies, (his Father having stocked it for him;) and Fanny presides with most excellent Management in his Dairy; where, however, she is not at present very able to bustle much, being, as Mr. Wilson informs me in his last Letter, extremely big with her first Child.

Mr. Booby hath presented Mr. Adams with a Living of one hundred and thirty Pounds a Year. He at first refused it, resolving not to quit his Parishioners, with whom he hath lived so long: But, on recollecting he might keep a Curate at this Living, he hath been lately inducted into it.

The Pedlar, besides several handsome Presents both from Mr. Wilson and Mr. Booby, is, by the latter's Interest, made an Exciseman; a Trust which he discharges with such Justice, that he is greatly beloved in his Neighbourhood.[3]

As for the Lady Booby, she returned to London in a few Days, where a young Captain of Dragoons, together with eternal Parties at Cards, soon obliterated the Memory of Joseph.

Joseph remains blest with his Fanny, whom he doats on with the utmost Tenderness, which is all returned on her side. The Happiness of this Couple is a perpetual Fountain of Pleasure to their fond Parents; and what is particularly remarkable, he declares he will imitate them in their Retirement; nor will be prevailed on by any Booksellers, or their Authors, to make his Appearance in *High-Life*.[4]

---

[3] A collector of the excise-tax levied on commodities during manufacture or retail. It was an unpopular tax: Johnson defines "excise" as "a hateful tax levied upon commodities, and adjudged . . . [by] wretches hired by those to whom the excise is paid." That the former peddler is "greatly beloved" in his new profession is either a testament to his uncommon virtue or Fielding's final irony.

[4] See Introduction, p. xviii.

CONTEXTS

The Romance Tradition

The basic plot of Joseph Andrews—*the adventures and vicissitudes of a pair of chaste lovers who come to understand their true identities and find in the end their proper home—goes back to the cosmopolitan Greek romances of the early Christian era. The longest and most complex work of prose fiction to survive from Greek antiquity is by Heliodorus, a work variously known as either* Ethiopian Story *or* Theagenes and Charikleia, *and dated to either the 3rd or 4th century CE. A 1717 translation by Charles Gildon, which Fielding may have known, is titled* The Adventures of Theagenes and Chariclia, a Romance. *In the passage from Gildon's translation reproduced here, the lovers' wise father figure, Kalasiris, discovers Charicia's true identity by reading the message written in Ethiopian script on a "fillet" or head-band that was found with Charicia when she was an abandoned baby.*

♣ Heliodorus
From *The Adventures of Theagenes and Charicia*[1]

I desired time to decypher it[2]; which being granted, I went strait to my Lodging, and the first thing I did, began to read the Inscription, which I found written, not in vulgar Letters, but in the Royal Ethiopic Character, not unlike that wherein our *Egyptian* Mysteries are engrossed. The Words were these:

Persina Queen of *Ethiopia* bequeaths this mournful Inscription as a last Legacy to her Daughter, whatever her Name may chance to be; a Daughter only known to her by the Pangs she felt in bringing her

---

[1] *The Adventures of Theagenes and Charicia, A Romance*, 2 vols. (London, 1717), 1:176–80.

[2] It refers to the "fillet" or head-band.

327

forth. [My Blood curdled *Cnemon,* upon reading *Persina's* name; however I went on.] The Sun is witness, that Great Author of our Race, that I expose thee not, my Child, upon any dishonorable account, nor did I conceal thy Birth from thy Father *Hydaspes* for any reason whereof I ought to be ashamed. But, Dear Child, if ever thou livest to read these Letters, accept the Apology which I make to Thee, and to him whom the Gods shall incline to take thee up, and to all Mankind, explaining the grounds of my unnatural Cruelty to thee.

Sol and *Bacchus* were our Ancestors among the Gods; among the Heroes, *Perseus* and *Andromeda,* and after them *Memnon.* These at several times built the Royal Palace, and adorned it with Statues and Paintings representing their own Atchievements; the public Rooms and Porticoes with some sorts, the Bedchambers with others: Particularly, the royal Apartment was hung round with the History of *Perseus* and *Andromeda.* There it happened that your Father, after we had been married ten years without a Child, retiring from the mid-day heat, came in and knew me, excited to it, (as he protested himself) by a Dream. Upon which I conceived, and not long after, found my self with Child. From that time, to my lying in, there were publick Feastings all the Kingdom over, and Sacrifices of Thanksgiving offered, for the hopes the King had of an Heir and Successor from his own Loins. Being brought to bed at the usual time, I was delivered of a white Child, a Colour new to the *Ethiopians*; of which I knew the reason to be, that during your Father's Embraces, my Eye chanced to be fixed upon the Picture of *Andromeda* naked (for *Perseus* had just taken her from the Rock) and the Powers of Imagination were so unfortunately strong in me, as to produce a Child of like Complexion with the Picture.[3]

However, as I was well assured that such a reason would find but little Credit for clearing me from the suspicion of Adultery I resolved, if Possible, to secure my self from the ignominious Punishment due to that Crime. And thinking it much better for thee, my Child, to have a chance for life, than be delivered up to certain

---

[3] This ancient theory of "maternal impression," according to which things seen or imagined by a woman during or soon after conception could imprint themselves on her unborn child, reappears in *Joseph Andrews,* Book III, Chap. 4 with Joseph's strawberry birth mark. Heliodorus's further assumption that dark-skinned parents could have a light-skinned daughter reminds us that essentialist racial categories were not in place in either the Hellenistic world or the early modern Europe that revived Heliodorus's romance (see Sujata Iyengar, *Shades of Difference: Mythologies of Skin Colour in Early Modern England,* University of Pennsylvania Press, 2005).

Death, under the scandalous imputation of a Spurious Issue, I pretended to my Husband, that the Child died as soon as it was born, and took care to have thee exposed with all the Caution and Secrecy that might be; at the same time exposing with thee great Riches, as a Reward to him that should find, and breed thee up. And among other things I adorned thee with, I added this Fillet, the melancholy Remembrancer of both our hard Fates, which in deep sorrow I stain'd with Blood and Tears.

And now, my sweet Babe, for some few Minutes only my Daughter, if Fortune spare thy life, remember thy high Birth, and let Chastity be thy chief Care, that greatest Ornament to Women, and to them especially who carry noble Blood in their Veins. In this imitate thy Parents, as in every other Character of a Princely Mind. Remember also to enquire after a Ring, which among other jewels was exposed with thee, and be very careful of it, being the same thy Father married me with: A royal Cypher is engraven upon it, and it is set with a *Pautarbe* Stone of hidden Virtues. These things I talk to thee by Letters, the dumb conveyors of my Thoughts, since Fate denies us a living Conversation. They may be of use some time or other, and they may prove only the idle results of a fruitless Care, since no one can sound the depths of Fortune. But O unhappy fair one, a reproach to thy Mother by being beautiful! should the Gods continue thee among the Living, thou wilt know by these Tokens who thou art; otherwise they may serve as a Mother's last Duties to her dearest Child, whose Death I pray, may never reach these Ears.

Upon reading this Inscription, *Cnemon*, I found what I wanted, and admiring the wise steps of Providence, was seised presently with a strange medly of Passions, both Joy and Grief blended together. I rejoiced much at the discovering things I knew nothing of before, and that the Oracle was thoroughly unfolded. But then I grieved no less at what I feared might happen, and I pitied human Nature, as weak, and wavering, and never at any Certainty; and I had no need of any other Example to verify the reflection, than *Chariclia's* Fortune.

✤ Cervantes
From *The History of the Renowned Don Quixote de la Mancha*

El Ingenioso Hidalgo Don Quixote de la Mancha was published by Miguel de Cervantes in 1605, with a second part appearing in 1615. The English version that Fielding most likely knew was the

1700–1703 edition arranged by Peter Motteux and translated anonymously ("by several hands," according to its title page). The two passages below are taken from the 1733 sixth edition of John Ozell's revision of the Motteux edition. The first passage, from Cervante's second chapter of Vol. 1, Book 1, depicts Quixote's first adventure: seeing the world through the distorting lenses of chivalric romances, he mistakes a plain inn for a turreted castle and two common prostitutes for beautiful aristocratic ladies. In the second passage, from Vol. 1, Book 4, Chap. 20, a canon (cathedral-official) from Toledo laments to a curate the effects of chivalric romances ("books of knight-errantry"), but ends by offering an ideal model of the romance as an epic in prose. The canon's discourse has evident echoes in Fielding's literary theory.

"OF DON QUIXOTE'S FIRST SALLY."[1]

He very calmly rode on, leaving it to his Horse's Discretion to go which Way he pleas'd, firmly believing that in this consisted the very Being of Adventures. And as he thus went on, I cannot but I believe, said he to himself, that when the History of my famous Atchievements shall be given to the World, the learned Author will begin it in this very Manner, when he comes to give an Account of this my early setting out; 'Scarce had the ruddy-colour'd *Phoebus* begun to spread the golden Tresses of his lovely Hair over the vast Surface of the earthly Globe, and scarce had those feathered Poets of the Grove, the pretty painted Birds, tun'd their little Pipes, to sing their early Welcomes in soft melodious Strains to the beautiful *Aurora* who having left her jealous Husband's Bed, display'd her rosy Graces to mortal Eyes from the Gates and Balconies of the Horizon of *La Mancha,* when the renowned Knight Don *Quixote de la Mancha,* disdaining soft Repose, forsook the voluptuous Down, and mounting his famous Steed Rozinante, entered the ancient and celebrated Plains of *Montiel.'* This was indeed the very Road he took; and then proceeding, 'O happy Age, O fortunate Times,' cry'd he, 'decreed to usher into the World my famous Atchievements, Atchievements, worthy to be engraven on Brass, carv'd in Marble, and delineated in some Master-piece of Painting, as Monuments of

---

[1] In *Don Quixote,* 6th ed., 4 vols. (London, 1733), 1:10–13.

my Glory, and Examples for Posterity! And thou venerable Sage, wise Inchanter, whatever be thy Name, thou whom Fate has ordained to be the Compiler of this rare History, forget not I beseech thee my trusty *Rozinante*, the eternal Companion of all my Adventures.' After this, as if he had been really in Love; 'O Princess *Dulcinea*,' cry'd he, 'Lady of this captive Heart,[2] much Sorrow and Woe you have doom'd me to in banishing me thus, and imposing on me your rigorous Commands, never to appear before your beauteous Face! Remember, Lady, that loyal Heart your Slave, who for your Love submits to so many Miseries.' To these extravagant Conceits he added a World of others, all in Imitation and in the very Stile of those, which the reading of Romances had furnish'd him with; and all this while he rode so softly, that the Sun's Heat increas'd so fast and was so violent, that it would have been sufficient to have melted his Brains had he had any left.

He travell'd almost all that Day without meeting any Adventure worth the Trouble of relating; which put him into a kind of Despair; for he desir'd nothing more, than to encounter immediately some Person on whom he might try the Vigour of his Arm.

Some Authors say, that his first Adventure was that of the Pass called *Puerto Lapice*; others, that of the Windmill; but all that I could discover of Certainty to this Matter, and that I meet with in the Annals of *La Mancha*, is, that he travelled all that Day; and towards the Evening, he and his Horse being heartily tir'd, and almost famish'd, Don *Quixote* looking about him, in hopes to discover some Castle, or at least some Shepherd's Cottage, there to repose and refresh himself at last, near the Road which he kept, he espy'd an Inn, as welcome a Sight to his longing Eyes as if he had discovered a Star directing him to the Gate, nay to the Palace, of his Redemption. Thereupon hast'ning towards the Inn with all the Speed he could, he got thither just at the close of the Evening. There stood by Chance at the Inn-door, two young female-Adventurers, *alias* Common-Wenches, who were going to *Sevil* with some Carriers, that happen'd to take up their Lodging there that very Evening: And, as whatever our Knight-Errant saw, thought, or imagin'd, was all of a romantick Cast, and appear'd to him altogether after the

---

[2] "Dulcinea del Toboso" is Quixote's romantic name for the plain country girl he loves and idolizes, Aldonza Lorenco.

Manner of the Books that had perverted his Imagination, he no sooner saw the inn but he fansy'd it to be a Castle fenc'd with four Towers, and lofty Pinnacles glittering with Silver, together with a deep Moat, Drawing-bridge, and all those other Appurtenances peculiar to such kind of Places.

Therefore when he came near it, he stopped a while at a Distance from the Gate, expecting that some Dwarf wou'd appear on the Battlements, and found his Trumpet to give notice of the Arrival of a Knight; but finding that no Body came, and that *Rozinante* was for making the best of his Way to the Stable, he advanc'd to the Inn-door, where spying the two young Doxies, they seem'd to him two beautiful Damsels, or graceful Ladies, taking the Benefit of the fresh Air at the Gate of the Castle. It happen'd also at the very Moment, that a Swine-herd chanced to wind his Horn to get his Hogs together; and Don *Quixote* presently imagin'd this was the wish'd-for Signal which some Dwarf gave to notify his Approach; therefore with the greatest Joy in the World he rode up to the Inn. The Wenches, affrighted at the Approach of a Man cas'd in Iron, and arm'd with a Lance and Target, were for running into their Lodging; but Don *Quixote* perceiving their Fear by their Flight, lifted up the Paste-board Beaver of his Helmet, and discovering his wither'd dusty Face, with comely Grace and grave Delivery accosted them in this Manner: 'I beseech ye, Ladies, do not fly, nor fear the least Offence: The Order of Knighthood, which I profess, does not permit me to countenance or offer Injuries to any one in the Universe, and least of all to Persons of your Ladyship's exalted Rank and Merit.' The Wenches look'd earnestly upon him; endeavouring to get a Glimpse of his Face, which his ill-contriv'd Beaver partly hid; but when they heard themselves thus complimented with the Title of Ladyship, an Honour to which their Condition never had the least Pretence, they could not forbear laughing outright; which Don *Quixote* resented as a great Affront. 'Give me leave to tell ye, Ladies,' cry'd he, 'that Modesty and Civility are very becoming in the fair Sex; whereas Laughter without Ground is the highest Piece of Indiscretion: However, added, he, I do not presume to say this to offend you, or incur your Displeasure; no, Ladies, I assure you I have ho other Design but to do you Service.' This uncommon Way of Expression, join'd to the Knight's scurvy Figure, increas'd their Mirth; which incens'd him to that Degree, that this might have carry'd Things to an Extremity had not the Inn-keeper luckily appear'd at that juncture.

"On Books of Knights-Errant and the Epic in Prose"[3]

'Believe me, Mr. Curate,' said he,[4] 'I am fully convinc'd, that these they call Books of Knight-Errantry, are very prejudicial to the Publick. And tho' I have been led away by an idle and false Pleasure, to read the Beginnings of almost as many of 'em as have been Printed, I could never yet persuade myself to go through with any one to the End; for to me they all seem to contain one and the same thing; and there is as much in one of them as in all the rest. The whole Composition and Stile resemble that of the *Milesian* Fables, which are a sort of idle Stories, design'd only for Diversion, and not for Instruction. It is not so with those Fables which are call'd Apologues, that at once delight and instruct. But tho' the main Design of such Books is to please; yet I cannot conceive how it is possible they should perform it, being fill'd with such a Multitude of unaccountable Extravagancies. For the Pleasure which strikes the Soul, must be deriv'd from the Beauty and Congruity it sees or conceives in those things the Sight or Imagination lays before it; and nothing in itself deformed or incongruous can give us any real Satisfaction. Now what Beauty can there be, or what Proportion of the Parts to the whole, or of the whole to the several Parts, in a Book, or Fable, where a Stripling at Sixteen Years of Age at one Cut of a Sword cleaves a Giant, as tall as a Steeple, through the Middle, as easily as if he were made of Past-board? Or when they give us the Relation of a Battle, having said the Enemy's Power consisted of a Million of Combatants; yet provided the Hero of the Book be against them, we must of necessity, tho' never so much against our Inclination, conceive that the said Knight obtain'd the victory only by his own Valour, and the strength of his Powerful Arm? And what shall we say of the great Ease and Facility with which an absolute Queen or Empress casts herself into the Arms of an Errant and unknown Knight? What Mortal, not altogether barbarous and unpolished, can be pleased to read, that a great Tower, full of armed Knights, cuts thro' the Sea like Ship before the Wind; and setting out in the Evening from the Coast of *Italy*, lands by break of Day in *Prestor John's* Country, or in some other never known to *Ptolomy* or discover'd by *Columbus*? If it shou'd be answer'd, That those Persons who compose these

---

[3] In *Don Quixote* 1:255–58.
[4] 'he' refers to the canon from Toledo.

Books, write them as confess'd Lies; and therefore are not oblig'd
to observe Niceties, or have regard to Truth; I shall make this Reply,
That Falsehood is so much the more commendable, by how much it
more resembles Truth, and is the more pleasing, the more it is
doubtful and possible. Fabulous Tales ought to be suited to the
Reader's Understanding, being so contrived, that all Impossibilities
ceasing, all great Accidents appearing easy, and the Mind wholly
hanging in Suspence, they may at once surprize, astonish, please
and divert; for that Pleasure and Admiration may go hand in hand.
This cannot be perform'd by him that flies from Probability and
Imitation, which is the Perfection of what is written. I have not yet
seen any Book of Knight-Errantry, that composes an entire Body
of a Fable with all its Parts, so that the Middle is answerable to the
Beginning, and the End to the Beginning and Middle; but on the
contrary, they form them of so many Limbs, that they rather form
to design a Chimera or Monster, than a well-proportion'd Figure.
Besides all this, their Stile in uncouth, their Exploits incredible, their
Love immodest, Civility impertinent, their Battles tedious, their
Language absurd, their Voyages preposterous and in short, they are
altogether void of solid Ingenuity, and therefore fit to be banish'd
a Christian Commonwealth, as useless and prejudicial.' The Curate
was very attentive, and believ'd him a Man of a sound Judgment,
and much in the right in all he had urg'd; and therefore told him,
That he being of the same Opinion, and an Enemy to Books of
Knight-Errantry, had burnt all that belonged to Don *Quixote,* which
were a considerable number. Then he recounted him the Scrutiny he
had made among them, what he had condemn'd to the Flames, and
what spar'd; at which the Canon laugh'd heartily, and said, 'That
notwithstanding all the Harm he had spoken of those Books, yet he
found one good thing in them, which was the Subject they furnish'd
a Man of Understanding with to exercise his Parts, because they
allow a large Scope for the Pen to dilate without any Check, describing Shipwrecks, Storms, Skirmishes and Battles; representing to us
a brave Commander, with all the Qualifications requisite in such
a one, shewing his Prudence in disappointing the Designs of the
Enemy, his Eloquence in persuading or dissuading his Soldiers, his
Judgment in Council, his Celerity in Execution, and his Valour in
assailing or repulsing an Assault; laying before us sometimes a dismal
and melancholy Accident, sometimes a delightful and unexpected
Adventure; in one Place, a beautiful, modest, discreet and reserv'd
Lady; in another, a Christian-like, brave and courteous Gentleman;

here a boisterous, inhuman, boasting Ruffian; there an affable, war-like and wise Prince; lively expressing the Fidelity and Loyalty of Subjects, Generosity and Bounty of Sovereigns. He may no less, at times, make known his Skill in Astrology, Cosmography, Musick and Policy; and if he pleases, he cannot want an Opportunity of appearing knowing even in Necromancy. He may describe the Sub-tilty of *Ulysses*, the Piety of *Æneas*, the Valour of *Achilles*, the Mis-fortunes of *Hector*, the Treachery of *Cinon*, the Friendship of *Euryalus*, the Liberality of *Alexander*, the Valour of *Caesar*, the Clemency and Sincerity of *Trajan*, the Fidelity of *Zopyrus*, the Pru-dence of *Cato*; and in fine, all those Actions that may make up a compleat Hero, sometimes attributing them all to one Person, and at other times dividing them among many. This being so perform'd in a grateful Stile, and with ingenious Invention, approaching as much as possible to Truth, will doubtless compose so beautiful and various a Work, that, when finish'd, its Excellency and Perfection must attain the best end of Writing, which is at once to delight and instruct, as I have said before: For the loose Method practis'd in these Books, gives the Author liberty to play the Epick, the Lyrick, and the Dra-matick Poet, and to run through all the other Parts of Poetry and Rhetorick; for Epicks may be as well writ in Prose as in Verse.'

❦ Paul Scarron
Le Roman Comique (1712)[1]

Scarron's novel recounts the adventures of a troupe of itinerant actors and the characters they meet in the city of Mans, including the dwarfish lawyer Ragotin. At the center of the narrative are the young man Destiny and the woman L'Etoile ("Star"), lovers forced into act-ing careers out of necessity, and disguised as brother and sister in part to mislead the villain, who seeks to abduct L'Etoile. In the action leading up to the following excerpt (from Part II, Chap. 10), the actors have been performing at a country wedding; here the groom's mother, Madam Bouvillon, attempts to seduce Destiny. The scene is interrupted by the arrival of Ragotin, announcing that the actress Angelica, earlier kidnapped, has been discovered.

The chapter evidently resembles, in tone and style, the scenes of Lady Booby's attempted seduction of Joseph (I.5 and 8); yet an

---

[1] From Paul Scarron's *Le Roman Comique* (1651–57), translated by Thomas Brown, a person identified only as "Mr. Savage," "and others" (London, third edition 1712).

*examination of the subtle differences between Scarron's comic art
(in translation) and that of Fielding's may also prove illuminating.*

FROM CHAP. X.—"HOW MADAM BOUVILLON COULD NOT
RESIST A CERTAIN TEMPTATION, AND BESIDES, HOW SHE
GOT A BUNCH IN HER FOREHEAD"[2]

Madam *Bouvillon* being thus left alone, either because she was tired,
or that she feigned to be so, or else by reason that no Horse was able
to carry her Weight, sent her Servant to Destiny to desire him to
come and dine with her, and whilst Dinner was getting ready spent
her time in dressing. First she curl'd and powder'd, then put on a
lac'd Apron and Nightrail, and afterwards took to pieces a *Point de
Venise* Cravat of her Son's to make her a *commode*. After this she
opened her Daughter-in-Law's Trunk, and took thence her Wedding
Gown and put it on: In a word, thus trick'd up and adorn'd, she
look'd like to any little *Venus* in a Cloud, tho' that somewhat of the
fattest. Now notwithistanding all these Preparations of hers, *Destiny*
had, no doubt, much rather have dined with his Companions; but
then how could he have obey'd the Commands of his very humble
Servant Madam *Bouvillon*? He therefore not knowing how to get
free, was forced to comply; but was not a little surpriz'd when he
saw his paramour so youthfully drest. She receiv'd him with a smiling Countenance, took him by the Hands to have him wash them,
and squeez'd him after a manner that meant something more than
ordinary. He for his part was less solicitous of his Invitation, than
the occasion of it, and therefore often neglected eating, which gave
her an opportunity to press it. He knew not what to say to her,
being naturally no great Talker; but which defect she plentifully
supply'd by her never ceasing Clack. She was but too ingenious to
suffer any Chasm in Conversation for want of something to say.
When a Woman that talks much, meets with a Man that says little
and does not answer her, she always talks the more, for judging of
her Friend by her self, and perceiving that he has not *reparteed* to
what she advanced, she presently believes he has not been pleased
with what was said: and therefore to mend the Matter, proceeds to
say a great deal more, which commonly proves as impertinent as
her first Discourse was ridiculous. The only way that I can propose

---

[2] In *The Whole Comical Works of Mon. Scarron*, 3rd ed. (London, 1712), pp. 160–63.

to deal with such Women as these, is to talk as much, if not more than they, for thereby if they cannot be silenc'd, their Voices may at least be drowned. As for the matchless *Bouvillon*, she was the most immoderate Talker of nothing that ever was known, for she not only talk'd to her self while she was in private, but would answer her self likewise. The silent disposition of *Destiny* giving her an Opportunity, she determin'd to divert him with some large Relation or other. The Subject she chose to speak of, was the Intrigues of *Laval*, the Town where she lived; but she never hapned to blame any Person or Action, but she always took thence an occasion to commend her self, protesting at every fling of Satyr on her Neighbour, that tho' she was guilty of many Faults, yet in that particular she was innocent. Tho' *Destiny* was extremely mortify'd at the beginning of her Discourse, and made her no Answer, yet he afterwards found himself oblig'd for quietness sake, to smile now and then, and sometimes to cry out, *Oh! that's Pleasant! oh! that's strange!* both which he often spoke, however *mal à propos*. As soon as *Destiny* had done eating, the voider³ was brought and the Table cleared. Then Madam *Bouvillon* clapping herself down at the Feet of the Bed, pulled him down by her, and her Servant (letting the Waiters of the Inn go out first) leaving her likewise, drew the Door after her, and shut it. This Madam *Bouvillon* perceiving, and thinking that *Destiny* had also observ'd it, said to him, *See this foolish Jade has shut the Door after her.* To which he reply'd, *If you please, Madam, I'll go open it. No,* said she stopping him, *let it alone; but you know* continued she, *when two Persons are lock'd up together, as they have an opportunity to do what they please. People will judge of them as they think fit. 'Tis not on such Reputations as yours, Madam,* reply'd *Destiny, for People to pass such Judgments. However, Sir,* quoth *Bouvillon, one cannot have too much Caution against Slander. Well, Madam,* reply'd *Destiny, but People will not talk without Grounds, and sure they can have none when they reflect upon the Inequality of our Conditions. Will you please therefore, Madam,* continued he, *that I go open the Door. By no means, Sir,* quoth she, going to bolt it, and adding withal, *For as long as People think it shut, it is better it were really so, that no body may come in upon us without our Consent.* Having said thus much, and

---

³ "A tray, basket, or other vessel in which dirty dishes or utensils, fragments of broken food, etc., are placed in clearing the table or during a meal" (*OED*).

perform'd the Office of a Friend for herself, she turn'd towards *Destiny*, giving him to understand by her large fiery Cheeks, and little sparkling Eyes, what Sport she had a mind to be at; then she proceeded to take off her Handkerchief from her Neck, and thereby discover'd to her Lover at least ten Pounds of exuberant Flesh; that is to say, near the third part of her Bosom, the rest being distributed in two equal Portions under her Arm pits. This ill Intention of her's causing her to Blush, (which sometimes the most impudent will do) her Neck was become as red as her Face, and both together might be well taken at any distance for a Scarlet[4] Riding Cap. All this made *Destiny* to blush too, but it was with Shame, when I'll give you leave to guess what might be the cause of Madam *Bouvillon's* blushing. Then she began to complain, *that she had something troubled her in her Back*, and therefore moving her self about in her Harness, as if she had itch'd, begged of *Destiny* to thrust his Hands down her Stays to scratch her. This the Youth immediately obey'd her in, trembling all the while, but whilst he was employ'd in pleasing her behind, she diverted herself with him before, handling his Sides thro' his Wast-coat, and asking him often, *If he was not ticklish?* Whilst these Lovers were thus pleasing each other, *Ragotin* came to the Door, and knocking and bawling like to any Mad-man, call'd out aloud to *Destiny* to open to him. This *Destiny* going to perform, drew his Hand all sweaty from *Bouvillon's* Back, but offering to go between her and the Table, as the shortest cut, chanced to trip against a Nail in the Floor, which brought him down with his Head against a Bench after that violent manner, that he lay sometime for dead. Madam *Bouvillon* in the mean time catch'd up her Handkerchief, and having thrown it over her Shoulders, made all the haste she could to open the Door, which having done, and *Ragotin* pushing against it with all his force at the same time, gave the poor Lady so cruel a Blow on the Face, that it almost flatted her Nose, and also raised a bump on her Fore-head, of the bigness of one's Fist. This made her to cry out, *she was dead*; which, tho' the little Rascal heard, he nevertheless made no excuse for, but leaping and bounding about the Room like a Mad-man, bawled out, *Mrs. Angelica 's found! Mrs. Angelica's found!* This he did the louder to provoke *Destiny's* Anger, who was all this while calling for Madam *Bouvillon's* Maid to come and help her Mistress, which she nevertheless could not possibly

---

[4] *Scarron's note*: Caps which county Men use, and button about their Necks.

hear, by reason of the Noise which *Ragotin* made. At length the Servant came, and brought Water and a clean Napkin, when between her and *Destiny* there was quickly some small Reparation made for the Damage done by the Door. But however great was *Destiny*'s Impatience to know what more News *Ragotin* had brought; he notwithstanding would not leave Madam *Bouvillon* till her Face was wash'd and anointed, and her Fore-head bound up with a Bandage. At last he offer'd to be gone, but that calling *Ragotin* a thousand Rogues for the Mischief he had done on the one Hand, while *Ragotin* drew him after him on the other, to give him a farther account of his Message.

Ethics and Theology

The selections in this section concern the proper relationship between ethics—that is, the study and practice of morality—and theology, the study of the doctrines of (here Christian) religion. Should ethics be independent from or dependent on theology? Within Christianity, should ethics be subordinated to theology, or is ethics the core of religion? These are questions explicitly raised in Parson Adams's conversation with Parson Barnabas (I.16–17) and implicitly pursued by Fielding throughout the novel.

My first selection is from John Tillotson (1630–94), archbishop of Canterbury (1691–94), whose sermons remained popular through Fielding's day. The sermon reproduced here suggests by its very title—"The Example of Jesus in Doing Good"—that for Tillotson ethics is the essence of Christianity. According to Tillotson, virtuous action recommends itself to us first of all on account of the "joy and delight" it brings with it. Only secondarily does Tillotson offer as a motive to do good the eternal, heavenly reward that awaits the virtuous person.

Our next author, Anthony Ashley Cooper, the third earl of Shaftesbury (1671–1713), is a philosopher who radically severed ethics from theology. Shaftesbury argues that to follow virtue for the sake of a reward, such as eternal bliss, is not to act virtuously but rather to act like a mercenary. Fielding alludes to Shaftesbury's notion of disinterested virtue when he claims, in an essay excerpted below, that "good nature" prompts us to act so as to bring about the good of others "without the allurements or terrors of religion"—that is, without thinking on eternal rewards and punishments. Yet Fielding adds that the good-natured person acts "without any abstract contemplation on the beauty of virtue," and so dissociates himself from Shaftesbury's corresponding doctrine that exercising

*goodness is not only delightful but also "beautiful" to "contempla-
tion." In Joseph Andrews we see the doctrine of virtue's "intrinsic
beauty" satirized within Mr. Wilson's tale (III.3).*

*The final selection in this section is from George Whitefield
(1714–70), one of the founders of modern Christian evangelicalism
and a popular, relentless preacher in both Britain and the American
colonies. Whitefield set theology before ethics: to be a good person,
he declaimed, falls short of being a Christian. For Whitefield, only
those who have been "born again" in Christ through the Holy
Spirit are true (as opposed to merely "nominal") Christians. Only
these will be saved, and they will be saved through Christ's atoning
sacrifice, not through any good works they may or may not do. Parson Adams calls this a "detestable doctrine" (I. 17).*

✤ John Tillotson
From SERMON XVIII, "The Example of Jesus in doing Good"[1]

ACTS X 38.

——*Who went about doing good*

WHEN Almighty God designed the Reformation of the World and
the restoring of man to the Image of God, the Pattern after which he
was first made, he did not think it enough to give us the most perfect Laws of holiness and virtue; but hath likewise set before us a
living Pattern, and a familiar example to excite and encourage us,
to go before us and shew us the way, and as it were to lead us by the
hand in the obedience of those Laws. Such is the Sovereign Authority of God over men that he might, if he had pleased, have only
given us a Law written with his own hand, as he did to the people of
Israel from Mount *Sinai*: but such is his Goodness, that he hath sent
a great Ambassador from Heaven to us, *God manifested in the
Flesh*, to declare and interpret his will and pleasure; and not only
so, but to fulfil that Law himself, the observation whereof he
requires of us. The bare Rules of a good life are a very dead and
ineffectual thing in comparison of a living Example, which shews us
the possibility and practicableness of our Duty; both that it may be

---

[1] From *The Works of the Most Reverend Dr. John Tillotson*, 3rd edition, London,
1701, pp. 190–99.

done, and how to do it. Religion indeed did always consist in an Imitation of God, and in our resemblance of those excellencies which shine forth in the best and most perfect Being; but we may imitate him now with much greater ease and advantage, since God was pleased to become man on purpose to shew us how men may become like to God. And this is one great end for which the Son of God came into the world, and *was made flesh, and dwelt among us*, and conversed so long and familiarly with mankind; that in his own Person and Life he might give us the Example of all that holiness and virtue which his Laws require of us. And as he was in nothing liker the Son of God than in being and doing good, so is he in nothing a fitter Pattern for our imitation than in that excellent Character given of him here in the Text, That *He went about doing good* . . .

To do Good is the most pleasant employment in the World. It is natural; and whatever is so is delightful. We do like our selves whenever we relieve the wants and distresses of others. And therefore this Virtue among all other hath peculiarly entituled it self to the name of *Humanity*. We answer our own Nature, and obey our Reason and shew our selves Men in shewing mercy to the miserable. Whenever we consider the evils and afflictions of others, we do with the greatest reason collect our Duty from our nature and inclination, and make our own wishes and desires and expectations from others a law and rule to our selves. And this is pleasant, to follow our nature and to gratify the importunate Dictates of our own Reason. So that the benefits we do to others are not more welcome to them that receive them, than they are delightful to us that do them. We ease our own nature and bowels, whenever we help and relieve, those who are in want and necessity. As on the contrary, no man that hath not divested himself of humanity can be cruel and hardhearted to others without feeling some pain in himself. There is no sensual pleasure in the world comparable to the delight and satisfaction that a good man takes in doing good. This *Cato* in *Tully* boasts of as the great comfort and joy of his old age, *That nothing was more pleasant to him than the Conscience of a well-spent life, and the remembrance of many benefits and kindnesses done to others*. Sensual pleasures are not lasting, but presently vanish and expire; but that is not the worst of them, they leave a sting behind them, as the pleasure goes off.

—*Succedit frigida cura*.[2]

---

[2] "Cold cares come next."

Sadness and melancholy come in the place of it, guilt and trouble and repentance follow it. But the pleasure of doing good remains after a thing is done, the thoughts of it lie easy in our minds, and the reflection upon it afterwards does for ever minister joy and delight to us. In a word, that frame of mind which inclines us to do good is the very temper and disposition of happiness. *Solomon,* after all his experience of worldly pleasures, pitches at last upon this as the greatest felicity of human life, and the only good use that is to be made of a prosperous and plentiful fortune, *Eccl.3.12. I know that there is no good in them, but for a man to rejoice and do good in his life.* And a greater and a wiser than Solomon hath said that *it is more blessed to give than to receive.*

To employ our selves in doing good is to imitate the highest Excellency and Perfection. It is to be like God *who is good and doth good,* and to be like him in that which he esteems his greatest glory, and that is, his Goodness. It is to be like the Son of God who when he took our nature upon him, and lived in the World, *went about doing good.* It is to be like the blessed Angels, whose great employment it is to be *ministring Spirits for the Good of others.* To be charitable and helpful and beneficial to others, is to be a good Angel and a Saviour and a God to men. And the Example of our blessed Saviour more especially is the great Pattern which our Religion propounds to us. And we have all the reason in the world to be in love with it; because that very goodness which it propounds to our imitation, was so beneficial to our selves: when we our selves feel and enjoy the happy effects of that good which he did in the world, this should mightily endear the Example to us, and make us forward to imitate that love and kindness to which we are indebted for so many blessings, and upon which all our hopes of happiness do depend.

And there is this considerable difference between our Saviour's Charity to us, and ours to others: He did all purely for our sakes and for our benefit, whereas all the good we do to others is a greater good done to our selves. They indeed are beholden to us for the kindness we do them, and we to them for the opportunity of doing it. Every ignorant person that comes in our way to be instructed by us, every sinner whom we reclaim, every poor man we relieve, is a happy opportunity of doing good to our selves, and of *laying up for our selves a good treasure against the time which is to come, that we may lay hold on eternal life.* By this principle the best and the happiest man that ever was, governed his life and actions, esteeming it *a more blessed thing to give than to receive.*

❧ Anthony Ashely Cooper, third earl of SHAFTESBURY
From *An INQUIRY concerning* VIRTUE AND MERIT[1]

NOW, as to the Belief of a DEITY, and how Men are influenc'd by it; we may consider, in the first place, on what account Men yield Obedience, and act in conformity to such a Supreme Being. It must be either *in the way of his* POWER, as presupposing some Disadvantage or Benefit, to accrue from him: or *in the way of his* EXCELLENCY and WORTH, as thinking it the Perfection of Nature to imitate and resemble him.

IF (as in the first Cafe) there be a Belief or Conception of a DEITY, who is consider'd only as *powerful* over his Creature, and inforcing Obedience to his *abolute Will* by particular Rewards and Punishments; and if on this account, thro Hope merely of *Reward*, or Fear of *Punishment*, the Creature be incited to do the Good he hates, or restrain'd from doing the Ill to which he is not otherwise in the least degree averse; there is in this Case (as has been already shewn) no Virtue or Goodness whatsoever. The Creature, notwithstanding his good Conduct, is intrinsically of as little Worth, as if he acted in his natural way, when under no Dread or Terrour of any sort. There is no more of *Rectitude, Piety,* or *Sanctity* in a Creature thus reform'd, than there is *Meekness* or *Gentleness* in a Tyger strongly chain'd, or *Innocence* and *Sobriety* in a Monkey under the Discipline of the Whip. For however orderly and well those Animals, or Man himself upon like Terms, may be induc'd to act, whilst the Will is neither gain'd, nor the Inclination wrought upon, but *Awe* alone prevails and forces Obedience; the Obedience is *servile,* and all which is done thro it, merely servile. The greater degree of such a Submission or Obedience, is only the greater *Servility;* whatever may be the Object. For, whether such a Creature has a good Master, or an ill one, he is neither more or less servile in his own nature. Be the Master or Superiour ever so perfect, or excellent, yet the greater Submission caus'd in this Case, thro this sole Principle or Motive, is only the lower and more abject Servitude, and implies the greater Wretchedness and Meanness in the

---

[1] From Shaftesbury's collection, *Characteristics of Men, Manners, Opinions, Times,* 3 vols., London, 1715. The following selections are from *An Inquiry concerning Virtue and Merit,* Book 1, Part 3, section 3 (2:54–56), and Book 2, Part 2, section 1 (2:99–108).

Creature, who has those Passions of Self-Love so predominant, and is in his Temper so vitious and defective, as has been explain'd.

As to the second Case. If there be a Belief or Conception of a DEITY, who is consider'd as *Worthy* and *Good,* and admir'd and reverenc'd as such; being understood to have, besides mere Power and Knowledg, the highest Excellence of Nature, such as renders him justly amiable to All; and if in the manner this Sovereign and mighty Being is represented, or as he is historically describ'd, there appears in him a high and eminent regard to what is good and excellent, a Concern for the good of *All,* and an Affection of Benevolence and Love towards *the Whole;* such an Example must undoubtedly serve (as above explain'd) to raise and increase the Affection towards Virtue, and help to submit and subdue all other Affections to that alone.

* * *

To begin therefore with this Proof, "THAT TO HAVE THE NATURAL AFFECTIONS (such as are founded in Love, Complacency, Good-will, and in a Sympathy with the Kind or Species) is TO HAVE THE CHIEF MEANS AND POWER OF SELF-ENJOYMENT: *And* THAT TO WANT THEM IS CERTAIN MISERY AND ILL."

WE may inquire, first, what those are, which we call *Pleasures* or *Satisfaction* from whence Happiness is generally computed. They are (according to the common distinction) either Satisfactions and Pleasures *of the Body,* or *of the Mind.*

THAT *the latter of these Satisfactions are the greatest,* is allow'd by most People, and may be prov'd by this: That whenever the Mind, having conceiv'd a high Opinion of the Worth of any Action or Behaviour, has received the strongest Impression of this sort, and is wrought up to the highest pitch or degree of Passion towards the Subject; at such time it sets it-self above all bodily Pain as well as Pleasure, and can be no-way diverted from its purpose by Flattery or Terrour of any kind. Thus we see *Indians, Barbarians, Malefactors,* and even the most execrable Villains, for the sake of a particular Gang or Society, or thro some cherish'd Notion or Principle of Honour or Gallantry, Revenge, or Gratitude, embrace any manner of Hardship, and defy Torments and Death. Whereas, on the other hand, a Person being plac'd in all the happy Circumstances of outward Enjoyment, surrounded with every thing which can allure or charm the Sense, and being then actually in the very moment of such a pleasing Indulgence; yet no sooner is there anything amiss *within,* no sooner has he conceiv'd any *internal Ail or Disorder,* any thing *inwardly* vexatious or distemper'd, than instantly his Enjoyment ceases, the pleasure of Sense is at an end; and every means of that sort becomes ineffectual, and is rejected as uneasy, and subject to give Distaste.

THE *Pleasures of the Mind* being allow'd, therefore, superiour to those of the *Body;* it follows, "That whatever can create in any intelligent Being a constant flowing Series or Train of mental Enjoyments, or Pleasures of the Mind, is more considerable to his Happiness, than that which can create to him a like constant Course or Train of sensual Enjoyments, or Pleasures of the Body."

NOW the mental Enjoyments are either actually the very natural Affections themselves in their immediate Operation: Or they wholly in a manner proceed from them, and are no other than their Effects.

IF so; it follows, that the natural Affections duly establish'd in a rational Creature, being the only means which can procure him a constant Series or Succession of the mental Enjoyments, they are the only means which can procure him a certain and solid *Happiness.*

NOW, in the first place, to explain, "How much *the natural Affections are in themselves the highest Pleasures and Enjoyments:*" There shou'd methinks be little need of proving this to any-one of Human Kind, who has ever known the Condition of the Mind under a lively Affection of Love, Gratitude, Bounty, Generosity, Succour, or whatever else is of a social or friendly sort. He who has ever so little Knowledg of human Nature, is sensible what pleasure the Mind perceives when it is touch'd in this generous way. The difference we find between Solitude and Company, between a common Company and that of Friends; the reference of almost all our Pleasures to mutual Converse, and the dependence they have on Society either present or imagin'd; all these are sufficient Proofs in our behalf.

HOW much the social Pleasures are superiour to any other, may be known by visible Tokens and Effects. The very outward Features, the Marks and Signs which attend this sort of Joy, are expressive of a more intense, clear, and undisturb'd Pleasure, than those which attend the Satisfaction of Thirst, Hunger, and other ardent Appetites. But more particularly still may this Superiority be known, from the actual Prevalence and Ascendency of this sort of Affection over all besides. Wherever it presents it-self with any advantage, it silences and appeases every other Motion of Pleasure.

No Joy, merely of Sense, can be a Match for it. Whoever is Judg of *both* the Pleasures, will ever give the preference to *the former*. But to be able to judg of both, 'tis necessary to have a Sense of each. The honest Man indeed can judg of *sensual Pleasure,* and knows its utmost Force. For neither is his Taste, or Sense, the duller; but, on the contrary, the more intense and clear, on the account of his Temperance, and a moderate Use of Appetite. But the immoral and profligate Man can by no means be allow'd a good Judg of *social Pleasure,* to which he is so mere a Stranger by his Nature.

NOR is it any Objection here: that in many Natures the good Affection, tho really present, is found to be of insufficient force. For where it is not *in its natural degree,* 'tis the same indeed as if it *were not,* or had *never been.* The less there is of this good Affection in any untoward Creature, the greater the wonder is, that it shou'd *at any time* prevail; as in the very worst of Creatures it sometimes will. And if it prevails but for *once,* in any *single* Instance; it shews evidently, that if the Affection were thorowly experienc'd or known, it wou'd prevail *in all.*

THUS *the* CHARM of kind Affection is superiour to all other Pleasure: since it has the power of drawing from every other Appetite or Inclination. And thus in the Case of Love to the Offspring, and a thousand other Instances, *the Charm* is found to operate so strongly on the Temper, as, in the midst of other Temptations, to render it susceptible of this Passion alone; which remains as the *Master-Pleasure* and *Conqueror* of the rest.

THERE is no-one who, by the least progress in Science or Learning, has come to know barely the Principles of *Mathematicks,* but has found, that in the exercise of his Mind on the Discoverys he there makes, tho merely of speculative Truths, he receives a Pleasure and Delight superiour to that of Sense. When we have thorowly search'd into the nature of this contemplative Delight, we shall find it of a kind which relates not in the least to any private Interest of the Creature, nor has for its Object any Self-Good or Advantage of the private System. The Admiration, Joy, or Love, turns wholly upon what is exteriour, and foreign to our-selves. And tho the reflected Joy or Pleasure, which arises from the notice of this Pleasure once perceiv'd, may be interpreted a *Self-Passion,* or *interested Regard*: yet the original Satisfaction can be no other than what results from the Love of Truth, Proportion, Order, and Symmetry, in the Things without. If this be the Case, the Passion ought in reality to be rank'd with *natural Affection*. For having no Object within the compass of the private System; it must either be esteem'd superfluous and *unnatural* (as having no Tendency towards the Advantage or Good of any thing in Nature) or it must be judg'd to be, what it truly is, "A natural Joy in the Contemplation of those *Numbers,* that *Harmony, Proportion,* and *Concord,* which supports the universal Nature, and is essential in the Constitution and Form of every particular Species, or Order of Beings."

But this speculative Pleasure, however *considerable* or valuable it may be, or however superiour to any Motion of mere Sense; must yet be far surpass'd by *virtuous Motion,* and *the Exercise of Benignity and Goodness*; where, together with the most delightful Affection of the Soul, there is join'd a pleasing Assent and Approbation of the Mind to what is acted in this good Disposition and honest Bent. For where is there on Earth a fairer Matter of Speculation, a goodlier View or Contemplation, than that of a *beautiful, proportion'd,* and *becoming* Action? Or what is there relating to us, of which the Consciousness and Memory is more solidly and lastingly entertaining?

We may observe that in the Passion of Love between the Sexes, where, together with the Affection of a *vulgar* sort, there is a mixture of the *kind and friendly,* the Sense or Feeling of this *latter* is in reality superior to the former since often thro this Affection, and for the sake of the Person belov'd, the greatest Hardships in the World have been submitted to, and even Death it-self voluntarily imbrac'd, without any expected *Compensation.* For where shou'd the Ground of such an Expectation lie? Not *here* in *this World, surely*; for Death puts an end to all. Nor yet *hereafter,* in *any other.* For who has ever thought of providing a Heaven or future Recompence for the suffering Virtue of Lovers?

We may observe, withal, in favour of the natural Affections, that it is not only when Joy and Sprightliness are mix'd with them, that they carry a real Enjoyment above that of the sensual kind. The very Disturbances which belong to natural Affection, tho they may be thought wholly contrary to Pleasure, yield still a Contentment and Satisfaction greater than the Pleasures of indulg'd Sense. And where a Series or continu'd Succession of the tender and kind Affections can be carry'd on, even thro Fears, Horrours, Sorrows, Griefs: the Emotion of the Soul is still agreeable. We continue pleas'd even with this melancholy Aspect or Sense of Virtue. Her Beauty supports it-self under a Cloud, and in the midst of surrounding Calamitys.

For thus, when, by mere Illusion, as in *a Tragedy*, the Passions of this kind are skilfully excited in us; we prefer the Entertainment to any other of equal duration. We find by our-selves, that the moving our Passions in this mournful way, the engaging them in behalf of Merit and Worth, and the exerting whatever we have of social Affection, and human Sympathy, is of the highest Delight, and affords a greater Enjoyment in the way of *Thought and Sentiment*, than any thing be-sides can do in a way of Sense and *common Appetite*. And after this manner it appears, "How much *the mental Enjoyments are actually the very natural Affections themselves.*"

Now, in the next place, to explain, "How they *proceed from them*, as their natural *Effects*:" we may consider first, That the EFFECTS of Love or kind Affection, in a way of mental Pleasure, are, "*An Enjoyment of Good by Communication. A receiving it, as it were, by Reflection, or by way of Participation in the Good of others.*" And "*A pleasing Consciousness of the actual Love, merited Esteem or Approbation of others.*"

How considerable a part of Happiness arises from the former of these Effects, will be easily apprehended by one who is not exceedingly ill-natur'd. It will be consider'd how many the Pleasures are, of *sharing Contentment and Delight with others;* of receiving it in Fellowship and Company; and gathering it, in a manner, from the pleas'd and happy States of those around us, from accounts and relations of such Happinesses, from the very Countenances, Gestures, Voices and Sounds, even of Creatures foreign to our Kind, whose Signs of Joy and Contentment we can any-way discern. So insinuating are these Pleasures of Sympathy, and so widely diffus'd thro our whole Lives, that there is hardly such a thing as Satisfaction or Contentment, of which they make not an essential part.

✣ Henry Fielding
From *The Champion* (March 27, 1740)[1]

Good-nature is a Delight in the Happiness of Mankind, and a Concern at their Misery, with a Desire, as much as Possible, to procure the former, and avert the latter; and this, with a constant Regard to Desert.

---

[1] In Fielding, *The Champion: containing a series of papers humorous, moral, political, and critical*, 2 vols. (London, 1743), 2:39–41.

Good-nature is not that Weakness, which, without Distinction, affects both the Virtuous and the Base, and equally laments the Punishment of Villainy, with the Disappointment of Merit; for as this amiable Quality respects the whole, so it must give up the Particular, to the Good of General.

It is not that Cowardice which prevents us from repelling or resenting an Injury; for it doth not divest us of Humanity, and like Charity, tho' it doth not end, may at least begin at home . . .

That to be averse to, and repine at the Punishment of Vice and Villainy, is not the Mark of Good nature but Folly; on the contrary, to bring a *real* and *great* Criminal to Justice, is, perhaps, the best-natured Office we can perform to Society, and the Prosecutor, the Juryman, the Judge, and the Hangman himself may do their Duty without injuring this Character; nay, the last Office, if properly employed, may be in Truth the best natured, as well as the highest post of Honour in the Kingdom . . .

Lastly, that as Good-nature is a Delight in the Happiness of Mankind, every good-natured Man will do his utmost to contribute to the Happiness of each Individual; and consequently that every Man who is not a Villain, if he loves not the good-natured Man, is guilty of Ingratitude.

❖ Henry Fielding
From "An Essay on the Knowledge of the Characters of Men"[1]

Men are chiefly betrayed . . . by a gross but common Mistake of Good-Humour for Good-Nature. Two Qualities so far from bearing any Resemblance to each other, that they are almost Opposites. Good-Nature is that benevolent and amiable Temper of Mind which disposes us to feel the Misfortunes, and enjoy the Happiness of others; and consequently pushes us on to promote the latter, and prevent the former; and that without any abstract Contemplation on the Beauty of Virtue, and without the Allurements or Terrors of Religion. Now Good-Humour is nothing more than the Triumph of the Mind, when reflecting on its own Happiness, and that perhaps from having compared it with the inferior Happiness of others.

---

[1] In Fielding, *Miscellanies*, 3 vols. (London, 1743), 1:189–90.

✤ George Whitefield
From *Sermon I*, "Of Our New Birth in CHRIST JESUS"[1]

2 COR. V. 17.

If any Man be in CHRIST, he is a new Creature

THE Doctrine of our REGENERATION, or NEW BIRTH IN CHRIST JESUS, tho' one of the most fundamental Doctrines of our holy Religion; though so plainly and often pressed on us in Sacred Writ, *that he that runs may read*; nay, though it is the very Hinge on which the Salvation of each of us turns, and a Point too in which all *sincere Christians*, of whatever Denomination, agree; yet it is so seldom considered, and so little *experimentally* understood by the Generality of Professors, that were we to judge of the Truth of it by the *Experience* of most who call themselves Christians, we should be apt to imagine they had not so much as heard whether there be any such thing as *Regeneration* or no. It is true, Men, for the most part, are Orthodox in the common Articles of their Creed; they believe there is but one GOD, and one Mediator between GOD and Man, even the Man CHRIST JESUS; and that there is no other Name given under Heaven, whereby they can be saved, besides His: But then tell them, They must be REGENERATE, they must be BORN AGAIN, they must be renewed in the very *Spirit, i.e.* in the *inmost* Faculties of their Minds, e'er they can truly call CHRIST *Lord, Lord*, or have any Share in the Merits of his precious Blood; and they are ready to cry out with *Nicodemus, How can these things be?*[2] or, with the *Athenians*, on another Occasion, *what will this Babbler say?*[3] *He seemeth to be a Setter-forth of strange Doctrines, because we preach unto them* CHRIST, *and the New Birth* . . .

IF he that is in CHRIST must be a *new Creature*, then this may check the groundless Presumption of another Class of Professors, who rest in the Attainment of some Moral Virtues, and falsely imagine they are *good Christians*; if they are just in their Dealings, or temperate in their Diet, and do Hurt or Violence to no Man.

---

[1] In *Sermons on Various Subjects* (London, 1739), pp. 5–24.

[2] John 3:9. John 3:1–8 concerns re-birth in the Spirit.

[3] Acts 17:18.

BUT if this was all that is requisite to make us *Christians,* Why might not the Heathens of Old be *good Christians,* who were remarkable for these Virtues? Or St. *Paul,* before his Conversion, who tells us, That then he lived in all good Conscience, and was, touching the Law, blameless? And yet, after his Conversion, we find he renounces all Dependance on Works of this Nature, and only desires to be found in CHRIST, and to know the Power of his Resurrection; *i.e.* to have an experimental Proof of receiving the HOLY GHOST, purchased for him by the Death, and insured and applied to him by the Resurrection of JESUS CHRIST.

THE SUM of the Matter is this: Christianity includes Morality, as Grace does Reason; but if we are only mere *Moralists,* if we are not *inwardly* wrought upon, and changed by the powerful Operations of the *Holy Spirit,* and our Moral Actions proceed from a Principle of a *new* Nature, however we may call ourselves *Christians,* it is to be feared we shall be found naked at the Great Day, and in the Number of those, who vainly depend on their own Righteousness, and not on the Righteousness of JESUS CHRIST, imputed to and inherent in them, as necessary to their eternal Salvation.

NOR . . . will this Doctrine less condemn those, who rest in a Partial Amendment of themselves, without going on to Perfection, and experiencing a thorough, real, inward Change of Heart.

The Psychology of Laughter

What does it mean to laugh at someone or something? Thomas Hobbes in his 1650 work *Human Nature* (IX.13) argued that we laugh only at persons or things that we consider beneath us. This Hobbesian argument was refined by Joseph Addison (1672–1719) in issue no. 47 of the immensely influential periodical series he conducted with Richard Steele, *The Spectator* (1711–12, revived by Addison alone from June to December 1714). An excerpted version of this essay appears below.

✤ From Joseph Addison
Spectator, no. 47 (April 24, 1711)[1]

MR. *Hobbs,* in his Discourse of Human Nature, which, in my humble Opinion, is much the best of all his Works, after some very curious Observations upon Laughter, concludes thus: 'The Passion of Laughter is nothing else but sudden Glory arising from some sudden Conception of some Eminency in our selves, by Comparison with the Infirmity of others, or with our own formerly: For Men laugh at the Follies of themselves past, when they come suddenly to Remembrance, except they bring with them any present Dishonour.'

ACCORDING to this Author, therefore, when we hear a Man laugh excessively, instead of saying he is very Merry, we ought to tell him he is very Proud. And indeed, if we look into the bottom of this Matter, we shall meet with many Observations to confirm us in his Opinion. Every one laughs at some Body that is in an inferior State

---

[1] In *The Spectator*, 2nd ed., 2 vols. (London, 1713), 1:178–81.

of Folly to himself. It was formerly the Custom for every great House in *England* to keep a tame Fool dressed in Petticoats, that the Heir of the Family might have an opportunity of joking upon him and diverting himself with his Absurdities. For the same Reason Idiots are still in request in most of the Courts of *Germany*, where there is not a Prince of any great Magnificence who has not two or three dressed, distinguished, undisputed Fools in his Retinue, whom the rest of the Courtiers are always breaking their Jests upon.

THE *Dutch*, who are more famous for their Industry and Application, than for Wit and Humour, hang up in several of their Streets what they call the Sign of the *Gaper*, that is, the Head of an Idiot dressed in a Cap and Bells, and gaping in a most immoderate manner: This is a standing Jest at *Amsterdam*.

THUS every one diverts himself with some Person or other that is below him in Point of Understanding, and triumphs in the Superiority of his Genius, whilst he has such Objects of Derision before his Eyes . . .

MR. Hobbs's Reflection gives us the Reason why the insignificant People above-mentioned are Stirrers up of Laughter among Men of a gross Taste: But as the more understanding Part of Mankind do not find their Risibility affected by such ordinary Objects, it may be worth the while to examine into the several Provocatives of Laughter in Men of superior Sense and Knowledge.

IN the first Place I must observe, that there is a Set of merry Drolls, whom the common People of all Countries admire, and seem to love so well, *that they could eat them,* according to the old Proverb: I mean those circumforaneous[2] Wits whom every Nation calls by the Name of that Dish of Meat which it loves best. In Holland they are termed *Pickled Herrings*; in *France, Jean Pottages;* in *Italy, Maccaronies;* and in *Great Britain, Jack Puddings.* These merry Wags, from whatsoever Food they receive their Titles, that they may make their Audiences laugh, always appear in a Fool's Coat, and commit such Blunders and Mistakes in every Step they take, and every Word they utter, as those who listen to them would be ashamed of . . .

THUS we see, in proportion as one Man is more refined than another, he chuses his Fool out of a lower or higher Class of Mankind; or, to speak in a more Philosophical Language, That

---

[2] "Strolling from market to market; wandering, vagrant, vagabond" (*OED*).

secret Elation and Pride of Heart which is generally called Laughter, arises in him from his comparing himself with an Object below him, whether it so happens that it be a Natural or an Artificial Fool. It is indeed very possible, that the Persons we laugh at may in the main of their Characters be much wiser Men than our selves; but if they would have us laugh at them, they must fall short of us in those Respects which stir up this Passion.

I am afraid I shall appear too Abstracted in my Speculations, if I shew that when a Man of Wit makes us laugh, it is by betraying some Oddness or Infirmity in his own Character, or in the Representation which he makes of others; and that when we laugh at a Brute or even at an inanimate thing, it is at some Action or Incident that bears a remote Analogy to any Blunder or Absurdity in reasonable Creatures.

BUT to come into common Life: I shall pass by the Consideration of those Stage Coxcombs that are able to shake a whole Audience, and take Notice of a particular sort of Men who are such Provokers of Mirth in Conversation, that it is impossible for a Club or Merrymeeting to subsist without them; I mean those honest Gentlemen that are always exposed to the Wit and Raillery of their Well-wishers and Companions; that are pelted by Men, Women, and Children, Friends, and Foes, and, in a word, stand as *Butts* in Conversation, for every one to shoot at that pleases. I know several of these *Butts* who are Men of Wit and Sense, though by some odd Turn of Humour, some unlucky Cast in their Person or Behaviour, they have always the Misfortune to make the Company merry. The Truth of it is, a Man is not qualified for a *Butt*, who has not a good deal of Wit and Vivacity, even in the ridiculous Side of his Character. A stupid *Butt* is only fit for the Conversation of ordinary People: Men of Wit require one that will give them Play, and bestir himself in the absurd Part of his Behaviour. A *Butt* with these Accomplishments frequently gets the Laugh of his Side, and turns the Ridicule upon Him that attacks him. Sir John Falstaff was an Hero of this Species, and gives a good Description of himself in his Capacity of a *Butt*, after the following manner; *Men of all sorts* (says that merry Knight) *take a Pride to gird at me. The Brain of Man is not able to invent any thing that tends to Laughter more than I invent, or is invented on me. I am not only Witty in my self, but the Cause that Wit is in other Men.*[3]

---

[3] Shakespeare, *The Second Part of King Henry the Fourth*, 1.2.

What Contemporaries Said

Joseph Andrews *received just one contemporary review, by the French cleric Pierre-François Guyot Desfontaines in his journal* Observations sur les écrits modernes *(July 1743), pp. 189–91. Desfontaines expressed admiration for the novel and soon after translated it into French. He remarked on the novel's acclaim among English readers: they consider it, he says, "at least equal" to* Don Quixote *and* Scarron's *Roman Comique. Be that as it may, English journals did not review the book, presumably because the romance or novel was not yet a reputable literary genre. Still, Fielding's novel sold well, 6500 copies in little more than a year. Fielding secured his prominence in 1749 with the publication of his next novel,* Tom Jones, A Foundling; *in 1751, an anonymous author, perhaps Francis Coventry, paid him the tribute of a book-length* Essay on the New Species of Writing Founded by Mr. Fielding, *excerpted below. My third selection comes from the Prologue to Part V of Sarah Fielding's novel* The Cry: A New Dramatic Fable, *3 vols. (1754), 3:121–24. Sarah here argues against the trend of seeing Parson Adams as an object of ridicule or butt of laughter. She censures those who fixate on farcical moments such as "the hounds trailing the bacon in his pocket" (*Joseph Andrews *III.6). We may note that one such person appears to have been James Hulett, whose illustrations to the third edition of the novel include a frolicsome rendition of this scene (reprinted in Illustration 6, p. 227). I conclude this section with an excerpt from James Boswell's* The Life of Samuel Johnson *(1791) that records Johnson's preference for Richardson over Fielding and Boswell's spirited rejoinder in favor of Fielding's moral art.*

✤ Pierre-Françoise Guyot Desfontaines[1]
Review of *Joseph Andrews* (July 1743)

There appeared in England last summer a work that the English place above all other novels that have ever existed, or deem at least the equal of *The Adventures of Don Quixote* and Scarron's *Roman Comique*. It is titled *The History of the Adventures of Joseph Andrews, and his Friend Abraham Adams, Written in Imitation of the Manner of Cervantes*, London 1742, in two 12 volumes. It is a judicious and moral novel, full of salt [wit] and pleasing qualities, without the least stain of libertinage either of mind or of heart; it makes us love virtue and is infinitely interesting. Both its central action and its embellishing episodes are charming. The denouement, although anticipated from the beginning, comes into view only in the last chapter, and cannot be guessed at earlier; thus up till the end the uncertain reader doesn't know what will be the outcome of the novel's ingenious imbroglio. The style is everywhere comic except for the passages which interest us in a tender and lawful love. *Joseph Andrews* is the brother of Pamela, who appears on the scene towards the end of the second volume, along with the English nobleman who has married her, and who brings about the most heart-warming state of affairs [at the novel's end]. Finally, I do not fear to assure you that England has never before produced so perfect a work in this genre. Moreover, this is not a vain and frivolous work; rather, it instructs the reader in English character and customs, which are not at all known in France, and it teaches a hundred particulars worth the attention of even the gravest persons. The author is Mr. Fielding, one of the best comic poets in England. The dialogue is another excellent part of the book. There are throughout depictions that are lively, natural, fine, even delicate, always pleasing and sometimes uproariously funny. This is the judgment I dare draw from the English original that has been sent to me, and that I read with great pleasure. If this excellent work should appear in French, as it seems likely it will, the reading public should hope that this service won't be rendered by some ignorant refugee[2] who will

---

[1] Review of *Joseph Andrews* from *Observations sur les écrits modernes* [*Observations on modern writings*] (July 1743), pp. 189–91. (Translated from the French by the editor.)

[2] *Réfugiés* were Calvinists who fled Catholic France to avoid religious persecution; many settled in Protestant England.

disfigure the novel, as most English novels have been disfigured by translators up to now. The English, to revenge their authors, often render our books the same service.

❧ Anonymous [Francis Coventry?]
From *An Essay on the New Species of Writing Founded by Mr. Fielding*[1]

I shall now begin to take a critical Review of these Histories in general, in performing which, if even Mr. *Fielding* himself does not confess that my Proceeding is impartial, I'll be content to send him my Name, that he may punish me *propria persona* in the next humorous Piece he publishes.

Sometime before this new Species of Writing appear'd, the World had been pester'd with Volumes, commonly known by the Name of Romances, or Novels, Tales, &c. fill'd with any thing which the wildest Imagination could suggest. In all these Works, Probability was not required: The more extravagant the Thought, the more exquisite the Entertainment. Diamond Palaces, flying Horses, brazen Towers, &c. were here look'd upon as proper, and in Taste. In short, the most finish'd Piece of this kind, was nothing but Chaos and Incoherency. *France* first gave Birth to this strange Monster, and *England* was proud to import it among the rest of her Neighbour's Follies. A Deluge of Impossibility overflow'd the Press. Nothing was receiv'd with any kind of Applause, that did not appear under the Title of a Romance, or Novel; and Common Sense was kick'd out of Doors to make Room for marvellous Dullness. The Stile in all these Performances was to be equal to the Subject— amazing: And may be call'd with great Propriety, 'Prose run mad.' This obtain'd a long Time. Every Beau was an *Orondates*, and all the Belles were *Stariras*:[2] Not a *Billet-doux* but run in Heroics, or the most common Message deliver'd but in the Sublime. The Disease became epidemical, but there were no Hopes of a Cure, 'till Mr. *Fielding* endeavour'd to show the World, that pure Nature could furnish out as agreeable Entertainment, as those airy non-entical

---

[1] *An Essay on the New Species of Writing Founded by Mr. Fielding* (London, 1751), pp. 13–20.

[2] Hero and heroine names from seventeenth century French romances. A "*Billet-doux*" is a love letter.

Forms they had long ador'd, and persuaded the Ladies to leave this Extravagance to their *Abigails*[3] with their cast Cloaths. Amongst which Order of People, it has ever since been observ'd to be peculiarly predominant.

His Design of Reformation was noble and public-spirited, but the Talk was not quite so easy to perform, since it requir'd an uncommon Genius. For to tread the old beaten Track would be to no Purpose. Lecture would lose its Force; and Ridicule would strive in vain to remove it. For tho' it was a Folly, it was a pleasing one: And if Sense could not yield the pretty Creatures greater Pleasure, Dear Nonsense must be ador'd.

Mr. *Fielding* therefore, who sees all the little Movements by which human Nature is actuated, found it necessary to open a new Vein of Humour, and thought the only way to make them lay down *Cassandra* would be to compile Characters which really existed, equally entertaining with those Chimæras which were beyond Conception. This Thought produced *Joseph Andrews*, which soon became a formidable Rival to the *amazing* Class of Writers; since it was not a mere dry Narrative, but a lively Representative of real Life. For chrystal Palaces and winged Horses, we find homely Cots and ambling Nags; and instead of Impossibility, what we experience every Day.

But as Mr. *Fielding* first introduc'd this new kind of Biography, he restrain'd it with Laws which should ever after be deem'd sacred by all that attempted his Manner; which I here propose to give a brief Account of. The first and grand one of all, (without which, in however regular a Manner the rest is conducted, the whole Performance must be dead and languid) is, that thro' the whole Humour must diffuse itself. But this can by no Means be perform'd without a great Genius, nay, even a particular Sort of one: for tho' Mr. *Bayes* informs us, any Man may commence Poet by his infallible Rules;[4] yet in this Kind of Writing he must be at a Stand without this grand Requisite. But to proceed.

The next Thing to be consider'd, is the Choice of Characters, which tho' striking and particular must be exactly copied from

---

[3] Stock name for a lady's maid.

[4] Bayes is a ridiculous figure in *The Rehearsal* (1671), a play by George Villiers, Duke of Buckingham; he expounds his rules for (bad) dramatic writing in Act 1, scene 1.

Nature. And who can doubt, when they see the Features of an *Abraham Adams*, or *Madam Slipslop*, faithfully delineated, but that Field will afford an agreeable Variety? Every Word they speak must be entirely consonant to the Notion the Author would have his Readers to entertain of them: And here it may not be amiss to remark the great Analogy there is between these Histories and Dramatic Performances, which Similitude I shall enlarge upon occasionally in the Progress of this Review. In regard to Character, after what I have mention'd as necessary, it would be the greatest Affront on the Reader's Understanding to point out the Comparison.

As this Sort of Writing was intended as a Contrast to those in which the Reader was even to suppose all the Characters ideal, and every Circumstance quite imaginary, 'twas thought necessary, to give it a greater Air of Truth, to entitle it an *History;* and the *Dramatis Personæ* (if I may venture to use the Expression) were christened not with fantastic high-founding Names, but such as, tho' they sometimes bore some Reference to the Character, had a more modern Termination.

At the same Time Mr. *Fielding* ordain'd, that these Histories should be divided into Books, and these subdivided into Chapters; and also that the first Chapter of every Book was not to continue the Narration, but should consist of any Thing the Author chose to entertain his Readers with. These if I don't forget, Mr. *Fielding* himself has nominated, the several Stages of his History, which he metaphorically calls a Journey, in which he and his Readers are Fellow-Travellers. His particular Success in these preliminary Essays demonstrates . . . that these are not the easiest Part of his Task: Which I believe, Mr. *Fielding* somewhere says himself.

The Story should be probable, and the Characters taken from common Life, the Stile should be easy and familiar, but at the same Time sprightly and entertaining; and to enliven it the more, it is sometimes heightened to the Mock-heroic, to ridicule the Bombast and Fustian, which obtain'd so much in the Romances. Of this Kind are his various Descriptions of the Morning, and his diverting Similes occasionally dispers'd thro' the Body of his Work. *Horace* tells us, *dulce est desipere*, but Mr. *Fielding* remember'd he added *in loco.*[5] For which Reason, he always takes care to indulge himself in these Liberties of Stile where the Story is least interesting.

---

[5] "It is sweet to be foolish—sometimes" (Horace, *Odes,* IV, xii. 28).

✤ Sarah Fielding
From *The Cry: A New Dramatic Fable*[1]

To travel through a whole work only to laugh at the chief companion allotted us, is an insupportable burthen. And we should imagine that the reading of that incomparable piece of humour left us by *Cervantes*, can give but little pleasure to those persons who can extract no other entertainment or emolument from it than laughing at *Don Quixote*'s reveries, and sympathizing in the malicious joy of the maid at the inn, when she had confined the poor knight in painful durance, by tying him up to the window by the hand, and letting the weight of his whole body hang on that small hold: and that strong and beautiful representation of human nature, exhibited in *Don Quixote*'s madness in one point, and extraordinary good sense in every other, is indeed very much thrown away on such readers as consider him only as the object of their mirth. Nor less understood is the character of parson *Adams* in *Joseph Andrews* by those persons, who, fixing their thoughts on the hounds trailing the bacon in his pocket (with some oddnesses in his behaviour, and peculiarities in his dress) think proper to overlook the noble simplicity of his mind, with the other innumerable beauties in his character; which, to those who can understand *the word to the wise*, are placed in the most conspicuous view.

That the ridiculers of parson *Adams* are designed to be the proper objects of ridicule (and not that innocent man himself) is a truth which the author hath in many places set in the most glaring light. And lest his meaning should be perversely misunderstood, he hath fully displayed his own sentiments on that head, by writing a whole scene, in which such laughers are properly treated, and their[2] characters truly depicted. But those who think continual laughter, or rather sneering, to be one of the necessary ingredients of life, need not be at the trouble of travelling out of their depths to find objects of their merriment: they may spare themselves the pains of going abroad after food for scorn; as they may be bless'd with a plenteous harvest ever mature and fit for reaping on their own estates, without being beholden to any of their neighbours.

---

[1] *The Cry* by Sarah Fielding with Jane Collier, 3 vols. (London, 1754), 3:121–24.

[2] *Joseph Andrews*, Book III. Chap. 7. The characters are an old half-pay officer, a dull poet, a scraping fiddler, and a lame *German* dancing-master. (Sarah Fielding's note.)

The greatest men, 'tis true, may have some oddnesses and pecu-liarities, which are indeed food for mirth and pleasantry: but the honest laughs which they create in the judicious and benevolent mind are such, as their own candor (if they are truly great men) will readily excuse; and their good humour, if they have any, will then induce them to join the mirthful chorus: and the result must be the charm of universal chearfulness and innocent mirth. We are very apt to do as manifest an injury to comic writers, as we do to the characters they represent; and because they here and there properly embellish their pictures with risible figures, we want to turn the whole into farce, by desiring to see nothing but the grotesque: we expect in every page to meet with such jests as shall distort our fea-tures into a broad grin; otherwise, let them paint the most agreeable images of human nature, let them ever so accurately search the inmost recesses of the human heart, there is a general outcry set up against them, that they are spiritless and dull.

But indignation at the malicious rather than ignorant absurdi-ties which we have heard vented on honest parson *Adams* hath led us into a much wider digression than we at first intended.

✤ James Boswell
From *The Life of Samuel Johnson*[1]

"Sir, (continued he,) there is all the difference in the world between characters of nature and characters of manners; and *there* is the dif-ference between the characters of Fielding and those of Richardson. Characters of manners are very entertaining; but they are to be understood by a more superficial observer than characters of nature, where a man must dive into the recesses of the human heart."

It always appeared to me that he estimated the compositions of Richardson too highly, and that he had an unreasonable prejudice against Fielding. In comparing those two writers, he used this expression; "that there was as great a difference between them as between a man who knew how a watch was made, and a man who could tell the hour by looking on the dial-plate." This was a short and figurative state of his distinction between drawing characters of nature and characters only of manners. But I cannot help being of opinion, that the neat watches of Fielding are as well constructed as

---

[1] *The Life of Samuel Johnson, LL. D.* (1791), 2 vols., 1:299.

the large clocks of Richardson, and that his dial-plates are brighter. Fielding's characters, though they do not expand themselves so widely in dissertation, are as just pictures of human nature, and I will venture to say, have more striking features, and nicer touches of the pencil; and though Johnson used to quote with approbation a saying of Richardson's, "that the virtues of Fielding's heroes were the vices of a truly good man," I will venture to add, that the moral tendency of Fielding's writings, though it does not encourage a strained and rarely possible virtue, is ever favourable to honour and honesty, and cherishes the benevolent and generous affections. He who is as good as Fielding would make him, is an amiable member of society, and may be led on by more regulated instructors, to a higher state of ethical perfection.

Further Reading

Alter, Robert. *Fielding and the Nature of the Novel.* Harvard University Press, 1968.

Backscheider, Paula R., and Catherine Ingrassia, eds. *A Companion to the Eighteenth-Century English Novel and Culture.* Blackwell, 2005. Contains three essays on or partly on *Joseph Andrews*: (i) Paula McDowell, "Why Fanny Can't Read: *Joseph Andrews* and the (Ir) Relevancy of Literacy," 167–90; (ii) Adam Potkay, "Joy and Happiness," 321–40; and (iii) Roxann Wheeler, "Racial Legacies: The Speaking Countenance and the Character Sketch in the Novel," 419–40.

Bartolomeo, Joseph. "Interpolated Tales as Allegories of Reading: *Joseph Andrews.*" *Studies in the Novel* 23 (1991): 405–15.

———. *Matched Pairs: Gender and Intertextual Dialogue in Eighteenth-Century Fiction.* University of Delaware Press, 2002.

Battestin, Martin C. *The Moral Basis of Fielding's Art: A Study of Joseph Andrews.* Wesleyan University Press, 1959.

Black, Scott. "Anachronism and the Use of Form in *Joseph Andrews.*" *Novel* 3 (2005): 147–64.

Campbell, Jill. *Natural Masques: Gender and Identity in Fielding's Plays and Novels.* Stanford University Press, 1995.

———. "Fielding's Style." *ELH* 72 (2005): 407–28.

Cruise, James. "Fielding, Authority, and the New Commercialism in *Joseph Andrews.*" *ELH* 54 (1987): 253–76.

Dickie, Simon. "*Joseph Andrews* and the Great Laughter Debate." *Studies in Eighteenth-Century Culture* 34 (2005): 271–332.

Frank, Judith. "The Comic Novel and the Poor: Fielding's Preface to *Joseph Andrews.*" *Eighteenth-Century Studies* 27 (Winter 1993–94): 217–34.

Goldberg, Homer. *The Art of Joseph Andrews.* University of Chicago Press, 1969.

Hunter, Paul. *Occasional Form: Henry Fielding and the Chains of Circumstance.* Johns Hopkins University, 1975, 94–116.

Knight, Charles. "*Joseph Andrews* and the Failure of Authority." *Eighteenth-Century Fiction* 4 (1992): 109–24.

Lynch, Deidre Shauna. *The Economy of Character: Novels, Market Culture, and the Business of Inner Meaning.* University of Chicago Press, 1998, 23–79 (on Fielding, Hogarth, and the question of what constitutes "character").

Lynch, James J. *Henry Fielding and the Heliodoran Novel: Romance, Epic, and Fielding's New Province of Writing*. Fairleigh Dickinson University Press, 1986.

McClish, Glenn. "Henry Fielding, the Novel, and Classical Legal Rhetoric," *Rhetorica* 14 (1996): 413–40.

McCrea, Brian. "Rewriting *Pamela*: Social Change and Religious Faith in *Joseph Andrews*." *Studies in the Novel* 16 (1984): 137–49.

Paulson, Ronald. *Hogarth: High Art and Low, 1732–50*. Rutgers University Press, 1992, 185–202.

———. *The Beautiful, Novel, and Strange: Aesthetics and Heterodoxy*. Johns Hopkins University Press, 1996.

Potkay, Adam. *The Story of Joy from the Bible to Late Romanticism*. Cambridge University Press, 2007. Chapter 4, "Ethical Joy," has a substantial section on *Joseph Andrews*.

Prytula, Nina. "'Great-Breasted and Fierce': Fielding's Amazonian Heroines." *Eighteenth-Century Studies* 35 (2002): 173–93.

Rawson, Claude. *Henry Fielding and the Augustan Ideal under Stress*. 2nd edition. Humanities Press International, 1991.

Richetti, John. *The English Novel in History, 1700–1780*. Routledge, 1999, 121–35.

Ruml, Treadwell, II. "Henry Fielding and Parson Adams: Whig Writer and Tory Priest." *JEGP* 97 (1998): 205–25.

Staves, Susan. "Fielding and the Comedy of Attempted Rape," in *History, Gender, and Eighteenth-Century Literature*, ed. Beth Fowkes Tobin. University of Georgia Press, 1994, 86–112.

Stephanson, Raymond. "'Silenced by Authority' in *Joseph Andrews*: Power, Submission, and Mutuality in 'The History of Two Friends'." *Studies in the Novel* 24 (1992): 1–12.

Tave, Stuart M. *The Amiable Humorist: A Study in the Comic Theory and Criticism of the Eighteenth and Early Nineteenth Centuries*. University of Chicago Press, 1960, 140–63.

Taylor, Dick, Jr. "Joseph as Hero in *Joseph Andrews*." *Tulane Studies in English* 7 (1957): 91–109.

Williams, Jeffrey. "The Narrative Circle: The Interpolated Tales in *Joseph Andrews*." *Studies in the Novel* 30 (1998): 473–88.